The Paranoid Vision

Deciphering the Mystery of Malevolence

Mark Dillof, Ph.D.

Mystical Kentuckian Press
Louisville, KY
2013

First Paperback Edition

ISBN: 978-0-9855953-3-3

This book emerged from the research that I undertook, as part of my Ph.D. degree program, from Union Institute & University, from 2001 to 2006. I wish to thank the members of my doctoral committee, as well as those who served as consultants to the committee. They include: Professor Emeritus John Tallmadge, Professor Elliot Robins, Professor Chris Hables Gray, Professor Bruce Douglass, Professor Emeritus Maurice Friedman, Professor April Boyington Wall, Professor Kathleen Damiani, Professor Ronald Miller, Professor Emeritus Donald Weiss, Professor Neil Kressel and Professor John C. Farrell. I owe them each a debt of gratitude for helping me to create a more cogent and better-written manuscript.

Although the members of the committee were unanimous in encouraging me to convert the dissertation into a book and then to have it published, each of them expressed disagreement over various ideas contained in these pages. They may well be correct in many of their criticisms. Consequently, any errors contained here, questionable assumptions and dubious conclusions are solely my own fault.

Finally, I would like to express my gratitude to my parents, clients, students and friends.

Book cover design: Glen Edelstein glenede@gmail.com

Cover photo: unaknipsolinafotografie // www.knipsolina.de   Getty Images

Book formatting: Janet Dooley janet@r5i.com

To:
those who suspect that things
are not what they seem

Table of Contents

Chapter One

Introduction: What is the Paranoid Vision?

"The mind is its own place and in itself can make a heaven of Hell, and a hell of Heaven."

— John Milton

The nature of evil is one of life's deepest mysteries, prompting many a perplexed person to inquire: What is its origin? What is the source of its allure? Can evil be overcome? For centuries, people turned to myths, dreams, and fairy tales for answers, and then to theology and moral philosophy. In recent years, psychiatrists have reduced evil to psychopathology. They have debated, for example, whether those people commonly regarded as evil are really sociopaths, necrophiliacs, or malignant narcissists.

In the chapters that follow, we shall examine evil from an altogether new perspective, that of epistemology. Philosophers mean by "epistemology" the investigation of the foundations of knowledge. "Epistemology," as used here has a more specific meaning — the investigation of the mind's power to shape our experience. Certain outlooks on life depict the world as benevolent. But people under the sway of "the paranoid vision" experience the world as infused with malevolence. Ironically, they increasingly resemble the demons that haunt their violent fantasies. That insidious transformation is the subject of our inquiry.

What, then, is the paranoid vision? Like clinical paranoia, it is characterized by delusions of persecution. Those subject to such fantasies are convinced that some nefarious group of people is plotting to harm them. They might fear, for example, that a cabal of dentists, who are working for the CIA, have conspired to implant mind-control devises in their fillings. Such fantasies are also indicative of delusions of grandeur, for why would the CIA be so interested in them in particular? Furthermore, paranoids project their feelings — which are frequently hostile, if not downright malignant — onto other people. They then imagine that it is other people, not themselves, who have evil intentions.

Paranoiac delusions are not, though, the exclusive province of the clinically paranoid. For example, if the internet is any indication, a fair number of people believe that the damage wrought by Hurricane Katrina was part of a plot by certain politicians to destroy the poorer sections of New Orleans, so as to alter the electoral landscape in their favor. Similarly, there are those who believe that Princess Diana was really assassinated by the British royalty.

What is the psychological origin of these and other conspiracy theories? We shall argue that they do not indicate the presence of psychopathology, since most conspiracy theorists are relatively sane. Rather, conspiracy theories derive from a certain worldview, i.e., from a way of interpreting reality, which we are calling the paranoid vision. Like all worldviews, the paranoid vision can be shared by a group of people, an organization, or by an entire society. Of course, worldviews are usually indigenous to a particular place and time in history. But the paranoid vision is perennial. It is as familiar to the human landscape as is love, hate, jealousy, sadness, laughter and longing.

What, then, is the connection of the paranoid vision to malevolence, or evil? We have referred to the mechanism of projection, which we shall have more to say about subsequently. Another clue to paranoia's potential for malevolence lies in the curious fact that it is contagious. It is, indeed, akin to a cognitive virus, restructuring how one sees the world. That is how entire organizations, religious sects, societies, and nations can be rapidly transformed. Horrifying examples of this are the genocides that occurred in Serbia and in Rwanda. In a relatively short time, friendly neighbors were transformed into homicidal maniacs. There is little indication, though, that the other personality disorders are similarly communicable. Entire organizations or societies have not, for example, quickly become obsessive-compulsive. This would confirm our argument that paranoia was more than a personality disorder, for personality disorders are not communicable, but visions of life, or worldviews, are.

How, exactly, is the paranoid vision able to spread? It must find narrative expression; i.e. it must consist of a story with a plot and characters. The story is then told by one person to another. The second and third chapters explore two types of paranoid narratives — conspiracy theories and apocalyptic fantasies. Such stories are like a Trojan Horse, secretly harboring the paranoid vision of life. The focus of our investigation is, more specifically, how an organization can become a breeding ground for such narratives and, thus, for the paranoid vision. We shall analyze several such organizations to illustrate that phenomenon. Moreover, we'll argue that the paranoid vision is the way of seeing, or worldview, behind political fanaticism, genocide, and terrorism.

Can the paranoid vision be overcome? When a person owns up to his or her negative projections — Jung calls this "the encounter with the shadow" — the paranoid vision collapses. Mythically speaking, the character Oedipus, in Sophocles' tragedy, did exactly that. It is devastating to realize, as did Oedipus, that the villain that one has so vigorously been pursuing is none other than oneself! For Oedipus it was a dark victory, as was symbolized by his blinding his eyes, for the eyes symbolize conscious understanding. To transcend such tragic wisdom requires that the paranoid vision be overcome not only on a personal level, but be defeated philosophically. Then there is not a blinding darkness, but greater illumination.

Of course, a worldview is not a consciously articulated philosophy, like those developed by Plato, Aristotle, Spinoza, Hegel, Whitehead, and other metaphysicians. On the contrary, those who are under the sway of the paranoid vision do not realize that that is how they see things, for worldviews operate unconsciously. The fact that one is not aware of having a worldview, or way of seeing, is what gives it its power. Why should this be so? Self-awareness precipitates questions and doubts, which constrain one's energies. Unawareness, by way of contrast, leaves one's energies and motivations unexamined and unchecked. That is what makes a worldview so powerful, and potentially so dangerous. And that is why paranoids rush in where angels fear to tread.

The antidote to any worldview, including the paranoid vision, is, therefore, to discern its structure and dynamics. That is because visions of life are creatures of the night that vanish before the light of conscious understanding. Our intent, then, is to uncover the "double helix," the essential structure, of the paranoid vision. In so doing, the epistemological roots of malevolence may be revealed.

Paranoia Dark and Paranoia Light

What, then, is the essence of the paranoid vision? It is that there exists an enemy who is conspiring to do one harm. There is much to suggest, though, that a certain continuum exists within the paranoid vision. Some paranoids have a vague sense of suspicion, and a mild proclivity towards believing in conspiracies. At the other extreme are those paranoids who are intensely suspicious, have wild delusions of persecution coupled with insane delusions of grandeur, and vilify other people, to the point of violence. This creates somewhat of a conundrum: Is it the case that the paranoid vision, in its essence, is malevolent? In that case, paranoia in its everyday milder forms— vague suspicion, but without any of the malevolent manifestations— might be viewed as a diluted form of the paranoid vision. Or is it that the paranoid vision is not essentially malevolent? In that case, there are other variables that would make it so.

What argument is there for the latter view of the paranoid vision? The great majority of its manifestations are relatively innocuous. For example, the films of Alfred Hitchcock and cinema noir in general, the stories of Franz Kafka and Edgar Allan Poe, and the novels of John Grisham and Dan Brown, are infused with the paranoid vision, but they are far from malevolent in their outlook. If one enjoys entering into the paranoid world of films of intrigue, it is because there is a certain metaphysical pleasure in imagining that one grasps the reality behind appearances, and there is also a relief that comes from cutting the Gordian knot of life's complexities, and reducing it all to a battle of good and evil. These authors are, though, involved with the subject of malevolence, i.e. murders, and other crimes, and their protagonists may inhabit a universe that is malevolent to varying degrees. Perhaps the paranoid vision, experienced with artistic or aesthetic distance, allows one to taste it, without becoming dangerously bewitched by it.

There are also many people who are obsessed with conspiracy theories, and there are other people who believe that the apocalypse is on the horizon. In regard to the latter, a survey by Time Magazine, conducted in 2003, concluded that about forty million Americans believe that end-time prophesies will come to pass in their lifetime. Conspiracy theory mongering and apocalypticism, while indicative of the paranoid vision, are usually not malevolent. According to Peter Knight (2000), the preoccupation with conspiracy theories is no longer a fringe phenomenon, but has gone mainstream. Those who belong to "conspiracy culture" are not just the stereotypic rightwing extremists described by Richard Hofstadter (1965; 1996). Knight goes so far as to say that, "...to some extent we are all conspiracy theorists now." (2000, p. 25)

The paranoid vision may also be elevated to a level where it reveals profound insights about life. William Farrell (1996) contends that paranoia is the predominant way of seeing of the great writers and thinkers of modernity, from Nietzsche to Freud. Why, then, are popular encounters with the paranoid vision — from conspiracy theories to novels of political intrigue — captivating and exciting? It may be because they resonate with profound truths. There will be more discussion of those truths, in Part III. Thus one can be under the sway of the paranoid vision, but neither be hostile nor clinically paranoid.

Understanding the paranoid vision as not intrinsically malevolent requires determining what factors would make it so. But understanding the paranoid vision as intrinsically malevolent requires determining what it is that dilutes it, sublimates it, or elevates it to a higher level. In the chapters that follow, we shall opt for the latter interpretation, i.e. the paranoid vision, in its very essence, is malevolent. But in Part III, "Beyond the Paranoid Vision," the question will arise as to whether the paranoid vision, in its very essence, is, indeed, a rather lofty vision of life, and only malevolent in its baser manifestations. For the sake of clarity, when we refer to the paranoid vision, at least in the first two parts, we mean it in all its malevolence, unless otherwise stated.

Finally, the paranoid vision is not the root of all evil, but whenever malevolence appears in the context of a group or organization it is invariably the case that the paranoid vision is present. The chapters that follow will determine if our thesis proves valid.

The Underlying Theme of the Paranoid Vision

If paranoia is a vision of life, it must be single, or unitary, but paranoia, clinically understood, is recognized by a diversity of symptoms. In the statistically based guidebook that many clinicians use to determine the presence of psychopathology in a person, called DSM-4, there is little effort to indicate how these symptoms are interconnected, other than to state that if four or more out of seven symptoms are in evidence, then that person could be judged to be paranoid. Even specialized texts on personality theory that present a general theory of paranoia leave many dots unconnected. Paranoia, like other psychological maladies, is viewed as a syndrome. The notion of syndrome merely points to the fact that certain symptoms are found together, without informing one as to the essential reason why.

Some personality theorists, including Theodore Millon, contend that, "No universal attributes may be spoken of as the 'essence' of the paranoid personality" (1996, p. 701). Millon is what is known as a nominalist, i.e., a person who denies the reality of universals and essences. He may be right about particular cases of individuals with paranoid personalities. After all, some people manifest only one or two of the symptoms of paranoia. Then again, if Plato is correct — that, here on earth, only imperfect representations of ideal types, or essences, exist—then it is not uncommon for people to display only some of the symptoms of paranoia.

The argument that we are making, though, is not that there exists a paranoid personality, but that there exists a paranoid vision. The paranoid vision is not merely a syndrome, for it possesses an underlying unity that logically accounts for why different symptoms are found together. In order to truly understand paranoia, one needs to grasp all of its manifestations as derivative of that single essence, or way of seeing.

Bearing that in mind, one may wonder: what, essentially, do delusions of persecution—as well as such related symptoms as hostility, bitterness, envy, umbrage, resentment, suspiciousness, and fear—have to do with delusions of grandeur? That extreme opposition—which Kraepelin, back in 1921, referred to as "...a combination of uncertainty with excessive valuation of self" (Millon, 1996, 693)—may provide a clue to the mystery of the paranoid vision. Nancy McWilliams, a psychoanalyst, explains that opposition:

> The main polarity in the self-representations of paranoid people is an impotent, humiliated, and despised image of the self versus an omnipotent, vindicated, triumphant one. A tension between these two images suffuses their subjective world. Cruelly, neither position affords any solace: A terror of abuse and contempt goes with the weak side of the polarity. While the strong side brings with it the inevitable side effect of psychological power, a crushing guilt. (1994, p. 214)

That inner opposition, in regard to self-image, almost sounds like a manic-depressive disorder, except that there is an important difference: the sense of one's ignominious position in life—as "impotent, humiliated, and despised," to use McWilliams's language—is blamed on other people. This same sense of humiliation could, of course, apply not solely to oneself, but to one's people, group or nation (Hofstadter 1965; 1996). That same poisonous sense of having been humiliated is spewed forth in Hitler's Mein Kampf and the speeches of Osama bin Laden.

Were one to examine the words, either spoken or written, of such individuals possessed by the paranoid vision, which will be the effort of subsequent chapters, and if one were to listen with "the third ear," one might hear something like this: "The grandeur and the happiness, that I — as well as my people (organization, society, etc.) — deserve, would exist today were it not for the machinations of a certain evil cabal, who ruined it all for us. I bitterly hate them for having robbed us of paradise, and resent them for enjoying what they have stolen. Furthermore, I fear their insidious power, and their nefarious plans to totally enslave, pauperize, defile, humiliate, or destroy us." That subtext of the paranoid vision might be summed up as "Paradise has been lost, and I know whose fault it is!"

Obviously, the paranoid is no stranger to hatred (or venom, animosity, choleric moods of all sort), but here is hatred of a certain type. Ordinary hatred is founded simply on the sense that someone is in my way of getting what I want. It lacks the grandiose claim of paranoid hatred—that happiness and greatness is one's birthright —and the consequent resentment and bitterness over paradise lost. Furthermore, paranoid hatred, i.e. malevolence, contains an admixture of another very dark emotion, which theorists of personality disorders, like Millon, have observed:

> Beneath the surface mistrust and defensive vigilance in the paranoid lies a current of deep resentment towards others who "have made it." To the paranoid, most people have attained their status unjustly; thus he or she is bitter for having been overlooked, treated unfairly, and slighted by the "high and mighty," the "cheats and crooks" who dupe the world. Only a thin veil hides these bristling animosities. (1996, p. 701)

Millon concludes that the reason for this resentment is that paranoids are unable to accept their own "faults and weaknesses." This is true, but it could be argued that this resentment derives from the sense of paradise lost, and that its loss is coeval with another person's, or group of people's, success. That is, the paranoid has the sense that a certain group of people have stolen paradise. Apparently, the paranoid does not believe in "win/win," but has a "zero-sum game" notion of success, which means that there is only so much wealth, success, or happiness to go around. Therefore one person's failure is predicated on another person's success, and one person's paradise is another person's hell. All this is no small matter, for, as C.S. Lewis (1961) makes plain in his analysis of John Milton's Paradise Lost, Satan — who is the very incarnation of evil — is motivated by envy, resentment, and wounded pride because Christ is regarded by God as superior to Satan. If envy, resentment, and wounded pride lie at the very heart of the paranoid vision, then, from a moral perspective, the paranoid vision is very much what evil is all about.

This envy, or resentment, has most unfortunate consequences when the paranoid vision finds expression on the political level, for envy is impervious to goodwill. As has often been observed, if someone hates you, and you act kindly to that person, his or her hatred towards you is likely to abate. But if a man's hatred is founded on envy, and you show kindness to him, his hatred will increase (Schimmel, 1997, pp. 55-82). For he will envy, resent, and hate you for your largesse of spirit, because it makes the paranoid appear all the more small-minded and petty. Furthermore, paranoids will suspect that your goodwill has a dark ulterior motive, and that what you are conspiring to do is far more sinister than if you had simply been directly aggressive. This bitter envy, resentment, and wounded pride leads the paranoid to vilify other people.

Vilification is reflective of another dimension of the paranoid vision. It has been said that President Richard Nixon — a case in point of a political paranoid — did not have opponents; he had enemies. Thus he had his infamous enemies list. When this sort of vilification involves not merely isolated individuals, but an entire group of people, the result is an us/them duality, a Manichean view of the world, in which "we" are completely good, pure, and noble, and "they" are completely evil, base, and iniquitous.

Like Richard Nixon, President Barack Obama has delusions of grandeur, as evidenced by his contempt for the constitutional limits placed upon the executive branch of government. But Nixon was merely temperamentally paranoid, whereas Obama uses the paranoid vision in a deliberative manner. Following Saul Alinsky's handbook for radical change, he foments class warfare amongst those prone to delusions of persecution, demonizes his political opponents and seeks to delegitimize the values of almost half the American electorate.

Obama's style is far afield of the loony rightwing conspiracy theorists that Hofstadter offered as examples of political paranoia. Rather he cloaks his animosity with feel-good banalities—such as hope and change—and empty promises, in the earnest and heartfelt manner that Americans have come to expect from their demagogues. Obama is, therefore, quite skillful in the strategic use of the various elements of the paranoid vision, in the service of his "progressive" agenda.

In any case, the paranoid has no patience for moral subtlety, i.e. no patience for people, as they almost always are—a mixture of good and bad; the emphasis here is on almost. It is not surprising that this Manichaeism leads to violence. After all, as Richard Hofstadter pointed out, "Since the enemy is thought of as being totally evil and totally unappeasable, he must be totally eliminated — if not from the world, at least from the theater of operations to which the paranoid directs his attention." (1965, p. 31)

Paranoia-infused Manichaeism is bereft of sympathy or tolerance for those whom one blames and vilifies for having ruined the possibility of paradise. As with paranoia in the clinical sense, in the paranoid vision one projects one's worst qualities—one's shadow, as C.G. Jung calls it—upon another group of people, who one then demonizes. Furthermore, one is always the least tolerant towards those who are a projection of one's own disowned qualities. Paranoid projection is indicative of a lack of self-awareness, and a lack of emotional maturity.

Let us summarize: the mood of the paranoid vision derives from a baseless claim to grandeur clashing with feelings of humiliation. Paranoids attribute the source of their humiliation to a certain group of people, who are then hated in an envious sort of way. As in all envy, there is a sense that other people have stolen what is rightfully one's own.

One's venom is then projected onto that scapegoated group of people, so that it appears that the scapegoats are the angry aggressors, rather than oneself. Indeed, the scapegoats are demonized. The consequence of these psychological maneuvers is an us/them, or Manichean, view of the world. That, then, is the subtext, the single essence, behind the multiple manifestations of the paranoid vision.

The Darker Side of Utopian Thinking

Paranoiac delusions of stolen grandeur often take the form of paradise lost or, to be more precise, "paradise stolen." The paranoid is, of course, under the illusion that it is theoretically possible for there to exist a paradise on earth. Sometimes the sense of loss becomes the motivation to actually build a utopian society or, more likely, to revive a utopia that supposedly once supposedly existed before "they" destroyed it. Such longings also lead to a desire for the millennium.

It is when moves are made to actualize such longings, that their deadly potential is revealed. After all, Nazi Germany, Stalinist Russia, and Pol Pot's Cambodia, were all founded on utopian ideals. Furthermore, the effort to realize utopian ideals often results in terror — as in the French Revolution — and terrorism. The driving force of Osama bin Laden's murder and mayhem was his wish to restore the Caliphate. If such movements are incredibly sanguinary, it is because they are infused with a sense that an apocalypse must precede the millennium.

To some extent, the dream of utopia would appear to be born of the universal longing to be free of the hardships, disappointments, and injustices that one suffers in this less than perfect world. Imaginative dreams of a better world appear to be, at worst, merely naïve, the idle speculations of philosophical dreamers. Sometimes utopian thinking has a positive value; it can awaken the human imagination to undreamed of possibilities, some of which can be a boon to mankind. Furthermore, writers like Ernst Bloch (1959; 1995) suggest that utopia gives us hope, and how can one live without hope?

But there is a darker side to such longings, just as there is a darker side to romantic, idealistic, and unconstrained longings in general. Utopian longings, i.e. the effort to restore a lost paradise, often derive, as we have suggested, from paranoid delusions of grandeur. Of course, such delusions are not unique to individuals with paranoid proclivities, but are universal. They originate from the earliest stage in human development, one characterized by egocentricity, or self-centeredness. Egocentricity is not the same as selfishness, for selfishness can only arise after the fall into self-awareness, when there has emerged a sense of competing interests, and an insistence on one's own. Egocentricity, on the contrary, is the sense of infinitude and unboundedness endemic to the innocence of early childhood, which wreaks havoc on the emotional life of teenagers when parents insist that they abandon childish longings, but which can be protracted well into adulthood.

The world has a way of puncturing one's illusions and delusions, and in a most ignominious way. Using Freudian terminology, we could say that the pleasure principle—with its oceanic feelings of unboundedness, and infinitude—must give way to the reality principle. It must give way, because of the demands of adulthood. The harsh encounter of self and world begins in the playground sandlot amongst one's rude peers, and the lesson is reinforced daily in grade school. The world does not recognize one's grandeur and, in moments of doubt, one wonders if the world's assessment might be correct. It is how one responds to the inevitable pricking of the delusive bubble of ego, and to the psychic deflation that follows, that is critically important. A particular type of morbid reaction to ego-deflation characterizes paranoid thinking.

The self-doubt, that undermines one's sense of grandeur, most often leads from egocentricity to egotism, i.e. selfishness, and then to what has been called "enlightened egotism," an awareness that one inhabits a world of competing interests, and that one can best satisfy one's own interests by cooperating with other people. Egotism, of any variety, may not be the final goal of psychological development, but it is an important advance out of the autism of childhood egocentricity. This is because it recognizes the existence of the world and other people, even though it maintains what Buber (1923; 1971) has called an "I-It" relation to the world and to other people.

But, ideally — from the standpoint of psychological development — doubts about one's grandeur should result in a shift from egocentricity, not just to egotism or to enlightened egotism, but to a "higher level" answer to the question of how to be. A higher-level answer is one that starts in the acknowledgement of one's finitude, the reality of other people, and a subscription to the reality of transpersonal values. The move from self-centeredness to concern for one's family, community, one's country, and concern with one's fellow human beings in other parts of the world, is an example of this shift.

Another example of this self-evolution is the shift from egocentricity to theocentricity. Unfortunately, all efforts to transcend ego can be subverted by subterranean motives. Religious faith, for example, can become a new and far more deadly arena for paranoid delusions. Like a deposed dictator, one's ego can wait for the opportune psychological moment—a moment of spiritual stress, a dark night when the soul is weak and susceptible to invasion—and then return, this time in the guise of sanctity, to recapture its lost throne. Apart from that untoward possibility, real transcendence allows one to regain the infinitude that one lost when egocentricity came clashing upon the shoals of reality. But the infinitude that one regains is not the infinitude of the ego, but of what mystics and transpersonal psychologists call "the Self."

The ego is not easily daunted by the clash between its delusions of grandeur and actual reality. Instead of maturing, it might imagine a future time when its dreams of exaltation, grandeur, happiness, love, respect, and fulfillment will be realized. Furthermore, this utopian state of affairs might be imagined not only for oneself, but for one's tribe, organization, people, nation, race, or for the entire world as in the case of communism.

From a psychological perspective, utopian thinking is essentially vain self-exaltation, a clinging to childhood egocentricity. This clinging has the effect of canceling, or at least deferring, the process of psychological maturation. It is an adolescent protest against facing the responsibilities, and the harsh realities, of adulthood. Adolescence mistakes the quixotic promptings and paradisiac images—that arise form puerility of spirit — for true idealism. Anything but innocent, this romantic, adolescent outlook has given birth to violent revolutions and cruel reigns of terror.

From a philosophical and theological perspective, utopian thinking is idolatry, an attempt to locate the infinite, absolute, and eternal in the realm of the finite. Instead of turning to a transcendent answer to the question of human suffering, one becomes a humanist, setting out with likeminded souls to build the Crystal Palace, or perhaps Babel. This utopian project is a rebellion. Milton believed Satan, a mutineer against God, to be the quintessential rebel, but Camus found a number of people, famous or infamous, to be essentially in rebellion. Psychologically understood, the rebellion is against those doubts that might undermine one's delusions of grandeur. That rebellion is usually not a positive development, for self-doubt is the very catalyst of psychological maturation.

But such doubts can abort. That is perhaps where projection—which is recognized by clinicians to be the fundamental defense mechanism of paranoia—emerges. One's doubts are projected onto other people, resulting in a bitter sense of insult and injury. As a consequence, the universe then falls into two camps: the true believers and the heretics who create anxious doubt and uncertainty. Furthermore, the perception of the immense gap between the real world and the utopian dream world breeds frustration and discontent, which then give way to hatred, resentment, wrath, and suspicion. Eventually, it leads to violent thoughts about how this gap might be bridged, and to violent actions.

If one understands this frustration, many of the paranoia-infused plagues of modernity—including terrorism, totalitarianism, apocalyptic visions, and conspiracy theories—might also begin to be intelligible. For example, a utopian or millenarian might conclude that our world is so hopelessly perverted in its iniquity, or so deeply sunk in confusion and ignorance, that the millennium is not very likely, through any practical course of action, to come about. There then emerges a longing for a savior who could magically transform the world. But instead of a savior comes an autocrat who seeks to repress independent thought and judgment. The autocrat, or totalitarian dictator, then spins the venomous narratives—conspiracy theories and apocalyptic fantasies—that become the organizing principles of paranoid movements.

Out of despair over not being able to transform the debased present state of affairs, one might also conclude that the only way for utopia to be realized would be if the world—or at least the evil part of the world—were to be destroyed, thus making room for a new creation, for the realization of a new world order. That is how apocalyptic visions figure into the picture. It is similarly the inspiration for apocalyptic terrorism.[1]

Furthermore, one might imagine that there exists a certain group of people preventing the realization of a utopian paradise. When delusions of lost or stolen grandeur combine with delusions of persecution, the result, quite often, is the emergence of virulent conspiracy theories. There are, then, significant reasons why utopian longings often give rise to a dystopia.

One can conclude, then, that the paranoid vision is a particular form of adolescent protest, a rebellion against the ego deflation that is part of psychological maturation. We have, it must be remembered, been focusing on the paranoid vision in its suspicious, angry, and hostile form. Of course, many paranoids are merely suspicious, but it is those who are also hostile who are of interest to us, for this is a study of malevolence.

One can also conclude, more generally, that paranoia is not an arbitrary concatenation of symptoms. It is not merely a syndrome, for there is a meaning and significance to the paranoid's feelings and behavior. Once the inner essence of the paranoid vision has been grasped, its various manifestations logically follow.

The Primacy of the Paranoid Vision

We all know people who, oddly enough, appear to be paranoid only in a certain realm. That realm is usually politics. Is it possible, then, for a person to be clinically paranoid, but only in regard to politics? Senator Joseph McCarthy—who, in the 1950s, achieved fame and then notoriety as a communist hunter—has often been cited as the prototypical political paranoid. But Mark Landis (1987) has argued persuasively that McCarthy was not clinically paranoid, but was really an impulsive personality type. More recently, Arthur Herman (2000) has argued that McCarthy was a manic-depressive. Psychohistory is always a speculative endeavor.

---

1 The current president of Iran, Mahmood Ahmadinejad, is a case in point of a madman imbued with the paranoid vision. Ahmadinejad does not claim to be the savior, but he is seeking to precipitate the apocalypse, i.e. a nuclear war, so that the savior — the Shiite's term for it is "the Mahdi" — can arrive. C.F. John von Heyking. (November 2005) "Iran's President and the Politics of the Twelfth Imam." Ashbrook Center for Public Affairs. <www.ashbrook.org/publicat/guest/05/vonheyking//twelthimam.html>

And yet, even if Senator McCarthy was not clinically paranoid as Landis and Herman contend, there was still something truly paranoid about him. The historian Richard Hofstadter had earlier offered a solution to this conundrum. He distinguished clinical paranoia from what he termed "the paranoid style," which is the subject of his seminal essay, The Paranoid Style in American Politics. Although Hofstadter was writing about paranoia in the context of American politics, his observations also apply to paranoia in organizations.

> In the paranoid style, as I conceive it, the feeling of persecution is central, and is systemized in grandiose theories of conspiracy. But there is a vast difference between the paranoid spokesman in politics and the clinical paranoiac: although they both tend to be overheated, oversuspicious, overaggressive, grandiose, and apocalyptic in expression, the clinical paranoid sees the hostile and conspiratorial world in which he feels himself to be living as directed specifically against him; whereas the spokesman for the paranoid style finds it directed against a nation, a culture, a way of life whose fate affects not himself alone but millions of others. (1965, p. 6)

Hofstadter is quite perceptive in his description of the paranoid, and excellent in distinguishing political paranoia from the clinical variety. But what exactly does he mean by style? Hofstadter states, "When I speak of the paranoid style, I use the term much as a historian of art might speak of the baroque or the mannerist style. It is above all a way of seeing the world and of expressing oneself" (1965, p. 4) Following Hofstadter's logic, we might say that just as Braque, Leger, and Picasso expressed the cubist style in their paintings, so it is that political fanatics express the paranoid style through their actions. To understand the cubist style, though, we would need to understand cubism as a theory of art. More fundamentally, we would need to understand the cubist vision of life. Otherwise, the particular type of lines, shapes, forms and colors endemic to the cubist style would be incomprehensible.

Similarly, to understand that form of behavior known as the paranoid style, we would need to understand the vision of life that found expression in that style. One would need to discern, for example, why representatives of the paranoid style, i.e. political fanatics, have a keen interest in conspiracy theories. Hofstadter wrote as an historian and did not attempt to explain matters on a psychological and philosophical level, so he leaves it to us to uncover the way of seeing that lies at the root of the paranoid style. We are, of course, maintaining that that way of seeing is the paranoid vision. How, though, are we to distinguish clinical paranoia from the paranoid style? Hofstadter distinction is helpful here...

> ...the clinical paranoid sees the hostile and conspiratorial world in which he feels himself to be living as directed specifically against him; whereas the spokesman of the paranoid style finds it directed against a nation, a culture, a way of life whose fate affects not himself alone but millions of others. Insofar as he does not usually see himself singled out as the individual victim of a personal conspiracy, he is somewhat more rational and much more disinterested. (1965, p. 4)

Thus, by Hofstadter's definition, what makes for psychopathology is the private nature of one's narrative. If, on the other hand, it can be shared with other people, then one is a representative of the paranoid style.

It might appear that paranoia, in the sense of being a style and a vision of life, is derivative of clinical paranoia. After all, everyone has heard of clinical paranoia, but only historians, political scientists, and other scholars are familiar with the paranoid style, and very few people conceive of paranoia as a vision of life. We would maintain, though, that the relationship between these variables is actually the reverse—paranoia, in the clinical sense, and the paranoid style too, are not primary, but derivative of the paranoid vision. Clinical paranoia, i.e. the personality disorder, is really the psychopathological manifestation of the paranoid vision. It is not our purpose here to answer the question of why some people who are under the sway of the paranoid vision are so out of touch with reality as to be clinically paranoid, while others share with their colleagues certain delusions, usually of a political nature, that makes them representatives of the paranoid style.

Since this is not a study of clinical paranoia, questions of individual psychopathology are relevant only in so far as they can shed light on the paranoid vision. The type of question relevant to the present study is not whether various dictators are clinically paranoid, or whether they are really manic-depressive, narcissistic, or necrophiliac. Nor is this an investigation of the influence of family history and genetics on the paranoid vision. Here a whole new set of factors comes into play. For example, power, greed, and immorality in general, can be paranoiagenic,[2] i.e., fostering, or inducing, the paranoid vision. Such factors are particularly paranoiagenic in an organizational setting, even if they are not relevant to the etiology of paranoia in a person's individual history.

It is interesting, for example, that those involved with psychohistory often allege that Stalin showed all the symptoms of being clinically paranoid, whereas they debate whether Hitler was paranoid. Fromm (1973) argued that Hitler was really a malignant narcissist and a necrophiliac. But what is of far greater importance to this investigation is that both dictators were under the sway of the paranoid vision. We are not, therefore, concerned here with the "where question," i.e. the question of origins, which is the province of psychohistory, but with the "what question," i.e. understanding what, more precisely, is the paranoid vision.[3]

In this section, we have distinguished the paranoid vision from the paranoid style and from paranoia in the clinical sense. We have seen that the paranoid vision is primary, and that paranoia in those other senses are derivative. The fact that paranoia can spread like a cognitive contagion—through conspiracy theories and other such narratives—confirms that it is essentially a vision of life. Bearing this new vantage

---

2   The term paranoiagenic derives from E. Jaques. Cf. A General Theory of Bureaucracy. (1976). The term subsequently appeared in Kernberg (1998). A chapter in Kernberg's book is entitled: "Paranoiagenesis in Organizations." We shall be extending the notion of paranoiagenesis, finding many more factors that cause paranoia.

3   Louis Sass makes this distinction between the "where" and the "what" question in his brilliant phenomenological analysis of schizophrenia (1994). The approach we take in our study of the paranoid vision is similarly phenomenological.

point in mind, when we use the word "paranoia," "paranoid," or "paranoiac" we mean it as a vision of life, unless otherwise specified.

When Paranoids are Right

"Sometimes paranoids are right," Golda Meir was reputed to have retorted when Henry Kissinger accused her of being paranoid. There have indeed been people incarcerated in mental institutions because their family or a totalitarian government claimed that they were paranoid, as an excuse to silence them. Furthermore, there have been actual conspiracies that initially were doubted. Watergate, the Iran Contra affair, and a number of CIA conspiracies come to mind. Proceed further back in history, and one will discover all sorts of conspiracies, from the assassination of Julius Caesar to the Dreyfus Affair. In regard to the business world, Adam Smith the intellectual father of modern capitalism, had this to say: "People of the same trade seldom meet together, even for merriment and diversion, but the conversation ends in a conspiracy against the public, or in some contrivance to raise prices." (1776; 1994, p.148) One commodity, then, never in short supply is conspiracies.

Let us evoke, once again, the ghost of Senator Joseph McCarthy. Here was a man who was thoroughly abrasive, a bully, a loose cannon, a person who embodied what Hofstadter considered to be the paranoid style, but he was not altogether wrong. There had been communist spies and fellow travelers in positions of power, almost to a shocking degree — particularly in the state department — and they did indeed have a damaging influence on American foreign policy. Much of the confirming evidence, in regard to McCarthy's allegations, is very recent, due to Moscow's permission for its secret cold war archives to be examined by scholars, thanks to Russian President Boris Yeltsin, and to the release of the classified Verona transcripts by the CIA and the NSA, thanks to the Freedom of Information Act (Haynes and Klehr 1999). In the eyes of certain historians, McCarthy is now vindicated (Herman 2000). Even a liberal and progressive, such as Ruth Price —in an article in *The Chronicle Review,* (July 7, 2005) about the spy, Agnes Smedley—begrudgingly admits as much.

But our point here is not about Russian spies; nor is it essentially about Senator McCarthy and other representatives of the paranoid style. Our point is that the accusation of being paranoid can be a form of ad hominem attack on one's opponent's arguments, and similarly a way of rewriting history so that it is in accord with one's present political agenda.

How open, then, to the possibility of conspiracy should one be? Might there, for example, really have been a conspiracy involving the assassination of President Kennedy? Is the Air Force really covering up the fact that space aliens landed at Roswell, New Mexico? How can one determine whether the man in a trench coat, who whispers some outlandish story in one's ear, is merely a false prophet, whose mind has been softened, over time, by exposure to too many conspiracy theories, or whether he is a true "Deep Throat," imparting some incredible, but valid and important, bit of information?

But this is the key to the whole affair, as far as the present study is concerned: even if a conspiracy theory turns out to be valid, it does not mean that those who subscribe to it are any less under the sway of the paranoid vision. In other words, even if paranoids were sometimes right—indeed, even if they were always right—they would still be under the sway of the paranoid vision. We state this because the present work is not a search for objective truth. It is, rather, an effort to understand a certain attitude, a habit of mind; more fundamentally, it is an effort to understand a certain vision of life. The belief in conspiracy theories, and the attitude of suspicion in general, is but one element in the paranoid vision anyway. This vision of life also includes hostility, delusions of grandeur, and much more.

There is a second point that requires clarification. The case examples are intended to open our eyes to paranoiagenic factors. It will become clear, for example, that the type of behavior that many people regard as immoral, is paranoiagenic. In those chapters, we shall not assume the stance of the moralist, bemoaning the loss of traditional values; nor are we going to suggest that it is a positive development. The intent is to be phenomenological, i.e. to observe the connection between two phenomena — immorality and possession by the paranoid vision.

Of course, the use of words like "immorality," and "evil" already implies a value judgment. Furthermore, the word "paranoid" implies a notion of normality, and the phrase, "distortion of reality" implies a view of reality. It is difficult to avoid such normative language. Too many qualifications such as the one made above—"that behavior, which many people would regard as immoral"—and our prose begins to sound rather prolix and stilted, as if one were an anthropologist from another galaxy observing the behavior of people on planet earth. All the same, such terms, like "immoral," will be used as self-critically as possible.

The Denial of Evil and the Unmasking of Two of Its Modern Disguises

Is malevolence, or evil, something real? That question must be addressed before we can decipher the connection of evil to the paranoid vision. The question of evil's reality is raised because certain words — evil, possession, demonic, satanic, and infernal—are currently met with a certain degree of skepticism, especially at the academy. The word "evil" often evokes the supernatural, a gothic melodrama or, even worse, it suggests the Manichean ontology endemic to the paranoid vision. Still, if one hopes to make sense of the malevolence of the paranoid vision, one cannot help taking the notion of evil seriously as something very real, for there is no cogent intellectual alternative. To designate as psychopathological those, who in previous centuries would have been regarded as iniquitous, creates merely an ersatz clarity. The mass murderer Pol Pot, for example, would appear to have been rather well-adjusted. Apropos is a recent article in The New York Times about a movement in psychiatry, especially those forensic psychiatrists dealing with serial killers, to reintroduce the notion of evil into discussions (Carey 2005).

If evil does exist, then to acknowledge that a group of human beings can become downright iniquitous does not make one paranoid, for to deny the existence of evil — as many of the British people did, under the leadership of Neville Chamberlain—can have dangerous consequences. That denial, although sometimes due to naiveté, most often stems from a failure of nerve. That failure hides behind the supercilious claim that one subscribes to a "nuanced morality," or some other form of moral relativism. That one's nerve would fail in the presence of evil is understandable, for the existence of evil flies in the face of rational understanding. Like any encounter with the irrational, or the uncanny, the encounter with evil can be disorienting, dizzying, and nauseating.

Hannah Arendt's notion of "the banality of evil," as embodied by the bureaucratic Eichmann, reduces evil to something more human, familiar, and understandable. Gone is the notion that evil is necessarily malevolent, let alone demonic. On deeper inspection, though, there may have been something more insidious about Eichmann than can be explained by Arendt's theory. In an article that recently appeared in Commentary (July-August 2005), Hillel Halkin argues that Eichmann was not the man described by Hannah Arendt—a mindless bureaucrat. Halkin, who studied the original film footage of Eichmann, concluded that Eichmann was highly intelligent.[4] The transcripts of the trial confirm Halkin's opinion.

Secondly, Halkin notes that there is a twisted expression on Eichmann's face, which had been observed by various journalists at the trial, and which Halkin interprets as a sour grimace. This is how Halkin describes Eichmann, "There is annoyance in this expression, and humiliation as well, mixed with hidden anger or rage—an anger or rage that the twisted lips fight to conceal, if not from himself, at least form the scrutiny of the judges..." (2005, p. 60). Halkin then proceeds to interpret the source of Eichmann's rage:

> Does this grimace, contrary to Arendt's view of him, make Eichmann a "monster"? Of course not; but it does hint at submerged depths that tell us there is more to the man than meets the eye. Again and again, the indignity of his position — he, the former Obersturmbannfuehrer, director of Section IV-B-4 of the Head Office for Reich Security, a once fearful figure to whose brutality several witnesses have testified, now incarcerated by the Jews, judged by the Jews — makes him wince with a revulsion that is at the same time an effort to remain reasonable and well-mannered. (2005, p. 60)

---

4 Halkin could have also supported his point by mentioning that Eichmann shrewdly used Kant's ethics in his own defense. (Bernstein 2002)

Why hadn't Arendt noticed Eichmann's true character? According to Halkin, it was because it would not have fit into her theory about the mindlessness of evil under totalitarianism. Halkin does not use the word "malevolent," but it is clear, from his descriptions of Eichmann, that he regards him to be so. There is, though, no contradiction in saying that Eichmann was both banal and malevolent, for even Milton's Satan, underneath all his demonic grandeur, was banal in his envy, pride, and all of his other personality flaws. On the other hand, evil itself, in contradistinction to those who commit evil, is a profoundly perplexing mystery.

There is, in addition to the mask of the bureaucrat, another mask —common to the modern world—used by those who are evil, or malevolent. It is the mask of the passionate idealist. An example of this type of person is the Dutch-Moroccan Mohammed Bouyeri, who murdered the film maker Theodore Van Gogh, simply because he felt that a film that Van Gogh had made about the oppression of women under Islam, had insulted that religion. At his sentencing, Bouyeri said to Van Gogh's mother, "I acted out of conviction—not because I hated your son" ("Suspect in Dutch," 2005).

Some have a tendency to view that breed of murderer as tragically misguided, but ultimately selfless. After all, like Bouyeri, they claim that they act not out of hate, but out of conviction. Eric Hoffer, who was never deceived by such true believers, observed that "It is the inordinately selfish who need self-forgetting most, hence their proneness to passionate pursuits" (1955, 125). The press, on the other hand, is deceived, which is why one very rarely hears suicide bombers, and terrorists in general, described as being "inordinately selfish," bloodthirsty, sadistic, mean-spirited, or malevolent. In the case of Bouyeri, it is not clear why "conviction" would prompt him to shoot Van Gogh not once, but fifteen times, then, after Van Gogh was dead, to stab him, finally slitting his throat. Obviously, there was something a lot darker than conviction involved. The supposedly mindless bureaucrat and the passionate "idealist," are very different psychological types, but they share the desire to camouflage their true nature. It has been long known that evil often is insidious in its efforts to conceal itself.

Murderers such as Eichmann and Mohammed Bouyeri are clearly evil. But are they also under the sway of the paranoid vision? Eichmann divided the world into those who are Aryans and those who are Jews. And Bouyeri divided it into Muslims and infidels. That sort of Manichaeism, coupled with the demonization of a certain group of people, is certainly indicative of the paranoid vision. There are further clues to the connection between evil and the paranoid vision that now warrant examination.

Evil and the Paranoid Vision

What, then, is the essence of evil? The eminent Indian scholar Ananda K. Coomaraswamy, in an essay entitled "What is 'Satan' and Where is 'Hell'?" (1947; 1977), cited a long tradition of philosophers and theologians, both East and West, who maintain that evil either derives from or is equivalent to individuality, egotism, and self-will. Among the many sources that he quotes is the Theological Germanica, the religious classic of the fourteenth century, which states "For there is nothing else in hell, but self-will; and if there were no self-will, there would be no devil and no hell" (1977, pp. 28-29).

Egotism, or self-will, is certainly indicative of the state of sinfulness. Indeed, it has often been pointed out that the seven deadly sins—greed, gluttony, lust, wrath, sloth, pride, and envy—are essentially the seven forms of egotism. Mystic that he is, Coomaraswamy attributes the problem not just to egotism, but, most fundamentally, to individuality itself, the implication being that selfhood comprises more than individuality. This philosophical tradition argues, then, that evil is not merely a function of bad upbringing. Nor is it confined to evildoers. On the contrary, evil lies at the heart of what it means to be a human being, at least in the immediate sense. When things go smoothly, dark impulses remain hidden, but when conflicts between individuals arise, be it even over trifles, it is fortunate that there are laws to discourage ordinary citizens from murdering each other.[5] Coomaraswamy also maintains that without individuality there would be no paranoid suspiciousness. If the paranoid vision has its roots in individuality, then it is always a latent possibility.

Another clue to the nature of evil can be found in the lives of people like the ancient Roman tyrants Nero and Caligula. They were possessed by sexual carnality, sadism, greed, gluttony, the lust for power, vanity, and a host of other dark emotions. Apropos is the New Testament's description of demons as "legion." That is an accurate description, for the evil person does not really possess a unified self, but a legion of moods, interests, and desires, all craving to be satisfied, despite any violence, to oneself or to others, that doing so might entail. Actually, "legion" would accurately describe the psychological life of the average person, even if it is somewhat less dramatic than that of a Roman emperor. What we are arguing is in accord with Buber's analysis of evil. Those who have fallen into temptation have, in essence, been sucked into "the vortex of possibility." (1953, p. 93) As Buber states,

> In the swirling space of images through which he strays, each and everything entices him to be made incarnate by him; he grasps at them like a wanton burglar, not with decision, but only in order to grasp the tension of omnipossibility; it all becomes reality, though no longer divine but his, his capriciously constructed, indestinate reality, his violence, which overcomes him, his handiwork and his fate. (1953, p. 92)

Bad as it is, what Coomaraswamy and Buber are referring to here is merely the ubiquitous garden-variety species of evil. There also exists something rarer, and far darker, which might be called true evil, or, as Kant called it "radical evil." It lies beyond the sinfulness intrinsic to egotism, self-will, and individuality. Buber refers to the first type

---

5 This dark view of human beings, which is not inaccurate, is beset with the mystery of how it is that people, from time to time, act magnanimously, indeed are capable of self-sacrifice and saintliness. Apropos is a recent biography of Abraham Lincoln by William Lee Miller, *Lincoln's Virtue: An Ethical Biography*. (Knopf 2002). Miller explores how it is that this Kentucky backwoodsman, lawyer, and then politician could evolve into a truly good person. In any case, we won't address this ethical problem here, other than to suggest that the existence of goodness indicates that selfhood can transcend egotism.

of evil, the type that we have just discussed, appropriately enough, as the evil of indecision, but refers to radical evil as the type involving decision, for there is a deliberate choice of the state of damnation.

The psychiatrist M. Scott Peck, in his seminal work, *People of the Lie* (1983; 1998) provides a perceptive analysis of radical evil: "It is not their sins per se that characterize evil people, rather it is the subtlety and persistence of their sins. This is because the central defect of the evil is not the sin but the refusal to acknowledge it." (p. 69) But what is involved here is more than a narcissistic refusal to acknowledge one's sins, for the truly evil person is, as Peck understands it, malignantly narcissistic:

> Evil is an opposition to life. It is that which opposes the life force... Evil is that which kills spirit. There are various essential attributes of life — particularly human life — such as sentience, mobility, awareness, growth...Evil, then, for the moment, is that force, residing either inside or outside of human beings, that seeks to kill life or liveliness. (pp. 42-43)

What is the origin of this death wish? It is, first of all, a function of the psychological mechanism of projection. Peck suggests that evil people project their iniquity onto other people, and then seek to destroy the evil that they imagine to exist in the other person. Here, then, is an effort to destroy in other people that which one dare not admit exists in oneself, for it would terribly wound one's pride. On a deeper level, though, the malignant narcissist knows it all too well. The paranoid vision is, of course, very much about that sort of projection, not only upon individuals, but upon other groups, organizations, peoples, societies, races, and nations.

There is a second reason for the evil person's death wish. It might be called "malignant nihilism," for it spawns not merely the meaninglessness intrinsic to nihilism, but also a hatred for life. The evil hate life, and would murder it, because it opposes their will, desires, and goals. Of course, life opposes everyone's will, but whereas life's adversities cause psychologically healthy people to mature, malignant narcissists rebel, becoming all the more bitter, resentful and hostile.

Like those who are simply egotistical, those who are possessed by radical evil suffer from the vortex of possibility. This is because there is, as we have suggested, a meaninglessness intrinsic to nihilism. Without meaning there is no direction, the effect of which is disorientation, an experience that cannot be endured for very long. Might the appeal of the paranoid vision be that it promises coherence and unity—as does any worldview—offering relief from the vortex of possibility? For now that one has an enemy, one's energies are focused, and one has a direction in life; i.e. to destroy one's enemy.

We earlier observed that the paranoid makes a claim to perfection (purity, grandeur, greatness, etc.) and yet simultaneously experiences a sense of humiliation, impotence, and degradation. This same type of opposition exists for one who is possessed by the spirit of malevolence. As Peck maintains "We come now to a sort of paradox. I have said that evil people feel themselves to be perfect. At the same time, however, they have an unacknowledged sense of their own evil nature. Indeed, it is this very sense from which they are frantically trying to flee" (1983; 1988, p. 74). The fact that both the paranoid and the evildoer suffer a similar contradiction would suggest that there is a structural similarity in the selfhood constituted by paranoia and by radical evil. Obviously, with a contradiction raging in one's soul, one will not know inner peace. So it is for both the paranoid and the evildoer. As Coomaraswamy states, "...for as long as he is not at peace with Himself, he can hardly be at peace with anybody else, but will 'project' his own disorders..." (p. 28)

In maintaining that a person can become possessed by the paranoid vision, and that such a person has become malevolent, one finds oneself beset by a conundrum: good and evil presuppose a moral agent who can freely choose between the two, but possession implies a lack of freedom. What sense, then, does it make to claim that a person possessed by the paranoid vision is malevolent and therefore evil? Would it be absurd to say that a person can freely choose to become possessed, or enslaved, to the paranoid vision? Although logically a contradiction, it isn't existentially, for that is actually what happens.

In truth, a person is never completely possessed, whether it be by lust, by jealousy, by the desire for power, or by the paranoid vision, for there is always exists a margin of self-awareness. That self-awareness, which is key to understanding evil, is usually greater at the beginning, before one has sunk ever deeper into the depths of depravity. That is why it is still at the beginning, before becoming a murderer, that Macbeth still has the wherewithal to ask himself:

> ...why do I yield to that suggestion
> Whose horrid image doth unfix my hair
> And make my seated heart knock at my ribs,
> Against the use of nature? (Act. I, Scene IV. Line 134)

Hitler offers us an example of the paradox of possession. There has been much debate about whether he really hated the Jews or was simply Machiavellian, i.e., using the Jews to manipulate the German people. (Rosenbaum 1999) Support for the former can, for example, be found in Mein Kampf (1925; 1999). It is clear from reading that book that he truly hated the Jews, and in a really visceral way. So great was his hatred that he was willing to risk losing the war so as to continue to have the Jews killed. After all, the German army desperately needed railway cars, which were in short supply, to transport troops during the war in Russia. But Hitler refused his generals' requests, for those railway cars were needed to transport the Jews and other "undesirables" to the gas chambers.

On the other hand, evidence that Hitler was Machiavellian can, for example, be found in his famous statement, "If the Jews did not exist, I would have had to invent them." In Mein Kampf, he writes about the "big lie." He knew clearly that he was using the Jews as a scapegoat. It would seem a contradiction to assert that both notions—that he truly hated the Jews, and that he was using the belief in the Jews in a Machiavellian way—were simultaneously true, and yet they were. He was self-aware enough to know what he was doing in regard to the Jews, but he deliberately chose to fall into the abyss of hatred, to let himself be possessed by the paranoid vision, in its most maleficent form. He was, therefore, evil because he allowed himself to be possessed, to become unfree. Perhaps the choice of un-freedom lies at the very heart of evil.

A Preview of Horrors

The main body of this work consists of three parts. The first explores the narratives of the paranoid vision. These narratives—which include conspiracy theories and apocalyptic visions—are mythic stories that are infused with the paranoid vision. Without these stories, the paranoid vision could not receive expression, and could not spread to other people. It is here that paranoids find a scapegoat to explain and to justify their sense that they live in a fallen world, and that a group of conspirators are responsible. Secondly, those who indulge in apocalyptic fantasies see the coming end of the world as rectifying the sense of injustice that they experience.

The chapter on conspiracy theories deals with the explanatory and justificatory power of conspiracy theories. Whereas explanation seeks to render the world intelligible, justification seeks to render the perplexities of human existence both intelligible and meaningful. For the purposes of analysis, we have distinguished the explanatory from the justificatory functions of conspiracy theories, but in actual fact, explanation and justification are of a piece, for those who subscribe to these theories presume that by stripping away appearances, they will also uncover the fundamental cause of their unhappiness in the machination of conspirators.

Part II explores four case examples of the paranoid vision. These include Freud's inner circle, the Rajneeshees, the Khmer Rouge, and radical Islam. They are intended to be diverse so that one might grasp the paranoid vision by seeing it from a multitude of perspectives. (In the last chapter, the conclusion, we also briefly consider a few more examples, such as that of Henry Ford.)

Sigmund Freud's inner circle is the story of what can happen when a group of intellectuals devote themselves to the ideas of a powerful intellectual, who himself has a proclivity for the paranoid vision. In fairness to Freud, it is far from being the only time that a group of intellectuals became a paranoid cult. For example, Ayn Rand's circle of followers was clearly a cult as Jeff Walker, in *The Ayn Rand Cult* (1999), illustrates. Furthermore, as Robert J. Lifton suggests, even a graduate department of a university, or a scientific movement, can become, in essence, a cult (Lifton, 1989). The choice of Freud and his inner circle was based on several factors. It was partially due to the fact that they were a particularly intriguing group of people. It was also because Freud was a seminal figure in the emergence of the paranoid vision in modernity, as John Farrell (1996) illustrates. It was partially because their history together is very well-documented. Finally, it was because if it could happen there it could happen anywhere, for these were people who were the very founders of psychoanalysis.

Making sense of the paranoiac beginnings of psychoanalysis requires dwelling on the darker side of Freud and his disciples. This does not mean, though, that we have joined the ranks of those critics who, out of an inability to endure a painful cognitive dissonance, fail to acknowledge that although great men and women often have great faults, it does not lessen the value of their accomplishments. The fact that they are deeply flawed makes all that they did accomplish all the more remarkable.

In any case, there have been tens of thousands of organizations as bad as, or a good deal worse than, Freud's inner circle. Intellectual groups, social organizations, political groups, businesses, non-profits, charities, universities —there are endless examples of organizations, of every type, being transformed by the paranoid vision into hellish places. What essentially happened in Freud's inner circle is far from uncommon. It should, therefore, be read and understood as a case example of a universal phenomenon.

Bhagwan Rajneesh's organization is representative of how a group of spiritual seekers, centering their lives around a person they regard as a sage, can transform into a paranoid cult. A far more egregious example of such a group of people could have been chosen. Rajneesh and his cohorts could not anywhere measure up, in regard to deadliness, to such cults as those of Charles Manson, Jim Jones or to Aum Shinrikyo. But what is intriguing about the Rajneesh cult, in contradistinction to the others, was that here was a man who, initially at least, really did have much to offer in terms of deep insight into the human predicament, coupled with the ability to invite other people to challenge those metaphysical assumptions that imprison their awareness. Rajneesh's writings reveal an intelligent and creative thinker, possessing a certain spiritual intensity. That is what makes his downfall, and that of his disciples, all the more poignant, and all the more telling, as a cautionary tale about the paranoid vision.

Pol Pot and the Khmer Rouge, the Cambodian communist party, is an example of the paranoid vision emerging amongst a group of radical intellectuals who were not content merely with intellectual discussion, but sought political power as well. The result was the creation of a lethal organization hell-bent on genocide. There are, again, many other examples that could have been chosen, but there are a number of things that seem particularly interesting about the Khmer Rouge. They are an example of a group of people motivated by a millennial vision, namely communism. What never ceases to intrigue those who study the history of the Khmer Rouge is the extent of their anti-intellectualism, the fact that they killed people who wore glasses, who had soft hands, or who spoke other languages.

The last case example, radical Islamism, is not about a single organization, but a movement that is a blend of religious fundamentalism and a totalistic ideology which, some would argue, either is, or bears a close resemblance to, fascism. All in all, it is a paranoid reaction to modernity. Radical Islam is a millennial movement, for it imagines that there had existed a Muslim utopia in the seventh century, during the time when Mohamed was alive. Daniel Pipes (1998b) points out the defensiveness of Osama bin Laden and other radical figures. This defensiveness grows out of the sense that paradise was stolen from them.

So it is that these case examples are all quite different. Needless to say, Freud and his colleagues were intellectuals, not genocidal murderers or terrorists. Yet they are compared here to groups like the Khmer Rouge. Once again, the purpose of these comparisons is not to blunt obvious distinctions, but to understand the paranoid vision by seeing a wide range of its expressions.

Part III, called "Beyond the Paranoid Vision," explores the possibility of transcending the paranoid vision. This transcendence takes two forms, the first of which is to elevate the paranoid vision to a "higher" level, where, freed of its malevolence, it might reveal deep truths about life. For example, Plato's Allegory of the Cave is viewed here as essentially a paranoid narrative, for it too suggests that there is an adversary who has conspired to do one harm. That harm consists in keeping one imprisoned in the cave of illusion and ignorance.

Secondly, transcendence could involve a shift from the paranoid vision to the comic vision. Why the comic vision? There is nothing more serious than a person under the grip of the paranoid vision. This is not surprising, for the paranoid vision is the polar opposite of the comic vision. Whereas the paranoid vision is grimly serious, the comic vision is lighthearted and playful. Whereas the paranoid vision offers a simplistic and reductive view of people and events, the comic vision embraces ambiguity, incongruity, and absurdity. Whereas the paranoid vision views humanity in terms of a Manichean dualism, the comic vision promotes a sympathetic inclusiveness. These reflections are important because the comic vision may be a cure for those who see life in terms of the paranoid vision. Thus the course of our journey will be into the depths of the paranoid vision, and then, hopefully, we shall find our way out into the sunlight.

Part I:

Narratives of the

Paranoid Vision

Chapter Two

Conspiracy Theories: Quest for Intelligibility and Meaning

"The belief in the Homeric Gods whose conspiracies were responsible for the vicissitudes of the Trojan War is gone. But the place of the gods on Homer's Olympus is taken by the Learned Elders of Zion, or the monopolists, or the capitalists, or the imperialists."

— Karl Popper (1963; 2002)

The core belief of the paranoid vision—that satanic conspirators have robbed one's group (clan, society, nation, etc.) of happiness, grandeur, and paradise—remains just an unfocused metaphysical pathos, until a story is hatched to give it substance and direction. Conspiracy theories are able to serve this narrative function because they are a mode of explanation in the philosophical sense. They are, in other words, a way of interpreting the world so that, wherever upon it one may gaze, it reflects back a certain vision of life, i.e. the paranoid vision. Conspiracy theories, therefore, are akin to myths, fairy tales, novels, metaphysical systems, theologies, scientific theories, apocalyptic fantasies, urban legends, and other representations of the mind's quest to make sense of the world. We stated that conspiracy theories are a mode of explanation, but it will become apparent that they are actually a curious perversion of the explanatory enterprise.

To explain is to render the spatiotemporal world intelligible, i.e., graspable by the mind. That which is intelligible must be definite and determinate. It must be something, have an identity, be a unity, for the mind cannot grasp a hodgepodge. Nor can it grasp what is different from one moment to the next. The mind can only fix upon that which is constant. The enterprise of explanation consists in positing that there exists something, amidst the world of multiplicity and change, that is unchanging, graspable and intelligible. What, then, satisfies that criterion? Scientific explanations posit a material substrate such as matter, energy, substance, or atoms. Matter, for example, is said to remain the same, despite its multifarious transformations. Or they posit scientific laws, which are believed to possess an unchanging eternality. For example, Kelvin's Law will not be any different next year.

Unlike metaphysical or scientific explanations, conspiracy theories do not seek to explain the spatiotemporal world. They seek to explain the social and political realm. The identity factor in a conspiracy theory is a group of people—for example, the Freemasons, the Illuminati, the Jews, the Imperialists, the Trilateral Commission, The Council on Foreign Relations, or the Bilderbergs—who are alleged to be secretive, powerful, nefarious, and the real force behind the tumult of world events.

There is a great satisfaction in being able to grasp, or to imagine that one grasps, the sociopolitical realm—a multiplicity of people, societies, nations, ideas, and much more, all suffused with change—by reducing it to a single idea, theme, or plot. One reads the newspaper, and suspects the dark truth, "Ah ha! It all makes sense. It's those powerful and fiendish Bilderbergs again, that international cartel of bankers, industrialists, and power brokers who control the world!" Like matter, or energy, the Bilderbergs, presumably, can assume a multitude of forms, guises, or disguises. Although terribly troubled by the evil that they perceive, conspiracy theorists also experience the joy of understanding, the satisfaction that derives from seeing it all come together, or at least seem to come together. False understanding can seem just as convincing to the mind as true understanding, at least initially, until doubts start appearing.

All explanatory theories are, therefore, founded on an appearance/reality distinction. Things are never what they seem. It may appear, for example, that a houseplant withered, disintegrated, and all but disappeared, but in reality—according to the chemist—atoms were merely rearranged. Similarly, it may appear that American astronauts walked on the moon, or that Islamic terrorists blew up the World Trade Center, but conspiracy theorists regard such notions to be the product of deceptive appearances and disinformation, and would gladly disabuse everyone of their illusions. They contend, though, that false beliefs are not simply a function of naiveté. On the contrary, they have been deliberately fabricated by a nefarious group of conspirators. In that sense, appearances in the realm of conspiracy theories are different from appearances in the realm of science, for the latter is not a function of a deliberate deception, although Descartes, in his *Meditations*, did consider the possibility that a cosmic trickster could be deliberately deceiving him.

In addition to multiplicity and change, there is another dimension of spatiotemporal existence that is in need of explanation. It is what philosophers refer to as contingency, and it is synonymous with chance, accidentalness, openness, and indeterminacy. Contingency is unintelligible because it means that there is no graspable reason why events occur; they are merely random. The opposite of contingency is necessity. Causal, or mechanical, necessity means that, for example, a billiard ball cannot move for no apparent reason, but has moves because another ball strikes it. Of course, for those who seek meaning in the world of events, causal necessity answers the "how" question, but not the "why" question. What they are seeking, therefore, is what Aristotle referred to as the teleological, or final cause. This sort of explanation seeks an ultimate purpose, a necessary reason, for why things happen.

The denial of contingency, and the search for necessity, is evident in all domains. Theological and philosophical explanations, for example, seek to reveal divine necessity. This is the necessity that

Hamlet intuited when he said, "There is a providence in the fall of a sparrow." Marcus Aurelius expressed it as follows:

> The whole divine economy is pervaded by Providence. Even the vagaries of chance have their place in Nature's scheme; that is, in the intricate tapestry of the ordinances of Providence. Providence is the source from which all things flow; and is allied with Necessity, and the welfare of the universe. (167 AD; 1964, pp. 45-46)

The pre-Socratic Anaximander's one extant fragment tells us that the four elements return to the Apeiron, the boundless, out of necessity, for having transgressed their rightful bounds. Plato's notion of a great chain of being—from the angels down to the lowest animals—is an attempt to establish that the existence of the world follows necessarily from God's agape (Lovejoy 1936; 1973). Hegel, in his *Philosophy of History* (1840; 1990), seeks to show that the history of the world, including its disastrous conflicts, is not merely arbitrary or accidental. On the contrary, it proceeds from a dialectical necessity, from "the cunning of reason." The pessimistic Schopenhauer of course, regarded Hegel's ideas as pure bunk, but even the atheistic Nietzsche discovered something akin to a providence, necessity, fate, or destiny, which entered into his philosophy as "amor fati."

The wish to deny the contingent dimension of spatiotemporal existence, and the insistence that events happen out of necessity, leads science to posit causal explanations. Encapsulating the effort of science to explain away the chance dimension of the world, Einstein said, "I refuse to believe that God plays dice with the universe." Einstein was objecting to the quantum physics of Heisenberg, with its claim that uncertainty and indeterminacy are intrinsic elements of reality (Zukier, 1987).

Conspiracy theories are, therefore, not unique in that regard, for they, too, seek to demonstrate that behind the appearance of contingency, accident, chance, and indeterminacy, lies necessity. They claim that none of the significant events of the social and political realm are free, unplanned, or accidental. On the contrary, these events are due to a nefarious cabal of conspirators operating clandestinely. If one thinks otherwise, then one has been deluded by appearances, and fooled into complacency by the conspirators. The notion that "nothing happens by chance" has reached absurd proportions in the Middle East. Daniel Pipes, an historian and theorist of conspiracy theories, and a Middle East specialist, offers examples, from the Arab counties and Iran, of conspiracy theories predicated on the notion that the Jews — and sometimes the Americans or the British—are behind just about everything bad that happens, including natural disasters like earthquakes and droughts. (Pipes 1989)

The conspiracy theories surrounding the Kennedy assassination offer an illuminating example of this effort to explain away contingency. There is something absurd about a lone gunman, a feckless loser of little consequence, assassinating the President of the United States. Essentially stated, the mind cannot compute that a relatively minor cause could generate a major effect. This is because the basis of intelligibility is that A=A, the law of identity, from which is derived what Leibniz called "the Principle of Sufficient Reason." It states that a cause must be equal in potency to its effect. Otherwise there is creation ex nihilo, something coming out of nothing, like magic, which is unintelligible to reason. Thus, only a conspiracy of colossal proportions—one involving the CIA, the Mafia, Castro, the Russians, Nixon, and everyone else who had a reason to hate Kennedy—could precipitate an event of such immense consequences.[6]

Might it be fair to say that scientific explanations seek intelligibility within the material realm, and that conspiracy theories seek intelligibility within the social and political realm? That is not quite true, for not all social and political theories hinge around a conspiracy. There are social and political theories, of the usual sort, that seek unchanging laws amidst the continually changing social and political realm. A theory of that sort might contend, for example, that the loss of Great Britain's colonies in the twentieth century was not something that happened for merely contingent reasons—for example, the fact

---

6   Robins and Post (1997) present a somewhat different analysis of why the lone gunman theory has been rejected, by many people, in favor of conspiracy theories about Kennedy's assassination. They contend that the actual facts of the case are not congruent with the myth of the young king murdered. Robins and Post are correct, but we would contend that mythic thinking is an effort to explain the world.

that Mahatma Gandhi appeared on the scene — but was due to long-term economic and geopolitical trends.

Such explanations differ from conspiracy theories in that the identity factors that they posit—a long term social trend (such as the aging of the population of a country), an economic law (such as the Pareto Principle), a geopolitical and social reality (such as the closing of the American frontier), or a cultural change (such as the rise of feminism)—are abstract and impersonal. In contrast to social and political theories, the identity factors posited by conspiracy theories — the secret and nefarious designs of a certain group of people — are particular and personal. That is the strange twist in conspiracy theories, their oddity as a mode of explanation, for instead of truly ascending to the abstract and universal, they conflate the particular and the universal. That is, after all, what is implied in suggesting that a particular group of people is the universal cause of all that is wrong with the world.

There obviously are philosophical, theological, and psychological theories about the origin of evil, but they do not attribute evil to a particular group of people. A noted scholar of conspiracy theories, Michael Barkun, has a somewhat different take on the function of conspiracy theories than the one offered here. Barkun states, "The essence of conspiracy beliefs lies in attempts to delineate and explain evil" (2003, 3). Barkun is correct that conspiracy belief defines what is often experienced as a vague apprehension of evil and, in so doing, makes it more comprehensible. But what conspiracy theories seek to explain and to justify is not evil, but human suffering, why this life of ours is not quite paradise. Evil is not what is being explained, but is the vehicle of explanation. More precisely, the existence of an evil group of conspirators is the vehicle of explanation, i.e. the identity factor behind the multiplicity of life's problems.

Why, for example, was there a pestilence that ravished the countryside, a tidal wave, or an earthquake? One can search for a scientific cause, a theological reason, or one can attribute it to an evil cabal of conspirators who have the technological know-how and power to cause such disasters. There has been, for example, a conspiracy theory, rife in many Afro-American communities, that the deadly

AIDS virus was created by the CIA, as a form of genocide against blacks. Thus an evil group of conspirators becomes the explanatory vehicle to make sense of suffering.

It should also be noted that although most scholars would agree that conspiracy theories are a form of explanation, the distinguished social psychologist Serge Moscovici begs to differ. His objection is worth considering:

"But, you will say, conspiracy theories grow out of the need to explain, which is the function of any theory...In order for any explanation to be valid, however, one must be willing to recognize certain limits to its applicability. If one can trace all effects to the same cause, one believes that one has explained everything. But a theory that explains everything really explains nothing. Thus I suggest that the function of conspiracy theory is not to explain an event through a cause. Rather, it responds to the need to integrate one's image of society in one cause...In other words, the import of the theory in question is that it integrates people's mind-set and prevents any "rupture" in their mentality...It is like saying 'You see, everything is clear,' or 'There is nothing bizarre or disconcerting about this; you are familiar with all this.'" (1987, pp. 156-157)

Moscovici is correct that the function of conspiracy theories is not really to explain, if by "explain" we mean investigating a phenomenon and then discovering its true cause. On the contrary, conspiracy theories "explain away" phenomena, particularly those events that might disrupt the ontological security of the members of a particular society. For example, many socially and politically backward countries blame their economic troubles on conspiracies by Western imperialists, thus explaining away those unpleasant facts about themselves that urgently need to be addressed, but if addressed would cause social disruption. Although Moscovici does not use the phrase "explain away," or "reductionism," it lies at the heart of his critique.

On the other hand, Moscovici is incorrect in distinguishing conspiracy theories from other theories on that basis, for in truth, to explain is always to explain away, and this is something that all theories do, more or less. The Freudians, for example, claim that human values are nothing but sublimated libido. Thus do they seek to explain away real guilt by reducing it to mere guilt feelings, as Buber (1964) suggests. Philosophical and scientific theories are no different in that respect. They explain away anything that is unintelligible, such as color and sound, by taking these phenomena out of the object, and placing them in that repository for "unreal" appearances, known as the subject (Meyerson 1908; 1973).

Naturally, some theories do more explaining away, are more reductionistic and, consequently, further afield of appearances, than others. At one extreme are explanations like that of Parmenides, who said that "Reality is a well rounded sphere." Despite the metaphysical brilliance of Parmenides, and his disciple Zeno, in audaciously following the logic of reason to the point of the reductio ad absurdum, one cannot help raising the pedestrian objection that subsequent philosophers raised, that the world sure doesn't look like a well rounded sphere.

At the other extreme of the explanatory spectrum lies the metaphysics of those who are interested in "saving the appearances," to use Owen Barfield's phrase. Alfred North Whitehead's process philosophy, for example, may be relatively congruent with common sense, but Whitehead has been rightfully accused of not explaining very much (Schilpp 1951). Where do conspiracy theories stand on the explanatory spectrum? They are way out there, on the far side of reductionism. They do not ignore appearances, but they radically interpret them such that the world appears far afield of anything approaching common sense.

Selling Life Short

The enterprise of explanation, therefore, seeks to show how that which is accidental, or contingent, is really necessary, in this case predetermined. Conspiracy theories offer a curious type of causal explanation for events whose outcome would otherwise not seem to be predetermined. For example, it would certainly appear that buyers and sellers in the stock market determine the price of stocks, that it is a free market. After all, the stock market is comprised of millions of shareholders, and billions of dollars change hands each day. The Securities and Exchange Commission does not have the staff to monitor thousands of individual securities, as well as the millions of transactions that occur every day. Insider trading is notoriously difficult to prove. Consequently, individual stocks have, at times, been manipulated. Furthermore, as happened in the case of Enron, the financial statements of a company can be falsified to deceive investors of a company's net worth. Enron was not the first, nor will it be the last, case of such fraud and investor deception, and for every Enron there have been many more such conspiracies that have never been exposed.

But it would be almost inconceivable that the entire market could be manipulated, that a group of conspirators could force the Dow, the S & P 500, and all else to go up or to go down at their command, without their collusive efforts being detected. After all, large-scale trades are required to be reported to the Security and Exchange Commission. Even without that reportage, it would be virtually impossible to keep such major manipulations a secret for very long. All the same, there have always been conspiracy theorists who have claimed that the market is manipulated. They have asserted, more specifically, that the entire stock market — not merely individual securities—is manipulated by a cabal of wealthy financiers, who conspire to manipulate prices for their personal gain, while maintaining the illusion of a free market.

In the late 1990s, when the bull market was reaching levels that some security analysts considered to be unrealistically high, one could detect, among investment analysts, an increasing sense of financial acrophobia, a fear of the Icarus-like consequences of the stock market's bold ascent to historically unprecedented levels. This fear was reflected in the warning by Allan Greenspan, then Chairman of the Federal Reserve Board, of "irrational exuberance" among investors. At that time, some conspiracy theorists who wrote and published investment newsletters were coming out with their usual very bearish predictions. That their predictions would be pessimistic is not surprising, since those with the paranoid vision are inclined, for reasons that shall be explored, towards an apocalyptic view of the future. They would eventually be vindicated, to some extent, for the market's bubble would burst, but that would not be for some time.

In the meantime, those bearish conspiracy theorists felt perplexed, frustrated and a bit embarrassed that the stock market kept on climbing to higher levels, despite their gloom and doom forecasts. To explain the stock market's strength, they maintained that a group of high-ranking government officials—such as the heads of the United States Treasury, the Federal Reserve Board, the New York Stock Exchange, and the Commodities Futures Trading Commission—had formed a "Plunge Protection Team." The team would, with government funds, make huge purchases of stocks during serious market sell offs, with the intent of stabilizing the market, so as to prevent it from dropping too precipitously and creating a serious recession or even a depression. That such a team supposedly existed was the secret to which the newsletter writers, and even the *Washington Post* (Fromson 1997), had somehow become privy. That sort of conspiracy theory was not, of course, nefarious. On the contrary, it was one that many investors would hope exist. There was, though, absolutely no basis for such a belief.

Why, then the existence of such a belief? Aside from relieving the anxiety over the bottom dropping out of the market, the belief fed into a certain paranoid delusion of grandeur. One imagined that oneself alone, or just a small handful of people, have, through their great powers of discernment, been able to decipher the actions of a powerful group of people, namely the stock market conspirators, and that one has been disabused of one's naïve belief in the free market.

In addition to the conspiracy theory about the Plunge Protection Team, there have always been conspiracy theories about secret cabals of investors who manipulate the stock market for their financial gain. Umberto Eco suggests another motive,

> Take stock-market crashes. They happen because each individual makes a wrong move, and all the wrong moves put together create panic. Then whoever lacks steady nerves asks himself: Who's behind this plot, who's benefiting? He has to find an enemy, a plotter, or it will be, God forbid, his fault. (1998, p. 513)

Eco has a point about sour grapes, for envy lies at the core of the paranoid vision, but the long and notorious history of conspiracy theories relating to financial institutions other than the stock market—such as those about international bankers, the Rothschilds, the Federal Reserve Board—would make us suspect that there was something in addition at stake. Here, from Lipset and Raab's book on extremism (1970), is a representative passage from Gary Allen, a writer whose books expounding conspiracy theories have sold in the millions. He indicates a collusion between international bankers and socialists:

> Why would international bankers and financiers be interested in promoting a Socialist World Government? Clearly, socialism is only the bait to obtain the support of the political underworld and to create the structure necessary to maintain dictatorial control. What this small group of financiers and cartel-oriented businessmen are interested in is in monopoly control over the world's natural resources, trade, transportation, and communications—something that despite their great wealth they could not achieve otherwise. Therefore, the supercapitalists become supersocialists realizing that only a World Government under their control can give them the power necessary to achieve their goal. Only this could explain why these extremely wealthy men would be willing to support movements which seem to be aimed at their own destruction, The financiers and cartelists do not seem to be injured by the socialists so long as they can manipulate them, using them for their own purposes. (Allen, as qtd. in Lipset and Raab, 1970, p. 260)

What is the origin, psychologically speaking, of Allen's contention that the international bankers are plotting—in the most farfetched manner imaginable, i.e. by instigating a socialist revolution—for dictatorial control? Might there be an underlying anxiety at play here, on the part of Allen and other paranoids? The psychiatrist David Shapiro provides us with a clue, when he refers to the paranoid as even more rigid than the obsessive-compulsive:

> The fact is that the unexpected, the surprising, the unusual, or even the new is no friend to any rigid person—neither to

> the suspicious person nor even to the dogmatic one. To a
> rigid person, the unusual or unexpected is threatening simply
> because it is unusual or unexpected, aside from whatever else
> it may be...It is not a concrete danger, but surprise that the
> suspicious person dreads most. (Shapiro, 1962, pp. 62-63)

What is the anxiety over being surprised essentially about? Shapiro does not say, but one may surmise that it is not simply evolutionary. That is, it is not a residue of primeval concerns about being suddenly ambushed by a tiger. To be surprised derives, rather, from an ontological anxiety. Such an anxiety is not about one's physical existence; it is about a threat to selfhood. To be surprised is to lose control, or to realize that one never was in control.

There are, of course, certain people, nervous about appearing not to be in control — senior corporate managers, for example — whose favorite phrase, upon hearing any sort of surprising news, no matter how shocking, is "I knew that." In such cases, the claim to prior knowledge operates partly as a way of convincing other people of one's omniscience, and partly as a defense mechanism, a way of hiding one's own insecurities from oneself. Of course, Shapiro is referring to a more pathological anxiety over the threat of being surprised than is found in the average person.

The fear of being surprised, the anxiety over uncertainty, and the dread of not being in control are, essentially, a species of a more fundamental anxiety, that of being disoriented, of falling into a state of chaos, and thus losing all control. This is one of the most primal and terrifying of anxieties. Apropos is Freud's insight that one seeks to transform anxiety into fear. Paradoxically, underlying the paranoid's fear of being controlled by evil conspirators is an anxiety over a total lack of control. The emotional logic runs like this: It is better to have a cabal of evil conspirators in control, and then to fear and hate them, than to have an anxious and un-grounding state of affairs in which no one is in control. Investigative reporter Jon Ronson colorfully expresses it, after a long search for supposed conspirators:

> "Let's face it," my Deep Throat had said to me, "nobody rules
> the world anymore. The markets rule the world. Maybe that's

why your conspiracy theorists make up all those crazy things. Because the truth is much more frightening. Nobody rules the world. Nobody controls anything." (2002, p. 321)

Let us see if our thesis can serve to illuminate the dark world of conspiracy theorists. It would appear that the conspiracy theorist feels ungrounded by the notion that the stock market and, for that matter, the entire global economy is not in the secure hands of a select group of highly ethical people with both superior knowledge and intelligence. On the contrary, the stock market is founded on something that is unplanned, open, indeterminate, and uncontrollable: the differing opinions and decisions of millions of buyers and sellers, each with a limited grasp of situations and events. It sounds like a recipe for a chaotic and anxious state of affairs.

It may, indeed, appear that the markets are always on the edge of chaos, but part of the conspiracy theorist's anxiety, in that regard, derives from a failure to understand, and to appreciate, how the world really works. Economist and political philosopher Friedrich A. Hayek explains:

> The enemies of liberty have always based their arguments on the contention that order in human affairs requires that some should give orders and others obey. Much of the opposition to a system of freedom under general laws arises from the inability to conceive of an effective co-ordination of human activities without deliberate organization by a commanding intelligence. One of the achievements of economic theory has been to explain how such a mutual adjustment of the spontaneous activities of individuals is brought about by the market, provided that there is a known delimitation of each individual. (Hayek 1960; 1978, 159)

Neither the totalitarian nor the conspiracy theorist believes that order can come about through individuals acting spontaneously without the imposition of a commanding intelligence. If the totalitarian, fearing chaos, believes that order must be imposed from without, the conspiracy theorist, similarly fearing chaos, believes that order already exists, behind the scenes, and is in full control of our world, even if it is the evil order of conspiratorial collusion. Neither has faith that order can emerge unplanned.

In point of fact, unplanned order—in the form of a naturally arising equilibrium — is intrinsic to the stock market, to the capitalist economy, and to economic, social, and political interactions in general. Not only are such unplanned equilibriums at play in the realm of business and economics, and social systems, they are also the foundation of the ecosystem of nature. As a matter of fact, "chaos theory" is really about the spontaneous emergence of order out of chaos on a molecular level (Gleick 1987).

It may be that a disbelief in the possibility of order, intelligence, and life emerging unplanned out of accident and contingency is ripe soil for the growth of the paranoid vision. The suspiciousness and distrust endemic to the paranoid vision, and the underlying anxious ontological insecurity, compel a person who sees life this way to fear unstructured situations, or to delusively imagine that control exists where, in fact, it does not. Disbelief in the possibility of unplanned order is likely a consequence of a lack of trust in life itself, for contingency lies at the very heart of life. Might it be, then, that the paranoid vision is the product of an existential crisis? That question will be left open for now.

The dreadful encounter with contingency gives rise to conspiracy theories not only in the economic domain, but in the realm of history too. Hofstadter felicitously expresses the paranoid sense of history as a conspiratorial plot:

> Unlike the rest of us, the enemy is not caught in the toils of the vast mechanism of history, himself a victim of his past, his desires, his limitations. He wills, indeed he manufactures, the mechanism of history, or tries to deflect the normal course of history in an evil way. He makes crises, starts runs on banks, causes depressions, manufactures disasters, and then enjoys and profits from the misery he has produced. (1966, p. 32)

The conspiracy theories that arose, particularly in America, after the French Revolution, illustrate Hofstadter's thesis. Historical research indicates that the revolution arose spontaneously. It was the result of a number of forces — social, political, economic, cultural, and intellectual—that had long been brewing, and which finally converged one fateful day in 1789. Of course, the fact that all of those factors converged when they did, and how they did, and with certain people leading the revolution, are all contingent factors. There was no historical necessity, for example, for the reign of terror occurring. Thus history is a combination of the determinacy of long term trends mated with indeterminacy, i.e. chance. But, as Hofstadter points out, conspiracy theorists claimed back in the eighteenth century, and still claim today, the contrary thesis, that the French Revolution had been preplanned by the Illuminati, a secret society, who saw how they could profit materially by fomenting revolution in France.

Conspiracy theories about history derive from a deficient understanding of the forces that guide history, just as they derive from a deficient understanding of economics. Daniel Pipes quotes two historians who offer implicit criticisms of the conspiratorial view of history. Herbert A.L. Fisher writes, "[T]here can be no generalizations, only one safe rule for the historian: that he should recognize in the development of human destinies the play of the contingent and the unforeseen" (qtd. in Pipes, 1997, p. 38). Lewis B. Namier writes, "The crowning attainment of historical study is a historical sense — an intuitive knowledge of how things do not happen" (qtd. in Pipes, 1997, p. 38). Namier means that conspiracies are not the major factors in history. Pipes also quotes the philosopher Karl Popper: "First [conspiracies] are not very frequent, and do not change the character of social life." (qtd. in Pipes, 1997, p. 39).

If anyone had an intuitive grasp of the way in which history works, it was Shakespeare, as he demonstrated in his plays. The way in which the conniving Richard the Third fails, in the end, is most enlightening. Richard loses his kingdom over what would seem to be a relatively minor detail, the lack of a horse. But the fact that Richard is defeated by a minor detail is not itself a minor detail! After all, accidents, contingencies, chance, and tricks of fate are the stuff of life. They defeat the conspiracy theory notion of history, which is founded on faith in the efficacy of perfect planning. Popper explains:

> Hitler, I said, made a conspiracy that failed. Why did it fail? Not just because other people conspired against Hitler. It failed, simply, because it is one of the striking things about social life that nothing ever comes off exactly as intended. Things always turn out a little bit differently. We hardly ever produce in social life precisely the effect that we wish to produce, and we usually get things that we do not want into the bargain. (1963; 2002, p. 166)

It is not that Hitler had nine lives. It is just that "mission impossible" scenarios are, with rare exceptions, indeed impossible. For example, the Israeli rescue at Entebbe—although overall an amazing success and a mission impossible if there ever was one—still resulted in the tragic deaths of an outstanding Israeli commander as well as one of Idi Amin's captives. As for warfare in general, the phrase "the fog of war" is certainly apropos. Modern, sophisticated warfare, conducted by the well-trained and technologically advanced American military, still has "friendly fire," which is responsible for a high percentage of casualties. Furthermore, although such factors as military genius, shrewd planning, intelligence, belief in the nobleness of one's cause, and sheer daring play a significant role in the success of any military campaign, the history of warfare indicates that simply managing to make fewer errors than the enemy also plays a very significant role. For example, Stalin was foolish enough to trust Hitler, when Hitler claimed that he wanted peace with Russia, despite the fact that Hitler had amassed over a million German soldiers on the Russian border! Yet Stalin still managed to win because Hitler was the bigger fool by attacking Russia during the winter, while being at war with England, and then by declaring war on America, thus waging a war simultaneously on three fronts. Here, then, it is evident that chance, accident, human stupidity, ignorance, delusion, and fate play a major role in history, contrary to the notion, shared by conspiracy theorists, that just about everything is planned.

Is history, then, nothing but a series of accidents? Certainly not. The historians quoted here are not denying that there are historical laws and that some sense can be made of the whole affair, although it is easier to do so retrospectively. The quest of the historian is to find such laws. Nor are they denying the existence of conspiracy theories. They are merely contending that the contingent, accidental dimension of spatiotemporal existence be taken into account in any attempt to understand the dynamics of history.

Ersatz Universality

All theories aspire to universality, for what is universal is necessary, rather than particular and contingent. In myth, universality is found in archetype. For example, Freud found that the struggles of King Oedipus, and those of Electra, are essential for the psychic development of all men and women. Of course, in Greek mythology, the gods are all too human, and so often lacking in universality, but the themes that emerge from those stories are, indeed, universal.

The same universality is found in literature, where theme transcends the particular characters and their struggles, the effect of which is to structure and render one's own experience meaningful. Consequently, William Faulkner recommended to the young writer to leave "...no room in his workshop for anything but the old verities and truths of the heart, the old universal truths lacking which any story is ephemeral and doomed—love and honor and pity and pride and compassion and sacrifice" (1950, 179).

In science, universality is found in laws and theorems. Newton's laws, for example, apply in Beijing, China just as they do in Binghamton, New York. In philosophy, universality is found in essence or idea. In all domains, only what is universal transcends time, conditions, circumstances, accidents, and contingencies, and can therefore serve as an intelligible and satisfactory explanation.

Do conspiracy theories, as a mode of explanation, possess universality? Now, this is the odd thing: as noted earlier, the identity factor in a conspiracy theory—namely a group of alleged conspirators—is specific, and therefore contingent. There is nothing necessary or universal about the Freemasons, nor any other group of alleged conspirators. People, groups, and organizations that actually exist, or once existed, are, by their very nature, particular, rather than universal. Furthermore, they are creations of time, and what is temporal cannot serve as a universal cause.

Even if it were somehow true that the evils that befall one were not a function of chance—but were prearranged to occur by a group of conspirators wielding enormous power, who could significantly influence the course of history — the very existence of the conspirators would be contingent upon the accidental circumstances endemic to spatiotemporal existence, and thus lack necessity. There is not a necessary reason why any particular person, group or organization—nefarious or otherwise—is destined to exist and to play a decisive role in shaping world events, Hegel to the contrary. Rooted in the vicissitudes of current events and history, the existence of a secret cabal lacks both the time-transcending universality, as well as the necessity required to serve as a satisfactory explanation of the evil, injustices, and suffering that one experiences.

That said, how is it that conspiracy theories do, in fact, have enormous explanatory power for many people, capturing their emotions, luring believers to suspend their critical thinking capacities, and sometimes propelling them into violent action? The explanatory power of conspiracy theories derives from the fact that they make an implicit claim to universality and necessity. Absurd though it may seem, their subtext is often that the alleged conspirators are the universal, necessary, and ultimate, source of evil in the world or, at least, the group of conspirators are believed to be Satan's earthly agents. Usually, the more malevolent the conspiracy theory, the more ultimate is the implicit metaphysical claim. Sometimes this claim to universality is even explicit, as in the conspiracy theory about Jewish plans for world domination—presented in the notorious forgery, commissioned by the Russian Tsar in the 19th Century—*The Protocols of the Elders of Zion* (Marsden, 1903; 2004).

How is it that conspiracy theories have been, and still are—despite their often being completely counterintuitive, if not downright absurd —powerfully persuasive to so many people, even to highly intelligent people? The answer lies in the symbolic, or mythic, power of conspiracy theories as a mode of explanation. To understand symbolic thinking, it might help to compare it to metaphorical thinking. In metaphorical thinking, a metaphor's meaning (its tenor) has been clearly discriminated from its vehicle (that which embodies its meaning.) One might say, for example, that a lion represents courage. Thus, in metaphorical thinking, the animal known as a lion and the concept of courage have clearly been distinguished.

But in the type of cognition characterized as symbolic—which is also called "mythic," or "archetypal"—the meaning of a symbol has not been distinguished from its particular representation. Thus, to a person experiencing life mythically, to eat the heart of a lion is literally to acquire courage. Similarly, for a devout Christian, baptism is experienced, quite literally, as being reborn. And similarly, in the communion ceremony, the Eucharist wafer does not represent Christ's flesh, and the wine represent Christ's blood; through the miracle of symbolic cognition the blood and the wine are experienced as literally Christ's flesh and blood. Thus, a person who is in symbolic consciousness does not distinguish the particular (the lion's heart, being immersed in water, the wafer and the wine, etc.) from its meaning (courage, rebirth, God, etc.)

Conspiracy theories are, actually, a curious hybrid of philosophical explanation and symbolic thinking, which is why we have suggested that they are a perversion of the explanatory enterprise. That is how it is possible for a conspiracy theory to evoke the sense that a particular group of people do not just have evil ways, but are perceived to be evil incarnate. That, then, would account for the curious absurdity of a contingent explanation—for example, "The Masons are behind everything"—appearing to be non-contingent, indeed the universal and necessary explanation of all of the evils in existence.

It is obvious, then, for a conspiracy theory to persuade one of its "truth," in the mythic sense, one cannot remain rational, discriminative, and analytical in one's thinking. One cannot use discursive reasoning to arrive at the truth of a matter for, if one did, one would perceive facts that were incongruent with the theory, wild improbabilities, and glaring contradictions within its logic. One might also question the motives, sophistication, and mental health, of those who were propagating the theory: Are the conspiracy theorists resentful hate mongers? Politically naïve? Psychologically unbalanced?

Imbued with the paranoid vision? What is their real agenda? All such thoughts would perplex one, prompting one to become skeptical of the conspiracy theory, or at least to entertain serious doubts about its validity. Conspiracy theories can only persuade one of their truth if one first falls for the temptation to regress to what has been called the symbolic, or mythic, level of cognition.

We use the word "temptation" in a way that is similar to how the social psychologist Dieter Groh used it in his essay, "The Temptation of Conspiracy" (1987). One can be tempted to believe in conspiracy theories because they provide a facile answer to ultimate questions that all people must face, questions that are difficult and problematic—Job, Arjuna, Hamlet, or Ivan Karamazov type of questions. Life's temptation is not just to believe in conspiracy theories. It is, more essentially, to regress to symbolic "answers" to life's ultimate questions, of which conspiracy theories are one species.

It is on the symbolic, or mythic, level of knowing that an alleged group of conspirators can be cast as the devil, or the Antichrist, in a cosmic morality play, with its Manichean bifurcation of the world into the forces of absolute good and absolute evil. Many scholars of conspiracy theories have noted this duality. J. M. Roberts believes that this type of Manichean thinking became increasingly prominent as a mode of historical explanation after the French Revolution:

> As events unrolled, they did so in a way which favored more and more a view of history as a whole as a struggle or a debate between two sides, one white, one black. The model became more and more persuasive, and even the struggles of Greek city states and the trumpeting of medieval barons were strained out of context and re-read as acts in the universal drama of Left and Right. Political Manichaeism resulted which has embittered our political life ever since. Today people still seek extensions of its wonderfully simplifying power and impose the terminology it has engendered on things as incongruous as the politics of modern Africa—just as, a century ago, they were imposed on the primitive convulsions of the Balkans. (1972, p. 358)

Some years back, while a graduate student, the present author attended a lecture in which this Manichaean view of history was offered. The speaker contended that the morass that the world was in was due to the defeat of Germany and the triumph of The Soviet Union in World War Two. He explained that this was because Germany was the embodiment of the masculine (The Fatherland) and The Soviet Union the embodiment of the feminine (Mother Russia). Although he acknowledged that Hitler was a madman who needed to be stopped, he still contended that Hitler's Germany was the last stand for the masculine in the modern world, and its defeat was responsible for the present ignominious state of masculinity, and the fallen state of our world. What about the conflict between liberal Western democracy and totalitarianism, which most historians would regard as the essential conflict? And what about Great Britain, Japan, Italy, the United States and other countries who were engaged in the conflict? He dismissed all this as insignificant, as a mere sideshow, because it lay outside the bounds of his Manichean worldview.

Of course, it is true that a particular group of people can become truly evil, and a dangerous menace, and they must be stopped. Ironically, though, it is most often those who have founded their ideology and their political aspirations on conspiracy theories who become a dangerous menace, for they engage in actual conspiracies. After all, Hitler, Stalin and Pol Pot were avid conspiracy theorists, as are the Islamic fundamentalists who commit acts of terror. This is not surprising since the use of terror stems from the Manichean view of the world, that finds expression in conspiracy theories.

This conflation of individual and archetypal is akin to idolatry. But rather than worshipping a finite human being or a particular thing as if he, she or it were God incarnate, the conspiracy theorist regards a particular group of people, the supposed conspirators, as if they were Satan incarnate, or at least the agents of Satan. This demonization could aptly be called "negative idolatry." Because they are viewed archetypally, and not as regular human beings, powers are attributed to the supposed conspirators that make them larger than life. One such power attributed to them is ubiquity. They seem everywhere, and involved with everything. If, for example, one believes that that an allegedly secret society like the Council on Foreign Relations are conspiring to control the world, then wherever one looks — at the international news, or what is occurring locally—one will suspect the hidden hand of the Council on Foreign Relations to be controlling events.

Lee Harris wrote an essay for Policy Review that discussed the danger of having an enemy that is imbued with a certain type of symbolic thinking. He stated that one needs to understand Al Qaeda's September 11th attack on the United States, not in terms of the conventional Clausewitzian model of war—a war with rational goals intended to further the political objectives of a nation—but as part of a "fantasy ideology," as a symbolic act that "transforms all parties into mere symbols." (Harris 2002, p. 13)

Harris states that Japan's attack on Pearl Harbor had conventional strategic goals; the Japanese saw that it was to their political and economic advantage to attack the United States, so as to discourage the United States from interfering with Japan's colonization of Manchuria. In contrast to Japan's military activities, the terrorism that occurred on September 11th was not part of a conventional war. Al Qaeda gained no geopolitical advantage. Rather, it took place for mythic reasons, as a product of the fantasy ideology of radical Islam. The United States had become a symbol to them of all that was evil about the modern world. The worse than expected destruction of the towers and injury to the Pentagon—both mighty fortresses of the Great Satan—was a sign that the radical Islamist's great faith and purity had resulted in divine intervention. This mythic tale was not itself a conspiracy theory, but was a product of that which is the mother of all conspiracy theories, the paranoid vision, with its duality of the blessed and the damned.

Troublesome Theoretical Incongruities

Paradoxically, the key to understanding a theory is to discern its limits, to ask: What is the theory unable to explain? Where does the theory fail in its claim to universality? There is always some element of reality that lies beyond the purview of a theory, outside the circle of interpretation. For example, the theory of atomism cannot explain human values such as love, justice, charity, and beauty. Efforts by atomists to do so are reductionistic; they attempt to "explain away" these values rather than admitting that their theory has a "leftover," that which cannot be explained by the theory. Similarly, the frequent claim made by a certain class of conspiracy theories, that "The Jews are all powerful, and control everything," cannot explain their persecution through the centuries, the Holocaust, nor how Jews are frequent targets of terrorism by Islamic fundamentalists.

What, then, to do with such contradictory evidence? In such realms as philosophy and science, it can be relegated to the realm of appearances, and is dismissed as insignificant. In the realm of conspiracy theories, the most direct way of dealing with it is to simply deny the facts. For example, some conspiracy theorists have adamantly claimed that the Holocaust never occurred, that it is merely a story concocted by certain conspiring Jewish groups to gain sympathy, as a means to gaining power. The same is true of the Turks who deny the existence of the Armenian genocide. If evidence is presented that contradicts the validity of a conspiracy theory, the conspiracy theorist, who uses the tactic of denial, will denigrate the evidence, claiming that it is fabricated. Indeed, there is no convincing those who are determined to deny facts that contradict their conspiracy theory. This is because their criterion of validity is not empirical evidence, reason, or common sense, but emotional appeal, the ability of their conspiracy theory to evoke for them the pathos of the paranoid vision.

What would happen were one to admit the exceptions to the theory, or to admit facts that contradict the theory? It may be that they cannot be acknowledged without the theory being refuted (Kuhn 1962; 1996). If, on the other hand, the exceptions are able to somehow be integrated into the theory without nullifying the theory, doing so will have the effect of qualifying the theory. The theory will now be considered true only under a finite range of conditions. That is what happened when classical physics acknowledged the significance of certain oddities—such as black box radiation—that it could not explain. The result, of course, was the emergence of quantum physics, and the realization that the truths of classical physics are true, but only under a finite range of conditions.

When qualifications are incorporated into a theory, it makes the theory a good deal more credible. After all, limiting conditions are intrinsic to spatiotemporal existence. The world is infused with contingency. Why then the resistance? The slightest qualification to a theory belies its claim to universality and to completeness, causing the theory to lose its explanatory power. This is because the intent of explanation is to grasp the all, the absolute, the totality. The historian of ideas Arthur O. Lovejoy (1936; 1964) informs us that the absolute is "the final terminus of thought." It is, therefore, the final terminus of explanation.

Qualified theories, like qualified ontologies or qualified theologies, lose their power to center people's lives, provide a ground for their existence, and direct their energies. Imagine if, for example, Saint John, in a more cautious mood, had said, "God is love...except when he has his bad days." Or Marx had informed us that Communism's material dialectic might not be inevitable after all, and recommended that the workers of the world hedge their bet by purchasing a good mutual fund. A qualified way of seeing the world would be more reasonable, but it would fail to satisfy the criteria of universality, completeness, absoluteness, and totality, and thus lose its ability to act as a center, a first principle, for a person's life.

A reluctance to admit qualifications is certainly potent in the case of the conspiracy theorist. Were qualifications admitted, the conspiracy theory would fail to impart an emotional drama, sense of conviction, and direction. Consequently, when one gazed upon the world, through the scope of a conspiracy theory—whose paranoiac potential had been diluted by acknowledging limiting conditions—the world so conceived would fail to reflect back to one the paranoid vision. Qualifications, then, precipitate a letdown from the animating paranoid vision into the mundanity of ordinary existence. Of course, in reality, conspiracy theories do not make relative, partial, contingent, explanatory claims, for the paranoid vision is founded upon a kind of fanatical thinking, akin to what Robert Jay Lifton calls "totalism," which he describes as "...all or nothing emotional alignments..." (1989, p. 129) Consequently, the conspirators must be regarded as all-powerful. Halfway villains won't do. It would be a weak conspiracy theory that contended that a cabal of conspirators did not have control over the entire world, but only controlled part of Northern New Jersey, and then only on weekends, and even then only when the head conspirator's meddlesome mother-in-law was not in town.

In some cases, though, it is possible to question the validity of a theory without rejecting it. There exists, indeed, a certain breed of conspiracy theorists who do remain uncertain about the validity of their theories. That is possible since the paranoid vision is not always imbued with malevolence. Thus it is that conspiracy theories, although fully infused with the paranoid vision, are not always malevolent. There are, for example, conspiracy theories about the US Air Force knowing that space aliens landed at Roswell, New Mexico, but covering it up. Such theories are generally benign. The mood is not one of intense hostility, resentment, and anger. It is rather one of longing to know the truth, uncertainty, and frustration over not knowing, coupled with a sense of distrust over a government that is believed to be deceitful. Jodi Dean, an expert on UFO beliefs, criticizes the notion that the conspiracy theorists are convinced that they have encountered a conspiracy. As Dean expresses it:

> ...conspiracy thinking is so uncertain that one is rarely convinced; instead one becomes involved in a reiterative back-and-forth that mobilizes doubt and reassurance in a never-ending, never-reconciled account of possibility...My claim is that conspiracy thinking operates prior to a final conversion; indeed, it is a sort of anxious pre-belief, a thinking that is a longing that one suspects, fears, and even desires will never be fulfilled. Ever suspicious, it disavows the closure of a final explanation, theory, or political and moral order. (2002, pp. 93-95)

Dean is making some perceptive observations here, but two of her points seem dubious. First of all she suggests that the belief in UFOs is a conspiracy theory. The belief that UFOs landed is not in itself a conspiracy theory, but the notion that the government (the Air Force) is covering it up, is one. More importantly, this openness to doubt, indeed open-mindedness, to which Dean refers, is true of only relatively non-malevolent conspiracy theories, like the ones involving whether there was a cover-up at Roswell. After all, most conspiracy theories about space aliens are not about finding the ultimate source of evil. They derive from the longing to make contact with the rest of the universe, which itself is due to that cosmic loneliness endemic to earthlings.

Along these same lines, there exists what might be called a certain postmodern sophistication regarding conspiracy thinking. Those who maintain this attitude are often ironical about their own conspiracy beliefs. An example of this stance, according to Peter Knight (2000), can be found in the film *Conspiracy Theory* (1997). The protagonist, the prototypical wild and wacky conspiracy theorist, played by Mel Gibson, is initially treated satirically by the screenwriter but, as the plot progresses, he is eventually taken seriously. The postmodern sense of things one derives from the film is, "Who knows?" In other words, since objective truth is a lost cause, one must maintain an openness to all possibilities, including far out conspiracy theories. This ironical attitude towards truth makes postmodern conspiracy theorists, unlike the classic conspiracy theorists to which Hofstadter refers, not malevolent, but skeptical and inquisitive. It is, indeed, possible to thoroughly enjoy conspiracy theorizing.

Perhaps it is even one's civic responsibility to maintain a certain skepticism and openness to the possibility that one's government, or the business for which one works, is involved with a secret plot. And then there is the ever-present conspiracy that Emerson warns one about, "Society everywhere is a conspiracy against the manhood of each of its members" (1981, 261). Conspiracy theorists of the malevolent kind, on the other hand, are not ironic, for irony requires distance and usually implies a certain playfulness. On the contrary, malevolent conspiracy theorists are closed, and they are deadly serious about it all. If they are open at all, it is in regard to the details of their theories, but the basic premises remain intact.

We have said that one can outright deny the limits of a theory, or one can accept those limits, to varying degrees, without questioning the original premise. There is a third way of dealing with those elements of reality that lie outside the limits of a theory: the theorist can attempt to swallow and digest the incongruous facts, modifying the details of the theory without diluting the theory's original premise. Consequently, the theory will be convoluted, bent this way and that way, so as to accommodate the incongruous facts. For example, the insistence that the sun revolved around the earth resulted in Ptolemy's complex and convoluted theory of epicycles. It was only finally rejected because Copernicus' theory proved far more parsimonious.

This convoluting of a theory is what most frequently happens in the realm of conspiracy theories. For example, Daniel Pipes (1998a) tells us that many Arabs admit that Jews are killed by Palestinian suicide bombings. Does this belie the Arab's notion that the Jews are all-powerful? Not at all, for they claim that the Israeli secret intelligence service, the Mossad, arranged for the terrorists to set off the bombs, so as to make the Arabs look bad. Another example involves those conspiracy theorists who are convinced that the Warren Commission's investigation of the Kennedy assassination was a cover-up. They sometimes wonder why the powerful Kennedy family didn't question the Warren Commission Report. According to a theory circulating on the internet for a time, Jacqueline Kennedy wanted the cover-up, for she was the one who shot and killed her husband on that fatal day.

Some years ago, the author witnessed firsthand the convoluting of a theory. He attended a discussion led by a brilliant and charismatic professor while at a college in California. This professor was convinced that the students in the 1960s had destroyed the country through their liberal attitudes. Bill Clinton, who was then president, represented to him everything that was detestable about the Woodstock generation.

At the time, there was a conspiracy theory circulating that President Clinton had murdered his former press secretary, Vince Foster. Some conspiracy theorists alleged that the President had ordered hits on hundreds of other people as well, including arranging for a busload of school children to crash. Apparently, the professor had obtained these ideas from various newsletters and websites devoted to discussing and disseminating conspiracy theories. He argued that those wild allegations were completely true. During the group discussion, the question was raised why it was that the President had never been caught; after all, the crime of murder was obviously far more serious than his affair with Monica Lewinsky. Surely, if the President had murdered people, the Republicans, and even some Democrats, would do everything in their power to uncover the facts. Furthermore, with so many people murdered, there was bound to appear a smoking gun, some bit of incriminating evidence, or someone who would talk to a reporter. Here, then, was an example of facts that were incongruent with the conspiracy theory that the President was a murderer.

The professor's response to the objection essentially consisted in convoluting his theory to accommodate the incongruous facts. He said that Kenneth Starr—the special prosecutor selected to investigate the allegations of President Clinton's misbehavior, and maybe serious malfeasance—was actually in cahoots with President Clinton! That was why the murders were being kept secret. Furthermore, Kenneth Starr's prosecution of the president on the Monica Lewinsky affair was just a red herring to distract the public from the murders. The professor had succeeded in incorporating the incongruous facts into the conspiracy theory, although the theory became a bit more convoluted, to say the least.

We can conclude that conspiracy theorizing is a desperate effort to make sense of the world. It is desperate because there is a great deal in life that is inexplicable, that must remain unintelligible. This is not, essentially, because each of us is endowed with limited intelligence, knowledge, and understanding. It is due, rather, to the limits of human cognition. In other words, these cognitive limits are not psychological. They are epistemological, meaning that they are intrinsic to what it means to know anything. The existentialist philosopher Karl Jaspers (1935; 1957)—in the tradition of Immanuel Kant who sought to describe the limits of human reason — stated that consciousness is "horizonal," meaning that there must, out of necessity, be a limit, or horizon, to what can be known. This limit is expressed, for example, in the fact that one can only see things from a certain point in history, and from the finite perspective of one's personality, life history, and limited knowledge and experience.

Consequently, even for the most knowledgeable person life is very much a game of blind man's bluff. One journeys though life, often unsure of the path, unsure of what fortune has in store, and uncertain of the future of the world. How can one plan ahead when the brightest people have been notoriously wrong in their predictions? Major events so often come as a surprise. The fall of the Soviet Union was not predicted by most of the brightest intellectuals. Neither was September 11th. The existential implications of Heisenberg's Uncertainty Principle are a source of ever-present anxiety.

It is how one responds to this uncertain state of affairs that is crucial to one's development as a human being. Kant recommended faith, the great difficulty of which was drawn out by Kierkegaard; i.e. one proceeds in "fear and trembling." Goethe's Faust is so unhappy over the limits of his ability to know that he considers suicide, but instead makes a pact with the devil, with the promise that he could attain complete knowledge. Humility and faith are qualities lacking not only in Faust, but also those under the sway of the paranoid vision. Out of their mental desperation, from being unable to attain certitude about life, paranoids begin to hallucinate those cognitive mirages known as conspiracy theories.

The Justificatory Power of Conspiracy Theories

Human beings, unlike animals, cannot simply be. They feel compelled to justify their actions, demonstrating how they are necessary, right, and valid, i.e. moral. More essentially, justification is the effort to connect one's actions to a higher law or purpose. Even those who commit heinous deeds are not indifferent to questions of good and evil, but seek to defend their actions, both to themselves and to others. Invariably that higher law, upon which they base their justifications, is self-defense. As the genocidal Slobodan Milosevic stated, "There is no Serb aggression...We are merely protecting ourselves" (qtd. in Morrow, 2003, 59).

Also, unlike animals, human beings cannot suffer without earnestly seeking to know why they suffer and, more generally, why anyone suffers. In this case, it is God's ways that are in need of justification. The effort to uncover the meaning of suffering finds expression in myths about the origin of evil, as well as in theology and philosophy. Major disasters — such as earthquakes, disease epidemics, tidal waves, and holocausts—invite questions of the role of fate versus chance versus providence in human affairs. Theological arguments, known as theodicies, seek to reconcile the existence of such disasters, which are considered to be a "natural evil," with the existence of God. Whether such arguments are cogent is another story.

All theologies, and those philosophies that address humanity's existential concerns, can, therefore, be considered as answers to Job who, in the Biblical story, felt that his suffering was not justified since he was a good, righteous man. When he asked God for an explanation, his three friends urged him to repent, even though there was no evidence for his culpability. What if Job's three "comforters," as they have been called, had been conspiracy theorists? They would have sought to cut the Gordian knot of the theological conflict by blaming neither Job nor God, but the Canaanites, or one of the other neighboring tribes. That would have been a letdown, for in attributing the problem to their neighbors, they would have prevented the energy of Job's question from reaching a critical mass, precipitating the moral and religious crisis that it had become, not just for Job, but potentially for anyone who has been deeply perplexed by apparently gratuitous suffering.

It is fair to say that without Job's crisis neither Christianity nor Jewish mysticism, nor other such product of this crisis of faith, would have appeared on the scene as answers to Job. Conspiracy theories and other products of the paranoid vision—by offering a spurious answer to the question of justification—have a retarding effect on the evolution of moral and religious consciousness, both in a person and in a society. Actually, even apart from conspiracy theories, the proclivity to assign blame — which is rife is our litigious society—has that retarding effect. The effort to pin blame on certain politicians, after a natural disaster, such as a flood or an earthquake, is a way to avoid encountering the tragic dimension of life and the depths of the questions about life's ultimate meaning that start to emerge.

Just as conspiracy theories, as a perverse form of explanation, are delusive, providing a simulacrum of intelligibility, so it is that they, as a perverse form of justification, provide a twisted morality. There may be, more specifically, a particular type of justificatory reasoning intrinsic to the paranoid vision. To understand this reasoning—which locates the source of life's problems in another group of people—consider, by way of contrast, the Judeo-Christian notion of original sin, as well as the tragic vision of life that flowered in ancient Greece. Both clearly place the blame for the fallen state of our world not on the gods, but on human beings. The fact that the snake deceived Adam and Eve does not exculpate them. Sophocles' Oedipus Rex reaches the same conclusion. Oedipus was unaware that the stranger that he encountered and killed on the road was his father, and that the queen was his mother. Is he still guilty even though he was at the mercy of fate conspiring against him? One can conclude, from Sophocles' play, that Oedipus is clearly guilty.

Is the source, then, of Oedipus's guilt some tragic flaw? Is it his bad temper (i.e. a lack of prudence and self-restraint, or sophrosyne)? According to Paul Ricoeur (1973), all that is beside the point, for there are tragic heroes who really do not have a fatal flaw. What flaw, for example, did Antigone have? Or Agamemnon? They were forced into double-bind situations. And yet the tragic vision posits that human beings, even though they are subject to fate, are still guilty. Perhaps, then, the really important thing for Greek tragedy is not the origin of suffering, but the value of suffering. That value could be summed up by Aeschylus in his play Agamemnon, "He who learns must suffer. And even in our sleep pain that cannot forget falls drop by drop upon the heart, and in our own despair, against our will, comes wisdom to us by the awful grace of God." (qtd. in Hamilton, 1937, p. 170)

Despite their significant differences in worldview, the Greeks with their tragic vision and the Hebrews with their moral vision conceive of suffering as punishment, purification, and atonement, the purpose of which is redemption. Christianity, similarly, sees the necessity for arduous efforts at self-purification and repentance, even if salvation can only come through the grace of God. True philosophers, who seek salvation through knowledge, are no exception, for Plato recommends, "that a man, ought to always live in perfect holiness" (Meno). The mystic, who seeks illumination or enlightenment, travels the same purgative path.

How different is the view of suffering that lies at the root of the paranoid vision. It is not founded on a conviction of original sin, nor on retribution for a transgression that had fractured the very cosmos, as in Greek tragedy. What justification can suffering have when one is fundamentally innocent, good, perfect, pure, and noble, simply by being affiliated with a certain group? If one is already perfect, there is no need for moral exertion, no continual struggle to walk the straight and narrow. The sense here, then, is that one's existence is justified. It is one's suffering that is not justified and not deserved.

A person would be right to infer that the paranoid vision derives from a sense of metaphysical rebellion, one that is particularly endemic to the modern age. Of course, to assault the universe, like Camus' rebel, does not mean that one is imbued with the paranoid vision. After all, self-righteousness—over the sense of having been insulted and injured —is far from uncommon among human beings. On the other hand, this sense of injustice, unfairness, and victimization readies the ground for the paranoid sense that some group of people, a cabal of conspirators, is the source of one's problems. For example, in 1919, after their defeat in World War I, if the Germans looked inward at all, it was relatively short-lived, for in 1939 they voted the Nazis into power. The Nazis attributed Germany's military defeat to the Jews and other groups, whom they slanderously accused of having betrayed Germany.

What is the origin of this sense of being innocent, pure, perfect, and great? The paranoid vision has its own version of the paradise lost myth. It attributes the fall neither to the gods, nor to natural or cosmic disasters, nor to the deficiencies within human beings, but to oppression by society. "Man is born free, but is everywhere in chains," states Rousseau. That society's chains can be broken is his version of "good news for modern man." The next step is to posit that Paradise was lost, not simply because of society in general, but on account of the evil machinations of a particular group of people. The implication is that paradise can be regained by vanquishing that group and destroying their treachery.

The ruthless regime of the Khmer Rouge, under Pol Pot, offers an example of Rousseauian longings for a return to an original innocence transformed into a horror show. The other totalitarian movements, including fascism, Nazism, and communism, were similarly founded on this quixotic, utopian optimism (Berlin, 1967). Terrorism — from the Jacobinism of the French Revolution's reign of terror, to groups like Al Qaeda in the present century—is rooted in this same facile optimism.

It would, indeed, seem counterintuitive to associate the paranoid vision with idealistic and utopian longings since paranoids are typically angry, bitter, fearful, suspicious, and cynical. This paradox is understandable, if one realizes that their dark worldview derives from feeling robbed of the felicity that they claim as their due. Is it correct, then, to conclude that disappointed paradisiac expectations lead to violence? They do not always lead there, which means that there must be some other precipitating factor present. Lance Morrow's insight into evil suggests what it might be:

> Evil portrays itself, almost without exception, as injured innocence, fighting back...I have wondered for months how, in the face of the world's condemnation and disgust, the Serbs could keep up a war conducted by rape, murder, and starvation of whole cities...They found a remarkable solution: They felt sorry for themselves. They marinated in self-pity; self cherishing, they fairly caramelized themselves in sentimentality. They solved their formidable moral problems by declaring themselves the injured party....Being a victim is the Rolls-Royce of self-justification, a plenary indulgence. (2003, p. 59)

It would seem, then, that disappointed expectations first turn into self pity before they erupt into violence. This is because self-pity vindicates self-defense, which provides a type of justification for violence. Often the sense of self-pity takes the form of feeling that one has been treated unfairly. Political psychologist Neil J. Kressel argues that such feelings are what motivated the Serbs to commit their atrocities in Bosnia:

> Serbs responded to Milosevic enthusiastically partly because many believed that history had treated them unfairly and that other groups would persecute Serbs if given half a chance. Many supported the nationalistic interpretation of twentieth-century history — that Serbia never got its just reward for

siding with the victorious allies in two world wars. (2002, p. 25)

The Jonah Complex

Freud, in "Mourning and Melancholia" (1915), proposed the novel thesis that paranoia was a defense mechanism against the paranoid's repressed homosexual desire for the father. Shapiro (1965) arrives at a similar conclusion in emphasizing not the desire of, but fear of, passive surrender on the part of the paranoid. Why, then, did Freud settle on homosexuality? Freud, quite perceptively, saw that the paranoid fears passive surrender. He was also perceptive in relating it to the father complex, for the father symbolically represents the sphere of morality and justification, which is the paranoid's real preoccupation. But there is another phenomenon that finds symbolic expression as passive surrender — religious consciousness, both as it emerges and develops. It is apparent that what the paranoid actually fears is surrender to God, and that Freud is misconstruing that surrender as evidence of homosexuality.

Freud had read the autobiographical account by Judge Daniel Schreber (1903; 2000) of his insanity. Schreber had risen quite high in the German court system. Then, in his middle years, he became insane and had to be institutionalized. He recovered, was released, returned to his family for many years, then relapsed into insanity again, finally dying in an insane asylum.

Schreber's story presents us with a bizarre but illuminating example of the symbolic conflation of the demands of religious morality — particularly in a Christian context, which emphasizes the idea of the marriage of man and God—and the fear of homosexuality. After all, Schreber's insanity—which Freud, who never examined Schreber, subsequently judged to be a paranoid psychosis—centered around Schreber's fear that God was trying to turn him into a woman, so that Schreber could become God's wife.

In Kierkegaard's Either/Or, the exponent of the ethical life is also a judge, the fictional Judge Wilhelm. Kierkegaard's choice of a judge is appropriate, because a judge believes that it is possible to be in the right relation to life by obeying laws. But by the end of the second volume of Kierkegaard's work, Judge Wilhelm is beginning to despair, for he sees the inadequacy of a life guided by moral precepts. He is ready, according to Kierkegaard's account, for a new stage on life's way, for the religious life. The difference between the ethical life and the religious life, according to Kierkegaard, is that those who are living a religious life cannot depend upon the moral law as a guide to life. Hence the "fear and trembling." After all, what moral precept would command a person to murder one's child? But that is the sacrifice that God demands of Abraham in the Biblical story.

But the essential sacrifice, according to Kierkegaard, is not of Isaac. It is of Abraham's understanding, his ability to make sense of it all. To masculine consciousness, which identifies with thinking and reasoning, the surrender of self-directive understanding for a life of faith seems feminizing. Judge Schreber is similarly ready for this shift from the ethical to the religious level of consciousness but, in his madness, he pictures what should be symbolic as something literal: that God is seeking to transform him, literally, into a woman. Madness often consists in literalizing what is meant to be symbolic or metaphorical (Carveth, 1999).

If it is the case, therefore, that what the paranoid really fears is not homosexuality, but surrendering to the divine, then the paranoid has what Abraham Maslow called a "Jonah Complex," which consists in a flight from one's calling, for fear of its demands. Jonah — when commanded by God to go to Nineveh to tell the people there to repent — took flight on a ship bound in the opposite direction.

Why the flight? From what is he really running? What is required in going through these "stages on life's way," as Kierkegaard called them, is a sacrifice of egocentricity, which is no small matter. Paranoia is but one modality of the Jonah Complex. Now, this is where the paranoid's longing for utopia enters the scene. It is the longing for a perfect state of affairs, where nothing is required. Therefore, sacrifice is not required! After all, there is no need to sacrifice one's earthly being for transcendent values, if heaven on earth has already come to fruition.

That, in point of fact, is the reason why Aristotle rejected socialism as a form of government. If the state provides to all who are in need, the act of charity becomes impossible. What is wrong with that state of affairs? Aristotle argues that charity is necessary for one's moral perfection. After all, the act of charity is a manifestation of the act of sacrifice. Socialistic visions—as well as millenarian and utopian visions in general—derive from a longing to be free of the need for sacrifice, undisturbed by the demands of morality.

In actuality, those who are utopian and millennial in their thinking do see the need for sacrifice. Here is the great irony of it all: Sacrifice is required to bring about a state of affairs in which sacrifice will never be required again. Reading between the lines, one can find this motivation in the writings of utopians, revolutionaries, totalitarians, and terrorists. For example, it is not unlikely that Mohamed Atta and the other September 11th terrorists—as lustful as other young men their age—half believed that the reward for their "martyrdom," as promised in the Qur'an, would be seventy-two virgins, sloe-eyed beauties for each of them, despite being fairly educated middle class men, whose thinking had been influenced by living in the West. Their reward would be, in essence, a state of guilt-free indulgence, free of the need for sacrifice. The ruthless totalitarians of the Twentieth Century sought to bring about a state of affairs in which not only they, but everyone as well, would never again have to sacrifice.

To bring about this future paradise on earth, they were willing to sacrifice the lives of millions of people. This paradise on earth is the supposed summum bonum that was used to justify the endless backbreaking labor, the loss of personal freedom, the separation from family, the resultant mass starvation, the torture of those who voiced dissent, as well as all the other forms of misery and horror that belonged to such great crusades as the Soviet Five Year Plans, under Stalin, and Mao's cultural revolution, both of which claimed the lives of many millions of people.

Behind the longing for utopia is the flight from sacrifice, but behind that flight is the flight from morality. Where, though, lies the negativity involved with morality? Becoming a moral being precipitates an inner conflict between the ego and moral self. This conflict is brought to bear upon everything that is done, at every moment of one's life, creating an inner divisiveness. As Sir Thomas Browne, in *Religio Medici* wrote, "There is a man within me who is angry with me" (p. 73).

Having a conscience is not only difficult, but also problematic. This is not because the moral imperative clashes with egotistical self-interest. It is because even when a person earnestly seeks to do what is right, he or she may be uncertain over the right course of action. Neither Kant's Categorical Imperative, nor the Golden Rule, can be a guide to action when moral demands clash with each other, as they so often do. Thus, when one considers the burden of conscience, with all of the doubts and torments that it can engender, the lure of utopia is certainly understandable.

Another lure related to the paranoid vision is the scapegoat. According to Rene Girard, in *Violence and the Sacred* (1977; 1979), the scapegoat is actually a universal phenomenon, and is not merely found in the type of sick organizations, groups, and societies that interest us here, for the scapegoat is a means for the members of any society to conceal their violent nature from themselves. Girard sees human beings as violent by nature. The scapegoat comes into being because of a repression: Human beings cannot acknowledge their aggressive urges, hence the need for a substitute, a scapegoat to whom such urges are attributed.

Girard states that, although scapegoating in the ritualistic sense is a universal phenomenon, many contemporary societies do not have such rituals. Lacking such cathartic channels, they are all the more aggressive. But Girard does not explore why, in certain societies, scapegoating can rage out of control, as it did, for example, in Pol Pot's Cambodia. The problem is that Girard understands human aggression somewhat along the same lines as does Konrad Lorenz, as analogous to animal aggression. Civilization is viewed as merely the velvet glove hiding the hidden claw. But if human aggression were fundamentally animalistic, as Girard suggests, there would be no need for human beings to repress it, or to disguise it. After all, the very fact that human beings, as Girard contends, repress the awareness of their aggression, by means of scapegoating, implies the existence of shame, which means that human beings, unlike animals, possess a moral sense. To make sense of scapegoating, one must understand it in that light.

Aggression, as it exists in the human realm, is not, therefore, simply a function of instinct. Unlike animals, human beings can be downright malevolent. It is also the case that animals are neither totalitarians nor fanatics. As Arthur Koestler stated, "...the trouble with our species is not an excess of aggression, but an excess capacity for fanatical devotion" (1976, 233-234). It would seem, then, that aggression in human beings is not so much biologically driven, as it is the manifestation of certain ways of seeing, such as the paranoid vision.

Furthermore, it would appear that not all scapegoating is an effort to repress aggression. For example, the distinguished historian of Islam, Bernard Lewis, in *The Roots of Muslim Rage* (1990), contends that Islamic fundamentalists scapegoat the United States so as to deflect attention from the social, economic, and political problems of their own nations. Here scapegoating is not about repressed aggression. If anything is being repressed — and not so well at that — it is feelings of humiliation, envy, and resentment. So it would seem that Girard's notion of scapegoating is too narrow.

What interests us about scapegoating is, of course, that it is the foundation of conspiracy theories of the virulent sort. The resultant conspiracy theories can then lead to a host of evils: slander, false accusations and imprisonment, lynchings, pogroms, wars of vengeance, genocide, etc. It is possible, though, for scapegoating to find less violent channels, ones not infused with the paranoid vision. For example, Northup Frye (1973) contends that, when scapegoating exists in comedies—and it often does—it might consist, for example, in driving an unsociable character out of town. Shakespeare's *Merchant of Venice* is a somewhat darker example of such comedic scapegoating, making it a bit of a problem play.

But any sort of scapegoating, even when it finds a socially acceptable outlet, suggests an inability of a group, organization, or society to come to terms with its darker side. What builds up on account of running from themselves is not pent-up aggression, but pent-up anxiety on account of the increasing awareness of one's failures. In any case, to understand the scapegoating that lies at the heart of the paranoid vision, one must understand projection.

Projection and the Localization of Evil

The wish to blame other people for paradise lost operates by means of a curious psychological mechanism. Projection, which the Freudians regard as a defense mechanism, involves the attribution of what are really one's own unacknowledged faults to other people. After all, how else could one explain how it is that the most notorious conspiracy theorists of the Twentieth Century, the grand accusers, were also the most horrible of monsters?

It is possible, though, to project one's best qualities onto other people. Apropos is Ludwig Feuerbach's notion that religion is founded on the projection of totality, (infinitude, absoluteness, eternality)—which Feuerbach considered to be a regulative principle of human reason, in the Kantian sense—onto the universe. Failing to realize that this is a projection, people bow down before what they imagine to be the embodiment of absoluteness.

If Feuerbach is correct, projection—in and of itself, apart from the uses made of it by the demon within—may be simply due to a lack of self-awareness. Furthermore, as the German idealists tell us, projection is a very necessary foolishness. It is by projecting oneself onto the world, and then realizing, like an awakening Narcissus, that what is being seen is but one's own projection, that one comes to see and know oneself. Those who catch on to what has been happening appreciate Pogo's oft quoted phrase, "We have met the enemy, and they are us," although Feuerbach's version of it would be, "We have met God, and he is us."

In the case of paranoid projection, what one finds is not deification of the universe, but demonization of other people. People project their worst, most distasteful, qualities—their faults, desires, and weaknesses, all that they cannot bear to admit in themselves—onto other people. What is essentially projected, according to C.G. Jung, is a person's "shadow," their unacknowledged dark side. They then castigate someone else for supposedly possessing the very faults of which they are guilty. In Jung's *Man and His Symbols,* he quotes someone as saying, "For over five years this man has been chasing around Europe like a madman in search of something he could set on fire. Unfortunately, he again and again finds hirelings who open the gates of their country to this international incendiary" (p. 181). One would have guessed that the quote was from someone like Churchill or Roosevelt referring to Hitler, but one reads on only to discover that it is a quote by Hitler referring to Churchill! Hitler cast a very large shadow indeed.

The psychoanalyst Nancy McWilliams believes that projection is the primary defense mechanism in clinical paranoia. "When a person uses projection as his or her main way of understanding the world and coping with life, he or she can be said to have a character that is paranoid" (1994, 108). If, as McWilliams contends, projection is not merely a function of naiveté, but a defense mechanism, then what is being defended is one's self-esteem. Those who engage in projection suspect that there exists something dark in themselves that needs to be addressed, something that they cannot bear to see.

Millon has said something rather intriguing about the evolution of paranoid projection: "...troubled by mounting and inescapable evidence of inadequacy and hostility, paranoids are driven to go beyond mere denial. They not only disown these personally humiliating traits but throw them back at their real or imagined accusers" (1996, 704). The words "mounting" and "inescapable" that Millon uses are important, for the implication is that paranoia is not a static state of affairs, but a dynamic one, that it has its own dialectic, its own internal evolution. What is happening is that despite efforts to keep self-knowledge at bay, it manages to slip past the repressive guards of the inner self, and steal into one's awareness. Here, then, is an example of "the demonic," as Kierkegaard calls it, an active flight from what one already knows to be true. People become fanatical in their accusations when they suspect that it is they, themselves, who are guilty.

Besides projection, there is another cognitive delusion endemic to the paranoid vision. It is what Thomas Sowell calls "the localization of evil." He contends that it is representative of "the unconstrained vision of life," the way of seeing that fails to recognize the limits of the possible, and which is, therefore, the soil for utopian dreams. According to Sowell:

This localization of evil is one of the hallmarks of the unconstrained vision. There must clearly be some cause for evils, but insofar as these causes are not so widely diffused as to be part of human nature in general, then those in whom the evils are localized can be removed, opposed, or neutralized so as to produce a solution. The specifics of this localization —whether in undemocratic institutions, in Godwin, or in capitalist economy, as in some modern writers—are less crucial than the localization itself, which makes a solution possible. Evils diffused throughout the human race can only be dealt with by trade-offs, through artificial devices which themselves produce other unsatisfactory side effects. (1987, p. 144)

The type of thinking that would localize evil by attributing it to specific causes and conditions (for example, capitalism) creates the perfect climate for the emergence of conspiracy theories. A conspiracy theory will attribute evil not merely to "undemocratic institutions" or to secularism. It will localize evil a good deal more, by attributing it to a particular person or group, such as Western imperialists, capitalists, or foreigners. Many Serbs, for example, believe that what caused the end of their imagined paradise was a battle that they had with the Turks that took place in the year 1389 (Anzulovic, 1999). Paul Berman astutely observes how the pernicious logic of utopian thinking works:

There was always a people of God, whose peaceful and wholesome life had been undermined. They were the proletariat or the Russian masses (for the Bolsheviks and Stalinists): or the children of the Roman wolf (Mussolini's Fascists): or the Spanish Catholics and the Warriors of Christ the King (for Franco's Phalange); or the Aryan race (for the Nazis). (2003, pp. 48-49)

Berman then states that there invariably is a group of people who are held responsible for the fall:

There were always the subversive dwellers in Babylon, who trade commodities from around the world and pollute society with their abominations. They were the bourgeoisie and the kulaks (for the Bolsheviks and the Stalinists); or the Freemasons and the cosmopolitans (for the Fascists and Phalangists): and sooner or later, they were always the Jews (for the Nazis, and in a lesser degree for the other fascists and eventually for Stalin, too). (2003, 48-49)

There is a perverse optimism to the notion that all that is wrong with the world could simply be remedied by removing a particular group of people from power, or by obliterating them altogether, as if then the world would be forever free of evil. That is the great appeal in localizing evil; it makes things appear so easy. Furthermore, as Isaiah Berlin argues, it justifies anything:

> If [the realization of a utopia] is possible, then surely no price is too heavy to pay for it; no amount of repression, cruelty, or coercion will be too high, if this, and this alone, is the price for ultimate salvation for all men. The conviction gives a wide license to inflict suffering on other men, provided it is done for pure, disinterested motives. (2003, p. 47)

Having localized evil either in institutions or in specific groups of people, utopians do not think that they are required to make arduous efforts at moral improvement, as did their ancestors. Nor do they see themselves as sojourners on this earth with the fate of their soul hanging in the balance. Nor do they need to suffer the deep questions that Job, Jonah, Hamlet, and Arjuna wrestled with. Instead, they take themselves as intrinsically good, as having already arrived, and thus with no need to evolve.

Is Crisis Paranoiagenic?

Is the paranoid vision more prevalent at certain times in history? Hofstadter contends that, "Catastrophe or the fear of catastrophe is most likely to elicit the syndrome of paranoid rhetoric" (1965, 39). It could be argued, though, that the paranoid vision can be precipitated by any type of crisis that, according to the social psychologist Carl F. Graumann, may be, "...economic (e.g. unemployment, inflation), political (e.g. repression, instability, threat of war), or religious (e.g.

reformation, schism, spreading heresy)" (1987, 248). The historian of conspiracy theories, J. M. Roberts, would agree that, "there exists always a readiness and perhaps even a need among men to take a distorted, even paranoiac view of society and that this is intensified at moments of great stress..." (1977, p. 359).

What then do these times of crisis, or great stress, have in common? Graumann suggests that, "...underneath these various manifestations of crisis the established value system of a group or society is at stake" (1987, 248). The threat to a value system is essentially a crisis of identity. There have always existed conspiracy theories throughout history, for there have always been such crises and the anxiety that they create. This is as true, for example, of ancient Rome and medieval China as it is for England during the 19th Century, and Iran during the present century.

Some historians have proposed a more controversial thesis: conspiracy theories did not become a serious plague until about 200 years ago—corresponding roughly to the advent of the French Revolution — and didn't reach full fury until the 20th century (Roberts, 1977, Pipes, 1993). It could be objected that the reason why there are more conspiracy theories is that the population is much larger than in ancient times, and so the argument that historians like Roberts and Pipes are making would be hard to prove. Although speculative, it is intriguing enough to at least consider. But if conspiracy theories really are more prevalent today, what would make them so?

According to Daniel Pipes, "Paradoxically, conspiracism acquired force just as it became less plausible" (1997, p. 68). What made conspiracism less plausible was the loss of centralized authority — and all the scheming that is a concomitant of centralized authority — due to increasing democratization. If Pipes is correct, then the decline in actual conspiracies, due to democratization, is the paradoxical reason why there are more conspiracy theories. After all, the loss in centralized authority led to the need to believe that someone, or some group, must be in control over events. Consequently, conspiracy theories appeared on the scene to satisfy that need.

By the same logic, the rise of conspiracism might be related to Nietzsche's proclamation, "God is dead." For if God is not in the driver's seat, is anyone? The vertiginous alternative is that the world has simply gone into an ontological free-fall. It could be then that the rise of conspiracy theories emerged as a surrogate for divine providence. The unconscious sentiment would be: If God is not in control, then at least Satan is. One could substitute for Satan any number of groups believed to be the evil force plotting behind the scenes. Conspiracy theories arise, then, as a quest for certainty, stability and order during times of stress. Is this effort a success? As Marvin Zonis explains:

> Conspiracy thinking proliferates during times of severe political, economic, and conceptual crisis...The most persuasive theories of the paranoid process emphasize that paranoia is the product of a failed attempt to reconstitute a meaningful social world, however painful that meaning may be, after a period of regression and disintegration. Paranoia, then — and by extension conspiracy thinking — can be seen as a means for individuals in the throes of a sense-making crisis to construct a meaningful world after a profound disturbance of self—self-object relationships. (1993, p. 287)

If Zonis is correct that paranoia and conspiracy theories arise as a "failed attempt to reconstitute a meaningful social world," it would account for the psychological instability of a person under the sway of the paranoid vision, for a conspiracy theory is an inadequate answer to the questions of meaning, value, and identity. It is true that a conspiracy theory propels a person in a definite direction, for he or she now has an object to fear, resent, and hate. But a definition of oneself, predicated on who one has as an enemy, is an insufficient answer to the ever-restless question, "Who am I?"

We may conclude that conspiracy theories have both an explanatory and a justificatory function—they seek to render the world intelligible and one's life meaningful. The intelligibility and meaning that they offer derives from the paranoid vision. Its subtext is that there is a group of conspirators who have stolen paradise and are responsible for the present fallen state of one's group, organization, or society. There are, as we have suggested, conspiracy theories that are relatively benign; they do not have that underlying subtext. It is the malevolent ones that interest us here.

Chapter Three

The Allure of Apocalypse

"...a collective sense of impotence and anxiety and envy
suddenly discharged itself in a frantic urge to smite the
ungodly—and by doing so to bring into being, out of suffering
inflicted and suffering endured, that final Kingdom where
the Saints,clustered around the great sheltering figure of the
Messiah, were to enjoy ease and riches, security and power for
all eternity."

— *Norman Cohn (1961)*

Apocalyptic and millennial fantasies, like conspiracy theories, are mythically-charged stories, whose primary purpose is to make sense of human existence, such that the events that comprise one's personal history, as well as those that comprise the history of the world, are no longer experienced as accidental, random, and meaningless, but are seen to have a divine purpose. That purpose has to do with the end of the world, and what lies beyond it. In this manner, history is rendered intelligible, and human suffering meaningful.

Apocalypticism is a highly significant aspect of human thought and belief, which should be viewed from a larger perspective before determining its relation to the paranoid vision. The three major monotheistic religions were—like most religious sects and cults that have sprung up through the centuries—originally apocalyptic, but their apocalypticism cooled as they became established and institutionalized. The fundamentalist strain in these religions has, though, remained apocalyptic. Along with fantasies about the apocalypse, there exist fantasies about the millennium, the thousand years of perfect peace and harmony that would follow the end of the world. They are an essential part of the apocalyptic narrative.

American culture is profoundly apocalyptic, particularly in the Christian context. The popular interest in apocalypticism is expressed, for example, in the "Left Behind" series (1996), by Tim LaHaye and Jerry B. Jenkins, which, at the time this is being written, has already sold over 60 million copies. There one finds other typical elements of apocalyptic and millennial fantasies, including the Antichrist (a demonic being who will initially be appealing because of his charisma, but will spread evil throughout the world, finally to be overcome by Jesus at the Second Coming) and the Rapture (the transporting of those who are good immediately to heaven, just prior to the apocalypse). But apocalypticism is a phenomenon that is not confined to a religious context. As Frank Kermode contends, it lies at the core of modernism, as expressed in art and literature:

> What we think of as truly Modern or Modernist is always relatively apocalyptic. Cezanne plotting against the world mountain, Kandinsky deserting appearances in favor of his abstract proclamations, the novelists with their unique plots against time and reality, all are apocalypticists... (1985, pp. 101-102)

Even those modernists who are avowed atheists—Nietzsche, Marx, and Freud, for example—espouse ideologies that have great apocalyptic potential. Such has been the case with all intellectual revolutionaries and iconoclasts. Not only have ancient prophets, as well as modern artists and intellectuals, been inspired by apocalypticism, much that is endemic to popular culture, such as UFO sightings and disaster movies, stem from apocalyptic anxieties and millennial longings. According to Hillel Schwartz (1989), such anxieties become all the more powerful at the end of centuries, so it may be that, in these early years of the new millennium, such anxieties are still potent. On the positive side, apocalyptic longings have saved a great many people from despair, inspiring them with hope for a renewed mode of existence. The chapter, "Paranoia in a New Key," will explore the elevation of apocalypticism, such that the real apocalypse is not the end of planet earth, but the end of one's mode of being.

We have suggested that apocalyptic fantasies seek to make sense of life and find meaning in human suffering. Such motives are certainly not malevolent. How is it, then, that apocalypticism has sometimes had such horrific consequences? Consider communism and National Socialism, both of which Norman Cohn (1961) identified as millennial movements: one promised universal equality, the other a thousand year Reich. Ralph Peters (2003) contends that terrorism can take pragmatic or apocalyptic forms. The former, murderous though it may be, is intended to serve a practical social, economic, or political purpose. The latter has no practical agenda but only seeks to fulfill as violent an apocalyptic scenario as possible. As recent world events would indicate, apocalyptic terrorism is dramatically on the rise.

Under what conditions, then, do apocalyptic fantasies emerge that are malevolent? It is when those fantasies are infused with the paranoid vision. The connection between apocalyptic fantasies and paranoia, both in the clinical sense and as a political style, has indeed often been observed. In the last chapter, we referred to that most famous of mental patients, Judge Daniel Schreber. Many of his psychotic fantasies were thoroughly apocalyptic. But, as one learns from research scientist Ronald K. Siegel in his popular book, *Whispers: The Voices of Paranoia* (1996), paranoid delusions can involve many types of stories — from invasion by giant bugs to the secret plots of evil dwarfs, Mafiosi, and CIA agents. While such psychiatrically-observed paranoid delusions often involve a conspiracy theory, they only occasionally involve an apocalyptic scenario. Furthermore, in books that deal with paranoia as a personality disorder there is often no mention of apocalyptic fantasies (Shapiro, 1965, Meissner, 1986, Millon 1996, McWilliams, 1994).

In regard to the paranoid style, on the other hand, the relation of apocalyptic fantasies to paranoia is well in evidence. Hofstadter's essay is replete with examples of conspiracy theories that are simultaneously apocalyptic fantasies. As Hofstadter states, "The paranoid spokesman sees the fate of this conspiracy in apocalyptic terms — he traffics in the birth and death of whole worlds, whole political orders, whole systems of human values." (1996, p. 29) Therefore, apocalyptic fantasies need not be about the end of the world, as predicted by Biblical prophets, as well as by the mythic literature of many different cultures. These apocalyptic fantasies are often about the end of a certain cherished way of life, as manifested in a form of government such as monarchy, theocracy, or democracy. Or they can be about the loss of certain values, such as community, piety, or liberty.

One noted scholar of eschatology, Paul Boyer, questions whether the term "paranoid," applied to apocalyptic fantasies, is helpful: "Some describe this conspiracy-saturated end-time scenario as 'paranoid,' but does the label further our understanding?" (1994, p. 271) Boyer argues that when a belief is shared by millions of people, it is not appropriate to apply a psychiatric label. The problem here is that Boyer is not distinguishing between paranoia in the clinical sense and paranoia as a style, or as a vision of life. Furthermore, if, in point of fact, millions of people share a belief system that has all the characteristics of paranoia, in any sense of the word, there is no reason not to label it as paranoid.

All the same, the reason for the connection between apocalyptic fantasies and paranoia remains not altogether clear. Lifton does offer some valuable psychological insights, such as the significance of the motif of purification in millenarian cults like Aum Shinrikyo. But the connection between apocalyptic fantasies and paranoia needs to be grasped from an epistemological and a moral perspective, as well, to fully understand it.

The Explanatory Appeal of Apocalyptic Fantasies

According to Boyer, Isaac Newton observed that, "...the central value of Bible prophecy is not that it enables one to foretell the future, but that its fulfillment offers 'a convincing argument that the world is governed by providence'" (Boyer, 1992, p. 294). Biblical prophecy, therefore, is a form of explanation that seeks to show how the events of this world, which appear to be random, accidental and contingent, really display God's providence. That is the foundation on which apocalyptic fantasies find meaning in history, and are able to supposedly uncover that same meaning behind the everyday events of our world. No longer is life "a tale told by an idiot," for world events manifest an ultimate purpose and importance.

Apocalyptic fantasies explain away the accidental and contingent aspect of life, not only because we now know the ending of the story, but simply by virtue of the fact that the story, indeed, has an ending. Knowing that it will end offers closure. Of course, while death is an ending, it is not necessarily meaningful, but can only be rendered meaningful as part of a larger story. From the perspective of apocalyptic theology, death is not the end of the story, for there is still the apocalypse, and then there is either hell or the enjoyment of the millennium, depending upon how one has lived one's life, and finally there is the last judgment.

The apocalyptic fantasy is different in kind than that other paranoid narrative, the conspiracy theory. Whereas conspiracy theories are secular, apocalyptic fantasies usually involve religious prophecy. For conspiracy theorists, seemingly ordinary events are the doings of a supposedly powerful person or group of some sort—the Freemasons, the Jews, the Trilateral Commission. For apocalypticists, on the other hand, seemingly ordinary events are signs that reveal the unfolding of Biblical prophesies. For example, when Mikhail Gorbachev became president of the former Soviet Union, there was talk by those involved with prophecy, that here at last was the Antichrist that had been predicted in Revelations. The main reason for this belief was that biblical prophesies had predicted that the Antichrist would have a mark on his forehead, and Gorbachev indeed did. Every new event involving the Soviet Union and the Middle East was then interpreted as a confirmation of scripture.

When contrary evidence began to grow, in relation to the choice of Gorbachev as Antichrist—when relations between the United States and the Soviet Union became more cordial because of détente, and then when it appeared that he was actually dissolving the Soviet Union, which had been viewed by them as Gog (the hostile nation described in the Bible, who will be part of the endtime drama)—those writers of apocalyptic scenarios, feeling disoriented and discomfited, sought to deny what was happening. Boyer captures the wonderful irony of it all: "With striking unanimity these writers dismissed the reforms of Mikhail Gorbachev and the improved U.S.-Soviet relations of the late 1980s and early 1990s. These were not the next act of the script they were following!" (1992, p. 177) The apocalypse, then, would have to wait, until another candidate for Antichrist could be found.

One's narrative, therefore, is, more fundamental in constituting one's world than historical facts. When the events of the world are interpreted mythically—through the vehicle of conspiracy theories and apocalyptic fantasies — the result is a distorted, and sometimes dangerous, view of reality. An example of that phenomenon is the "fantasy ideology" of the 911 terrorists. Berdyaev (1944) warned, "myths can enslave;" a mind so enslaved longs for apocalyptic violence.

The distinction between conspiracy theories and apocalyptic fantasies is not, though, so cut and dried, for the former do have an implicit apocalyptic meaning—or at least are "apocalyptic in expression" as Hofstadter suggests. Furthermore, apocalyptic fantasies are themselves a kind of conspiracy theory, a cosmic conspiracy theory, in which the conspirators often include supernatural personages, such as the Antichrist and Satan, with God himself secretly running the show. Indeed, the word "apocalypse" comes from the Greek word "apokalypsis," which means to unveil, uncover, disclose or reveal, which is what conspiracy theories promise to do. What is revealed in an apocalyptic fantasy are secrets that had only been known in Heaven.

The historian George Herman states, "From the apocalyptic perspective, the things in this world are never as they seem..." (1997, pp. 18-19) As is the case with conspiracy theories, apocalyptic fantasies are predicated on an appearance/reality distinction. The appeal of both modes of paranoid fantasy lies in penetrating that veil of appearances and finding intelligibility and meaning. They are, therefore, modes of explanation and justification. Also, like conspiracy theories, apocalyptic fantasies are a curious hybrid of myth and metaphysics, or perhaps a missing link between the two, for like myth they are in the form of a story, but like metaphysics they posit an appearance/reality distinction.

In the pages that follow, "apocalyptic fantasies," will not mean ancient prophecy as found, for example, in *Daniel, Revelations,* or other biblical books. It will mean the interpretation of contemporary events in terms of those Biblical prophesies. Both the original prophesies and the derivative fantasies are products of the paranoid vision, and are paranoiagenic, but our focus here is on the interpretation and acting out of ancient apocalyptic fantasies in the light of present-day events.

From Eternity at the Beginning to Eternity at the End

The advent of the apocalyptic worldview constituted both a new view of time, as well as a new hope for the end of time. There would be an end to time, history, death, as well as all of the evils of human existence, for the world itself would soon be coming to a catastrophic end. Contrasting it to another mode of time transcendence can highlight the significance of the apocalyptic worldview. Before the advent of apocalypticism, human beings had sought to transcend time, suffering, and death by looking backwards to an imagined beginning of time, to a golden age—to what Mircea Eliade called illo tempore, the timeless realm before history began. Indeed, they more than looked back; they sought to connect themselves, in their actions and in their very being to the eternal beginnings. According to Eliade, the life of "primitive" people is devoted to repeating the archetypal actions of the gods, demigods, or heroes of legend who inhabit that timeless realm:

> In the particulars of his conscious behavior, the "primitive", the archaic man, acknowledges no act which has not been previously posited and lived by someone else...What he does has been done before. His life is the ceaseless repetition of gestures initiated by others. ...[His] gesture acquires meaning, reality, solely to the extent to which it repeats a primordial act. (1978, p. 5)

If, for example, a member of such a society builds a canoe, it is built in the fashion in which the inhabitants of the eternal realm, the gods or heroes, had built canoes. If one goes courting, one does it in the manner in which the legendary hero had done so. On this mythic level of consciousness, where the subject/object discrimination is minimal, one becomes the being who one imitates. Those who imitate the action of a mythic hero, become that hero. In so far as a person is able to live in accord with such archetypes, he or she is transported from the "falleness" and transiency of secular existence to the sacred and eternal realm of the gods and heroes.

According to Eliade, "...the primitive, by conferring a cyclic direction upon time, annuls its irreversibility" (1978, p. 89). The New Year's ritual—in which time is miraculously renewed—would be an example of a cyclical notion of time that has continued, although in a diluted and degraded form, into the present day. Cyclic time seeks to overcome the "terror of history," to use Eliade's apt phrase. The terror of history lies in its contingency and transiency. Thus the emphasis, in "primitive" societies, is in repeating archetypal gestures so as to annul historical time.

Eliade contends that an event can occur—in a culture, society or nation — that truly is unique. It cannot be understood in terms of an archetypal precedent. The birth of Abraham, Moses, Buddha, Christ, Mohammed, are examples of something truly new appearing in people's lives to create history. History can also emerge because of a calamity of some sort, such as a terrible earthquake, a pestilence, or an invasion. For example, the burning down of the temple in Jerusalem, by Nebuchadnezzar of Babylon in 586 B.C., was one such unique and catastrophic event that, Eliade suggests, propelled the Jews out of cyclical time and into an historical consciousness.

When the eternality of beginnings is lost to a certain culture or society, and they have entered into history, with its challenges, hardships, and the loss of contact with archetypes, a new approach to transcending time may dawn on some minds. They posit that true reality, eternity, perfection, i.e. the millennium, awaits them, not at the beginning, but at the end of time! The perfected state of being, in which good deeds will be rewarded and evil ones punished becomes the telos whose purpose is to justify all suffering. [7]

What is most obvious, then, about apocalyptic fantasies is that they picture the world as having an ending, one that is not arbitrary or accidental, but is predicted, prearranged, and meaningful. Their sense of time is neither historical nor circular, but linear: it has a telos, a prospect of fulfillment and consummation. Therefore, all human suffering finally does amount to something, to a state of being that is just and perfect, whole and complete, intelligible and meaningful. Suffering is redeemed by the paradise that awaits the good.

This shift in time consciousness has an important bearing on the effort to overcome evil. The mythology of the Babylonians presented a circular notion of time. The archetypal hero Marduk triumphs over Tiamat, who represents the waters of chaos, but his victory is never final, for the waters of chaos are always threatening to break free, and so must be subdued again. Marduk's victory over the forces of chaos —which are essentially the forces of evil—is simply repeated annually. In that ritual, the Babylonians would drive a pole through the head of a snake, symbolizing that Marduk had vanquished Tiamat (chaos, evil) once again. In that sense time is circular; no end to this cycle is possible and, as Ricoeur, in *The Symbolism of Evil* (1967), points out, the victory over evil, in the Tiamat myth, is always only temporary.

Apocalyptically infused cultures, by way of contrast, believe that the cosmic circle can be broken. Chaos, and therefore evil, can be finally and ultimately vanquished. According to Norman Cohn (1993), the emergence of end time dramas began with Zoroastrianism, which predated Judaism. It is there that a shift occurred from a notion of circular time to that of linear time. In Zoroastrian cosmology, as Cohn contends, "The world was a battlefield, the battle was still in progress, but it would have an end...cosmos would be rid forever of the forces of chaos" (1993, pp. 82-83). The old combat myth was thus transformed by Zoroaster from one in which the enemy was temporally defeated

---

7 A similar dialectic occurred in philosophy. See the chapter in Arthur O. Lovejoy's The Great Chain of Being (1973) entitled, "The Temporalization of the Great Chain of Being." The Platonic worldview corresponds to the illo tempore to which Eliade refers, and the Hegelian one corresponds to the endtime narratives.

to one in which the enemy was totally and forever defeated. The final victory over chaos would be, according to Cohn, "…The end of 'limited time' and the beginning of an eternity of bliss" (1995, 28).

This is where dark clouds enter into the landscape. Such high hopes, for an "eternity of bliss," breed a sense of frustration. Children, having been promised that Christmas is just around the corner, and still waiting thousands of years for it to happen, would similarly grow a bit impatient. This negativity is a necessary consequence of their linear view of time, in which fulfillment must wait until the end of time for the big payoff. That sense of disappointment then invites a paranoiac self-pity, resentment, bitterness, blame, and all things malevolent. If one is promised that paradise is on the way, then it inevitably follows that some group of conspirators must be responsible for the delay.

Consider, by way of contrast to the apocalyptic view of time, the resigned but calmly philosophical attitude towards life of Homer, who offers a cyclical view of human existence:

> As the generations of leaves,
> so the generations of men.
> Down to earth the wind shoots the leaves,
> but forest trees burst forth again
> in the hour when spring is born:
> so one generation of men
> dies off while another grows strong.
>
> The Iliad, VI.146-149

Homer's poem, like the *Book of Ecclesiastes,* suggests that since history repeats itself, anything that develops is not really new, but is part of the larger scheme of things. The Trojan War may have been a momentous event, but it was not the war to end all wars. That is a rather sober-minded and constrained vision of the possibilities open to humanity.

The basic premise of endtime fantasies, on the other hand, is that this generation is not just one of many generations. On the contrary, these days and this generation are unique. People living today and the events that they are witnessing are the culmination and conclusion of all that went before. These are the last days, and the faithful living today have been chosen to be in the vanguard of the battle against the forces of the Antichrist and the Devil. The consequence of this battle will decide the fate of the world. Psychologically understood, this scenario is an expression of the wild delusions of grandeur endemic to the paranoid vision.

It should be noted, though, that sometimes the apocalyptic mood is not primarily due to the paranoid vision being evident. It simply happens, from time to time, that there is born a generation who, lacking in historical perspective, believe that their age is totally unique, and that their passing means the end of the world. There are, indeed, as Arthur Schlesinger (1986) points out, cycles in American history. There are times when the equanimity that comes from knowing the wisdom of Ecclesiastes—that the sun will set, but that it will rise again, and that life goes on—is a scarce commodity. The humorist Joe Queenan comments on the apocalyptic forebodings among his generation:

> Baby Boomers are well known for their End of Days mentality, always rattling on about the last picture show and the last man standing and the last action hero and the last of the brave and the end of history: They are intoxicated by hyperbolic millennialism, by the all-consuming belief that after us comes the deluge, when in fact after us will simply come more stuff. A deluge did come after Louis XV, but it is highly unlikely that it will come after 'Louie Louie.' (2002, p. 148)

We might add that the current concern with global warming, or "manmade climate change," derives from apocalyptic anxieties. What is rarely considered is the existence of naturally occurring solar cycles, resulting in periods of heating and cooling, which take place over the course of millennia. Alas, this larger perspective lacks the emotional appeal of a paranoid morality play, one is which the oil companies take the role of the Antichrist, and former Vice-President Al Gore plays the savior.[8]

---

8 More recently, though, Mr. Gore has begun to appear less like the savior and more like Harold Hill, the protagonist of The Music Man (1957), thus ruining a perfectly good paranoid narrative.

What is of importance, then, is not the apocalypticism that derives solely from a lack of historical perspective. It is only when that lack of perspective is combined with the paranoid vision that human beings grow dangerously restless.

The Dread of Possession

Frank Kermode contends that, "...our sense of endings has its origins in existential anxiety" (1995, p. 254) In truth, "existential anxiety" is a tautology, for all anxiety is existential. In other words, all anxiety, including what has been called "neurotic anxiety," is the psychophysical concomitant of a threat to the existence of the self. The endings that Kermode is referring to are apocalyptic. These endings are both a manifestation of anxiety and a way of dispelling one's anxiety. Discerning the particular character of that anxiety might prove valuable. One would then know how it distorts the explanatory and justificatory enterprises, such that what results is a conspiracy theory or an apocalyptic fantasy of the malevolent sort. More than likely, the anxiety in question is the same anxiety that lies at the root of the paranoid vision in general.

A clue to this anxiety might be found in the clinical literature about paranoia, for there may indeed exist a micro/macro relation between clinical paranoia and the paranoid vision. The psychiatrist David Shapiro states that the paranoid is characterized by "...an exceedingly frail autonomy, one that, because it is so frail, can be maintained only in this remarkably rigid and exaggerated form" (1962, p. 80). Those who are anxious in this way experience their borders as constantly under siege, their very sense of identity threatened by invasion from without. To acquire a visceral sense of that anxiety, one might view a classic horror film suffused with paranoia, *Invasion of the Body Snatchers* (1956). In that frightening story, both body and mind are threatened with possession by alien life forms.

Apocalyptic fantasies are very much about the dread of possession. There is, for example, the image of the Antichrist who, according to Bernard McGinn, "...differs from the devil in being conceived of primarily as a human agent. The issue raised by belief in Antichrist, then, is that of the relation between human agency and evil, especially the possibility of a completely evil human being" (2002, 2). Invariably, this very incarnation of evil is a man who has political power, or who has control over the lives of other people in some other fashion. Images of the Antichrist have included dictators such as Nero, Napoleon, Mussolini, Hitler, and Saddam Hussein. A dictator makes sense in that regard, for the anxiety about social and political enslavement is an expression of the paranoid anxiety over loss of autonomy and possession.

According to Boyer, other candidates for Antichrist have included a number of Popes, as well as Gorbachev, Kissinger, Saladin, Sadat, Juan Carlos, Servan-Schreiber, Moshe Dayan, Sun Myung Moon, John F. Kennedy, and Ronald Reagan. Thus the choice for Antichrist depends upon one's political persuasion, and who happens to be in power at the time.

What explanation is there for the centuries long history of the Pope being accused of being the Antichrist? To a certain extent, it is simply because the Pope is a powerful man, but it is also related to a certain animus against Catholicism by Protestants. This anti-Catholic sentiment, at least as it exists in the United States—which Hofstadter notes in his famous essay—is present in some well circulated present-day conspiracy theories, such as the one by conspiracy theorist Milton William Cooper in his best selling book Behold a Pale Horse (1991). How can one understand this animus? Michael Barkun states that, "Opposition to the Catholic Church was a function not only of its allegedly foreign character—believers and clergy were said to owe fealty to a distant pontiff—but of its rituals as well" (2003, pp. 127-128).

The foreignness and ritualism of Catholicism contributes to the suspicions that this religion engenders among Protestants, but the essential reason for this animus against Catholicism lies in the very nature of Catholicism in contradistinction to Protestantism. Catholicism is founded, for the most part, on unquestioning obedience to higher authority, namely, the hierarchy from the priests to the Pope. Early on in their religious education, Catholics memorize the catechism, which consists of the Church's answers to fundamental questions. Thus it is that thinking on one's own is discouraged.

Protestantism, too, has its dogmas, as well as its rituals, but to a significantly lesser extent. Furthermore, the tradition that runs from Luther to Kierkegaard to Barth to Tillich insists on an encounter with God unmediated by a Priest and by any body of dogma. This directness of encounter places the emphasis on individuality and free thought. The rituals of Catholicism inspire awe, but awe can be a way to overwhelm the questioning mind, which is why Protestantism did away with many rituals. Indoctrination invites paranoid fears of mind control. Thus it is not surprising that the Pope, and Catholicism in general, have often been the subject of conspiracy theories. It also explains why the Pope has often been viewed as the Antichrist in apocalyptic scenarios.

A related motif in apocalyptic fantasies is that the Antichrist is conspiring to bring about a one-world government. One-world government would, of course, mean the end of autonomy for each nation. When President Bush the elder began to use the phrase "new world order" as shorthand for the post USSR world, it precipitated a spate of conspiracy theories, which still circulate on the internet, revolving around that fear. That fear also manifests itself in current conspiracy theories in which the Antichrist turns out to be the Secretary General of the United Nations. In such scenarios, the United States merges with a one world government and loses its independence and national sovereignty. For example, a website devoted to end time prophecy warns us about the United Nations. The urgency of their warnings is expressed in their habit of using bold type and all capitals — which is evident in the next few quotes — for what they feel are key words:

> It becomes apparent that this "Global Governance" (synonymous with World Government) intends to aggressively assert itself in the internal affairs of nations it perceives to be in need of changes. At first, universal acceptance of these notions might be founded on the public's perceived concern about smaller nations in crisis. But we may eventually be horrified to find that the same liberties may be taken in nations not WANTING intervention, including the United

States. (Emphasis in original) (Raggio 2003, p. 1) kenraggio. com/KRPN-Superpower.htm

Another website offers an even more dire warning about the dangers of one world government, in a page entitled "The Rise of a One-World Government":

> One major final sign of the very end predicted by many prophets which is yet to be fulfilled, is the rise of a powerful One World Government! Right now this "New World Order" is already taking over the world by stealth, by destroying traditional law, order and values of separate sovereign nations and cultures based on family, religion, local economy and national government. At the same time it gathers up the "failing" broken pieces by the scheme of "Globalisation" into "succesful and ideal" global institutions like the UN, World Court, UNESCO, UNHCR, Worldbank, IMF and numerous others. Similarly, smaller businesses are being bought up and centralised into multi-national giants, putting the little guys out of business. Eventually this "New World Order" and its ten powers nucleus, will be led by a bestial dictator who will eventually get fully possessed by Satan himself!— The Antichrist! The World will turn to this false Messiah, desperate to save them when their World Economy finally crashes and the threat of nuclear war forces them to unite in a One World Government! (Deep Truths. Articles from David Berg and the Family International.
>
> deeptruths.com/articles/final_signs.html
> http://www.powerpointparadise.com/endworld/fin-signs/frame-b.htm)

The writer, presenting a dystopian sense of things that is actually quite intriguing, goes on to warn us to beware of the utopian promises, which he regards as Marxist, of those who advocate a one world government:

> At first this capable and powerful united global government will be much better than today's chaotic conditions: A World of relative peace, of controlled peacetime economy instead

of a war economy, a World of fair distribution--"share the wealth, take from the rich to feed the poor", etc. Under man's most ideal leader and his World government, there will finally be a proper apportionment of the World's resources, "from each according to his ability unto each according to his need," of both fuel, food and other necessities, as well as an end to today's extravagant waste and unfair distribution of the World's supplies.

For awhile it will seem like absolute Heaven on earth, but the price to pay will finally be not only compliance with the World government and the total control of freedom and personal religion and so on, but the eventual aim of the Enemy--the Devil himself who controls it--will be: "Fall down and worship me, or you cannot enjoy this great Heaven on Earth that I have created!"--And that's where the rub's going to come! Luke 4:5-7 (Emphasis in original) (Deep Truths. Articles from David Berg and the Family International. deeptruths.com/articles/final_signs.html.)

The fear of all nations becoming one is a symbolic representation of the paranoid anxiety about losing autonomy through losing one's identity. This is not to deny that there are cogent arguments against foreign entanglements — as can be found, for example, in Washington's Farewell Address — and cogent arguments against becoming entangled with the United Nations, and warnings by thinkers within the dystopian tradition about the dangers of one world government. But the argument against involvement with the United Nations, predicated on the Secretary General supposedly being the Antichrist is expressive of a paranoia-infused mythic drama.

Paranoids have long been fearful of internationalism, in general, for the same reason that they are against the United Nations. In the Nineteenth Century conspiracy theories abounded about the Rothschilds. They were bankers, and people feared that the creation of a central bank would exert control over their lives. Of course, the fact that the Rothschilds were Jewish did not help their cause any. There have, of course, been many reasons for anti-Semitism, including the fact that the Jews, owing to their cosmopolitanism, represent the internationalism that those imbued with the paranoid vision find so dreadful. In more recent times, paranoids have been suspicious of such organizations that promote international relations as The Council of Foreign Relations, The Trilateral Organization, and the Bilderberg Group, and many websites can be found on the internet devoted to tracking the supposed machinations of these organizations. Paranoids, on both extremes of the political spectrum, have been against globalization for that same reason.

The fear of technology, which is common among paranoids, has a related origin. If one searches the web, one can find a great many websites devoted to disseminating information about how Bill Gates is supposedly the Antichrist, although less now that he has become a generous philanthropist. Why Gates? He is the richest person in the world, and had been the head of a powerful organization, Microsoft, whose Windows operating system is a virtual monopoly, and monopoly — especially in regard to an area that involves the ability to control, manipulate, and disseminate information, which is what computers can do — suggests illegitimate and demonic power to control people's minds. Not surprisingly, one of the candidates for Antichrist, according to Boyer, was a giant computer (Boyer, 1992, p. 283).

But the paranoid's luddism is not just in regard to the computer. Mass production means that the individuality that belonged to handcrafted things is lost. Due to technology, communications media, such as radio and TV, can become powerful propaganda tools, the result of which is that all minds subscribe to the same ideas, and individuality is lost. Of course, this is not merely a paranoid fantasy, nor merely the dystopian nightmare of writers like George Orwell. The propaganda potential of the mass media is a reality. But, again, what is a genuine concern is distorted into a panic, after it has been filtered through the paranoid vision.

Not only luddism, but anti-intellectualism in general has a number of causes, but it often derives from a paranoid anxiety of being invaded by foreign ideas, and thus of losing one's identity. The long-lasting conspiracy theories about Freemasonry and about the Illuminati, a late eighteenth-century group of intellectuals who were interested in promoting the ideas of the European Enlightenment, is a case in point. Anti-intellectualism has been a staple of the political right, as Hofstadter pointed out in Anti-intellectualism in American Life (1966), but Dowbiggen (2000) contends that it now very much belongs to those on the left, if one considers that an apparent intellectuality can sometimes be a mask for a more fundamental close-mindedness, otherwise known as political correctness.

In some paranoid groups and organizations, emotions too can be feared, for, like ideas, they can possess a person, belying his or her claim to autonomy. The Taliban, the 9/11 suicide bombers, and other radical Islamic groups prohibit music, dancing, and sensuality. These activities draw one into feelings, resulting in a loss of self-possession and autonomy. The fear of the emotions belongs to the ascetic dimension of religious consciousness. One even finds that fear expressed by Plato in *The Republic,* who would expel the poets from his utopian republic.

What makes groups, like the Taliban, paranoid is that they project all that they fear—the life of feelings and desire, and the consequent loss of self-possession—onto the United States, whom they then castigate as the Great Satan, as a prostitute luring them into sensuality. Were paranoids aware of themselves they would think, "I have weak ego boundaries. I am projecting my anxiety about loss of autonomy onto the world." On the contrary, they think, "They're coming in on me!" According to Nancy Kobrin, a psychoanalyst and an Arabist, radical Islamists seek to deny the Jewish and Christian roots of their religion by either converting or killing Jews and Christians. Why do they wish to deny their roots? As Kobrin states it, "The unacknowledged fear is the fear of losing their identity in the other. Think: enmeshment" (2005, 8). Here again, then, is the anxiety about loss of autonomy through possession.

It can be concluded, from these examples, that apocalyptic fantasies—and conspiracy theories, too, for that matter—are a product of the enterprise of explanation and justification distorted by anxiety. But apocalyptic fantasies also have an anxiety-relieving function. They present a horrifying scenario, one in which individual autonomy will be violated—which is a central anxiety of those under the paranoid vision — but then suggest that there is a way out, through salvation. In the end, the Antichrist and his totalitarian control over the world will be overcome, and then the millennium will follow.

There is an important qualification that needs to be made in regard to the anxiety over loss of autonomy that appears in apocalyptic fantasies. While it is true that the paranoid has an overriding concern for preserving his or her autonomy, it is also true that the paranoid, like everyone else, is a being of contradictions, and consequently desires opposite things. The paranoid fears the loss of autonomy, but how curious is the picture of what Christ's future kingdom will be like, as imagined by Scofield, the nineteenth century American millennialist. According to Boyer:

> Enforcing his unity and harmony will be Christ himself. As Scofield insisted, the "tranquility, blessedness, and peace" of the Kingdom Age will be possible only because "the government will be a theocracy" committed to "instant destruction of the insubordinate or rebellious." (1992, p. 322)

Boyer then adds that there is a similar sentiment expressed by another millennialist who was very popular at the time, "'Jesus will be an absolute dictator,' wrote Herbert Vander Lugt; 'He will displace one of our cherished freedoms—that of religion. He will not permit the practice or propagation of false religion in any form'" (1992, p. 323). One might object that these observations are applicable only to two men, Scofield and Lugt, who were, of course, highly influential in American evangelism and apocalypticism. But an exploration of case examples will reveal that this ambivalence in regard to freedom—an anxiety over losing one's autonomy, and a concomitant anxiety over gaining it—plays an important role in the psychology of a person under the sway of the paranoid vision.

Dictators, and even cynical politicians, capitalize on that ambiguity. They offer to safeguard their countrymen's autonomy by protecting it from foreign invasion, or from the invasion of foreign ideas, while simultaneously helping them do away with troublesome freedom through total conformity to the totalitarian state. In that sense, they are very much like Dostoevsky's Grand Inquisitor.

There is, finally, another irony—and a beautiful one at that—in regard to those under the sway of the paranoid vision: the one form of possession that they have every reason to fear, they do not fear! Paradoxically, they do not fear possession by the paranoid vision itself. They do, of course, have moments of relative lucidity and the self-doubts that follow, for there is always a certain self-awareness present, if marginal, even as the voice of madness screams all the louder, in an effort to drown it out.

The Dread of Defilement

What is the origin of disgust, nausea, and even horror over that which is slimy? One might recall one's earliest experiences of the slimy. It could, for example, have been from touching some substance, such as mud, or from observing an insect, or seeing some creeping crawling creature in a horror film, or from a slimy food such as the yellow from the yoke of an egg dripping onto one's plate. Sartre offers a clue to the mystery of this revulsion, "The first experience that the infant can have with the slimy enriches him psychologically and morally" (1943; 1988, p. 144). If Sartre is correct, the revulsion towards that which is slimy is due to the fact that evil, or immorality, is first experienced not as an abstract concept, not as the breaking of a commandment, but as something quasi-physical.

Sartre's intuitions about the slimy are confirmed by Paul Ricoeur, who does not write about the slimy, but of that which the slimy could be considered a species, namely the defiling. In *The Symbolism of Evil* (1986), he analyzes the defiling in terms of religious symbolism from the Old Testament, and sees it as both an infection and a mark of moral fault. Thus to be slimed—and, similarly, to be stained, soiled, sullied, or infected—is to experience evil not as a concept, but as an actual thing or substance.

For orthodox Jews, for example, nonkosher meat is defiling. Even if they should discover that they had been deceived into eating nonkosher meat, they will feel morally impure. The fact that they did not know better is irrelevant to the sense of being defiled, for on that level of consciousness, intention, or the lack of it, does not enter into moral judgments as a consideration. This is because the notion of intention presupposes the emergence of a subject who is separate from his or her body. If that separation exists, one could assert, "My body is not the inner me; it is not the real me." But this inner/outer discrimination does not exist on the defilement level of awareness.

Many people, whose consciousness has evolved to more elevated levels of morality still retain vestiges of defilement consciousness. One might feel, for example, that a certain person has a lubricious character, and a slimy handshake to go with it. Or a man may experience a sense of defilement when he notices that he has gotten mustard on his new necktie. The sense of disgust—which is derivative of defilement consciousness, along with the related experience of shame—may even, by some accounts, be a requirement for the advancement of human culture (Orwell, 1937, Miller, 1997).

According to Ricoeur, if evil on the level of defilement is prototypically represented as a stain, evil on the level of sin is represented as a deviation from the path of righteousness, which, more precisely, consists of the breaking of a moral law, such as one of the Ten Commandments. Thus evil on the level of sin requires a deliberate action on one's part, a misdeed, a straying from the straight and narrow. An interior subject has emerged on this level of awareness, and so a person's intentions, in contradistinction to the purity or impurity of their body, are relevant in moral judgments.

Let us suppose that a person does obey all the moral laws, but is inwardly proud and arrogant. Furthermore, lacking love, one is empty inside, "as sounding brass, or a tinkling cymbal," as it says in Corinthians. On this level of morality, which Ricoeur associates with guilt, doing the right thing is not sufficient to be a good person. When evil is experienced as guilt, in contrast to defilement or sin, the emphasis falls on having a pure heart, which means not even thinking impure thoughts.

The sense of evil, experienced as sin, can lead to subtle moral distinctions, requiring the services of a rabbi or a priest to determine if someone is at fault in a certain situation. It requires that people search their souls to know if they are guilty of the sin of pride, for example, despite having been rigorous in their obedience to the moral law, and despite their outward show of piety. Or maybe they were slothful in not offering their aid to others more vigorously, and so they are guilty on that score.

But morality on the defilement level of consciousness is much simpler—one is either pure or impure. It is the primitiveness of evil, represented as defilement that lends itself to that equally primitive defense mechanism, endemic to paranoia, projection. Of course, one could project one's sin or guilt. But those more nuanced levels of morality are such that one's accusations can easily boomerang, as the harsh winds of accusation suddenly shift their direction.

Bernard McGinn has stated that, "The apocalyptic worldview leaves no room for moral ambiguity" (2000, p. 16). The lack of ambiguity — which derives from defilement consciousness, coupled with the Manichean tendencies of the paranoid, along with the defense mechanism of projection—promotes the sense that, "We're clean. They need to be purified, and the apocalypse will bring it about." Even worse, there is a sense that, "Those impure people can defile us. We had better quarantine them, and kill them for our own protection." The "ethnic cleansing" that occurred in Bosnia is a terrifying manifestation of defilement consciousness, Manichaeism, and projection, resulting in genocide. This dread of impurity would also explain the death sentence fatwa that was issued against the writer Salman Rushdie by Iranian Islamic fundamentalists. According to Adam Kirsch:

> More than any writer of our time, Mr. Rushdie has been a foe of purity, of the belief that virtue demands restriction and purgation, severance and taboo. The Islamic ideologues who placed Mr. Rushdie in fear of his life for nine years, and who managed to wound or kill his Japanese, Norwegian, and Italian translators and publishers, recognized that this conviction made him their foe, as well. (2005, p. 1)

We suggested that there is evident in the apocalyptic literature a tone of impatience, the effect of which is to inflame the campaign against impurity. The impatience, and resultant feelings of wrath, stem from the perception that the world needs to be purified of evil before the arrival of the apocalypse, and then the millennium, but that there exist people who, by virtue of their impurity, are delaying matters. The consequences of this notion are deadly. Throughout the centuries, it has commonly meant, for example, that the Jews, Moslems, and other heathen need to convert before Christ will return. Writing about the Taborites, a fanatical religious group from the Middle Ages, Norman Cohn states that, "...massacre was seen as clearing the way for the Millennium... [The Taborites] were utterly convinced that the earth had only to be cleansed of sinners for Christ to descend from the heavens in majesty, whilst they, the Saints, soared through the air to greet him" (1961, p. 226)

One comes across these images of impurity and the need for cleansing repeatedly in the apocalyptic literature. How do such millenarian groups propose to cleanse the world of sinners? Does it mean leading the supposed sinners to the path of righteousness? On the contrary, it means killing them. A group that existed between the years 1290 and 1329, called the Brethren of the Yellow Cross, is typical in that regard. According to Cohn:

> As usual the route to the millennium leads through massacre and terror. God's aim is to free the world from sin. If sin continues to flourish, divine punishment will surely be visited upon the world; whereas if sin is once abandoned, then the world will be ready for the Kingdom of the Saints. The most urgent task of the Brethren of the Yellow Cross is therefore to eliminate sin, which in effect means to eliminate sinners. (1961, p. 116)

What makes matters even more perverse is that such fanatics feel justified in their murders, for they feel that they are purifying or saving not only themselves, but also those whom they murder. Apropos is a title of a book by Lifton, *Destroying the World to Save It* (2000). Lifton argues that Aum Shinrikyo, the apocalyptic cult that was responsible for the notorious poisonous gas attack on the Japanese subway system, became driven by the notion of "killing to heal." Here, again, is the motif of defilement and purification, but notice that here it is on a global scale:

> Altruistic mass murder depended, in turn, on a fourth
> characteristic: the relentless impulse toward world-rejecting
> purification. Here Aum drew upon its version of karma as
> ubiquitous defilement...reality itself was a defilement. With
> both matter and reality, indeed all human life, so defiled, the
> process of purification could be achieved by nothing short of
> killing on a planetary scale. (Emphasis in original) (2000, p.
> 204-205)

Elsewhere Lifton draws parallels, in regard to the defilement motif, to the Nazi's genocide, and beyond that omnicide, or world destruction, which echoes the Gotterdammerung of German mythology. Lifton also finds this theme in other apocalyptic cults, including that of Jim Jones who, as part of the Christian apocalyptic tradition, brings the Antichrist into the discussion: "Capitalist America was absolute evil: America's system is representative of the mark of the Beast and America is the Antichrist. Nuclear holocaust, he believed, would bring about a cataclysmic purification that would result in "total annihilation of all life in America'" (2000, 286). Lifton also sees the relation of the defilement and purification motif to the desire for racial purity. Referring to *The Turner Diaries*, the book that influenced Timothy McVeigh to destroy the Federal Building in Oklahoma City, he says:

> The book elaborates, proudly and affectionately, on the
> technical knowledge and steadfast racial totalism needed to
> carry out a project approaching global omnicide. First there
> is a vast "cleansing" of America's blacks, Jews, and white
> "race traitors" through a variety of massacres culminating in
> nuclear attacks on American inner cities...Then the cleansing
> is extended to all the global nonwhite populations, until finally
> a white racial utopia is ushered in. (2000, p. 333)

The Turner Diaries is, of course, a recrudescence of the apocalyptic racial purity-seeking of the Nazis. In any case, the notion of genocide, omnicide, or apocalypse as a form of purification has a long and notorious history, and includes a great many horrors, from the Spanish Inquisition, to the burning and drowning of witches at Salem, to the Holocaust, to the 911 suicide bombers. It is perhaps not insignificant that the preferred means of destruction, by apocalyptic movements, involves water or fire, with their suggestion of purification or renewal. It, therefore, makes a certain dark archetypal sense that the 911 terrorists would seek to turn the World Trade Center into a giant incinerator.

We have explored two paranoid anxieties: possession and defilement. Both are antithetical to the notion of original sin, as well as to the notion of "radical evil," that flaw or blemish which Kant believed is inherent in "the twisted timber of humanity." This is because evil represented as possession or as defilement is experienced not as something inherent in human beings, but as something external, something that comes in on us, to rob our autonomy, or to defile our purity. A third paranoid representation of evil is that of the devil. Here, too, evil is viewed as something external; it is not part of one's very being.

The fundamental assumption in all these representations of evil is that one is originally pure, and neither inherently sinful, nor twisted, nor blemished, nor imperfect in any way. The corollary is that one possesses purity, perfection, goodness, nobility, and grandeur. Long before Rousseauan romanticism argued that imperfection and evil are extrinsic to human beings, those under the sway of the paranoid vision had assumed exactly that about themselves. There is, of course, a significant difference between blaming society for one's fallenness as opposed to blaming a supposedly nefarious group of people, but the assumption of original innocence is the same.

We might conclude that apocalyptic fantasies have explanatory, justificatory, and anxiety relieving functions. It would appear, though, that they are the product of other powerful motives as well. For example, as Cohn suggests, in regard to a number of millenarian cults that emerged in Germany and in Holland during the Middle Ages:

> Thus in each of these areas in turn a collective sense of impotence and anxiety and envy suddenly discharged itself in a frantic urge to smite the ungodly—and by doing so to bring into being, out of suffering inflicted and suffering endured, the final Kingdom where the Saints, clustered around the

great figure of the Messiah, were to enjoy ease and riches,
security and power for all eternity. (1961, p. 32)

It is the sense of impotence, anxiety, and envy that makes
apocalypticism so potentially dangerous. There is yet another reason
why people are entranced by apocalyptic fantasies. As Boyer notes,
"In 1914 Walter Lippmann perceptively wrote of the way such theories
can suffuse the monotonies of everyday life 'with an alert and tingling
sense of labyrinthine evil'" (1992, p. 270). Thus, that which to many
people is the only thing worse than anxiety, namely boredom, comes
into play. Both conspiracy theories and apocalyptic fantasies are very
much a flight from boredom. That apocalypticism is driven by a welter
of motives is understandable enough, for it is rare that any human
enterprise does not arise out of a mixture of motives.

The Apocalyptic Temptation

Like conspiracy theories, apocalyptic fantasies promise to provide
intelligibility, direction and meaning. They do so by seducing one into
a passionate mythic drama, which provides an implicit explanation
of the world and a justification for human suffering. The temptation
of apocalypse lies in believing the fantasy that the destruction of the
world will create a better one, that humanity will have the chance to
begin all over again, and that the world may attain the purity that
it supposedly had in a mythic golden age. The longing for rebirth is
intrinsic to the human condition. The apocalyptic temptation is to
reify an inner transformation, thus mistaking it for an outer drama.
It is the temptation to seek to change the world as a surrogate for the
task of changing oneself.

There will always be certain elements of reality that cannot
be incorporated into a theory for—as Gödel's first and second
incompleteness theorems prove mathematically—a theory cannot
be both consistent and complete. We saw that to be the case with
conspiracy theories. Are apocalyptic fantasies narrow, or constricted,
in their worldview? Is there an element of reality that cannot be
explained? A study of a millenarian cult, which appeared in the 1950s,
may offer a clue.

The study was done by a team of psychologists, who acted as participant-observers of a group of people who had, over the course of several months, become like a cult. They were convinced that there was going to be a great flood, and it was imminent. A spaceship would arrive in time to take this group of people to another planet, but everyone else would drown. Needless to say, the spaceship never did arrive. Fortunately, the members of this space cult did not meet with a tragic end, unlike the members of the Heaven's Gate cult, who were similarly awaiting a rocket. They just ended up rather disappointed, especially about having to ask their former bosses if they could have their old jobs back, after having resigned, on grounds that they were leaving the planet for good. More generally, they were disappointed about having to live in this less than perfect world.

The psychologists then wrote a book based on their experiences as participants and on their observations called *When Prophecy Fails* (1956). What interests us here is a particularly telling statement made by one of the former spaceship cult members, a young man named Fred. He had a sort of epiphany about the limits of the apocalyptic drama, and why it is founded on a constricted view of the world:

> Fred says that he doesn't believe that this disaster will ever occur. The way he put it was: "When you stop and think of it, it seems rather cruel to drown all these people just to teach them a lesson, doesn't it? The way to teach people a lesson or the way to educate people is to educate them slowly; you can't educate them with one big jolt.." (Festinger, Riecken, Schachter, 1956, p. 220)

To understand Fred's insight, consider the story of Noah, which is one of a number of apocalyptic stories that appears in the Bible. Noah is told by God to build an ark, to bring aboard his kin, and two of each animal species. Then it rains for forty days and nights. Everyone drowns except for those aboard the ark. Why the need for a flood? God was angry at the iniquity of mankind and concluded that the great flood would purify the earth. It would wipe away all the dirt, slime, and iniquity that were defiling the purity of God's creation. Then the world that he created could get a fresh start with Noah and his kin; drowning everyone would teach them a lesson that they would never forget, to say the least.

Did God—or at least the mythmaker who wrote down the story —really imagine that humans would be any different after this apparently fresh start? No matter how many times God threatens mankind with punishment — by sending prophets with their minatory warnings, by visiting mankind with plagues, by destroying cities, etc. —nothing seems to work. If anything, people conclude that if they are dissatisfied with other people, then they are justified in exhibiting holy vengeance. They, too, can seek to purify the world by destroying it. The result is akin to what sometimes happens when a father beats his son for misbehaving. The son then learns to beat other people when they do something that he does not like. Freud called this behavior "identifying with the aggressor." Although God's inscrutable ways cannot be known, it is unlikely that hatred towards other people was the lesson that God intended to teach, but unwittingly He, or the mythmaker, did. This unintended consequence is one of religion's supreme ironies.

One must sympathize, though, with God's wrath, and with the longing for severe retribution that finds expression in the Bible, for this world is often cruel and unjust. It is galling, for example, that mass murderers like Stalin and Idi Amin die peacefully of old age, and their terrible atrocities go unpunished. Of course, those are just egregious examples of a world that has always reeked with injustice. To make sense of life, one posits an afterlife or a millennial kingdom of some sort, a realm where all accounts are finally paid, and with interest. To a large measure, the dispensing of justice is the appeal of apocalyptic fantasies.

The vision of life, presented in these apocalyptic tales, is a constricted one, as evidenced by its Manichean dualism, which eschews shades of gray. It should, therefore, come as no surprise that those who engage in apocalyptic fantasies tend to be self-righteous and unforgiving, attitudes that often lead to projecting one's shadow onto other people. The image of God that emerges in apocalyptic fantasies —whether from the Bible or elsewhere—is a reflection of their own narrowness of perspective.

What makes this view of the world narrow is that it ignores transformative dimension of human existence. Human beings are, as has often been said, really "human becomings." Everyone knows this, for they see children grow—physically, emotionally, and intellectually—and, if one is perceptive, one can also see adults go though many transformations in their lifetime.

To undergo these transformations means making mistakes, sometimes tragic ones, but such is the path to wisdom. In contrast to the punitively apocalyptic sense of things, that is endemic to the paranoid vision, there exists, then, an evolutionary view of human existence. It intuits that even death and damnation might not be the last word, as suggested by the ancient saying, "God's providence as regards Pharaoh was not terminated by his drowning." This view does not, though, deny the reality of evil, nor the need for punishment, but it also sees the possibility of penitence, grace, forgiveness, and rebirth. The evolutionary perspective is fundamental to Hinduism and Buddhism. These religions posit that if you do not get it right in this life, you will keep on returning until you do. A popular version of this is presented in films like *Defending Your Life* (1991) and Groundhog Day (1993). Therefore, the notion that each human being evolves is the antithesis of the apocalyptic sense of things, with its finality, its notion that when you are damned, you are damned forever.

In one very fundamental sense, the Bible, taken as a whole, is the expression of an evolutionary perspective, for God himself evolves.[9] The evolution of morality and religion is certainly evident, for example, in The Book of Job, but it is most dramatic in the shift from the Old Testament to the New Testament. What essentially happens is this: Finally, after thousands of years of hurling lightning bolts, creating floods, raining down locusts and hailstorms, and implementing various other forms of holy destruction, God gets a revolutionary new idea: he will demonstrate what needs to be done, then maybe humans will finally get the message. So he suffers on the cross and dies for our sins.

This new approach certainly has a better chance of moving the hearts of human beings than do lightning bolts, but it too proves

9 For a discussion of God's evolution, see C.G. Jung's Answer to Job (1978). For a discussion of the evolution of Zeus, see Carl Kerenyi's Prometheus (1997).

problematic, for sometimes it succeeds—as is illustrated by the story of the bishop's candlesticks, from Victor Hugo's *Les Misérables*—but often it fails. Instead of imitating Christ, most people think, "Great. He did it for us, so now we don't have to." Out of frustration with mankind for not getting the message of Christ, comes *The Book of Revelation.* It is essentially *The Book of Daniel,* or the story of Noah in *Genesis,* redux, an atavism to an earlier notion of seeking to make humankind good through apocalyptic threats and punishment. At least Noah and the flood was an enjoyable story, appealing to children with its tale of all those animals boarding the ark. *The Book of Revelation,* on the other hand, is horrific. So after all the talk of love and forgiveness that one finds in the Gospels, the paranoid vision is back in town, like the return of the repressed.

Apocalyptic fantasies are a product of the paranoid vision, but they are also an answer to the question—How can human beings be changed so that they could become righteous? The assumption behind the question is that if humans would be good, then finally heaven on earth can come about. Why not the route of education? The millenarian is impatient with education, for it takes a long, long time and it is unlikely to ever produce saints on a grand scale. Even under the best of circumstances, its outcome is uncertain. Education can even enhance a person's villainy. The treacherous Alcibiades had one of the greatest of teachers, Socrates. All of Heidegger's immense learning could not prevent Heidegger from joining the Nazi Party, nor could it induce him to apologize, years later, for having done so. The alternative to education is the school of hard knocks, but that, too, takes a very long time, and its outcome is equally uncertain. So the millenarian remains impatient.

Many thoughtful people, out of perplexity, have been prompted to ask such perennial questions as, "Why is it that times change, but humans are always the same? Is there no hope for mankind? If human beings cannot change, how can I come to terms with this bloody horror show called history?" There are answers to such questions, but they are only meaningful to those who have suffered in the crucible of transformation long enough to emerge with a radical shift of perspective. Without this deeper understanding, the frustrations that come from living in this imperfect world will leave a person in a spiritually precarious state. It can lead to a desperate wish to precipitate the apocalypse, and all the other manifestations of the paranoid vision that follow in its train. Frustration, then, can be paranoiagenic.

We have investigated two of the major narratives of the paranoid vision, conspiracy theories and apocalyptic fantasies. It is now time to explore how these and other manifestations of the paranoid vision find expression in various organizations and movements.

Part II:

Manifestations

of the

Paranoid Vision

Chapter Four
Freud's Inner Circle

"Power can infantilize those who wield it as much as those who submit to it."

— *Paul Roazen (1969; 1971)*

A common mission united the members of Freud's inner circle, which was comprised of his closest disciples: to develop and promote psychoanalysis. Here was a revolutionary new theory of the psyche and of human behavior, as well as a therapy that promised to liberate neurotics from their emotional conflicts. Ironically, the members of Freud's circle found themselves embroiled in emotional conflicts with each other, and with Freud. Not only were those conflicts miserable in themselves, they were also a harbinger of what was to come: the inner circle was to metamorphose into an organization thoroughly possessed by the paranoid vision.

What thus emerges—from the records, journals, books, articles and correspondence of the members of the inner circle—is an unsettling account of how a group of brilliant intellectuals devolved into something resembling a cult. Perhaps the inner circle had become more akin to a church in the midst of an inquisition, as a number of cultural historians have argued, including the psychiatrist Anthony Storr:

It has often been remarked that the squabbles about psychoanalytic theory which resulted in so many of the members of Freud's inner circle resigning or being expelled as heretics seemed like doctrinal disputes within a Church rather than scientific disagreements. The latter can certainly be bitter; but seldom involve the character assassination and pejorative language which Freud used to describe those adherents who later disputed his theories...When his associates remained faithful disciples, Freud gave them his approval; but when they disagreed, he abused them, or accused them of being mentally ill. Adler was described by Freud as a paranoiac; Stekel as unbearable and a louse; Jung as brutal and sanctimonious. Psychoanalysis became more and more like a religious cult, and Freud himself applied the term heretics to defectors. (1996, p. 117)

Abuse, slander, the excommunication and demonization of heretics—what a far cry from the high ideals of scientific inquiry! If the psychoanalytic movement, supine on our consulting room couch, could recount the details of its early childhood, its nightmarish family dramas and traumas, we might come to know the answer to the fundamental question—How did this happen?

Paranoid Tales from the Vienna Woods

In 1902 Freud invited several of his followers to meet with him on a regular basis to discuss psychoanalysis. That group, often referred to as the inner circle, initially called themselves "The Wednesday Psychological Society," later renaming themselves "The Vienna Psychoanalytic Society." The membership included a number of individuals who would become distinguished in the early psychoanalytic movement including Alfred Adler, William Stekel, Ernest Jones, Karl Abraham, Hans Sachs, and Sandor Ferenczi. Otto Rank would later be introduced to Freud by Adler, and become a member.

After some years, a group of Swiss psychiatrists joined, including C.G. Jung, who was about twenty years Freud's junior. Freud invested a great deal of hope in Jung, whom he saw as his heir apparent, and who became known as "the crown prince of psychoanalysis," the person who would eventually become Freud's successor. Although Freud was only about fifty years old when he created his inner circle, the need to have psychoanalysis continue on in the world after he was gone was obviously of crucial importance to Freud.

By all accounts, Freud and Jung were very impressed with each other, and quite fond of each other too. Jung writes about how they talked together for thirteen hours, nonstop, during their initial meeting. It was also apparent from their correspondence that a strong father/son relationship had developed between them, which they both acknowledged and encouraged, actually addressing each other as father and son in some of their letters. This should not be surprising, since it would appear that Freud had a paternal relation to all of his disciples. It was just that Jung had quickly become his favorite son.

Jung was certainly brilliant, ambitious, articulate and capable, and that may have been sufficient for Freud to choose him to be his successor. But Freud, always with an eye to public relations, had another reason for favoring him. Jung was not Jewish, unlike almost all of the other members of the inner circle, including Freud himself. Freud thought that by having a gentile at the helm of the Psychoanalytic Society, psychoanalysis would not be dismissed by anti-Semites, both European and American, as merely a Jewish phenomenon. Of course, Freud could have chosen Ernest Jones for he, too, was a Christian, but apparently Freud did not have the same confidence in Jones as he did in Jung.

During those weekly meetings of Freud and his disciples, there was much debate over theoretical issues, and often Freud would act as a mediator. It was one thing for disagreements to remain within the confines of Freud's theoretical system. It might be acceptable, for example, to argue that infantile sexuality began at age two-and-three months, rather than at age two. But that there existed such a thing as infantile sexuality was not itself debatable for, by most accounts, Freud could not tolerate disagreement about his fundamental ideas. As Paul Roazen contends, "Although [Freud] admired originality and talent, he had difficulty tolerating anyone with ideas of his own. As he freely admitted, 'I have no use for other people's ideas when they are presented to me at an inopportune moment.' Thus Freud repeatedly drove away his best pupils" (1971a, p. 181). As in all cults and totalitarian groups, the leader's opinions and ideas are regarded as gospel, as official doctrine.[10] The most important point of unspoken dissension was, of course, Freud's opinion that sex was at the root of all human behavior. To suggest otherwise was regarded by him as a personal affront, indeed, as a betrayal. Freud regarded the questioning of the basic axioms of psychoanalysis as nothing short of heresy. What existed, then, was not creative dialogue, but the kind of demand for ideological purity that Lifton suggests is endemic to those movements that are totalistic, i.e., those that promote an ideological totalitarianism.

The majority of Freud's circle accepted the party line, at least outwardly. But Freud's circle also included some independent, creative thinkers who were finding it increasingly difficult to suppress the dictates of their personal ideas and vision. Consequently, those creative individuals found themselves hemmed in and oppressed by the limits of Freud's conceptual schema. Adler, for example, might wish to discuss the possibility that a certain patient's dream was really expressive of power issues, rather than about repressed sexual libido, and that feelings of inferiority and social interests also played an important role in an individual's psychic economy. And Jung would contend that there were religious and spiritual longings at the root of human behavior, as well.

It was becoming apparent over time that Adler was drifting away from doctrinaire Freudianism. His writings indicated that he did not subscribe to the fundamental axioms of psychoanalysis such as infantile sexuality and the importance of the Oedipus Complex. It will be necessary to go into more detail about what led up to these conflicts, but suffice it to say for now that Freud decided to put his foot down. At one meeting, he arranged to humiliate Adler by presenting a paper in which he aggressively attacked Adler's ideas. Roazen reminds us of how much this conflict was like that which might exist in a church:

10 Ernest Jones (1955) contends that Freud did get along with Binswanger, who dissented with Freud's opinions, and that proves that the fault lay with the other members of Freud's inner circle. Like most issues, this one is not black and white, but Jones did have a history of partisanship in favor of Freud. We must consider the opinion of the other historians, as well as the writings of Jung, Adler, and the other members of the inner circle.

> Freud outwardly denounced Adler. It was a trial and the charge
> was heresy...As Sachs, who voted with Freud, remembered,
> Freud "did not spare his opponent and was not afraid of
> using sharp words and cutting remarks..." The penalty was
> excommunication, and Freud set out to ostracize Adler and
> his sympathizers. (1971a, p. 184)

This soon led to Adler's resignation, along with several of his
friends and supporters, including Stekel. If Freud imagined that
his problems would be over now that the "traitorous" Adler and his
sympathizers were gone, he was sorely mistaken. Over time, Freud
and Jung's relationship grew increasingly strained. It is apparent
from Jung's correspondence with Freud, that Jung was becoming
oversensitive, almost in a paranoid way, to the smallest hint that
Freud had slighted him. These misunderstandings were followed by
reconciliations, followed by new tensions and conflicts. Freud did all
that he could to patch things up, but that always meant leaving the form
of their relationship intact, i.e. keeping it as father/son relationship.
It was becoming apparent, though, that Jung no longer wished to be
Freud's "son." Jung's letters reveal that he may have been trying to
hide from himself his ambivalent feelings about independence, under
the guise of hostility. This is understandable, for it must been a terrible
emotional trial for Jung to break away from the mentor with whom he
had been so close, and to set out on the uncertain path before him.

The final break with Jung was also very distressing for Freud,
for it dashed his hopes for an ideological heir who would be able to
carry the torch of psychoanalysis. Freud believed that without an heir,
the psychoanalytic movement would founder and maybe not survive.
Apparently, he did not have much confidence in anyone else in the
inner circle to replace Jung, nor, it would seem, did Freud believe that
his ideas could survive in the world on their own merit. Of course,
ideas in the world, like children in the world, are subject to all sorts
of permutations; they can evolve in ways that their creator cannot
control.

Freud, though, believed that he could control the future of his
ideas. This is not surprising, since those under the sway of the paranoid

vision—with their continual anxiety about threats to their autonomy —are desperate in their efforts at maintaining control. To have his ideas out there and not to be able to manage them was, therefore, experienced by Freud as a dreadful assault on his autonomy.

The departure of Jung not only meant to Freud that he had lost his successor, the person who would be the shepherd and guardian of his ideas, but it also meant that Jung had now become, in Freud's eyes, a serious threat. This was because Jung was espousing a rival psychological theory. At that time there were, of course, other schools of psychology, including Adler's Society for Individual Psychoanalysis. What was it about Jung's theory that Freud found so threatening? Jones quotes a letter that Freud wrote to Ferenczi on January 5th, 1913, that expresses the tenor of Freud's fears:

> Naturally everything that tries to get away from our truths will find approbation among the general public. It is quite possible that this time we shall be really buried, after a burial hymn has so often been sung over us in vain. That will change a great deal of our personal fate, but nothing that is of Science. (qtd. in Jones, 1955, p. 148)

Freud's belief that the general public was against his ideas was simply not true; on the contrary, Freud's ideas were becoming increasingly popular. It was Freud's cynicism, impatience, and lack of faith in life that made him too easily despair. Freud's letter also suggests that Jung's departure would lead the public to conclude that psychoanalysis was not a science. A science, in Freud's mind, was a unified body of knowledge, and having contending schools of psychoanalysis would belie its scientific claims. But hasn't science always had contending schools of thought? Of course, if one totalizes one's theories—and makes them into something akin to religious gospel, rather than seeing them as scientific hypotheses — one will feel threatened by rival theories, as did Freud in regard to Jung's ideas.

Furthermore, the notion that the public's realization of this would lead to the death and burial of the inner circle was a baseless fear. There was a sense on Freud's part of martyrdom, which derives from a paranoid delusion of grandeur. All this is important, because those who are under the sway of the paranoid vision see themselves as acting defensively, and therefore feel justified for behavior that is downright hostile, as was the behavior of Freud and his followers.

In response to the bitter disagreements, angry conflicts and unceremonious departures that ensued—including those of Adler, Stekel, and Jung, and the insecure and anxious sense it created—Freud and his remaining disciples felt the need to close ranks. In 1912, they formed a secret committee consisting of Otto Rank, Karl Abraham, Max Eitingon (who had been part of the Swiss contingency), Ernest Jones, Sandor Ferenczi, and Hans Sachs. It continued in operation until 1926; its purpose was to protect psychoanalysis, and to safeguard Freud's legacy after he died. In other words, this "band of brothers," as it has been called, was to serve the purpose that a single disciple, like Jung, had been intended to serve. Freud gave each of the members of the committee the gift of a finger ring that represented their fealty to Freud. Up until the formation of the committee, one could say that it was only Freud who was paranoid. It could be argued that Freud's disciples formed the committee just to please their teacher, and perhaps humor him, while realizing full well that he was paranoid, but it is unlikely. Their loyalty and belief in Freud was still very strong, such that they began to see the world as he did, i.e., they too fell under the sway of the paranoid vision.

When Jung had his final break with Freud, he was still president of an organization that Freud had created years before, the International Psychoanalytic Society. Indeed, Freud had nominated him to that position. The fact that Jung was still its president engendered a great deal of fear on the part of the Committee. They feared that Jung would use his position to cause trouble for everybody, so they conspired to do what they could to destroy Jung's professional reputation. This was a multifaceted campaign. It involved, among other things, Freud's writing a book, On the History of the Psycho-Analytic Movement that would serve to denounce Jung. Francois Roustang describes the very violent language that was used by Freud and the other members of the Committee to describe their plot,

...the book was to be "vigorous and plain-speaking." It would be a "bombshell" which should have a great effect. Freud's correspondent understood perfectly, since he wrote, "I have already written to you about the 'History,' I have read it over and over again and have increasingly come to see how important a weapon it is." And a little later, "Your 'History' will result in the resignation of Jung." In the meantime, Abraham himself is working on a criticism of Jung's works which Freud applauds and says deserves "a civic crown" (doubtless because it will greatly help to eliminate the traitor) and is "excellent, cold steel, clean, clear and sharp." The steel from which daggers are made. ...[Freud] sums up the whole affair with triumphant impudence: "I enclose Jones's letter. It is quite remarkable how each one of us in turn is seized with the impulse to kill, so that the others have to restrain him." (1998, pp. 251-252)

It is almost easy to forget, from the violent language, that this was a group of intellectuals discussing a former member of their organization. As Richard Webster writes, "At the height of the conflict with [Jung] intellectual distaste for his views was converted into something approaching physical revulsion and he and his followers were hunted down with an attitude which is almost reminiscent of that shown by Stalin towards Trotsky" (1995, p. 383) These early psychoanalysts who were members of the Committee had, indeed, become thoroughly infused with all the suspiciousness, malevolence, and Manichean us/them projection and hostility that belongs to the paranoid vision. The psychological gain in this was that it allowed Freud and his disciples to abandon their petty and exhausting squabbles with each other, and to be united against a common enemy.

As it was, Jung resigned from the International Psychoanalytic Society by his own choice, so all of the Committee's plans proved quite unnecessary. Perhaps it was even a bit of a letdown when Jung resigned, for with the enemy gone, the group's principle of unity was lost, and the old rivalries and animosities became prominent again.

Some years latter, the question of loyalty appeared again, this time with Otto Rank who was himself a member of the Committee. Although living in America, he was still very close to Freud, and would visit him during his trips to Europe. The trouble began when Rank wrote a book, which he dedicated to Freud, on the birth trauma. The emphasis here was not on the child's relation to the father, which it had been for Freud, but on the child's relation to the mother (Webster, 1995). Initially, Freud was encouraging of Rank's novel ideas. But the other members of the Committee realized that Rank's birth trauma theory was contrary to orthodox Freudianism. They were very concerned by this, and did not let Freud alone until he too was concerned. As a result Rank felt obliged to write an abject letter of apology to the entire Committee for having written his book. As Grosskurth describes it:

> What were Rank's choices? He was like a cornered rat. Freud had warned the American analysts that Rank's theories in no way represented his own. The Committee had closed ranks against him, and even his friend and collaborator Ferenczi no longer supported him. Without the imprimatur of official psychoanalysis, scientific journals would be closed to the exposition of his ideas, students would be unavailable, and he would receive no referrals.
>
> Freud seemed to have acted as the Grand Inquisitor, and Rank's groveling "confession" could have served as a model for the Russian show trials of the 1930s. Did Rank ever mutter "eppur si muove"? He believed with all his heart in his theory, but managed to avoid discussing it in the letter. The emphasis is placed completely on his state of mind. He addresses the Committee as though it were a Star Chamber, not a group of fellow analysts. He admits to moral turpitude, but about what? The real question of his theory and technique are totally ignored. (1991, pp. 167-168)

In Rank's letter of confession, he states that the reason for his having espoused a theory that was contrary to Freudian orthodoxy, and obviously false, was that his own psychological problems at the time drove him to write it! It is indeed the case that whereas a religious organization would consider heresy a sin, Freud and his loyalist disciples considered ideological heresy to be due to psychological illness. This is, in fact, how Jones—who was, most likely, expressing the party line on this point — explained the formation of divergent psychoanalytic theories:

> Theoretically, it should have been possible to anticipate the possibility of relapses among analysts such as we were familiar with in our patients, but nevertheless the first experiences of the kind were unexpected and startling. Nowadays we are less astonished.
>
> When an analyst loses insight he had previously had, the recurring wave of resistance that has caused the loss is apt to display itself in the form of pseudo-scientific explanations with the name of a "new theory." Since the source of this is on an unconscious level it follows that controversy on a purely conscious scientific level is foredoomed to failure (1955, p. 127).

In other words, divergent theories, such as those of Adler and Jung, are not to be taken seriously in themselves because, by virtue of Jones' argument ad hominem, they are merely the product of their creators having a psychological relapse. What had happened to psychoanalysis? Supposedly, it was intended to be a form of psychological healing, but was transformed by the Committee into a weapon against heretics! The inner circle had truly devolved from an intellectual circle into something akin to a cult.

Dehumanizing one's opponents—by declaring them insane and their theories a product of that insanity—is a way of maintaining a fanatical hold on the group's truth. This dehumanization belongs to the Manichaeism that derives from the paranoid vision, for the world is split up into "we the sane/they the insane." An even more precise division would be: "we are capable of knowing the truth since our minds are free and unclouded by mental illness/your mind is clouded by mental illness hence, from the standpoint of truth, your ideas are but the meaningless babblings of a madman, and only have significance from a psychiatric point of view." Eventually, though, Rank drifted away from Freud, and Rank too would be officially excommunicated.

In considering these events, one might wonder, "Did the increasingly doctrinaire, cultish, and totalistic nature of the inner circle make it a breeding ground for the paranoid vision, or did the paranoid vision cause the inner circle to devolve into a cultish and totalistic organization?" In all likelihood, there was an interaction between both factors. Cultish, totalistic organizations are paranoiagenic. And possession by the paranoid vision by the leader of an organization, and eventually by some of his or her followers, invites a devolution of the organization into a cult or totalistic organization. There exists, then, a vicious circle, with totalism feeding into the paranoid vision, and the paranoid vision feeding into totalism.

The Paranoiagenic Power of Tyranny — Intellectual Totalism and Authoritarianism

Could it be that there is a certain kind of theory that lends itself to being held as holy writ, and which then leads to all that then follows, including the anathematizing of heretics? Any theory can engage people's passions. One might recall, for example, Louis Pasteur's battle to have the scientific community consider the merits of his germ theory. All the same, the theories that are defended with the most passion are usually those that are totalistic, they seek to explain absolutely everything. Such theories, although they appear to be science, are really metaphysics. Consequently, nothing less than meaning, purpose, and indeed reality itself, are at stake.

There is another factor that is intrinsic to totalistic theories. In contending that sexuality is the first principle of human behavior — in its repressed form it is at the root of neurosis and in its sublimated form, it is at the root of social, cultural and intellectual achievements — Freud was not making a scientific observation, one that could be tested through experimentation. Totalistic theories are not ultimately subject to empirical verification.[11] In point of fact, whether or not Freud was correct in his interpretations, he sought to support them on data derived from a small number of theoretically controversial case studies — Anna O., the "Wolf Man," Dora, Little Hans, Shreber, etc. In the case of Judge Shreber, he never even met the man, but merely read Schreber's notorious diary. Indeed, many of Freud's theories were not

11 There have, of course, been many efforts to verify psychoanalysis through experimentation, but the results have been inconclusive. Rieff suggests that this is because facts can be proved or disproved through experimentation, but concepts cannot (Rieff 1959). It is really explanatory concepts that cannot be proved or disproved through experimentation.

even derived from case studies, but from myths or tragedies such as Oedipus. Even if, at times, Freud's interpretations were brilliantly perceptive, they lacked anything even vaguely approaching scientific objectivity. His results were not duplicable, for how could they be when his conclusions were based on abstruse speculation or on intuition? If Freud was not doing science, what, then, was he doing? He was using psychoanalysis as a form of philosophical explanation. As Barbara Von Eckardt states, "[Freud] seems to have believed that a theory could be justified solely on the basis of its explanatory power" (1998, p. 108).

Explanatory principles are not what one experiences, but how one experiences the world, and they are totalistic because they seek to explain everything. They are not the world that a person sees, but the glasses with which he or she sees the world. Freud, then, was using sexuality as an explanatory principle, as a first principle in the philosophical sense, whose purpose was to make sense of everything else. The great mass of phenomena that comprise human reality were to be rendered intelligible by means of the conflicts and crises that belong to a sexual being. If totalistic theories, then, such as Marxism or psychoanalysis, are not subject to empirical verification, it is because they are essentially explanatory principles.

Indeed, Donald P. Spence (1982) makes the case that Freud, in his various interpretations of dreams, neurotic symptoms, etc., was not discovering historical truth, i.e. the actual experience that the patient had been through. On the contrary, Freud, in conjunction with his psychoanalyzed patient, would create a narrative truth, an interpretation that was constituted out of the various fabrics of the patient's experience so as to be in accord with psychoanalytic theory. Thus, the psychoanalyst is not so much a pattern finder as a pattern maker. To interpret or make patterns out of one's experience is at the heart of the enterprise of explanation.

If patients were cured it was not necessarily because their experience had been illuminated. It may be, as some have argued, that the mere act of creating a coherent story out of one's experience is healing. That is probably true, but there is a more fundamental reason why. It was healing because Freud's patients had switched from one mode of explanation to another, i.e. from their Victorian way of seeing the world, in which morality and guilt were very much of a possibility, to a Freudian way of seeing the world, in which God had been reduced to one's superego, and a guilty conscience had been reduced to socially-imposed guilt feelings.

Switching over to the Freudian mode of explanation did get rid of guilt feelings, but guilt feelings became replaced with feelings of meaninglessness. After all, the inevitable consequence of the secularization of the universe is meaninglessness, emptiness, boredom, and Weltschmerz. Weber called the loss of mystery that results from this secularization and rationalization, "disenchantment." Whole new schools of psychotherapy then emerged—humanistic, Logotherapy, existential therapy, etc.—in an effort to solve the loss of meaning that psychoanalysis had engendered.

Freud was, then, really a metaphysician, for the wish to explain how everything is one, i.e. monism, is the longing of every metaphysician. Freud did, of course, make empirical observations, and some very perceptive ones at that, but there was usually a gap, what one might call an "ontological non sequitur" between his empirical observations and his theories. In any case, Freud's psychological monism was a form of totalism. That is why Freud rejected the ideas of Adler, Jung, Rank, and everyone else who would modify psychoanalysis. The notion that there could be multiple determinants of human behavior — power, religious longings, the birth trauma, etc.—would have meant that sexuality would no longer be regarded as the first and only principle.[12]

Freud's psychological monism, or totalism, is the equivalent in politics of totalitarian tyranny, for where there is monism — whether it be on a philosophical, theological, scientific, social, or political level—there is bound to be little tolerance for dialogue and debate. Monism is, to borrow Popper's expression, an enemy of the open society. Perhaps that is because everything is invested psychologically in one's first principle. It is one's orientation, or "center," which saves one from disorientation, chaos, and the void.

12 Interestingly enough, in his later years Freud became a dualist. In Beyond the Pleasure Principle he contended that, in addition to Eros, there existed Thanatos, the death instinct; both were responsible for human behavior. It was supposedly World War I, in all of its shocking grisliness that inspired Freud to believe that there must be a death instinct. It is interesting how the perception of immense suffering will drive a person to dualism, for now evil (Thanatos, for Freud) becomes a separate metaphysical principle. Freud, thus, had become, in essence, a follower of philosophical Manichaeism.

Broadly speaking, to a religious person, God serves the same purpose that the first principle does to a philosophical person like Freud: it is the principle of orientation. The intellectual totalizes an idea, and the romantic totalizes another person. It would be fair to say that psychoanalysis was Freud's absolute, his god. That was why Freud did not merely criticize those with different theories, he anathematized them, and the language that he used was that of religion; i.e. they had committed heresy. Apropos was the distinguished psychiatrist Eugen Bleuler's letter to Freud explaining his reason for resigning from the International Psychoanalytic Society, which Gay quotes:

> This "who is not for us is against us," he declared to Freud in 1911, upon resigning from the International Psychoanalytic Association, "this 'all or nothing' is in my opinion necessary for religious communities and useful for political parties. There I can accept the principle as such, but for science, I consider it harmful." (1998, p. 215)

Those who desperately cling to their first principle, refusing to acknowledge their inner doubts, become fanatics. Fanaticism is paranoiagenic because one's self-doubts are projected onto another person or group of people, just as the Catholic Church projected their own emerging doubts about their theocentric worldview onto Galileo. In the case of the inner circle, Freud projected his inner doubts on those heretics who proposed rival theories of psychopathology. Once the defense mechanism of projection is activated, and once those who are fanatical see themselves as merely acting defensively, the other manifestations of the paranoid vision follow suit.

Kant states that the reason for his having written The Critique of Pure Reason was to overcome dogmatism, the type that had been found in philosophical theories, for he saw that dogmatic theories were a foe of freedom and tolerance. (He also wanted to make room for faith, but that is another story.) Apparently, Kant's efforts were in vain, for his critique became the soil from which sprung many new schools of philosophy, all of which are no less dogmatic, than those that Kant had criticized.

What interests us here is that psychologists like Freud have proposed psychotherapies that are as theory-laden and dogmatic as any metaphysical theory. The behaviorists, those who subscribe to the medical model of psychopathology, the Jungians, indeed almost all schools of psychotherapy are probably far less theoretically self-critical than the Freudians and at least as doctrinaire. Psychology still needs its Kant, although it is not clear whether really anything would free psychology from the tyranny of un-self-critical metaphysical assumptions.

In addition to theoretical totalism, another oppressive and paranoiagenic force that plagued the early psychoanalytic movement was authoritarianism. It is related to the paranoid need for loyalty. Freud once wrote to his new Swiss disciple Max Eitingon, "We are a little handful that includes none of the godly, but no traitors either" (qtd. in Gay, 1998, p. 180). That the question of loyalty should become so significant an issue, and that fear, suspiciousness, and malevolence had reached the point where a committee, no less a secret committee, was deemed necessary to protect this group of psychoanalysts from "enemies" and "traitors" would strongly suggest that the inner circle had become possessed by the paranoid vision.

The quest for complete loyalty is really a manifestation of the authoritarian need for complete control — over people, circumstances and events—which is symptomatic of the paranoid vision. What, though, is the source of the need for complete control? It is the flip side of the paranoid fear of losing autonomy (Shapiro, 1971).

Perhaps the problem for those under the sway of the paranoid vision is not that they have a weak sense of autonomy, but that they experience their autonomy as weak, although it be no weaker than anyone else's. After all, it belongs to the human condition to be faced with a multitude of imponderables, and this necessary openness before the unknown qualifies anyone's claim to complete freedom and autonomy. But those under the sway of the paranoid vision cannot accept that open, uncertain, and insecure state of affairs. That, again, is why there are conspiracy theories, with their effort to render intelligible the sheer contingency and unpredictability of current events, and the course of history.

Authoritarians are also unsettled by the uncertainty that belongs to relating to other people. That is why they seek to control that most unstable element in human beings—their freedom. It may, then, be that the demand for loyalty—which is a manifestation of the authoritarianism that is endemic to the leaders of such cultish organizations — stems from an inability to accept the uncertainties and unknowingness that belongs to the human condition. The demand for loyalty may stem from those uncertainties regarding one's relation to those often fickle, and sometimes perfidious, creatures called human beings.

Authoritarian leadership invariably creates a downward spiral. Its repressive nature invites challenges, treachery, the departure of the members of an organization, and other forms of opposition. The encounter with opposition then causes the leader to become more authoritarian which, of course, creates greater opposition. The negative result confirms the paranoid's sense of the untrustworthiness of human beings and vindicates the paranoid's own malevolence. It becomes, in other words, a self-fulfilling prophesy. That downward spiral found expression in Freud's inner circle, for as certain members left the organization, the question of loyalty became an increasingly prominent issue, as reflected in the symbolism of the finger rings.

Authoritarians who have absolute power, such as Stalin, can stifle opposition through terror; that, of course, is not possible in an intellectual circle. But conformity was enforced by the fear of being disapproved by Freud, ostracized by one's colleagues, and perhaps excommunicated for committing heresy. As Paul Roazen states it, "Quarrelling with Freud was the most dreadful possibility imaginable. To be cast out by him meant expulsion from the chosen few, psychic death. The book would be closed, the candle snuffed out" (1971 b. p. 7). Lifton termed this same phenomenon, "the dispensing of existence" (1989), a phenomenon that is intrinsic to cults. As he describes it, "The most literal example of such dispensing of existence and nonexistence is to be found in the sentence given to certain political criminals: execution in two years' time, unless during that two-year period they have demonstrated genuine progress in their reform" (1989, p. 433). Freud's inner circle dispensed existence in a figurative sense. Being "excommunicated" meant utter failure. This is because the perception, among the members of the inner circle, was that history was being made and not to be there was to miss the boat. Missing that boat was enough to drive at least several exiled members of that circle to suicide.

Roazen states how Freud's eventual rejection of Victor Tausk — one of his most brilliant early disciples—was a major factor in Tausk's suicide at the age of forty. Freud's reaction to Tausk's suicide was heartless, revealing a good deal about how he saw his disciples and everyone else. Farrell quotes Freud's letter to Lou-Andreas Salome:

> In his letter to me he swore undying loyalty to psychoanalysis, thanked me etc. But what was behind it all we cannot guess. After all he spent his days wrestling with the father ghost. I confess that I do not really miss him: I had long realized that he could be of no further service, indeed he constituted a threat to the future. (1996, p. 79)

Freud refers to Tausk's pledge of undying loyalty, which was what the authoritarian Freud demanded. Apparently, though, that pledge coupled with his suicide was not sufficient to win Freud's love and approbation. This was because, as the letter indicates, people were only significant if they could serve Freud, which is why he uses the phrase, "...I had also realized that he could be of no further service." The historian Paul Johnson (1990) once defined an intellectual as someone who considers ideas more important than people. Johnson is perhaps being a bit hyperbolic, but his remark is certainly accurate in regard to Freud.

In any case, Roazen also points out that another early disciple, Herbert Silberer, also killed himself over being rejected by Freud. And Stekel, too, after his final rejection by Freud killed himself, although there might have been other factors involved, such as Stekel's declining health. There is obviously something wrong with that picture: a group of brilliant intellectuals has turned into a cult, i.e., a dysfunctional family whose leader has become a demanding and castrating father, with self-negating disciples competing for his approbation and love, and sometimes committing suicide like forlorn lovers if they do not receive it. That is the type of soil that undermines ego-stability, and makes one more prone to the fanaticism endemic to the paranoid vision. Freud's authoritarianism drew people who had a proclivity to be true believers, but the creative and independent part of a person's personality can be in conflict with his or her longings to have a directive father. Many of Freud's disciples were plagued by that conflict. As a result, the inner circle turned into one big unhappy family.

Let us now examine the father/son conflict in more detail, for as we shall see, the unresolved inner conflicts that people bring to an organization precipitates certain interpersonal conflicts, which make an organization a breeding ground for hyper-suspiciousness, mutual vilification, and all else associated with the paranoid vision.

The Father/Son Conflict and Its Paranoiagenic Power

It is obvious, then, that the disagreements that Freud had with his disciples were not simply about ideas, or about explanatory principles. There existed a more fundamental conflict involving father/son dynamics. According to Phyllis Grosskurth, "The early psychoanalytic movement took the form of an extended family whose origin was the idealized family of the Committee. It was a male family of sons led by a patriarchal father, but conspicuous in its lack of a nurturing mother." (1991, pp. 15-16) Apropos of these masculine tensions is the fact that Freud got along in a much easier way with some of his women disciples. Although neither Lou Andreas-Salome nor his daughter, Anna Freud, were members of Freud's inner circle, they were active in the various psychoanalytic associations and very close to Freud. Francois Roustang indicates why the men had a problematic relation to Freud, but the women less so:

> Personal obedience was not enough to guarantee faithfulness to the Freudian way of thinking nor to sustain what was necessary for the analysis. When one considers on the one hand the mysticoclinical ideas of Lou Andreas-Salome, which Freud hardly criticizes and even encourages, and on the other hand the reductive interpretations of Anna Freud, which subvert psychoanalysis in the most decisive way, one is convinced that the confidence Freud had in these women is

equal only to their admiration of him and their submission to him. They explicitly questioned neither Freud nor his work, thanks to which they could transform psychoanalysis into a Russian novel or a school textbook... (1998, pp. 255-256)

Roustang suggests, then, that unorthodox psychoanalytical ideas, in themselves, did not disturb Freud; it was unorthodox ideas coming from men that caused trouble. Consequently, even to be obedient to Freud was not sufficient to ensure his love and approbation, if one were a man, for the sheer act of being a man made one a potential subject, thinker, knower, intellectual contender, and critic.[13]

Thus, in addition to the Oedipal tension between Freud and his disciples, there was the tension involved with each disciple wanting to be the favorite son, all of which turned out to be highly paranoiagenic. Let us now flashback to the time when Adler and Jung were still members. The advent of Jung and the other members of the Swiss contingency caused serious discord in the organization; it was clear that Freud favored the Swiss over his original Viennese members. Adler and several of his friends in the inner circle felt slighted when Freud chose Jung to be the head of his newly formed International Association for Psychoanalysis, and threatened to leave the organization. So, as a gesture of reconciliation, Freud limited Jung's presidency to two years, made Adler president of the Viennese Psychoanalytic Society and Stekel the vice president, as well as making Adler and Stekel the editors of that organization's new journal.

It was only a relatively short time, then, for the inner circle to turn into a politicized organization with factions and bitter conflicts between them. Those conflicts about position, status and power undermined the strength of the inner circle, for if their original intent and mission was to introduce psychoanalysis to the world, that intent was being diluted by ego-driven interests, creating an infirmity of organizational purpose. A weakened intent and loss of purpose can have many manifestations in an organization, from an increase in pettiness, cliquishness, malicious gossip and gratuitous backstabbing

---

13   Rajneesh, who is the subject of the next case example, went further than Freud. He assigned all of the important executive roles, in his organization, to several of his female disciples, and pretty much surrounded himself with women.

to a disorienting malaise. It is that last factor, disorientation—the sense of, "Why am I here?"—that makes one prey to the ersatz orientation promised by the paranoid vision.

The inner circle was truly a hotbed of envy, contention, and hostility. That there is a tendency for this sort of behavior to occur is not in itself the fault of the leader of such a group. To a large extent, this contention is simply due to the many garden varieties of egotism. Conflicts get more psychologically complicated, though, when archetypal relationships enter in, i.e., competition for the love, regard, approval and approbation of the father.

In one of his early correspondences to Jung, Freud actually suggested that Jung treat him like an equal, but Jung wrote back that he wished to relate to Freud as a son. Since Freud was a generation older, any other relation might have felt strained for Jung and the others. Gay speculates that Jung knew that Freud had some trouble with friendships — his former friendships with Breuer and then with Fliess had been bitter disappointments — and so Jung sagely concluded that a father/son relationship might be a better bet than a friendship or a collegial relationship.

The problem, though, was that these psychologically familial relations tended to draw out emotions of a puerile nature and had the long-term effect of infantilizing many of the members of the inner circle, such that they became incapable of doing or thinking anything without getting Freud's consent, while squabbling with each other like siblings in rivalry for their parent's attention. Then, of course, they become resentful and rebellious adolescents. Perhaps it was the very nature of the intimate investigations of each other's childhood conflicts that invited that type of psychological regression. As Gay states:

> The rubbing up of sensitive, often labile, individuals against one another was bound to produce sparks of hostility. What is more, the provocative subject matter of psychoanalytic inquiry, rudely touching on the most heavily guarded spots in the human psyche, was taking its toll and generating a pervasive irritability. (1988, p. 177)

To a large extent, one must sympathize with Freud; his disciples had to emerge as mature individuals, and it may be that the dynamics of cultish organizations like the inner circle tend to retard one's emotional maturation. A good leader, on the other hand, will seek to dissolve the resultant personal and interpersonal tensions that arise in such an emotionally-charged atmosphere, but a leader with a dark agenda will capitalize on those tensions, often unconsciously. There are a number of subterranean motives for doing so. First of all, it is flattering to see other people compete for one's approval and love. A second motive for inviting rivalry is this: the leader knows, whether consciously or unconsciously, that this sort of competition for his approval breeds conformity and obedience amongst his disciples, which is what an insecure leader desires. If receiving the leader's good opinion requires demonstrating that one uncritically accepts his doctrine, then the disciples will compete with each other to see who can conform the most. That would appear to be exactly what happened in Freud's inner circle.

The downside of such dynamics is that the hostility and conflicts that it generates can get out of hand, threatening to irreparably fracture the group. Also, a leader is apt to lose respect for and grow contemptuous of such adoring disciples. This contempt invites a sadism on the part of the leader. Extrapolating on a quip by Groucho Marx, the leader might say, "I wouldn't want to be associated with any association that was willing to make me its leader." As Roazen states, "Freud's male members wanted his love, but he gave it only if they came close to castrating themselves as creative individuals" (1971b, p. 113). There were those willing to be Freud's intellectual eunuchs, but others resented the idea and eventually left.

It would appear, then, that the leader of a cultish, or totalistic, organization is rarely a truly good father who prepares his children to think and judge for themselves, and thus to become adults with strong independent lives. On the contrary, he encourages their dependency, and subverts any moves that they might make to independence. It is interesting that when relations between Freud and Jung began to turn bitter, Freud tried to appease Jung, but he only ended up exacerbating the situation. What Freud could not realize, though, was that Jung no longer wished to be the crown prince of psychoanalysis, i.e., Freud's psychological son. In the language of psychoanalysis, Jung had an unresolved Oedipus Complex, at least in regard to wanting to kill his father. Jung could not admit this to either Freud or to himself, for the only way that he could break away from Freud was through a hostile break.

One of the ways that Freud sought to encourage the dependence of his disciples was to psychoanalyze them. If they disagreed with Freud about anything involving, for example, an interpretation of their behavior or Freud's interpretation of a dream, their disagreement was attributed to "resistance" or repression, or some other defense mechanism on their part. In this way, Freud disqualified his followers to be free thinkers, capable of independent judgment. Consequently, they became all the more dependent upon Freud—whose thinking was supposedly unclouded by psychological complexes—for insights into themselves, and the eventual psychological freedom.

Of course, the end never came, for as Grosskurth states, "The subtext of psychoanalytic history is the story of how Freud manipulated and influenced his followers and successors. Their general passivity caused them to remain in thrall to an interminable analysis" (1991, p. 15). Jung, among others, caught on to the hermeneutical bind[14] that Freud was using to control his followers, and accused Freud of doing exactly that. Freud's response is significant, for he adamantly denies it, and then, almost immediately in the same letter does the very thing that he just denied. In a letter to Jung, dated 1913, Freud writes,

> Your allegation that I treat my followers as patients is demonstrably untrue. . . It is a convention among us analysts that none of us need feel ashamed of his own neurosis. But one [meaning Jung] who while behaving abnormally keeps shouting that he is normal gives ground for the suspicion that he lacks insight into his illness. Accordingly, I propose that we abandon our personal relations entirely. (Freud 1913, p. 1)

---

14 The Marxists seek to put their opponents in the same sort of hermeneutical bind. If you disagree with their theories, they will disqualify your statements because you are a slave to the thinking of your social class.

Some of Freud's followers were, indeed, coming to see that Freud was not the good father they hoped to find. On the contrary, Freud was really akin to the mythical father Chronos who eats his children, nullifying their existence as independent beings. But this domineering could only go so far. Zeus and his siblings finally overcame Chronos. In Freud's circle, a conflict emerged between Freud and some of the members of his circle, who wanted to be "fathers," i.e. creative in their own right, which meant having their own ideas seriously considered. Archetypally speaking, their ideas were their children. To have ideas of their own, therefore, was to become fathers themselves. But the Chronos-Freud could not allow that, for in his mind there could only be one father—just as there could be only one god—and it had to be him.

Apropos of these struggles is Freud's theory, from *Totem and Taboo* (1962), that there had literally existed, in the ancient past, a domineering primal father. The curious parallel between Freud's theory and his relation to the members of his inner circle gradually became evident to some of Freud's disciples, including Ernest Jones. According to the cultural historian John Farrell, "Jones remarked to Freud after reading *Totem and Taboo* that the theory of the primal father seemed to have 'an unusual personal significance' for Freud" (1996, p. 235). One learns from Freud's book that the primal father keeps all of the women of the tribe for himself. He was what is referred to today as the "alpha male."

Freud believed that, at one decisive point in history, the sons finally plot to overthrow the primal father, and they succeed. Farrell observes, "...the primal father Freud discovered at the bottom of human nature was a thinly disguised version of himself" (1996, p. 58). Apropos are the famous incidents in which Freud fainted twice, three years apart, in the presence of Jung. Some scholars contend that these fainting episodes were due to Freud's Oedipal fear that his psychological son would usurp him. After all, Jung was not just any disciple. Freud had selected Jung to be the heir apparent, the crown prince of psychoanalysis.

It is also significant that Freud, like the mythical father of *Totem and Taboo*, would hoard the females. Freud would psychoanalyze his disciples' wives, fiancés and girlfriends. The analysis often had the effect of dissolving his disciples' relationships with these women. It also resulted in drawing these women close to Freud. Freud wouldn't have love affairs with these women, but it is evident from his correspondence that he did enjoy their adulation. He was clearly in competition with his disciples in that respect. We earlier referred to Freud's relation to his disciple Victor Tausk, who had been involved with Lou Andreas Salome, a woman whom quite a number of illustrious men had known, including Nietzsche. The same competitive dynamics were evident there.

It was therefore the case that a very real source of tension in Freud's circle was this: they wanted to be approved by Freud, which meant being a "good son," i.e. obedient and sycophantic. They wanted that for they had a strong desire to acquire direction, purpose and meaning in their lives. An authority figure promises, either implicitly or explicitly, to provide that by appealing to a great cause. Of course, this meant entering into a relation to that higher authority, or authoritarian figure, as a son. But each member of the inner circle also wanted to be a father of ideas in his own right. This tension could either be resolved by leaving the group, as some eventually did, or by remaining in the group and participating in certain perverse group phenomena whose purpose was to expel, through scapegoating, heretics in the group or attack the "enemies" of psychoanalysis outside the group. Let us explore how this happens.

The Paranoiagenic Power of the Inner Circle's Conflicts

We suggested earlier that the unresolved tensions among the members of Freud's inner circle, created by the father/son conflict, had a paranoiagenic potential. As Farrell contends, "...Freud 'projected,' in the most uncomplicated sense of the term, his own hostility onto the surrounding intellectual community, imagining that it was peculiarly enraged by his findings" (1996, p. 53). There was more involved there, however, in terms of projection. It is rather common, not only for a single person to project, but for an entire group to project. The unresolved anxiety and hostility that they feel towards each other, and particularly towards their leader for having psychologically castrated them, is channeled into fear, suspicion and hatred towards imagined enemies outside the group. This way intra-group tensions get dissolved for a time as they turn into inter-group tensions.

Thus, the growing discontent, frustration and hostility experienced by the members of the inner circle were translated into a paranoid sense of being persecuted by the enemies of psychoanalysis. This is nothing new, for it has been said many times before that organizations seek out external enemies, scapegoats onto which to discharge their poisons, so as to maintain their own cohesiveness. This sense — that the enemies of progress and enlightenment are at the gate, and it is up to the paladins of psychoanalysis to overlook their petty disagreements with each other so as to defend psychoanalysis — is a manifestation of the us/them, Manichaean sense of opposition that is intrinsic to the paranoid vision. Freud, of course, encouraged this sort of us/them sense of things, and the strategy actually worked for quite a long time.

But hadn't there actually existed a good deal of opposition to psychoanalysis, especially to the notion of infantile sexuality? Is this a case of paranoids being right about their fears? According to Roazen, "[Freud enticed] followers by exaggerating the degree to which his supporters were an embattled minority" (1971b, p. 47). Roazen is correct, for Freud, in his paranoid manner, downplayed in his mind the fact that psychoanalysis was slowly but surely gaining adherents all over the world.

Gay, on the other hand, interprets this behavior on Freud's part as masochism: "[Freud's] habit of dramatizing his intellectual isolation testifies to this disposition." (1998, p. 140) Freud's sense of martyrdom, of being persecuted for his greatness, was a delusion of grandeur. It was flattering for Freud to see himself as a hero willing to courageously defend the truth in the face of the world's violent antagonism. The actual prospect of success, though, to a person like Freud—who sees himself as a courageous liberator, willing to be a martyr for the truth—can be troubling, for as Rieff states:

> So congenial was the stance of an emancipator that Freud
> could not cope with the victory that was his during the last
> period of his life. As he tried to ward off the easy ascent of
> patients as itself a sign of resistance, so Freud could not
> acknowledge the extent to which his own views had actually
> vanquished the prudery against which they were aimed. He
> had been prepared for a long struggle of ideas: like the sick
> individual, he wrote, the sick society is "bound to offer us
> resistance." (1979, p. 337)

Apropos of Rieff's observation is what Freud experienced in America. We shall preface this tale by noting that it sometimes happens that an event occurs that does not fit in with a person's basic life narrative (i.e. the story that explains why the world is the way it is, and why one is suffering). Something similar happened to Freud. He was feeling his usual terrible frustration because of the slow lack of recognition that psychoanalysis was receiving, for he hoped that he would, like Darwin, become an instant intellectual star, but it was not happening that way. Then, unexpectedly, Freud received an invitation to speak at Clark College, in Worcester, Massachusetts. When Freud arrived, Stanley Hall, the president of Clark, awarded him an honorary doctor of letters. Some very eminent American psychologists, including William James, attended the four lectures that Freud gave there.

According to Peter Gay, Freud was taken by surprise by the whole affair. At least in America, or at least at Clark College, psychoanalysis was receiving the recognition, honor and respect that Freud so badly craved. Freud, though obviously very pleased by the honors bestowed upon him in America, discounted the whole event by disparaging America—in the way that European intellectuals did back then and still do today—for being primitive, shallow, devoted exclusively to money, and all the other familiar anti-American stereotypes. Freud told his disciples how happy he was to be leaving America and returning to Vienna.

But was it really Vienna that Freud missed? He had always told everyone how much he disliked that city, even though he chose to remain there. That discrepancy should make any psychologist suspicious. What, then, really was it about America? For one thing,

America was becoming a good deal less prudish than Victorian Vienna, thus belying Freud's notion of the stubbornness of repression and the immense resistance to psychoanalysis that he had anticipated. In addition, success, recognition, and respect in America did not fit with his martyrdom narrative. Neurotic that he was, he had projected a whole mélange of tenebrous feelings relating to martyrdom onto Vienna. In other words, Freud missed inhaling the un-salutary miasma of the paranoid vision.

Freud also realized, probably unconsciously, that external opposition, i.e., an enemy—whether real or imagined—was necessary to keep his divisive group of disciples together, and not at each other's throats, nor at his. Apparently, he feared the Oedipus complex breaking out among his disciples more than he feared the Nazis. Indeed, Freud would have stayed on in Vienna and would have, most likely, been murdered by the Nazis, for they had entered that city and already burned copies of his books months before. Fortunately, Ernest Jones had, at serious peril to himself, flown into Berlin and then to Vienna to arrange for safe passage to England for Freud, his family, and other members of the inner circle.

Apropos of all this, one might ask: could it be that the paranoid vision thrives on opposition? Certainly, Freud was a person who thrived on opposition. As Roazen states:

> Freud thrived on opposition — whether it came from teachers, the resistances of patients, deviating pupils, or the outside world. He is said to have remarked to a favorite patient that "open opposition, and even abuse, was far preferable to being silently ignored." "Many enemies, much honor," he wrote, "If the time of 'Recognition' should arrive it would compare with the present as the weird glamour of the Inferno does with the blessed boredom of Paradise. (Naturally I mean this the other way round.) (1971a, p. 196)

Roazen is correct that Freud craved opposition, but it was really because opposition was the fuel which fed his paranoid vision. Opposition confirmed his dark sense of reality, his pride at being a conquistador and a martyr, and it enabled him to lead a cult by having them project and discharge their growing resentment onto the outer world.

Is it any surprise, then, that Freud did not like England? The British, in their relative liberality and tolerance, were too respectful and open to his ideas. England was, therefore, not a place where Freud's inner drama of heroic resistance to persecution could find confirmation in the objective world. Only the paranoid vision, with its sense of a threatening external enemy, could keep his inner world together, and his inner circle together.

Psychoanalysis as Conspiracy Theory

The "hermeneutics of suspicion," is Ricoeur's notion that beneath the surface of human existence there lies something more fundamental, more primitive, darker. It is repressed from conscious awareness by means of the prettified lies and rationalizations of civilization. Since it is being repressed, it takes a courageous intellectual to dive into the sewers of human existence and bring the monstrosity to light. For Nietzsche, that special something that he dug up was power (and maybe also resentment). For Marx, it was class struggle. For Freud, it was sex (and maybe also instinctual aggression).

Such hidden forces belie one's claim to autonomy. One thinks that one is acting freely, but one is really under the constraint of a "hidden hand" that has designs of its own. All such theories are predicated on a simplistic appearance/reality distinction. What makes it simplistic is its reductionism, i.e., it seeks to reduce the great complexity of phenomena to some basic aspect of psychological or social reality.[15]

This is not to deny that there are, indeed, valuable gems of truth to be found in the discoveries of these "masters of suspicion," as they have been called. Power motives, for example, can be repressed, and sexuality, too. Those and other darker forces are sometimes the hidden motivators behind phenomena that seek to wear an appealing, socially acceptable mask. Resentment, for example, often does lie behind the rage for equality, as Nietzsche informs us. The problem with these

---

15 Is Hegel's notion of "the cunning of reason" another example of a metaphysical conspiracy theory? It would be an example. But, unlike the theories of Nietzsche, Marx, and Freud, Hegel's theory is not reductionistic. That is because Hegel does not explain that which is higher in terms of that which is lower.

theories, however, is that by totalizing the forces that they uncover, i.e., by seeking to make them explain everything in a reductive manner, they present a distorted image of reality. Part of the ideological dispute that Jung had with Freud involved Freud's reduction of religion to "the projection of an infant's helplessness." Jung's far more nuanced theory of religion has its serious problems, too, but at least it is not absurdly reductive, like Freud's theory of religion.

Could it be, then, that these suspicion-laden theories—with their simplistic appearance/reality distinction—are, in essence, metaphysical conspiracy theories? The hidden hand of some unseen metaphysical force, would, then, be the real conspirator. Metaphysical conspiracy theories have the same fundamental appeal as the garden-variety conspiracy theory: they offer a flight from the ambiguity, uncertainty, complexity, and disorder that belongs to human existence.

For a person who reads Freud and becomes seduced into seeing the world in his way, everything begins to make sense, or at least it seems to make sense, owing to its facile reductive logic. It is a giddy feeling, like that of uncovering a conspiracy or a supposed conspiracy, when everything—from slips of the tongue, to dreams, to neuroses, to great works of art, to the forces behind political struggles—becomes understandable and intelligible, for they are all of a piece; it is all about the id, in conflict with the superego, and the demands of the social world. In exchange for the great delight of (false) comprehension,

one's entire world has been degraded, for the principle of unification is the lowest metaphysical common denominator, a quasi-material principle such as libidinal energy (also called "psychic energy" or "instinctual energy").

We earlier suggested that Freud was a metaphysical monist by virtue of the fact that what is ultimately real in human psychology is instinctual energy seeking release. Ernest Jones contends, to the contrary, that Freud was not a monist since everywhere in Freud's psychology conflict exists, such as the basic conflict between the instincts and the demands of the social world. This means, to Jones, that there are multiple determinants of human behavior in Freud's psychology. In that sense, Jones is correct.

For Freud, however, everything cultural, intellectual, or spiritual has been reduced to a dimension of social reality. In other words, culture does not arise organically, but is imposed on us from without, by parents and educators. For example, one gathers from Freud that if one's parents did not impose religious beliefs on the child, that he or she would not naturally develop them. The suggestion is that the products of culture and spirit are artificial, or have merely a utilitarian value.

Just as the cultural, intellectual, and spiritual have been reduced to the social, so it is that the social has been reduced to the instinctual. It follows, then, that the products of culture are not what they seem, for if one were to strip away their mask one would discover that they are sublimated libidinal energy. Thus the products of culture are unreal, or less than real, compared to the instinctual. That is why, in the metaphysics that underlies Freud's psychology, there is only one true reality, and that is the libido.

Thus Freud shares this with all thinkers who subscribe to various versions of the hermeneutics of suspicion: they all contend that when one strips away the veneer of civilized falsehoods, which exist to protect human vanity, one finds—underlying goodness and virtue—self-interest, baseness, ruthlessness. There is no longer any "higher." It is merely a sublimation of that which is "lower." Goodness, kindness, decency, and idealism are seen as illusory, for they are, at best, sublimations — and at worst repressions—of that which is truly real, namely libido.

Not all Nihilists Dress in Black

Is psychoanalysis, by virtue of its undermining of traditional values, nihilistic? Let us see if we can answer that question by examining the words and actions of its founder. An observation by Farrell is illuminating in that light: "[Freud declared] altruism that might have characterized his life as something mysterious and not necessarily admirable: 'Why I, and incidentally my six adult children as well, have to be thoroughly decent human beings is quite incomprehensible to me.'" (1998, p. 243) Those who are simply immoral still seek to argue that their actions are really noble. Freud, by contrast, is seeking to undermine the very notion of goodness, decency, or morality. At least judged from the quote above, it would appear that Freud was growing increasingly nihilistic.

Freud was probably closer to Sandor Ferenczi than to any other of his disciples, although he, too, would later break away from the master, as he developed his own ideas. Webster quotes Ferenczi's clinical diary: "[Freud] said that patients are only riffraff. The only thing patients were good for was to help the analyst make a living and to provide material for theory. It is clear we cannot help them. This is therapeutic nihilism." (qtd. in Webster 1995, p. 354)

Was Ferenczi correct in his harsh assessment that Freud was a therapeutic nihilist? Apropos is the story of Horace Frink. He was, strange to say, both a very gifted American disciple of Freud and also one of Freud's patients. When Frink traveled to Vienna, he both trained with Freud and underwent therapy with him. Although Frink was a depressive, with suicidal tendencies, Freud still sought to have Frink become head of the New York Psychoanalytic Society! How can one explain that surprising choice of someone who was mentally unstable to be Freud's American representative? According to Crews, "[Readers] would be less surprised, however, if they understood how shorthanded Freud was for emotionally stable disciples. Between 1902 and 1938, at least nine of the 149 members of the Viennese Psychoanalytic Society died at their own hands." (1998, p. 261)

As Lavinia Edmunds, who has done an extensive investigation of the Frink story states, "Freud, [Frink's] mentor and analyst, had pronounced his analysis complete, refusing to see him further, even as Frink's depression was deepening. Freud had promised Frink happiness once he left his wife, Doris Best, and two children for New York heiress Angelika Bijur." (Edmunds, 1998, pp. 260-276) Freud's advice to Frink was, furthermore, not merely a promise of happiness but a threat. According to Crews, Freud told Frink that he should, "get divorced and remarried to a rich woman, or you will turn homosexual" (1998, p. 261). That sort of quackery sounds almost farcical, were it not for its tragic consequences. Freud also insisted to Bijur about the rightness of her leaving her husband to marry Frink. To make matters even worse, Bijur was Frink's former patient!

What was the outcome of Frink's marriage to Bijur? According to Edmunds, "In no time, the supreme happiness had degenerated into a hopeless mismatch" (1998, p. 262). The events that transpired resulted in ruining Frink's first marriage as well as Bijur's first marriage. Both Frink's ex-wife and Bijur's ex-husband were devastated. The situation also created broken homes, for there was children caught up in the mess. Judging by the letters of everyone involved, it released a tremendous flood of heartbreak, and in all likelihood it significantly contributed to the premature deaths of several of the parties involved.

What was Freud thinking? It is apparent from his correspondence with Frink that Freud believed in sexual satisfaction and emotional fulfillment through romantic love, no matter what the cost; he was surprisingly contemporary in that regard. Furthermore, ever in need of money to promote psychoanalysis, Freud saw that Frink marrying into money could mean generous donations for psychoanalysis. Edmunds quotes a letter that Freud sent to Frink:

> May I suggest to you that your idea Mrs. B. had lost part of her beauty may be turned into her having lost part of her money... Your complaint that you cannot grasp your homosexuality implies that you are not yet aware of your phantasy of making me a rich man...let us change this imaginary gift into a real contribution to the Psychoanalytic Funds... (qtd. Edmunds, 1998, p. 270)

Freud used the need to have psychoanalysis succeed in the world as his vindication for being mercenary, and for his manipulation of Frink and the other parties to this drama. Perhaps those who are able to justify their actions in such a manner are not really nihilists. After all, they do value something, namely the success in the world of their movement, whether it be, for example, Marxism, National Socialism, Radical Islamism, or Psychoanalysis. The theologian Paul Tillich (1957; 2001) maintains that if a person has "an ultimate concern," then he or she has a set of values and is religious. Freud, by that definition, had a set of values, and upheld them religiously. We would contend, though, that if, in adopting such an ultimate concern, one refuses to let anything stand in one's way, one is nihilistic. An example from literature is Ahab, in his pursuit of Moby Dick. He had an ultimate concern, all right, but his desire for vengeance was so extreme that it cost the lives of almost all of his men and his own life too.

Eugene Rose (2001) understands nihilists to be the "terrible simplifiers." After mentioning the simplifications of Lenin, Stalin, Hitler and Mussolini, he states, "More profoundly, Nihilist 'simplifications' may be seen in the universal prestige today accorded the lowest order of knowledge, the scientific, as well as the simplistic ideas of men like Marx, Freud, and Darwin..." (Rose, 2001, p. 38). It is the simplistic nature of totalistic creeds that make them nihilistic, for in their rush to explain how it is all one, they place the world on a Procrustean bed, thus destroying life, for life is invariably complex.

Another aspect of nihilism is the adoption of a teleological ethics. Any goal whose vindication is an end-justifies-the-means, or teleological ethics[16] (also known as consequentialist, instrumentalist, or utilitarian ethics) is, to coin a word, nihilistigenic. I.E., teleological ethics is not in itself necessarily nihilistic. It is pretty near impossible to live without justifying one's actions by virtue of certain ends. The classical example is that it may be necessary to lie or to steal in order to save somebody's life.

But teleological ethics is potentially nihilistigenic. In jettisoning all moral codes, if necessary, just so long as certain earthly ends can be achieved, the belief in the moral realm is undermined. The contempt for everyday scruples—simple things such as displaying civility—precedes actual violence, whether that violence be cruel words, physical brutality, or murder. Apropos is Camus' distinction between crimes of passion and crimes of logic. Crimes of logic are always founded on a teleological ethics.[17] The fanatic is the person who commits crimes of logic.

---

16   Teleological ethics may be contrasted with those ethics that Kant called "deontological." In the latter, one follows a moral maxim regardless of consequences. Kant's morality has the virtue of treating people like ends in themselves, rather than as means to an end. Kant's ethics, however, also runs into many other serious difficulties. We wont go into those difficulties here, other than to say that such ethics are unlivable. But at least Kant's ethics is not nihilistigenic.

17   Is it not the case, according to Kierkegaard, that the teleological suspension of the ethical lies at the heart of religious consciousness? That is true, and thus religious consciousness walks along the edge of the abyss of nihilism and is always in danger of falling in. For example, in the Abraham and Isaac story, God commands Abraham to sacrifice his son. That command, according to Kierkegaard, obviously cannot be justified in terms of any ethical law. But couldn't any religious

A stereotype of the nihilist is a person who wears all black, recites the poetry of Baudelaire, and is contemplating suicide, but if that image has any validity, it is of the outwardly despairing species of nihilist, of the person bereft of an ultimate purpose. The nihilist is thought to be the antithesis of the true believer. It could be argued, though, that the latter has simply gone from being despairing to being engaged, while still being a nihilist. After all, has the apostle of a blind faith, the dogmatist, the uncritical fundamentalist, and the fanatic, really overcome nihilism?

The true believer, a nihilist at heart, is, on the contrary, on a terrified flight from the ever-lurking void. What rescues the nihilist from the threat of meaninglessness is a goal of sort, a telos, one that it regarded as being infinitely important to fulfill. Bringing about the just society would, for example, be one such end.

What makes nihilism relevant to this discussion is that it is paranoiagenic. Metaphysical conspiracy theories, such as psychoanalysis, are both ideological expressions of the paranoid vision, as well as being themselves paranoiagenic. In reducing the complexity of human existence to power, economics, sexuality, or aggression, they cause a society to lose any moral compass that it had, further disorienting it. Philip Rieff (1959; 1987) has had many positive things to say about psychoanalysis, but he also warned of its antinomian and nihilistic cultural implications, its potentially corrosive effect on public morality, not because of its emphasis on sexuality, but because of its materialistic reductionism.

We are not arguing here for a return to traditional values, but merely observing that a society bereft of "higher" values, leaves its members disoriented, inviting the orientation that the paranoid vision promises. If psychoanalysis is a metaphysical conspiracy theory, it is an answer to the confusion, chaos, and meaninglessness that it created! The story of the inner circle would certainly support the notion that nihilism is paranoiagenic. It immiserated everyone

---

fanatic appeal to the teleological suspension of the ethical? See, for example, Jon Krakauer's Under the Banner of Heaven, (Random House 2003) which explores how two Mormon brothers, infused with millenarian longings, claimed that they heard a revelation from God, and that it commanded them to kill people. This is a philosophical problem that must be faced if the problem of fanaticism is to be overcome.

involved—founder, disciples, patients, and all else—in unpleasant dramas, the way that the paranoid vision tends to do.

A Countervailing Factor

There may have been, though, a countervailing factor at the heart of Freudian psychoanalysis that has militated against its paranoiagenic tendencies. In contrast to Marxism, for example, which is clearly millenarian and utopian, Freudian psychoanalysis has a far more constrained vision of life. As Bruno Bettelheim pointed out, "Freud called into question some deeply cherished beliefs, such as the unlimited perfectibility of man and his inherent goodness;..." (1983, p. 15) In that sense, Freud's sobering view of life stands in sharp contrast to the unconstrained millennialism, which—in the form of communism and fascism—was becoming a dangerous force in the world during the 1930s and 1940s, and is dangerous still today. Certainly that accrues to Freud's credit.

Indeed, psychoanalysis is, to a large extent, predicated on a pessimistic vision of life. It does not contend that one can ever return to the infinitude of the "pleasure principle," the idyllic life that he posited to exist before the onset of adult responsibilities. One cannot return to that state; nor does it lie in the future. As Freud indicates in Civilization and Its Discontents (1930; 1989), to be a mature adult, one must accept the limits, and the finitude of the "reality principle."[18] One need not have to suffer from a neurosis, but the price of civilization will always be a certain degree of discontent. Freud has essentially proposed a psychoanalytic notion of the biblical fall, but without a future state of blessed redemption. After all, as Phillip Rieff (1979) reminds us, Freud saw the repressions of civilization as necessary; there is no freedom from sexual constraint to be found in Freud. None of this is millenarian or utopian.

The historian of psychoanalysis Richard Webster contends, though, that Freud was a messianic leader, and that everything about psychoanalysis makes it a religion—Freud was the Pope, and psychoanalytic sessions are really a form of religious confession.

18 That is why Freudian psychoanalysts came to be called "shrinks." Patients had those infinite aspirations — that derived from the pleasure principle — shrunken so that they could live in accord with the reality principle.

Furthermore, there is, according to Webster, an apocalypticism implicit in psychoanalysis and also in Jung's ideas. As Webster writes:

> Jung's vision here, like that of Freud, is characteristic of the apocalyptic religious thinker who sees himself and his followers as islands of purity surrounded by a sea of corruption and filth. Jung would latter write with seeming objectivity about how Freud describes psychoanalyses as a wall of truth "against the black tide of mud." (1995, p. 377)

Webster makes a cogent case for Freud's messianism and apocalypticism. He is perceptive to see the connection here between the paranoid quest for purity and apocalypticism. The chapter on apocalyptic fantasies explored the relation of the notion of purity to the notions of original innocence and the primitive notion of fault. They are all key elements of the paranoid vision. There is a curious conflation between Freud's sense of ideological purity and an actual physical sense of purity.

Webster does not, though, state anything about psychoanalysis having a notion of a millennium or of a utopia. If Freud is the messiah, what good news does he bring for modern man? There really does not seem to be any, other than maybe the possibility of psychological health. If that constitutes an implicit millennialism, it might be the millennialism of child psychologists, social workers, or educational reformers, who imagine creating a world where parents and educators will learn to say and do the right thing so that future generations will grow up free of neurosis. But if that could be considered to be millennial, it is lukewarm and not very emotionally captivating to most other people.

Furthermore, since Freud believes that conflict between the instincts and society is inevitable, neurosis will always be a very real possibility. There is, then, in psychoanalysis, an odd blend of messianism and apocalypticism—both of which are often manifestations of the paranoid vision—coupled with a tragic sense of things,[19] the latter acting as a sobering wet blanket over any potential flames of millennial or utopian hopes.

Some of the post-Freudians—Jung, Fromm, Marcuse, and Maslow, for example—abandoned the tragic sense of psychoanalysis' founder. They contended that it is possible to live as a civilized human being without repression, and that one's lost infinitude can be regained. Norman O. Brown, in the apocalyptic 1960s, was a post-Freudian who advocated a return to polymorphous eroticism, which is a vision of life without repression. Consequently, post-Freudian psychoanalysis, in offering a sanguine view of human possibilities, tends towards millennialism. But the fact that the post-Freudians' worldview is not founded on a hermeneutics of suspicion mitigates the paranoiagenic potential of their millennialism. Our next case example, which is about Bhagwan Rajneesh, will illustrate the darker side of post-Freudian millenarianism.

---

19   We used the phrase "tragic sense of things," rather than "tragic vision," for the tragic vision has a transcendent dimension to it. Such transcendence is lacking in psychoanalysis. There does exist, though, paradoxically enough, a certain comic vision in psychoanalysis. As Rieff contends, "The undertone of tragedy in [Freud's] doctrine of immutable conflict has superimposed on it the comic solvent, therapy. [...] Freud...characteristically transforms the tragic themes into comic arrangements in which guilt and aspiration are to be appeased and placated" (1979, p. 63). It would, indeed, seem true that psychoanalysis does partake of the comic vision, by such psychic compromises. What is missing, though, is the transformative power of comedy, not just to offer compromises but to liberate. There will be more said about the comical in our chapter called, "From Paranoid Vision to Comic Vision."

Chapter Five

The Rise and Fall of the Rajneeshees

> *"Adolph Hitler, in his autobiography, Mein Kampf, says that if you want a nation to be strong, create enemies all around it; otherwise, people relax. Keep them continually in paranoia, fearing that there is danger all around."*
>
> — *Rajneesh (Autobiography)*

I n 1966, the Indian guru Bhagwan Rajneesh began offering a path to enlightenment to those who would become his disciples. From his efforts emerged an organization with thousands of members. Like Freud, Rajneesh had a small cadre of loyal followers, an inner circle. They, and the rest of his disciples, were far less individuated than were Freud's inner circle. The primary distinction of Rajneesh's disciples was simply their notoriety. On the other hand, they were not slackers. A high percentage of them had graduate degrees and were successful working professionals. Many of them were earnest in their quest for spiritual wisdom. Their history together, though, makes those misdeeds that occurred in Freud's circle pale in comparison, for the Rajneeshees devolved into a cult, in the popular sense of the word, one that became a serious menace to society.

The last chapter explored how the paranoid vision can emerge from within an intellectual circle. Here is an example of the paranoid vision emerging out of an organization devoted to spiritual fulfillment, awakening, self-realization. Rajneesh actually referred to what he had created not just as an organization, but as a movement. It certainly had the millenarian spirit endemic to such movements. For a time, when its membership was rapidly growing, it seemed that way.

One discovers here the usual manifestations of the paranoid vision—conspiracy theories, apocalyptic fantasies, an us/them dichotomy followed by projection, and scapegoating. One also finds here the millenarian utopianism that proves so paranoiagenic. What is particularly interesting are two other factors that proved to be paranoiagenic — the loss of moral compass, and Rajneesh's anti-tragic worldview.

A Brief History of the Rajneeshees Versus the World

Like Freud's inner circle, here was an organization with a highly charismatic leader. One can derive some sense of the mind and personality of the Indian guru Bhagwan Rajneesh from his many published writings. Typical of them is Awareness: The Key to Living in Balance. The reader discovers that its author, Rajneesh, had an incisive intellect and was quite learned, both in the wisdom traditions of the East, as well as in Western philosophy, psychology and literature. He had actually been a philosophy professor in India for a number of years prior to declaring himself a guru.

Since Rajneesh's books were predominantly compiled from transcriptions of his public lectures, one gathers that he must have been a fascinating and compelling speaker. Those who attended those lectures and subsequently wrote about the experience confirm this. Of course, Rajneesh's charisma did not only derive from his ability to engage the minds of his readers and his audiences. Rajneesh also knew how to use his voice to have a mesmerizing effect on his listeners. His very presence, particularly his large eyes, as well as his charming manner, added to the effect.

Rajneesh claimed to have achieved enlightenment, and he offered to bring his disciples to that higher state of consciousness. Initially, the path that Rajneesh laid out for them involved various forms of Eastern meditation. But he became increasingly eclectic over time, culling his ideas from the wisdom traditions of Hinduism, Buddhism, Taoism, and Sufism, as well as a variety of Western sources, such as the teachings of Gurdjieff, Alan Watts and those therapies that were becoming popular at the time.

There were many other reasons for Rajneesh's popularity. He appealed to people's longing for meaning, purpose, and direction in life. He also appealed to their need for community, a need that was particularly acute among those Westerners who, although well educated and often materially quite successful, still felt alienated from the mainstream of their societies. Furthermore, Rajneesh offered a millennial vision of a utopian society. The communes that he created, in India and in Oregon, were founded on that vision. Enlightenment, meaning, purpose, direction, community, and millennium—Rajneesh could appeal to almost anyone.

It is, therefore, not surprising to learn that by the early 1970s, Rajneesh's movement comprised thousands of enthusiastic disciples, whom he referred to as "sannyasins."[20] By some estimates, there were over 600 Rajneesh centers worldwide, and over 200,000 sannyasins when the movement was in its heyday, in the early 1980s (Milne, 1987, p. 11). Many of these sannyasins resided at or near his main retreat center, initially located in Bombay and then in Poona, India. Thousands more disciples were affiliated with auxiliary Rajneesh centers worldwide. The very rapid growth of Rajneesh's organization, and the large income it produced from its many ventures—from selling books and tapes of Rajneesh's lectures, to offering meditation retreats, to courting wealthy donors—did not occur by accident. Rajneesh was a very shrewd businessman, an entrepreneur who knew how to capitalize on people's longing for enlightenment.

Furthermore, Rajneesh was receiving praise from various observers of his movement, from the distinguished journalist Bernard

---

20 "Sannyasin" is a Hindu word meaning, "a wandering mendicant and ascetic." In point of fact, Rajneesh's sannyasins were neither wandering nor mendicants, and they certainly were not ascetic.

Levin to the Dalai Lama. This is not to suggest that Rajneesh and his disciples did not have their critics, who accurately perceived Rajneesh's movement to be essentially a very large cult, and who perceived that there existed the beginnings of trouble in paradise. All in all, though, it seemed to many of the movement's disciples, observers, and even critics, that Rajneeshism had a most promising future.

Rajneesh and his associates eventually bore witness to a remark attributed to Cyril Connolly, "Whom the gods would destroy they first call promising." This is because the gift of promise, talent, or genius, especially when other people applaud it, invites hubris. That danger turned out to be all too real. By virtue of a long series of increasingly ill-conceived actions on the part of Rajneesh and his inner circle, it all ended rather ignominiously.

It ended, more precisely, in 1986, in a Gotterdammerung of civil suits and serious criminal charges, resulting in Rajneesh's flight from justice, his arrest, trial, and deportation from the United States. Jail sentences were given to some of his closest associates. Rajneesh's 64,000-acre farm and its buildings in central Oregon, as well as everything else—including his Rolls-Royces—were auctioned off to pay their many creditors. Rajneesh did return to his native India to teach for several more years until his death in 1990, and Rajneeshism continues, in a much different form, to the present day. But the disgrace, precipitated by those dishonorable events, will probably forever haunt the movement.

It would be helpful to recount the events that lead to the downfall of the Rajneeshees. This requires backtracking just a bit. In his autobiography, Rajneesh indicates that he was a very rebellious child growing up in India, and that he continued to be rebellious years later when he became a college professor. Rajneesh was an agent provocateur. As he expresses it, "With or without reason, I was creating controversies...there seemed even if just for fun, a necessity to create controversies." (qtd. in Carter, 1990, p. 44) But controversy leads to conflict, and Rajneesh deliberately proposed ideas and recommended courses of action that were intended to foment conflicts with various elements of society. These conflicts set up an us/them opposition, which, in turn, gave rise to all of the other paranoid phenomena that follow from that duality.

After teaching for several years, he was becoming too controversial and was running afoul of university administrators. Rajneesh quit the university and set out as a traveling lecturer. He realized, early on, that by making his lectures controversial—by railing against the beliefs, values, and consuetudes of Indian society, and by making inflammatory remarks about those in political office, whether justified or not—he would attract a large audience, which he did. It is already clear that Rajneesh was no saint, for he fell for the temptation to achieve worldly success by engaging in the type of publicity-creating theatrics endemic to demagoguery.

When Rajneesh claimed that he was enlightened, he began to attract a following, as would any guru. He and his new disciples looked for a place where Rajneesh could just offer his wisdom, without having to travel, and they found it in Poona, India. Like many towns and cities of India, Poona was a fairly provincial and conservative place. The Rajneeshees, a large percentage of whom were Westerners from Europe and America, managed to offend the local residents. A major cause of offense was, not surprisingly, Rajneesh's advocating of unrestrained sexuality as a path to enlightenment. Rajneesh encouraged his disciples to flaunt their sexuality in public. The women disciples walked through town dressed in a very revealing manner. The Rajneeshees would also dance in the streets, and publicly display their affection for each other. Many Hindus condemned Rajneesh's claim — that enlightenment could be attained by orgiastic sexuality— as heresy. Many of the cult's conflicts with the neighboring community and notoriety simply derived from their not paying their bills. These conflicts were unnecessary, but, again, Rajneesh was drawn to fomenting them.

In order to support themselves in India and to pay their tuition at Rajneesh's ashram, some of the Rajneeshees found work in India in a variety of professions. Others relied on savings. But some engaged in prostitution and drug running (Storr 1996, p. 57). If Rajneesh did not actually sanction those activities, he certainly did not condemn them either, perhaps feeling that the end—the acquisition of money that would be spent on gaining wisdom from Rajneesh—justified the means. Well in evidence here is teleological ethics, with its nihilistigenic potential. Furthermore, it was obvious enough that Rajneesh, the antinomian rebel, was very contemptuous of society. He had little concern for the common weal, and probably he enjoyed that his disciples exploited those whom he held in contempt. These illegal activities on the part of some of his disciples did not endear the Rajneeshees to the members of the neighboring community.

Furthermore, Rajneesh liked to make remarks in public that he knew would offend the powers that be, in Indian politics, religion, and in other areas. This included vitriolic attacks on a powerful politician, Moraji Desai, the Prime Minister of India. Those attacks ended up hurting Rajneesh in many ways, for Desai eventually saw to it that Rajneesh's organization lost their tax-exempt status. As a result, they owed back taxes estimated at five million dollars, which was one of the primary reasons for their leaving India. All this disagreeable behavior on the part of the Rajneeshees turned out to be their undoing.

Rajneesh's Oregon Adventure

The cult had gotten into so much trouble in India, coupled with the back taxes, that Rajneesh's inner circle concluded that it was time to emigrate—perhaps "abscond" is the appropriate word—to another country. They chose the United States, and ended up purchasing a 64,000-acre ranch in central Oregon, which they named "Rajneeshpuram." The Rajneeshees would work the land, and construct various buildings that would be part of their operation, but their work would be a kind of meditation, for they would work with a high degree of mindfulness; furthermore, the interpersonal conflicts that arose at the ranch would be used for self-knowledge. The disciples' life in Oregon was in sharp contrast to what it had been in India. Gone was all sense of looseness and laxness. Now they were working 14-hour days, seven days a week.

James Gordon, a psychiatrist, journalist, and former disciple of Rajneesh, indicates that the purpose of the ranch was to "...serve as the birthplace for the 'new man'" (1987, p. 221). As Rajneesh expressed it, "With the new man there will come a new world, because the new man will perceive in a different way. He will live a totally different life, which has not been lived yet. He will be a mystic, a poet, a scientist, all together" (Osho 2000, p. 254).[21] Thus the goal of their enterprise was not simply to provide a context where enlightenment could be achieved. Rajneesh and his disciples were clearly caught up in millenarianism, although of a certain modern type — a quasi-Nietzschian notion of bringing about the birth of the superman. Here, then, was an incongruous mixture of motives — enlightenment, bringing about the millennium, and as it turned out, using the ranch as a moneymaking operation.

When millennial enthusiasm is in the air, paranoia can never be far behind. This is understandable because delusions of grandeur about the glorious affair that life is supposed to be, but isn't because the millennium has not yet arrived, invariably lead to disappointment, bitterness, and resentment over why the millennium has been delayed. Then someone, or some group of people, is made into a scapegoat. Through the process of projective identification, the scapegoat is provoked, making it easier for the scapegoat to become a projection of the cult's malevolence. Then the cult feels vindicated since they are only acting defensively. It would be good to keep that in mind, as we examine the events that unfolded in Oregon.

The actual paranoia-infused drama begins when the "us" encounters the "them." The "them" had been the inhabitants of India, but now the "them" was to be the inhabitants of the Oregon town of Antelope, the closest town to Rancho Rajneesh, about ten miles from the entrance of the ranch. Needless to say, the townspeople were suspicious of the cult, for they had heard about what happened when they were in India — the sexual promiscuity and the financial shenanigans, for example. Then there was the anti-Christian paganism that this Hindu cult represented to members of the outlying community. There was also a concern that people had that the sannyasins were involved with brainwashing. (The memory of brainwashing during the Korean War was still alive.) Adding to all this was the fact that Rajneesh had the same "in-your-face, flaunt your sexuality or your wealth" attitude that he had in India. Rajneesh may have simply liked Rolls-Royces, but

---

21 Rajneesh latter changed his name to "Osho."

purchasing ninety-three of them naturally seemed to his neighbors to be showing off a bit. It was bound to alienate most people and make them suspicious that Rajneesh was a con artist. If the townspeople were a bit paranoid themselves, it was not that their suspicions were not justified.

Initially, the cult sought to mollify the suspicions of their neighbors, so they told them that only forty people would be moving to Rajneesh's commune, and that they would be working the land. Despite their differences, it briefly appeared that the Rajneeshees would get along with their neighbors. But then the Rajneeshees started purchasing buildings in the neighboring town of Antelope, for it was the case that they had much larger ambitions. In time, what was supposed to be forty inhabitants swelled to about 2500. The townspeople felt betrayed, then sought to limit purchases by the cult through zoning ordinances. This was fair enough, for the water in the region was seriously limited and could not accommodate so many people. It certainly could not accommodate a city, which was what the cult intended to build on their property. As a result, legal battles between the cult and the neighboring township ensued.

Exacerbating matters terribly was Sheela, the Indian woman Rajneesh put in charge of the entire commune. Many people left the commune because they could not stand her manipulative and tyrannical ways, for she was exploiting everyone with endless work, demanding what money they had or their family had. During meetings with the townspeople, and when appearing on TV, Sheela came across as loud, abrasive, threatening, cruel, and malicious. One would be hard pressed to imagine that Rajneesh could have picked a worse person to run the commune, and to be its spokesperson. As we shall see, Rajneesh's choice of Sheela says a lot about him.

In any case, the legal battles also led to the cult — which, in terms of population, was now a majority — gaining control of the city counsel. They changed the name of the town from Antelope to Rajneesh, changed all of the familiar street names to those Hindu names associated with their cult, raised taxes, and took over the school system requiring the non-Rajneeshian inhabitants of Antelope to bus their children to another district fifty miles away. During the course of these events, the cult members harassed their neighbors, whom they obviously held in contempt, using the new police force that the cult created, and using intimidation to motivate the neighbors to sell their homes. The cult's initial strategy of maintaining a low profile was abandoned because the confrontation became major news, not just in Oregon, but nationally.

The continual complaints about the cult, as well as well as the publicity that this conflict was receiving, invited investigation. It didn't help Rajneesh any that he was not a US citizen, but was merely a visitor, who claimed to be a religious worker, who would be in the United States only for a short time. Furthermore, the Immigration and Naturalization Service was getting wind of the fact that the various marriages that had occurred at Rancho Rajneesh were essentially fraudulent. They had been made merely for the purposes of obtaining citizenship for many of the inhabitants of the ranch, who were foreigners. This might have gone unnoticed or been ignored were it not for the fact that it was blatant, with so many people having entered into these pseudo-marriages. The Attorney General began investigating the complaint that the transformation of the town of Antelope into the town of Rajneesh violated the separation of church and state.

Rajneesh had instilled in his followers apocalyptic concerns about finding a place that would be far enough from a big city so as to be free of devastation if there were a nuclear war. That was one of the reasons that they chose central Oregon. They would need to survive, for they, the Rajneeshees, would be the future hope of mankind. Around this time, in 1983, Rajneesh issued apocalyptic warnings that appeared in the cult's newspaper, the Rajneesh Times, for several months in a row. As Gordon states:

> The period of crisis will be between 1984 and 1999...There will be every kind of destruction on earth including natural catastrophes and man-manufactured autosuicidal efforts... The holocaust is going to be global...There will be floods which have never been known since the time of Noah... (1987, p. 131)

The way in which the Rajneeshees could save themselves would be "a Noah's Ark of consciousness." (Gordon, 1987, p. 131) Furthermore, the Rajneesh meditation centers in Los Angeles and San Francisco were closed down because of the prediction that these cities would be destroyed. The emergence of AIDS reinforced such apocalyptic fears. The apocalyptic atmosphere—ultimately created by the Rajneeshees' clash with the world, a clash that the Rajneeshees precipitated — led to a fearful siege mentality and to the cult becoming an armed camp. Indeed, they had a very large security force that possessed hundreds of assault weapons, including machine guns and Uzis. According to Milne, "The ranch now had eleven armed watchtowers, and a whole series of checkpoints to ensure that no unwanted visitors could get in and sannyasins could get out" (1987, p. 348). No one was trusted: the sannyasins had both their incoming and outgoing mail opened, read, and sometimes destroyed. People's telephone lines were tapped, their rooms bugged, and there were spies everywhere. Those Rajneeshees accused of being disloyal were "...subject to psychological intimidation and verbal assaults" (Gordon 1987, p. 134).

There were many other such incidents, including Rajneeshees poisoning a salad bar with salmonella so that local townspeople would be absent for an election that involved an important zoning decision affecting the cult. Over 700 people got sick, an incident, which is considered to be the first instance of bio-terrorism in the United States since Lord Amherst sold smallpox-infested rugs to the Indians. There were many other criminal incidents including the attempted assassination of state and federal officials who were prosecuting the case against the cult. There were anti-Semitic caricatures made in The Rajneesh News of the Attorney General who was Jewish. If all that was not bad enough, Rajneesh gave a press conference in which he made terrorist threats. According to Gordon, Rajneesh said, "...they cannot do any harm here. People can also hijack American planes..." (1987, p. 186).

There were also conspiracy theories that developed, one of which alleged that the federal government had put out a half million-dollar contract on Rajneesh's life. (Gordon, 1987, p. 242) But not all the conspiracy theories referred to people in the outside world who would harm the cult. Some of them were about things that were going on in the cult. One former Rajneeshee told FitzGerald that "...there might be an esoteric death cult in the commune: a Sannyasin who had just left the ranch had told him that there were rumors of an inner sanctum where the goddess Kali was worshipped and where there had been a human sacrifice." (1986, p. 345) For there to have been conspiracy theories about what went on at the commune, rather than outside the commune, the spirit of things must have really devolved so that there became a strong us/them distinction between Rajneesh's inner circle of disciples, and the rest of the Rajneeshees.

Once again, the defense mechanism of projection is at the core of this extreme paranoid reaction on the part of the Rajneeshees, not only to their neighbors, but to each other. Here, then, is another example of projection becoming prominent in an organization when certain psychological and interpersonal tensions are not able to be resolved other than by the members leaving the group. The unresolved tensions in Freud's inner circle involved the father/son conflict. Such tensions proved to be paranoiagenic, for there was a tendency to seek release from such internal tensions by attributing their source to "heretics," or upon those elements of society that were supposedly the enemies of psychoanalysis. Did this same phenomenon occur in Rajneesh's organization? There is an interesting passage in Milne that would suggest as much:

> The anger and frustrations that any normal person would feel in such a patrolled and regimented environment was turned around by the sannyasins and focused on the outside world. As the Rajneeshees started to lose court cases and the zoning plan for the new city started to look in extreme doubt, hatred and paranoia were increasingly turned outwards. (1987, p. 345)

FitzGerald has an intriguing observation, in that regard "The explanation now current among county officials and ranchers was that the Rajneeshees were quite deliberately making enemies for the sake of their own internal cohesion" (1986, pp. 339-340). Milne's description implies that the process by which Rajneesh's disciples externalized their frustration occurred naturally, but, according to FitzGerald, the ranchers and county officials believed that it was a deliberate strategy on the part of Rajneesh. Which explanation is true? Both are true, for the paranoid process of projecting the source of one's anger and frustrations occurred naturally, but Rajneesh knew how to exploit these feelings, how to fan the flames of anger, and how to direct the anger towards certain targets. There is some support for this by James Gordon, when he states that Rajneesh had, in those turbulent years at the commune, expressed admiration for Hitler and the Nazi propaganda minister Goebbels. Apropos is an interview that Gordon had with Rajneesh that appeared in The New Yorker, and which then appeared in Rajneesh's autobiography. Gordon asks:

> In my meeting with Sheela, certainly one could see her intelligence, at least in very practical matters, in her cleverness about things, but you could also see her very oppressive side, the very mean-spirited side as well. You must have seen that being in contact with her everyday? (qtd. in Osho, 2000, p. 254)

Rajneesh's answer to Gordon's question is startling and most revealing:

> I know! But it was needed for all those mean politicians all around. I could not put the commune in the hands of some innocent people — the politicians would have destroyed it...only bad people could have managed [the commune in Oregon]. Good people could not. (Osho 2000, p. 254)

What Rajneesh's answer reveals is his extremely cynical justification for using evil people to serve his purposes. His justification is defensive. He does not see that the politicians and his neighbors in Oregon acted the way in which they did because of the outrageously poor behavior that Sheela and the members of the commune had displayed to them.

Over time, the commune was transformed into something resembling an extremely repressive, fascistic, totalitarian theocracy. Carter quotes Mills and Kaplan, who described Rajneeshpuram as "... the closest thing to an Eastern Bloc experience in the United States..." (1990, p. 7) Carter, a sociologist who had spent several years as a participant observer of the cult when it was in Oregon, was struck by how extremely regimented life at Rajneeshpuram had become. Carter describes how he, and the staff that had accompanied him, reacted to what they experienced at the commune,

> We were perhaps too embarrassed by the constraints of our well-socialized notions of how social scientists "ought" to think and talk to compare the structure of Rajneeshpuram to a "fascist state" as Bhagwan was latter to do). Our rhetoric tended more to noting that the structure was "authoritarian" and that it displayed a preoccupation with total control, daily life regimented and regulated even in minutiae. (1990, p. 31)

The curious thing is how what it had become, namely a "fascist state," contrasts with the original ideals of freedom and openness. Once paranoia had become a contagion, it was inevitable that the cult would become a control-oriented organization—one characterized by an extreme degree of regulation and regimentation — for control is a way of handling the anxious uncertainty of the paranoid person and the paranoid organization.

The Rajneeshees might have succeeded with their commune, but they were becoming an increasingly serious menace to society. The cult might have gone out with a big apocalyptic bang were it not that Rajneesh's network of spies (Gordon, 1987) in the government alerted him that he was going to be arrested. He attempted to flee the country, was arrested at the airport, tried for various crimes, convicted, and deported from the United States, thus finally ending the whole ugly, sordid, and criminal affair.

What Happened?

Those who had been members of Rajneesh's cult, those who had observed it over the years, or who were familiar with its history, have been prompted to ask the question that the perplexed protagonist of *The Sand Pebbles* (1966) posed at the end of that film, "What the hell happened?" After all, Rajneeshism certainly did not have to come to a disgraceful end. Apropos is a statement by Jeannie, a disillusioned disciple of Rajneesh, where she refers to Rajneesh and his ruthless assistant Sheela:

> It's the old angry guru trip all over again...He's just lashing out at all comers. Now the people he and Sheela have been walking all over are hitting back and it's beginning to get messy. You can't fool the federal government for long without getting your fingers rapped. All this non-payment of bills, this lying, the PR deceit — why do we have to do it this way? We could have had our paradise legally and above board, and built our commune in complete peace. This way of doing things just makes me sick. (qtd. in Milne, 1987, p. 314)

Jeannie has gotten to the heart of this crazy affair — the Rajneeshees "could have had [their] paradise legally." Although "paradise" is a huge millennialist overstatement, it is true that Rajneesh's commune could have been viable had he adhered to his initial mission, the cultivation of enlightened beings, rather than the ruthless exploitation of his disciples' labor. According to Anthony Storr, "...Rajneesh is surely a telling example of the truth of Lord Acton's maxim: 'Power tends to corrupt, and absolute power corrupts absolutely.' Rajneesh degenerated into a monster of greed" (1996, p. 63).

Rajneesh was undoubtedly greedy, but there were other corrupting factors involved as well. There is much to suggest that Rajneesh had a "Citizen Kane complex," for like the protagonist of Orson Welles' film (1941), Rajneesh very much liked to collect things. According to his biographers, he collected everything from pens to expensive watches to 93 Rolls-Royces—so as to compensate for what he had, way back in India, but could never recover, his "Rosebud," i.e. a purity, innocence, and love that was forever lost to him. (Some biographers have connected that lost love to Rajneesh's grandfather, who had raised Rajneesh, as well as to his childhood sweetheart who had died.)

In addition to power, greed, and the compulsive desire to collect, there was something else that drove Rajneesh. As Milne indicates, "...Bhagwan loved publicity. He was addicted to it" (1987, p. 189). Perhaps the craving for fame is ultimately the wish to be loved, but it is that wish gone awry, for it is one thing to be loved as a human being, but to be loved as a god, by scores of disciples, is prompted by a delusion of grandeur.

If the lust for wealth, power, and fame were not enough to distract Rajneesh from his original mission, he was further driven off course by his rebelliousness, which ranged from iconoclasm to an aggressive hostility. In his autobiography, Rajneesh makes a rather telling comment upon his driving, "I am a terrific driver. And I don't believe in any rules—I may drive right, I may drive left, I may drive in the middle — so my poor people had to create a road just for me so I could drive anywhere, any way, at any speed." (Osho, 2000) A number of reports from those who had known Rajneesh indicate that he would often drive through red lights and engage in similar dangerous maneuvers. Rajneesh clearly had a reckless disregard for the safety of anyone else who might be on the highway. His disciples inherited his arrogant, disdainful and irresponsible attitude towards people in the outlying community. Anthony Storr classified Rajneesh as a narcissist, a classification which makes sense. But Milne's observations might qualify Storr's psychiatric classification:

> He had little compassion or regard for the feelings of others. There were to be many deaths in the ashrams, both from suicide and from hepatitis and other diseases that could have been cured with proper medical attention. Rajneesh never gave enough money for food in the ashrams, and was not concerned when we worked too hard or slept too little. (1987, p. 105)

It would appear, then, that if Rajneesh was, as Storr claims, a narcissist, Rajneesh had the type of narcissism—manipulating other people, being bereft of conscience, and lacking in compassion—that is characteristic of the personality disorder known as sociopathy. If one considers the criminal activity that the cult became involved in over the years, it would lend credence to that interpretation.

According to FitzGerald, this is what Rajneesh said about his native India just before emigrating to the United States, "'India,' he said, was 'an old, ancient, and rotten country, and many parts of this rotten goddamned country have to be removed...it stinks.'" (1986, p.

307) Rajneesh soon had an equally belittling view of the United States, and particularly of the state of Oregon. As Milne rightly perceives, "Even by early 1982 I could not see any way that the commune could succeed. Bhagwan simply could not restrain himself from punching authority in the eye." (1987, p. 274) There is, indeed, much evidence to suggest that Rajneesh possessed an aggressively hostile attitude towards society, both in India and America, which he expressed by flouting its laws and customs.

It would appear that Rajneesh was more concerned about getting his licks in, condemning and tormenting that element of society that he held in contempt — for being conservative, provincial, repressed, or repressive — than he cared about helping his disciples. Furthermore, Rajneesh's hostility significantly contributed to the us/them duality that developed between the Rajneeshees and the rest of humanity. When society finally reacted, the Rajneeshees then projected their own hostility onto society, and acted like victims. That is the fertile soil from which grow delusions of persecution, conspiracy theories, apocalyptic fantasies, and all the rest.

We have been exploring the question, "What happened?" It is apparent that Rajneesh's original intent, to bring people to enlightenment, was derailed by a variety of desires and animosities. Storr is correct that power corrupted Rajneesh although it must be added that the desire for fortune and fame did so as well. What is it about such desires that corrupt a person? They are intoxicating by virtue of being images of infinitude. The infinitude that they promise is not that which belongs to religious, philosophical, or mystical transcendence, but the infinitude implied in the notion of being free of the limits that belong to the human condition. If, for example, one has all the money, there are no limits to one's purchasing power.

The lure of the false infinite—of being infinitely wealthy, powerful, or famous—fills the mind with delusions of grandeur, causing one to lose all sense of what it means to be human. It is in that sense that wealth, power, and fame are disorienting, intoxicating, and un-grounding. Rajneesh's arrogance, disdain, and aggressive animosity towards society similarly evince a hubristic disregard of the limits intrinsic to the human condition. To be arrogant, in that way, is to regard oneself as king of the universe, and everyone else as subjects.

We have considered a number of disorienting factors in Rajneesh and his organization—greed, power, lust for fame, arrogance, and a malicious hostility. But there was one more that played a critically important part. Surprising to say, higher consciousness can be quite disorienting. As Goethe had observed, "Any growth in consciousness without a corresponding growth of self-control is pernicious" (Goethe, # 504). That could be Rajneesh's epitaph, as well as that of his disciples, for their elevated consciousness was not supported by a growth of self-control. True spiritual teachers or gurus balance spiritual intensity with self-control, sobriety, and morality. They put all other interests— fame, fortune, power, frustration and anger towards society, sleeping with female disciples, etc.—aside, for they are resolute in bringing their disciples to enlightenment. This is manifested both in their teachings and, most importantly, in their everyday lives. This does not mean that they must become joyless and humorless, but lightness of spirit must be balanced with focused intensity of purpose.

When gurus start imagining that they are Nietzschian supermen, beyond good and evil, it only leads them to self-inflation, and to madness. Whatever higher consciousness Rajneesh and his disciples had attained had the effect of dangerously unbalancing anddisorienting them. That unbalance and disorientation had, as we shall see, a paranoiagenic effect.

From Immorality to Madness to Self-Destruction

Might it be possible that immorality[22] is paranoiagenic? That is the conclusion that can be drawn from these case examples. Of course,

---

22 There are those who might object to the use of the word "immorality," for it sounds like value judgments are intruding into this psychological discussion. But the approach here is really phenomenological, for questions of morality psychologically impact human beings. One could, perhaps, use the psychologically phrased expression, "the perception that one is acting immorally," rather than "immorality," but that would be reducing morality to perceptions or to feelings, i.e. to psychology, something to which Martin Buber had strenuously objected. If a psychologist were to suggest that a certain person were suffering from guilt feelings, Buber might respond with something like, "No, my good doctor, the man is not suffering from guilt feelings; he is suffering because he is guilty."

not all paranoia is due to immorality, nor does all immorality leads to paranoia, but it is a relatively easy slide from immorality to possession by the paranoid vision. This slide might occur more frequently in groups or organizations than in individuals. Of course, one could argue that all organizations are a bit mad, for as Nietzsche observed, "Madness is rare in individuals—but in groups, parties, nations, and ages it is the rule" (1885; 1989, p. 90). But we are not referring here to the many garden varieties of madness that plague most organizations, but rather to a certain malevolent species of madness endemic to certain organizations, i.e. possession by the paranoid vision.

Furthermore, it may be that the madness of the paranoid vision is a stage in a larger dialectic. The ancient Greeks believed that there exists a cosmic force that seeks retribution for moral transgressions, which they called "nemesis." Could it be that paranoia is the middle term between immorality and nemesis? If so, one can begin to understand a notion that is as old as Sophocles, "Those whom the gods would destroy, they first drive mad." If the downward slide from ambition, or hubris, to becoming possessed by the paranoid vision (i.e. madness), to devastation (i.e. nemesis)—terrifyingly rendered by Shakespeare in his play *Macbeth*— is a perennial theme in literature,[23] it is because it is a fear that resonates in everyone. And it is always easier when the plunge into the depths of insanity is taken with other people.

That sequence—from a state of relative psychological stasis to hubris (the overweening pride that lies at the heart of immorality) to madness (paranoia) to destructive punishment — makes sense, if one realizes that the hubristic individual or organization is one who has become possessed by those delusions of grandeur that are

---

23   "When falls on man the anger of the gods, first from his mind they banish understanding." Lycurgus (In Leocratuem. Chapter xxi. Sec 92.)

"When divine power plans evil for a man, it first injures his mind." Sophocles (Antigone)

"Those whom God wishes to destroy, he first deprives of their senses." Euripides (Fragment, — Boswell, Life of Johnson 1783, Notes)

"Whom fate wishes to ruin she first makes mad." — Publilius Syrus, Sententium No. 479.

"For those whom God to ruin has design'd, He fits for fate, and first destroys their mind." John Dryden (Hind and Panther iii, l. 1093)

"Whom the Gods would destroy they first make mad." Henry Wadsworth Longfellow. (Mask of Pandora Pt. Vi, 1.58)

associated with madness, i.e. with paranoia. Nemesis need not take the form of physical death, but can have varied expressions, such as social disgrace, financial ruin, legal prosecution, and invasion by an enemy army. But whether or not this punishing destruction has an objective manifestation, it always involves a loss or death of the soul (Diel, 1980),[24] i.e. the loss of those life energies that have the power, as Socrates suggests, to transport us beyond ourselves, to the higher reaches of spirit. When the soul dies, the possibility of such transcendence is gone. An analysis of Rajneesh and his movement, his rise and fall, may help us to understand this dark dialectic — particularly the significance of that intermediate term, the paranoid vision.

Immorality is a deviation from what is regarded as right or just. An immoral person is egocentric, indifferent to the feelings, concerns, and rights of other people. There is, though, another aspect of immorality that has been particularly germane to our discussion. In addition to being egotistical, those who are immoral are dissolute. Their energies are unfocused, dissipated amongst a multitude of desires, goals, and objectives. Of course, truly evil people are as resolute as are those who are truly good. Lady Macbeth, for example, encouraged Macbeth to be resolute. She told him: "Screw your courage to the sticking place." Lacking that sort of resolution, Rajneesh, although immoral, was neither a thoroughly evil person, nor a good person.

Perhaps, at one time, as a young man in Bombay, he was resolute; he had but one desire, and that desire was to achieve enlightenment. And perhaps, afterwards, Rajneesh was resolute in seeking to teach other people to attain that state of awareness. But, in examining the history of his movement, one sees that Rajneesh became dissolute, for he also had a lust for power; he philandered with his female disciples, he became greedy for money; he craved world fame, he sought martyrdom; he became preoccupied with attacking society for its

---

24   Some writers, particularly of popular business books, concerned with the lack of motivation at workplaces, have referred to the loss or the death of the corporate soul, or of the organizational soul. Perhaps the metaphor does make a certain sense, for it quite possible for an organization to become, in a way that Gogol would have recognized, a place of "dead souls." Of course, the soul of a person, or that of a company, may die for reasons, other than immorality. It may die from a sclerosis of its creative energies due to excess bureaucratization. It may also die from the withering power of shallowness. For a recent account of soul death amongst college students, due to shallowness, see Tom Wolfe's new novel, I am Charlotte Simmons. (2004)

provincial ways; he was drawn to being an outrageous and notorious iconoclast; he sought to bring about the millennium, etc.

Kierkegaard wrote a book entitled, *Purity of Heart* (1847; 1981). The book's argument is that purity of heart is to will one thing. Rajneesh, on the other hand, willed everything. Consequently, what might have once been a focused self became but a legion of incompatible selves. Going through life as a plurality of selves might make for an interesting existence, although a schizophrenic one, but it is not exactly the intensely focused, straight and narrow path along the razor's edge. With a rather weak moral compass, with no allegiance to a code of ethics, Rajneesh was thrown off course by every desire and dark emotion that blew his way, and his organization suffered grievously on account of that. It became transformed from a forum for self-discovery into a narrow-minded, nasty, and paranoid cult.

There has always been much debate, by both journalists and scholars, about who Rajneesh really was. There are those who have viewed Rajneesh as a con artist, or huckster, as the "sex guru," and later as the "Rolls-Royce guru." That, indeed, he was. On the other hand, there are those who have regarded Rajneesh as a sincere spiritual seeker and brilliant teacher of Eastern wisdom to Westerners. That he was, too. Some who have written perceptively about the Rajneesh movement—for example, Gordon (1989), Milne (1987), and Storr (1997)—and who have been able to tolerate large doses of cognitive dissonance, contend that Rajneesh was both sincere as well as a huckster. Such contradictions abide, for the dissolute self has no overarching unity.

Using the word "dissolute" to describe Rajneesh's sense of self, opens one to the criticism of being retrograde. After all, from a postmodern, deconstructionist standpoint, there is no core self. Hadn't David Hume abolished the notion of a unified self, way back in the eighteenth century? Postmodernism values diversity, richness, and plenitude rather than unity. Its advocates, in essence, Whitman's declaration "Do I contradict myself? Well I contain multitudes." It is important to add that since the charismatic Rajneesh was the paradigm of selfhood for his disciples; they sought to follow in his postmodern ways.

Perhaps, for the same reason, the analogy with Macbeth might be considered retrograde, for Macbeth—and Lady Macbeth, too—had a conscience, although a guilty one. But questions of good and evil, of leading the right life, would no longer seem to be a serious concern when the normative dimension of life is no longer regarded as the path to reality, but as merely a set of socially imposed rules enforced with violence. We are neither affirming nor denying here the validity of the notion of morality as social construct. We are merely commenting upon its likely psychological implications, as well as the implications for an organization founded on that notion of morality.

If there is no longer any belief in the notion of a unified self, nor any inner subscription to morality as a guiding principle in human affairs, the consequence is a far profounder dissoluteness than there would be for those who still believe in selfhood, as well as in good and evil, but have chosen to take the road to perdition, as did Macbeth and Lady Macbeth. Another way of saying it is that for Macbeth there existed a moral touchstone, although he strayed far afield of it, but for Rajneesh there was no touchstone.

Now this is the question: why would immorality—in the sense of dissoluteness—be paranoiagenic? Dissoluteness leads to inner turmoil and disorientation. The experience of inner turmoil, and the frightening threat of psychic chaos, is a painful state of affairs, and cannot be endured for very long. When people become disoriented in this way, they desperately seek orientation, i.e. they seek to make sense of their experience. They thus become susceptible to the ersatz order, meaning, and intelligibility promised by conspiracy theories, apocalyptic fantasies, Manichean vilifications, and the like. The dissolute self, which is now painfully disoriented, thus becomes lured to the false orientation promised by the paranoid vision.[25]

Haven't conspiracy theories, apocalyptic fantasies, and all else that is expressive of the paranoid vision been around long before the advent of modernity, let alone postmodernism? After all, Norman Cohn (1957; 1979) writes about paranoid cults existing in the Middle Ages. Since that objection is certainly valid, the matter requires clarification.

---

25 There are, of course, many other possibilities in regard to the search for orientation, including that of finding genuine meaning in life, which then becomes one's guiding star. We shall not expatiate on that hoped for possibility, for our concern here is with darker matters.

Those paranoid cults about which Cohn writes were imbued with the antinomial spirit, i.e. they were opposed to the notion that moral laws are obligatory. In that sense, the antinomianism that was espoused and practiced by those medieval cults was really a precursor of postmodernism. Or, one might say that postmodernism is but another form of the antinomianism that has been around for centuries.

Furthermore, both might be considered to be but species of Protagorean relativism, with its notion that, "Man is the measure of all things." It is a position that Socrates argued against along epistemological lines, as he had with the extreme Heracliteans. After all, if the very words that people use are in constant flux, there can be no intelligibility. If Whitehead is correct, Protagoreanism, antinomianism, postmodernism, and nihilism in general — as well as a hundred and one other forms of value relativism that have appeared throughout the centuries—are but "a series of footnotes to Plato."

The Paranoiagenic Potential of Anti-Tragic Teachings

It should come as no surprise that not only was Rajneesh's personality and his actions in the world paranoiagenic, but so were his very teachings. As was evident in the case of psychoanalysis, paranoiagenic ideas have dangerous consequences. It is important to get some sense of the essence of those teachings if their impact on Rajneesh's organization, and on the events that unfolded, is to be fully understandable.

What made Rajneesh really unique among Indian spiritual teachers was that he did not advocate an ascetical life. On the contrary, he championed a free, indeed orgiastic, sexuality as a path to enlightenment. (Once again, some of the medieval antinomian cults that Norman Cohn wrote about come to mind.) Needless to say, Rajneesh's teaching was quite popular, especially with the young, for it claimed to transcend the immemorial conflict between spirituality and sexuality, and promised a route from their dissatisfied lives to a state of innocence before the fall into self-consciousness, sin, and guilt.

Rajneesh also distinguished himself from other spiritual teachers who had advocated the renunciation of material goods, and who saw poverty as the path to God. Rajneesh, on the contrary, viewed asceticism, renunciation, and voluntary poverty—all that belonged to the Hindu tradition of wandering mendicant—as masochism, and contested that wealth is a prerequisite to spirituality. Here, too, Rajneesh promised that another ancient conflict, the one between God and Mammon, could easily be transcended.

Rajneesh, in viewing the origins of such conflicts as being merely due to social conditioning, is an heir to Rousseauan utopianism, with its shallow notion of an original human innocence. Such utopianism has proven to be paranoiagenic. It was pleasant to imagine that one could find heavenly peace without letting go of one's egotistical claims upon this world. It was an effort, in other words, to have it both ways. Needless to say, the notion of seeking self-transformation, without having to sacrifice any desire or inclination, is a bit suspect—as is any such effort to have one's cake and eat it, too—and suggests a puerility of spirit. FitzGerald rightly judges such ideas to be indicative of the "me generation," who cling to the belief that they can have it all, that no element of reality needs be renounced or sacrificed.

Of course, the Rajneesh's disciples claimed that they had sacrificed their egocentric orientation when they surrendered to their master, which was the initial requirement for becoming a disciple.[26] But what essentially is this surrender to Rajneesh? If the Rajneeshees had experienced this surrender as liberating, it is only because they had abandoned the burden of moral responsibility, by virtue of handing over their will to another person. In truth, such surrender is idolatry and slavery, for it involves forsaking one's autonomy and one's responsibilities. Balthasar Gracian, the worldly-wise seventeenth century monk, wrote that, "Slavery does not lose its vileness because it is disguised by the nobility of its lord and master" (1637; 1993, pp. 160-161).

But this surrender to Rajneesh was not only vile; it also had a retarding effect on his disciples' emotional, moral, and spiritual development. For inner development only takes place in the crucible of everyday decision-making, where higher values and egotistical

---

26 As symbolic of this surrender, they had to dress in the orange robes of the Sannyasin, wear a mala with Rajneesh's picture around their neck, and be renamed with a Hindu name assigned to them by Rajneesh.

concerns invariably come into conflict. When the disciple's character and integrity has become atrophied or never develops in the first place, he or she becomes psychically weakened and susceptible to a host of spiritual scourges. For just as nature abhors a vacuum, so it is that the human heart abhors the void. The paranoid vision is a futile effort to fill that void.

There is a tragic dimension of human existence that finds expression in writers like Aeschylus and Shakespeare, in the existentialists, and in Freud. These thinkers call attention to the limiting conditions of human existence, especially the ineluctable fact that human beings are mortal. But most of the post-Freudians denied the tragic, as has the human potential movement, the new age movement, and Rajneeshism. They particularly denied the tragic dimension of sexuality, the intimate connection between love and death. The liberated person, in their opinion, would be uninhibited, free of the guilt and all of the emotional baggage that belonged to sexuality.

The very notion of guilt-free indulgence is predicated on the notion that one does not have to be under the constraints of moral consciousness, and the guilt that belongs to it. Rajneesh framed the whole effort to be free of such constraints not in post-Freudian terms, but in the language of Eastern mysticism; he spoke of the goal of such efforts being the letting go of attachments. He even found a precedent for it in Tantric sexuality, which is derivative of Hindu mysticism, but the connection between what Rajneesh taught and Tantra seems dubious. Although couched in the language of nonattachment and of Eastern religion, Rajneesh's teaching about sexuality was really all in the service of egotistical freedom in the world.

It makes sense, then, that Rajneesh's disciples nicknamed him "Zorba the Buddha"—named after the protagonist of the novel *Zorba the Greek* (Kazantzakis, 1946; 1996)—for Rajneesh sought to combine a kind of Zorba life-affirmation with Buddhism. This effort to overcome the conflict, that many people experience between the sacred and the secular, found expression everywhere, including in the daily discourses that Rajneesh delivered to his assembled disciples. According to Gordon, "[Rajneesh] might interrupt a long and eloquent discourse on Buddha's Heart Sutra with a joke from *Playboy*..."

(1987, p. 12). And according to FitzGerald, Rajneesh would cite "... Gurdjieff, Socrates, and Bob Hope all in a single lecture" (1986, p. 291). Rajneesh's lectures, for that reason, must have been quite entertaining, and had some of the comic spirit that we shall have more to say about in Chapter Nine.

Rajneesh's effort to overcome the conflict between the sacred and the secular necessarily involved a condemnation of Christianity, which contends that this world and heaven are in opposition, and that the sacrifice of earthly being is necessary if the truth of heaven is to be affirmed. In a very telling passage from one of his discourses, Rajneesh states:

> "The Real Jesus," he went on, "never died on the cross. That which dies is not really part of you." Christ was not the name of a person but "the name of the ultimate state of consciousness. It is exactly what we call in the East Buddhahood. Jesus was one of the Christs. Abraham was one, Moses was one, Lao-Tzu one, Krishna was one. Identifying with Jesus as a figure on the cross is simply a way for people to project their sadness." Jesus became "an excuse for people to become miserable," and the worship of his suffering was a form of pathology perpetuated by hysterical saints and repressed priests. (Gordon 1987, p. 31)

Never died on the cross?! This is, of course, a false rendition of the Christ story, for the whole point of the story was that Christ, although the son of God, was still a man, which is why He is tempted, and which is why He cries out in despair, "Lord, why hast Thou forsaken me?" If Christ was like Rajneesh claimed, immortal, Christ's sacrifice would have been an exercise in futility, and Christianity would be meaningless.[27]

Of course, the Christ story is not a tragedy, for Christ is resurrected. But for Rajneesh the tragic is simply denied by a facile recourse to an Eastern mysticism whose meaning he has similarly misconstrued. Rajneesh's radical misinterpretation of Christianity is a glaring

---

27 Chapter Seven explores radical Islamism. There, too, one finds a denial of the crucifixion. In the Qur'an, Mohamed states that, at the last minute, someone was substituted for Jesus. Both radical Islamism and Rajneeshism must deny the crucifixion, for they advocate a triumphalism.

example of a false effort at transcendence, one that simply refuses to recognize the limits and finitude of human reality.

There is another important element in Rajneesh's teaching that is related to his championing of uninhibited sexuality— his Nietzschian antinomianism, his disdain for the morality, mores, consuetudes, and laws of society. Dave Frohnmayer, the Oregon Attorney General who had investigated Rajneesh's cult, had some revealing opinions, in that regard, about Rajneesh. James Gordon, who interviewed Frohnmayer, has this to say:

> Frohnmayer, who had written his Harvard honors thesis on Nietzsche and Lenin, saw in Rajneesh the same "individual self-aggrandizement," the same "relativity of truth," the same "disengagement from ethics," that he had discovered in Nietzsche's concept of the Superman. "I wanted to say to Bhagwan," he told me, "I've read your book." Rarely, he told me, had he seen people who were "genuinely evil," but from what he could tell, Rajneesh and Sheela fit in that category. (1987, p. 210)

Rajneeshism was a teaching that did not encourage compassion, or what the Buddhists called Karuna, the selfless love for all sentient beings. On the contrary, it encouraged guilt-free indulgence, individual self-aggrandizement, and a smugness about being on a spiritual path, coupled by a supercilious, disdainful and, indeed, hostile attitude towards other people. Here, again, was an example of dark ideas having dark consequences.

Rajneesh's ideas, taken as a whole, may be self-serving, and even sinister in their implications, but are they paranoiagenic? In so far as they are founded on a worldview that is unconstrained in its perception of human possibility, his teachings unwittingly promote delusions of grandeur. In that sense his teachings are, indeed, paranoiagenic. Nietzsche himself was aware that many people would not be up to his philosophy of living beyond good and evil.[28]

We have been suggesting that Rajneeshism is essentially Rousseauan optimism redux. Perhaps the problem with such facile

---

28 Although arguments ad hominem are suspect, Nietzsche himself went mad and succumbed to delusions of grandeur; he would sign his name "Dionysus."

optimism is that it is founded, paradoxically enough, on a fundamental repression. When Freud used the term, "the return of the repressed," he was referring to sexually charged psychic events, to the Oedipus Complex and other dark matters. But here is a curious thing: when such sexually-infused content is no longer repressed—as is the case in our permissive society—other dimensions of human reality become repressed, a phenomenon that the existential psychologist Rollo May noted. (1969). What becomes repressed in such teachings is an awareness of the depths of human existence.

More specifically, what is repressed is an awareness of one's finitude, morality, the tragic dimension of sexuality and of life, the connection of sexuality with love and with death, and the inescapable sin and guilt connected with being a human being. When delusions of grandeur are in season—and they often have been in season since the 1960s — the awareness of the finitude that belongs to the human condition is repressed in this fashion, as it was in Rajneeshism.

But the awareness of finitude—mortality, the tragic, sin, guilt, and all else that constrains human aspirations—does emerge, and when it does, the paths that it then takes are often sinister. This reemergence may have many manifestations, of which the paranoid vision is one. It makes sense that the paranoid vision would emerge, for when that which has been repressed is finally recognized, the attitude of one who comes to see it may be a bitter resentment towards life, and then hatred towards some group of people who are blamed for having deflated one's delusions of grandeur. That is the sort of bitterness that Dostoevsky's Raskolnikov—perhaps the model for Nietzsche's pale criminal—experienced, when his inflated view of himself, his sense that he was a superman, came to grief. But Raskolnikov, thanks to Sonya's love and perhaps a sobering jail sentence, is saved from being tempted by the paranoid vision.

The downfall of Rajneesh and his organization, due to an immense hubris—its descent into paranoia, into criminality, into a life that was becoming increasingly like a prison camp—has the structure of a classical tragedy, the structure explored at the beginning of this chapter. It is as if that which had been repressed — such as the awareness of mortality, sin, and guilt—had reemerged in a rather demonic fashion to pursue the Rajneeshees. Except that for Rajneesh and his cohorts, the avenging Furies took the form of the Attorney General, the Immigration and Naturalization Service, the county sheriff, and other embodiments of the law, whose unstated mission it is to cure people of delusions of grandeur, paranoid or otherwise.

It might be said, then, that some are born paranoid, some achieve paranoia, and some have paranoia thrust upon them. Freud was born under the sway of the paranoid vision. Rajneesh, on the other hand, through a degeneration of spirit, opened himself up to possession by the paranoid vision. And the unfortunate disciples of both men had the paranoid vision thrust upon them. The paranoid vision can, therefore, have multiple etiologies.

Chapter Six

The Khmer Rouge

"But in the end paranoia, not enemies, was most responsible for bringing down the regime."

— *Elizabeth Becker (1986)*

ere we find the paranoid vision inspiring an event of horrifying enormity, the Cambodian genocide. A fuller understanding of its origins would require an historical and cultural analysis of Cambodia and its people, stretching back many centuries. It may be sufficient, though, to begin in 1941. That was the year that Prince Sihanouk began ruling Cambodia, as both king and as "elected official." He would remain in office for approximately the next thirty years. Sihanouk was a relatively benign dictator, certainly compared to what was to follow.

In the early 1970s, Sihanouk sought to nationalize the mostly foreign businesses and industries that supported his nation's economy. This was congruent with his overall philosophy of isolationism, economic self-sufficiency and, as Elizabeth Becker suggests (1986), a resistance to the forces of modernism. Considering that Cambodia had just freed itself from the yoke of ninety years of French colonialism, that it had suffered land grabs from Vietnam and Thailand, and that it was betrayed by the nations who promised freedom in exchange for their alliance in World War II, one can understand Sihanouk's sentiment about wishing for Cambodia to remain insulated (although, he was also motivated by wishing to maintain the monarchy, i.e. his own power). But Sihanouk's economic program had an adverse effect on Cambodia's economy. No doubt, the Cambodian economy was also dislocated, to some extent, by the American bombing raids of the Cambodian countryside designed to root out Viet Cong.

General Lon Nol staged a successful coup, with the aid of the United States. The U.S. had gotten involved because it wanted Sihanouk's assistance in its war against the Vietnamese, but Sihanouk had insisted on remaining neutral. When in power, Lon Nol proved to be far more corrupt than Sihanouk, and a far more ruthless and repressive dictator. Around that time, the Cambodian communist party, the Khmer Rouge, had formed a guerilla army, and began fighting the forces of Lon Nol. After a bloody civil war, the Khmer Rouge was victorious. These partisans then sought to transform Cambodia—which had been a predominantly Buddhist nation—into a communist utopia. Here is where the enigma of what happened begins, for as Becker states, "Cambodia became synonymous with misery, death, destruction, and despair. And with mystery" (1986, p. 19). The mystery, as Becker understands it, was how, after the devastating war that had ravaged the country, the Khmer would engage in an effort at social engineering that had such horrific consequences.

Certainly, the economic goals of the Khmer Rouge were wildly unrealistic, as utopian goals invariably are. Indeed, as Karl D. Jackson states, "Rice production was expected to treble in a single year if only enough enthusiasm and heroism could be mobilized to overcome the material obstacles" (1989, p. 62). The failure of the Khmer Rouge's ideologically-driven goals had paranoiagenic consequences. Robins and Post offer an illuminating example of this:

> The relation between programmatic failure and paranoid belief and behavior was best exemplified in Cambodia's most productive area, Battambang and its environs. The leadership ordered that the groups there be at least doubled. This improvement would be accomplished by the ethnically pure workers inspired by the new communist government and freed from the "servitude" of receiving material reward for their work. They would also be freed from Western fertilizers and insecticides. Of course, the brutalized, ill-fed, and often

inexperienced workers were not up to meeting the previous production level, much less doubling or tripling them. Productivity plunges. But for the leaders, failure did not lead to doubt of their ideology. Rather, they assigned the blame to ingrained capitalist habits and to traitors in the party. (1997, p. 250)

What is most significant, as Robins and Post indicate, is that in an effort to make sense of their failings, the leaders of the Khmer Rouge did not question the validity of their Marxist-Leninist economic and social theories. On the contrary, they fell entirely under the sway of the paranoid vision, with its specious explanatory and justificatory power. It was under the influence of that distorted way of seeing that the Khmer Rouge, between the years 1975 and 1979, murdered, by most accounts, over 1.7 million of their fellow Cambodians. Those who managed to survive the genocide had to endure an unimaginably repressive tyranny, one in which almost the entire population was essentially enslaved, had their family units destroyed through collectivization, and were in continual fear for their lives, lest they were found guilty of violating the slightest rule, such as showing up late to a meeting, or accidentally breaking a farm implement when working. Let us, then, examine how a nation can be transformed, almost overnight, into a nightmare realm, through the alchemy of the paranoid vision.

The Khmer are ethnic Cambodians. The Khmer Rouge (Red Khmer) were the communist party of Cambodia, whose leader, Saloth Sar, was known as Pol Pot.[29] They had actually been in existence since 1952, but only came into power in 1975. There are a number of scholars who contend that the United States' ruthless campaign of carpet bombing the Cambodian countryside — to rout out the Viet Cong, during the war in Viet Nam — was responsible for Cambodia's political destabilization, and that is what made it possible for the Khmer Rouge to come to power. Indeed, Kiernan (1996) contends that that bombing is the primary reason why the Khmer Rouge came to power, and why they became radicalized. There are, though, some

---

29 Sar chose the name Pol Pot because it was so common, like "Smith" or "Jones" to Americans. It was, therefore, congruent with the Marxist egalitarian ideal.

problems with that explanation. For one thing, the bombing ended in 1973, two years before the Khmer Rouge came to power.

Furthermore, Peter W. Rodman (1996) argues, in an article that is critical of Kiernan, that the Khmer Rouge's tyranny and murder were merely the implementation of an ideological vision that they had articulated way back in 1959, namely Marxism. No doubt the regime of Pol Pot was not pure Marxism, but Marxism with admixtures of the ideas of Jean Jacques Rousseau and Robespierre, strong elements of fascism, and the unique sadism of the Khmer Rouge. Secondly, communism was supposed to grow out of a developed stage of capitalism, something lacking in Cambodia. Lastly, it would appear that the leaders of the Khmer Rouge rejected the grand narrative endemic to classical Marxism of economic progress leading to a communist revolution. The Khmer Rouge were not interested in advancing beyond capitalism, but in immediately returning to a supposedly idyllic agrarian way of life.

Then again, there was never a regime—whether it be that of Lenin, Stalin Mao, Castro, etc.—that Marxists regard as pure Marxism. The key here is that they aspired to be Marxists, and it is that aspiration that is what is dangerous. More universally, one could say that it is not utopia—which never comes about anyway—but the aspiration to utopia that is dangerous.

Then there are those scholars—most notably Michael Vickery (1984) —who contend that the Khmer have always been a violent people, and what happened under the reign of Pol Pot was merely a continuation of this violence. Anthony Daniels disagrees with that view:

> Most writers, though, take the view that without ideology, without the ideas that Saloth Sar (later Pol Pot) and his small group of associates picked up in Paris in the 1950s, the history of Cambodia would have been very different and much less brutal. True, Cambodians have a record of brutality, perhaps even brutality of a particular kind — but is there any people that has not? Ideology raises brutality to a new level, and surely it isn't very difficult to see threads that connect Pol

Pot's regime to other Marxist regimes, as well as to Marx
himself. (2003, p. 1)

As both Rodman and Daniels suggest, at the very core of who
the Khmer Rouge were, and what they intended to do, was their
Marxist ideology. Marxism, like all utopian worldviews, has the
power to foment the paranoid vision. This is not to deny that there
were other significant factors that contributed to the Cambodian
holocaust. American bombing raids were merciless and played a part
in radicalizing the populace, as scholars like Short (2005) argue. The
character of the Cambodian people, no doubt, also played a part;
a number of scholars contend that Cambodians have a history of
bellicosity and cruelty, as is evident in their folk stories, even though
many visitors to Cambodia have found the people there to be warm
and friendly. Also influential was Cambodian nationalism, as well
as the extremely hostile xenophobic and racial attitude that Pol Pot
and his cohorts had towards other groups of people, especially their
neighbors, the Vietnamese. But, as will be evident, the primary
paranoiagenic factor was, indeed, Marxism.

The Khmer Rouge's economic goals were not only wildly
unrealistic; so were their social goals. Even by Marxist standards,
their goals were extreme, certainly in comparison to those of previous
Marxist regimes, such as those of Lenin, Stalin, Mao, Ho Chi Min, or
Castro. As David Chandler describes it:

> After emptying the cities, the revolutionary organization
> embarked on a program of social transformation that affected
> every aspect of Cambodian life. Money, markets, and private
> property were abolished. Schools, universities, and Buddhist
> monasteries were closed. No publishing was allowed;
> the postal system was abolished; freedom of movement,
> exchanging information, personal adornment, and leisure
> activities were curtailed. Punishments for infractions were
> severe, and repeat offenders were imprisoned under harsh
> conditions or killed. (1992, p. 1)

What can one derive, more essentially, from the Khmer Rouge's
brave new world? First of all, their notion of utopia is founded on a

primitivism, on a belief in an original innocence, of a very radical sort. As Francois Ponchaud states about the leadership of the Khmer Rouge, "As was true for many Khmers educated in the French tradition, the leaders held in admiration the work of Jean Jacques Rousseau, exalting the 'noble savage' corrupted by society" (anthologized in: Jackson, 1989, p. 160). This is the same sort of primitivism that inspired the Rajneeshees in Oregon, and which will be encountered again when we explore radical Islamism. It follows that the Khmer Rouge were anti-intellectuals, for they believed that thinking, knowledge, and all of the products of civilization destroy that original innocence.

Some years back, there appeared a book on the bestseller list by Robert Fulghum entitled *All I Really Need to Know I Learned in Kindergarten* (1993; 2004). Fulghum's book title could have been the political slogan of the Khmer Rouge, except that the Khmer Rouge took the idea literally; they actually abolished schools and universities. Apropos of this emphasis on innocence is the fact that the Khmer Rouge soldiers were very young; most were adolescents, and most were totally uneducated boys from the countryside. Many were in awe when they invaded Phnom Penh, and saw a city for the first time.

The Khmer Rouge put to death intellectuals, as well as anyone who was educated in a trade or profession, such as doctors, lawyers, college professors, and engineers. Mao also had always spoken disdainfully of the learned class. But Mao was just engaging in politically motivated revolutionary rhetoric. He was not so foolish as to actually kill those with an education, for he knew that his country needed such people. But Pol Pot brooked no such compromises with life's necessities. As Karl D. Jackson observes, "The truly extraordinary aspect of the Khmer revolution is the doctrinaire literalism with which they applied these [Marxist-Leninist] abstract principles without regard for the awesome costs to Cambodia in terms of diplomatic isolation, economic devastation, and massive human suffering" (1989, p. 44).

Consequently, anyone wearing glasses, or who had soft hands, or who spoke French or English, was branded an intellectual and was immediately dispatched to what became known as "the killing fields." All of these people, who were regarded as hopelessly corrupt —actually, they were referred to as animals, as lice, as germs, or with similar such imprecations—had to be killed if the millennium was to come. Apropos of this quest for the millennium, the Khmer Rouge created a new calendar, and regarded the present year, which then was 1975, as the year zero.

One of the Khmer Rouge's most notorious acts follows from their primitivism and their disdain for civilization (as symbolized by the city.) Shortly after seizing power they evacuated approximately three million people, the entire population of the city of Phnom Penh. Everyone was forced, at gunpoint, to abandon his homes, businesses, and profession. People who were very old, or who were being treated in hospitals, had to walk, along with three million other people, miles and miles into the countryside. Many died along the way. Those who survived then had to eke out a desperate existence, working twelve to fourteen hours a day, seven days a week—enduring malnutrition because of the extreme shortage of food, and disease because the doctors had been killed—in one of the many agricultural collectives that had been established throughout the land.

The pretext for this forced evacuation was that American planes would be dropping bombs on the city, which simply was not true. What, then, was the true reason for the evacuation? According to Jackson:

> The forced evacuation of Phnom Penh and the other major cities immediately after the victory of April 17, 1975, was for the outside world the single most inexplicable event of the Cambodian revolution. Understanding this policy requires reference to the paramount goals of political, economic, and cultural self-reliance. For the Khmer Rouge, the cities were the centers of foreign domination. (1989, p. 46)

Jackson is, no doubt, correct in his analysis. To the Khmer Rouge, the city represented foreign domination, for it was inhabited, as were the other Cambodian cities, by a wide variety of foreigners, and their influence was felt. But there may also be a symbolic reason for evacuating the cities. Pol Pot and his inner circle viewed the city as having a corrupting influence. They believed that not only Phnom Penh, but Cambodia itself, should be decimated, if necessary, so that it could be purified and saved from the defiling influence of foreigners. The title of a book by Robert J. Lifton is apropos to this discussion, *Destroying the World to Save It* (2000). There will be more to say about the symbolism of the city in the chapter on Radical Islam. Suffice it to say that the mystique of purity belongs, as we have seen, to the paranoid vision.

One can derive from Chandler's description of the Khmer Rouge's social and economic revolution not only its primitivism, but its extremism. There are a number of factors that contributed to this extremism. First of all, Cambodia had long been regarded as an economically backward country, one that was not yet part of the modern world. As Margolin states, "It was as though the real weakness of the regime, which went quite unrecognized, and the consequent feeling of insecurity that it engendered could be compensated only be an increase in violence" (1999, p. 632). Furthermore, Pol Pot lacked both the theoretical and the administrative brilliance of a Lenin, Mao, or even a Ho Chi Minh. Might there not be an inferiority complex at play here?

The sense of inadequacy and inferiority often leads to envy, and then to the need to prove one's worth. In regard to their sense of inferiority in relation to the Vietnamese, Short states, "The result was more than mere racial antipathy. It was a national inferiority complex, which took refuge in dreams of ancient grandeur" (2004, p. 25). The sense of inferiority can, therefore, lead to those delusions of grandeur that are associated with the paranoid vision. It is for that reason that Cambodia, under the Khmer Rouge, needed to prove that it was on the cutting edge of the communist revolution, no matter how many people were exterminated in the process.

A second reason for the insane pace of social transformation under the Khmer Rouge was a sense that change could only be accomplished through speed. After all, the revolution in China was traumatic enough, but Mao had made the Chinese undergo a relatively gradual transition to communism. Pol Pot, on the other hand, declared by fiat the existence of the new order of things. According to Margolin, the Khmer believed that the reason why China's Great Leap forward and the Cultural Revolution had failed was as follows:

...the Chinese had stopped at half-measures; they had failed to sweep away every counterrevolutionary obstacle: the corrupt and uncontrollable towns, intellectuals who were proud of their knowledge and presumed to think for themselves, money and all financial transactions, the last traces of capitalism, and "traitors who had infiltrated the heart of the Party." (1999, p. 632)

In that essay, Margolin also suggests that the extremism of the Pol Pot regime stemmed from a feeling of desperation. Pol Pot and his comrades suspected that they were late arrivals. They sensed that they were living in an age in which communism was in the throes of revisionism. That revisionism was due to the various communist regimes increasing awareness of the unbridgeable gap between Marxist-Leninist theory and the realities of the actual world. They realized that unqualified communism was proving to be problematic and unworkable in the Soviet Union, China, and elsewhere. Pol Pot and his cadres may not have suspected this in the 1950s, when they were students in Paris, full of the blinding idealism of youth. But they must have realized as much by the 1970s. It has been said that a fanatic is a person who redoubles his efforts when he suspects that what he is doing is impossible. That might be Pol Pot's epitaph. If communism was failing in other parts of the world, and was becoming subject to revisionism, then he must be all the more extreme, all the more ruthless, in his efforts to make it succeed in Cambodia.

Patrick Raszelenberg offers another interpretation of the extreme radicalism of the Khmer Rouge. He suggests that it was politically motivated, particularly in regard to Viet Nam:

"...the Khmer Rouges intended to attain communism by leaping over the socialist stage of development. Theirs would be the first truly communist society on earth, completely independent and self-reliant. Only then would Cambodia be able to withstand Vietnamese pressure and embark on a more aggressive policy toward its neighbor. Elements of this policy included the revindication of southern Vietnam as well as the expulsion of the Vietnamese from this area. After the initial

> internal stabilization of the situation, the Khmers Rouges
> pursued a policy of direct confrontation with the Socialist
> Republic of Vietnam, culminating in the explicit desire to
> wipe the Vietnamese off the face of the earth. (1999, p. 62)

Of course, this leads us to the question: why the need to exterminate the Vietnamese? The Khmer Rouge's racism derives from their paranoiagenic notion of an original purity, a purity made possible by the eradication of all that was foreign. Only when purity was achieved would the Khmer millennium arrive. Consequently, they sought the expulsion or eradication of everyone living in Cambodia who was not a Khmer, including those who were Vietnamese, Chinese, Thai, French, or American. Furthermore, Cambodian citizens who were not of Khmer descent were considered foreigners, and were dealt with in a similar fashion. A large number of these non-Khmer Cambodians, many of whom were of Vietnamese descent, and many of whom were Islamic Cambodians, were brutally killed. So it was that there were, for the Khmer Rouge, several classes of the impure. Most prominently they were the educated and the foreign, and the land had to be made pure through "ethnic cleansing."

Also rife were conspiracy theories about traitors within Khmer society, who supposedly had plotted with foreigners to overthrow the Khmer Rouge. Many of these theories revolved around the accused person working for the CIA. Since the foreigners were now gone, the only people left for the Khmer Rouge to blame were their fellow Khmer Cambodians, which led to what has been called an "auto-genocide," i.e. Cambodians killing Cambodians.

Like true paranoids, the Khmer Rouge projected their own ill will upon other people and other ethnic groups. Eventually, of course, their paranoid suspiciousness became a self-fulfilling prophesy, for their aggressiveness towards the Vietnamese — manifested by the repeated military incursions of the Khmer Rouge into Vietnam — prompted the Vietnamese army to invade Cambodia in 1979, which led to the end of the reign of the Khmer Rouge. Ironically, it was their avowed enemy who unwittingly ended their auto-genocide, probably saving an untold number of Cambodian lives.

As Becker reminds us, though, "But in the end paranoia, not enemies, was most responsible for bringing down the regime" (1986, p. 274). Becker then explains how those who might have been useful to the regime, and necessary in bringing about the renewal of Cambodia, were murdered, out of fear that they might be dangerous enemies. Here, again, is the ancient dialectic that was explored in the last chapter— immorality (the most egregious example of which is genocide) leading to paranoid madness (which results in indiscriminate murder), then leading to nemesis (invasion by an enemy army).

Tuol Seng Secret Prison (S-21)

As Foucault (1995) and other theorists have suggested, one can learn much about a society from its prison system. In the case of Cambodian society, during the nightmare years of 1975-1979, what one can learn is most revealing in terms of paranoid ideology. The Khmer had hundreds of detention centers throughout the countryside, which were essentially torture and death camps. But at the very heart of the Khmer Rouge horror show was their central prison, a secret detention center used to interrogate mainly those higher-ups in the Khmer Rouge, and their families, suspected by the Khmer Rouge of treachery. Indeed, eighty percent of those prisoners had been members of the Khmer Rouge. Tuol Seng, which was also known as S-21, might be viewed as a microcosm of the entire Cambodian nightmare. It can also, more generally, offer us insight into the mind of the conspiracy theorist, and into the paranoid vision.

As far as can be determined from the meticulous records that were kept, the overwhelming majority of these prisoners had been falsely accused of treason. There are a number of mysteries here. First of all, why falsely accuse those who obviously did not commit crimes? The analogy that David Chandler makes between Stalin and Pol Pot — especially in regard to the great show trials of 1938 in Moscow that preceded Stalin's purge — might help to answer that question:

> The elaborate confessions extracted in Moscow were orchestrated to please Stalin. They confirmed his often

> inchoate fear, preempted "enemy" initiatives, and strengthened his authority. In this respect, the Soviet purges and the confessions stemming from them closely resembled those extracted at S-21. (1999, p. 122)

What is particularly interesting is Chandler's notion that the trials confirmed the inchoate fears of these paranoids. Freud had said that human beings seek to transform anxiety into fear, for a fear is manageable, whereas anxiety is not. Similarly, the paranoid seeks to transform inchoate fears—which, one might say, are really paranoia-infused anxiety—into concrete conspiracy theories, with their perpetrators apprehended, put on trial, and then executed. This sort of scapegoating is a way of dealing with anxiety, although not a successful way, for it never confronts the real origin of that anxiety.

Would it have mattered to Stalin and Pol Pot—from the standpoint of managing their paranoia-laden anxiety—whether or not those about to be killed were actually guilty? Would it even have mattered whether, in all likelihood, those who were convicted of crimes were innocent? Apparently not, for the mere act of killing people instilled fear in their respective kingdoms and made these dictators feel more in control. Furthermore, totalitarian dictators are generally of the opinion that it is better to be safe than sorry; it is better to kill people just in case they are traitors.

All the same, how can one understand the fact that the Khmer Rouge murdered many young children, who were relatives of accused prisoners? The Khmer Rouge believed that young children were guilty because they were related by blood to the accused. There would appear to be a crude biologism and racism involved here. It may also be the case that the murder of the innocent was a symbolic way of propitiating the Moloch god of the totalitarian state. For the state to become renewed, the god demanded the pure blood of the innocent (Neumann 1970; 1995).

The accusations of treachery by their jailors might range from being counter-revolutionary to plotting the overthrow of their regime. It was not the only such prison run by the Khmer Rouge, but it was notorious for its brutality. Of the 14,000 prisoners who had been held there—which included men, women, and children—only seven were freed. The rest were severely tortured and interrogated, until they confessed to crimes that they did not commit. They were also tortured into implicating other innocent people. Finally, each prisoner was taken out into a field, beaten over the head with a metal club until dead, and buried in a shallow grave.

More specifically, they had to write a confessional autobiography, detailing how they had betrayed the party, and they had to invent some scheme of how they had gone about it. It was a kind of macabre creative writing project, in which the inducement for a lack of creativity was more severe torture. The final document then served as their last will and testament.

Each of the prisoners was, in essence, forced to create a conspiracy theory about himself or herself, and to implicate other people into their conspiracy. These forced confessionals then became the material in support of an elaborate super conspiracy theory. A man nicknamed Duch, the notorious head of S-21, was in charge of finding a thread among the many conspiracies contained in these confessionals. David Chandler, who interviewed over 500 former members of the Khmer Rouge after their regime collapsed in 1979, was able to assess Duch's role as head of S-21:

> Duch's neatly written queries and annotations, often in red ink appear on hundreds of confessions. They frequently correct and denigrate what prisoners confessed, suggest beatings and torture, and urge interrogators to unearth the buried "truth" that the prisoners are hiding. Duch also summarized dozens of confessions, pointing out the links he perceived with earlier ones and suggesting fresh lines of inquiry. (1999, p. 22)

Like all conspiracy theorists, Duch is a kind of primitive metaphysician, for the "reality" behind the appearance/reality distinction is a nefarious plot of some sort, which is buried and hidden. The fact that Duch had worked as a math teacher, i.e. he was a mathematician, was not insignificant, for we have seen that the prototypal conspiracy theorist is an abstract sort of person, with a top-down, a priori, way of seeing the world, a person who favors theory over experience, and who will gladly jettison the world of appearances in favor of the "real" world of theory. After all, experience is riddled with absurdity, but the world of theory is intelligible, or at least it seems that way.

All metaphysicians seek to explain how an apparent multiplicity is really one. The goal of conspiracy theorists is similarly to explain how all subplots are part of the one plot. Duch's "The Last Plan" was his conspiracist version of Einstein's Unified Field Theory. As Chandler describes it,

> The most elaborate of his memoranda, written in 1978, was titled "The Last Plan"; it attempted to weave two years worth of confessions into a comprehensive, diachronic conspiracy that implicated the United States, the USSR, Taiwan, and Vietnam. Like the late James Jesus Angleton of the CIA, Duch was mesmerized by the idea of moles infiltrating his organization. As a mathematician, he enjoyed rationally pleasing models. "The Last Plan" was his chef d'oeuvre. (1999, p. 22)

Chandler and other scholars of the Khmer Rouge have noted the comparisons to the confessions and conspiracy weaving that occurred during the Stalinist trials in Moscow in 1938. As noted earlier, coherence is the conspiracy theorist's criterion of validity. Of course, the dark irony is that a coherent theory need not, to their way of thinking, correspond to objective reality. Tucker and Cohen highlight the coherence thinking that was behind the Moscow purge trials of 1938, and compare that thinking to that which takes place in a paranoid delusional fantasy. In the introduction to their book about those trials, Tucker surmises:

> What unfolds before us in the trial, then, is a gigantic texture of fantasy into which bits and pieces of falsified real history have been woven along with outright fiction. It forms an elaborate unified system in the sense that everything hangs together in a coherent, logical, and internally self-consistent whole. The master theme running through it all and giving it a dramatic unity is the great anti-Soviet conspiracy. It furnishes

the motivation and therewith the explanation for hundreds
of events and incidents spoken of in the trial, many of which
really happened. Now this scheme bears a definite, and I
suggest further on, understandable resemblance to textbook
descriptions of a paranoid delusional system. (1965, p. xxiii)

Tucker is critical of Hannah Arendt, for he contends that it is not
totalitarianism as a system that lead to these trials, but merely the
psychopathology of Stalin. Tucker might appear to be right. After all,
had Trotsky, Bukharin, or someone else who had been in Lenin's inner
circle attained power, the history of the USSR, and of the world, would
have been far different. On the other hand, as political scientist Chris
Hables Gray points out, "Bakunin predicted a Stalin would arise from
Marxism and its pretense of scientism. Rosa Luxembourg predicted a
Stalin would arise from Leninism" (Gray 2005). If Stalin emerged out
of Marxism by a horrid dialectical necessity, then Tucker's criticism of
Arendt is incorrect.

Furthermore, in regard to Pol Pot's regime, how is one to explain
the fact that history repeats itself—in regard to the confessionals that
became part of a huge conspiracy—with the advent of the Khmer
Rouge? It is no doubt true that Pol Pot and the other higher-ranking
Khmer Rouge were influenced by Soviet history and admired Stalin.
That is one way to explain it. But most likely the reason why history
is repeating itself here is that both Stalin and the Khmer Rouge
shared a way of seeing, i.e., the paranoid vision. One must not dismiss
the possibility that totalitarianism was an essential cause of what
transpired in both the USSR and in Cambodia, for it may be that
totalitarianism, as a form of government, is not only a product of the
paranoid vision, but is itself paranoiagenic, and thus will eventually
give rise to a Stalin, as Bakunin and Luxembourg suggest.

There was a prisoner who did survive S-21 and wrote a book about
it, and what he has to say may further illuminate the Khmer Rouge
prison system, and the nature of their way of seeing. The ethnologist
and expert on Buddhist culture, Francois Bizot, who had been doing
field research on Cambodian Buddhism, was captured by the Khmer
Rouge and accused of spying for the CIA. Duch came to believe in
Bizot's innocence, and eventually had him freed. During the course of

his stay at Tuol Seng, Bizot had an opportunity to speak to Duch, and to try to understand him. Bizot's view of Duch is that he was anything but a cynic, for Duch was convinced that bringing communism to Cambodia would be the country's salvation. Ironically, Bizot saw that Duch was leading an "ethical life," one of honor and sacrifice, although for a wrong cause and committing atrocities to serve that end. Bizot even developed a certain fondness for Duch, whom he presents in his book as anything but a monster. In one passage, Bizot has a philosophical conversation with Duch, where he confronts the assumptions of all totalitarians:

> You are dreaming of a system intended to make man happy in spite of himself. When will we stop allowing men to die in the name of man? This notion of Man, with a capital M, lies at the root of so much suffering. The individual is always alone beneath the heavens; it's pointless to try to make him master of the world. (2003, p. 117)

As Bizot sees it—and he follows a long tradition of thinkers who have pursued this line of thought, from Dostoevsky to Camus—the problem with that type of true believer who become totalitarians lies in their abstractness. Apropos is an article that appeared in Atlantic Monthly about the Unabomber, Ted Kaczynski, another mathematician (a Harvard mathematics professor for a time). According to Alston Chase, here again is an abstract thinker, an idealist, who became a paranoid conspiracy theorist. Chase perceptively relates Kaczynski's way of seeing the world to the totalitarian worldview that ravaged the twentieth century. He mentions Stalin, but Duch and Pol Pot fit his picture:

> The real story of Ted Kaczynski is one of the nature of modern evil—evil that results from the corrosive powers of intellect itself, and its arrogant tendency to put ideas above common humanity. It stems from our capacity to conceive theories or philosophies that promote violence or murder in order to avert supposed injustices or catastrophes, to acquiesce in historical necessity, or to find the final solution to the world's problems—and by this process of abstraction to dehumanize

our enemies. We become like Raskolnikov, in Crime and Punishment, who declares, "I did not kill a human being, but a principle!"

"Guided by theories, philosophies, and ideologies, the worst mass killers of modern history transformed their victims into depersonalized abstractions, making them easier to kill. Much the way Stalin, citing Communist dogma, ordered the murder of millions of peasants toward "the elimination of the Kulaks as a class," so Kaczynski rationalized his murders as necessary to solve "the technology problem." (June 2000, pp. 41-65)

It is darkly ironic but understandable, then, that idealistic people like Duch, who become possessed by abstract, utopian ideals—and who have an unquestioned faith in the ability of social engineering to realize those ideals—end up becoming political mass murderers. Camus' notion of crimes of logic is relevant here again. Apropos is a curious comment that Stalin once made, "A single death is a tragedy, a million deaths is a statistic." It would seem that a proclivity for engaging in political abstractions coupled with a blind faith in social engineering is, from a moral perspective, the soil from which grows the most pernicious flowers of evil. From a psychological and epistemological perspective, such conditions are highly paranoiagenic, for they set up the Manichean us/them opposition that makes it possible to dehumanize and then to kill the enemy.

Why All the Blood?

Why is it that, after confessing, the prisoners were killed by the Khmer Rouge? After all, in China, Korea, and in Viet Nam, political prisoners were usually "reeducated," i.e. indoctrinated, or brainwashed, with the party's dogma. But there were no such reeducation efforts made by the Khmer Rouge. Death was the only option, and death was the punishment for even the smallest infraction, from stealing a piece of fruit to being related to someone who had already been executed by the Khmer Rouge. Even by the brutal standards of totalitarian political parties, the Khmer Rouge stands out as unique. There have been a number of theories put forth to explain the extreme horror of Pol Pot's regime, and why death, rather than reeducation, was considered the only option. Certainly, a clue may lie in the language that was employed by the Khmer Rouge to describe prisoners. As Chandler states:

> Pol Pot and his colleagues thought of Cambodia's internal enemies as intrinsically foreign and impure. Internal enemies could wreak enormous damage. In his "Last Plan," Duch compared their strategy to "the way the weevils bore into wood" or "the way oil permeates" and likened them to "worms" (dongkeau) or germs (merok) that had come from the CIA, Vietnam, and so on to attack healthy, revolutionary people. (1999, p. 44)

The fact that metaphors suggesting impurity, germs, infection, and disease are used is rather significant, for there is more than mere metaphor behind the language used. The language is the manifestation of a powerfully symbolic level of moral consciousness; i.e. what Ricoeur calls "the defilement level." In an earlier chapter, it became clear that both evil experienced as possession and as defilement are —in contrast to the notion of original sin, or perhaps what Kant called "radical evil"—experienced as something external that robs one's autonomy, or infects one with impurity.

The assumption, on that level of morality, is that one is originally pure. The sense of an original purity and an original grandeur, that were somehow lost—invariably because of other people—lends itself to utopianism and all the serious consequences that follow from utopian longings. The fact that evil on this level of moral consciousness is experienced as a quasi-material substance that infects a person, means that a person's thoughts, goals, and intentions, whether they be good or evil, are irrelevant regarding issues of fault.

If a person is viewed as completely infected, then there is no hope for reeducation or for ideological indoctrination, since the problem is not conceptual; it is quasi-biological. As Chandler states, "Once infected, anyone could infect others. Counterrevolution, unless it was nipped in the bud could become an epidemic" (1999, p. 44). Epidemics are serious affairs. With so much at stake, it is not surprising that death was considered the only option.

And yet, in Maoist China, this notion of defilement was also present, although the language used to describe prisoners was not as virulent. Furthermore, the Maoists had a notion of purification, and they believed that this purification could come about by reeducation. As to why, then, the Maoists believed in reeducation but the Khmer Rouge held a darker view is not entirely clear. It may be due to a failure of imagination on the part of the Khmer Rouge, a failure to imagine that anything more is possible for human beings. But if their death-dealing was due to a failure of imagination, this failure may itself be due to the utter extremism of Pol Pot's program, and to an impatience on account of that extremism.

There is another factor that might explain why reeducation was not an option. In our discussion of Rajneesh, we determined that he was a person with mixed motives. It does not bode well for the success of an enterprise when the leader of an organization, or a group of people in power, have mixed motives, for it usually means that one will succeed in neither objective. So it was with Pol Pot and his cadre. They wanted to bring about a Cambodian paradise, but they also had a darker motive. As Margolin states,

> It was much easier for the revolution in Cambodia to define what it opposed than actually to announce a positive program. For the most part, the Khmer Rouge sought revenge, and it was through this intention that they found most of their popular support, which then gained new impetus through radical collectivization. (1999, p. 619)

The desire for revenge often derives from the feeling of envy, or that impotent form of envy called "resentment," which Nietzsche perceived to lie at the root of much of what made the modern world go round. As Helmut Schoeck writes, "...the envious man does not so much want to have what is possessed by others as yearn for a state of affairs in which no one would enjoy the coveted object or style of life" (1966, p. 270). Certainly that desire to level down distinctions between people is the darker side of communism's rage for equality. That is often the root of the terrible violence in communist revolutions, and it was certainly a spur to the vengeful violence in Cambodia. Needless to say, Pol Pot was sinister enough to capitalize on that envy. As Quinn states, "Pol Pot sought out those from the bottom rung of society — those who were so envious of persons with more wealth that they would willingly strike them down" (1989, p. 236).

This desire for vengeance was a case of the have-nots envying the haves, but not simply in the material sense. There was a revengeful envy towards anyone who had any skills, who was educated in any way. As Margolin states, "Undoubtedly the aim was to crush anyone who showed exceptional qualities or the slightest sign of a spirit of independence..." (1999, p. 586) In any case, the envy that is the darker side of communism, which creates a sharp Manichean duality between haves and have-nots, is highly paranoiagenic. With that malevolent attitude in place, a program of reeducation would be out of the question, for it would militate against the longing for vengeance.

Thus the extreme violence of the Pol Pot regime stemmed from a mélange of dark feelings, including feelings of desperation, inadequacy, inferiority, impatience, and vengefulness. On the other hand, the extremism of the Pol Pot regime, its desperation, and the terror that it engendered — although bloodier than Maoist China30 — was really not all that unique. Lenin and his cohorts were also desperate, extreme, and murderous. What Stephane Courtois writes about Lenin and the Bolsheviks could just as well have been written about the Khmer Rouge:

> In a desperate attempt to hold onto power, the Bolsheviks made terror an everyday part of their policies, seeking to remodel society in the image of their theory, and to silence those who, either through their actions or by their very social, economic, or intellectual existence, pointed to the gaping holes in the theory. Once in power, the Bolsheviks made Utopia an extremely bloody business. (1999, p. 738)

In regards to a paranoia-inspired desperation, Pol Pot bears an even closer resemblance to Stalin. As Kenneth M. Quinn states,

---

30 A great many more people died in Maoist China than died in Cambodia during the period when Pol Pot was in power. A certain percentage were murdered, died in prison, or died from having to participate in long marches. But most died due to Mao's agricultural economic policies — which Mao derived from his reading of Marx — the result of which was massive starvation, and the unnecessary death of approximately 20 million people.

"...it appears that early Soviet practices influenced [the Khmer Rouge's] behavior regarding the use of violence. In short, Pol Pot was implementing Mao's plan with Stalin's methods." (1989, 236) It is clear, then, the path that the Khmer Rouge took, from desperation to murderous methods.

The Intellectual Origins of Pol Pot and Friends

Unlike Freud or Rajneesh, Pol Pot was not charismatic. In that sense, he would not appear to be the prototypal paranoid leader. Then again, one of the most paranoid leaders of all time, Joseph Stalin, was said to have had a rather bland personality. Pol Pot went even further than that; he actually sought obscurity. Apparently, during the first year that he was in power, few people even knew that the Khmer Rouge had a leader. He was simply referred to as Brother Number One. This makes sense within the organizational culture of the Khmer Rouge, for there was a strong need for egalitarianism, or at least to believe that it existed. It would appear, then, that a cult of personality is not requisite for the existence of a paranoid organization.

Furthermore, Pol Pot did not have the personality characteristics typically associated with paranoids. He was not "outwardly" suspicious, hostile, fearful, and all the rest. A number of historians went to Cambodia after the Khmer Rouge were routed and removed from power by the North Vietnamese. They did interviews with people who knew Pol Pot, and reported that most people regarded him as rather friendly, if not saintly. Short's description of Pol Pot (Saloth Sar until 1970), is quite amazing:

> To all appearances, he was still the same soft-spoken, smiling, amiable man who, as a student in Paris, was remembered for his sense of fun and good companionship; who later, as a teacher in Phnom Penh, had been adored by his pupils; and who finally as a communist, was valued for his ability to bring together different tendencies and groups. His revolutionary alias in the 1960s reflected his reputation. He called himself Pouk, meaning 'mattress', because his role was to soften conflicts. (2004, p. 190)

All this is very perplexing, for how could someone like this be a monster? That is the same question that one derives from reading Bizot's description of Duch, the head of S-21. There is no doubt, though, that he was pathologically paranoid, as was Duch, and there was no doubt about the depth of his moral depravity.

Greater knowledge about Pol Pot's childhood and insight into his personality would have been helpful, but all such information might be beside the point anyway, for the key to understanding Pol Pot, as well as his closest associates in the Khmer Rouge, lies in their ideas. Although these people were anti-intellectuals in a way that only intellectuals can be, ideas for them were not merely academic. On the contrary, they took ideas seriously enough to wager their lives on some of them.

What were their intellectual influences? It is common knowledge that as young men in the 1950s they studied philosophy in Paris, at the Sorbonne. As professor Gregory H. Stanton, founder and director of the Cambodian Genocide Project states, "The Khmer Rouge leaders read the Marxist theorists of the day, people like Jean-Paul Sartre..." (1987, p. 1) Actually, they learned about existentialism as well as communism directly from their esteemed professors, Jean-Paul Sartre and Maurice Merleau-Ponty.

Sartre, at that time, was seeking to reconcile existentialism with Marxism, an effort that resulted in his book Critique of Dialectical Reason, which he started writing in 1957, and published in France in 1960. Merleau-Ponty's Marxist sympathies had emerged earlier in his book Humanism and Terror published in 1947. Pol Pot was also influenced by the ideas of France's leading communist thinker at the time, Louis Althusser. What, of course, interests us in the ideas of these philosophers is the paranoiagenic potential of their ideas.

In an intriguing essay, the philosopher Waller Newell explores the roots of Pol Pot's thinking. The connection that Newell makes between postmodernism and Pol Pot would seem to be dubious, for postmodernism rejects all "grand narratives," including that of Marxism. More convincing is the connection that Newell makes between Heidegger on the right, and Frantz Fanon[31] on the left, to Pol Pot. As Newell understands it:

> Following Heidegger and Fanon, leaders like Lin Piao, ideologist of the Red Guards in China, and Pol Pot, student of leftist philosophy in France before becoming a founder of the Khmer Rouge, justified revolution as a therapeutic act by which non-Western peoples would regain the dignity they had lost to colonial oppressors and to American-style materialism, selfishness, and immorality. A purifying violence would purge the people of egoism and hedonism and draw them back into a primitive collective of self-sacrifice. (2001, p. 2)

Purifying violence? That is a rather disturbing notion! Unfortunately, it is far from an unusual notion, finding expression since ancient times, and most prominently in the twentieth century in fascistic myths of nationalistic rebirth, or what the scholar of fascism, Robert Griffin, calls "palingenesis," or national rebirth (1991). Perhaps what is disturbing about the notion of purifying violence is not simply that it reeks of death, but that it is a demonic perversion of a high-level enterprise: the religious and philosophical effort to purify one's soul, not by violence, but of violence! Violence, murder, and terror became means to bring about the perfect society.

Dostoevsky has often been attributed with the quote "If there is no God, everything is permitted." Although neither Dostoevsky, nor even his character Ivan Karamazov, actually said that, it is fair to say that it is derivative of Ivan's ideas. It also derives from Sartre's atheistic brand of existentialism, which removes all ultimate grounding from one's actions. Pol Pot's inner circle did not have any trouble realizing the implications of such ideas.

For Sartre, one's identity does not have a divine, eternal, or transcendent dimension. On the contrary, one's identity (one's essence) is determined by one's actions (one's existence). There is nothing in Sartre's philosophy to suggest that human life has any intrinsic value apart from what one makes it through one's actions.

---

31   Fanon was a proponent of violent revolution to overcome colonialism. Sartre had written an introduction to Fanon's book, The Wretched of the Earth (1965). In a footnote, Jackson states, "Fanon, in turn, is related to an older apostle of apocalyptic violence, Georges Sorel." p. 246). What is intriguing, from the standpoint of the paranoid vision, is that notion "apocalyptic violence."

The notion that human beings can create value may initially seem liberating, but it is really rather dubious. It is, as Kierkegaard suggested, like Baron Munchausen trying to literally lift himself up in the air by his own bootlaces. In other words, a ground, meaning, or purpose is that which transcends a person; if it is not ultimate, it is, from the standpoint of serving as an organizing principle for human existence, really worthless. It is absurd to imagine that one can be one's own ground.[32] But this is where the rubber meets the road: the loss of the transcendent or eternal standpoint means that human life does not possess an intrinsic value.

If human life has no intrinsic value—a value that had formerly been founded on the possibility of human beings partaking of the infinite and the eternal—what separates human beings from the other members of the animal kingdom? Whatever were Pol Pot's ideological assumptions, he was confronted by that question, and his conclusion, apparently, was that nothing at all separates the human realm from the animal realm.[33] As Erik von Kuehnelt-Leddihn trenchantly states, "[Pol Pot], like his red colleagues, took to its final logical conclusion the Marxist philosophy that deems man a 'higher animal,' a cousin, if a remote one, of rats, bedbugs, earwigs, and other pests susceptible to extermination" (1990, pp. 318-319). [34]

Marx determined that violence was often necessary for a communist revolution to succeed. Apparently, Sartre agreed with Marx on that score, for he was an apologist for Stalin, and he was for the FLN murdering European civilians in Algeria. Furthermore, in a magazine article, Sartre justified the killing of eleven Israeli athletes

---

32 Kierkegaard had referred to the effort to be one's own ground as "the despair of defiance," for the effort to defy the entrance of the divine into the realm of the human is hopeless, and soon plunges anyone who takes this false path through the labyrinth of life, into despair. The problem, for our purpose, is when such despairing individuals attain power over other people's lives.

33 There are many others who are confronted by this same question, such as the behaviorists and, more generally, the many other varieties of materialists, in addition to Marxists. But we shall not expatiate on that here.

34 Were von Kuehnelt-Leddihn alive today, he might find that there exists at least one other group who have taken Marxist materialism and egalitarianism to its logical conclusion, namely the radical ecologists, some who engage in acts of terrorism, who would seek to preserve -- even at the cost of human life -- rats, bedbugs, and earwigs, should they become endangered species.

by Palestinian terrorists at the 1972 Olympics in Munich (Sartre, 1972). He also supported Castro who has had many people murdered. We are, of course, uncertain as to what degree, if any, Sartre's ideas influenced Pol Pot and his student friends. What is likely, though, was that the ideas of Sartre, Merleau-Ponty, Althusser, and other thinkers were in the air, so to speak. It was part of the intellectual milieu of the Sorbonne at the time. Marxism was in the air, which is understandable because these Cambodians were seeking to rebel against French colonialism, and Marxism seemed to provide the necessary ideology.

Short claims that earlier revolutionaries, like Robespierre, had seen violence as a means to an end. As Short states, "But in Cambodia in the mid-1970, the glorification of violence went further. In Pol's mind bloodshed was cause for exaltation." (2004, p. 248) Short then quotes the sanguinary Khmer Rouge's revolutionary anthem:

> Bright red blood covers the towers and plains
> Of Kampuchea[35] our motherland,
> Sublime blood of the workers and peasants,
> Sublime blood of the revolutionary men and women fighters!
> The Blood changes into unrelenting hatred
> And resolute struggle.
>
> [Which] frees us from slavery. (qtd. in Short 2004, p. 248)

It is not clear why Short feels that the glorification of bloodshed is unique to the Cambodian revolution. After all, consider some lines from the French national anthem, The Marseillaise:

> Arise you children of our motherland,
> Oh now is here our glorious day!
> Over us the bloodstained banner
> Of tyranny holds sway!
> Of tyranny holds sway!
> Oh, do you hear there in our fields
> The roar of those fierce fighting men?
> Who came right here into our midst
> To slaughter sons, wives and kin.

---

35 "Kampuchea" is another name for Cambodia.

REFRAIN
March on, march on!
And drench our fields
With their tainted blood !

It would appear to be the case that the sense of bloodshed, in both revolutions, and as expressed in both national anthems, has a purgative or cathartic sense to it. If evil is to be experienced in the quasi-biological sense as a stain, or infection, then it follows psychologically that the cure for evil will involve a cleansing or purification, and that it will have that blood letting sense to it. Of course, even the revolutionary Thomas Jefferson said, "The tree of liberty must be nourished by the blood of patriots." But Jefferson saw this as a necessary evil, not a virtue in itself.

It has been noted that Marxists have a proclivity to argue that the murder and mayhem found in any particular Marxist regime — from Lenin's to Pol Pot's — is a mere aberration, an exception, and not true Marxism. But when every single Marxist, or communist, or social democratic regime is regarded as an exception, one has to become a bit suspicious. Consequently, one must concur with the historian Richard Pipes who states, "Just as the Holocaust expressed the quintessential nature of national Socialism, so did the Khmer Rouge rule in Cambodia (1975-78) represent the purest embodiment of Communism: what it turns into when pushed to its logical conclusion..." (2001, p. 132).

What part, then, did the paranoid vision play in the Cambodian holocaust and other such social and political catastrophes? First of all, there exists a discrepancy between millennial, or utopian, visions— such as those that derive from Marx—and the actual spatiotemporal world, in all of its fluidity, which countermands the realization of such monolithic ideals. That discrepancy, between ideals and reality, engenders the disappointment and bitterness that is paranoiagenic.

Secondly, there exists another class of ideas that are not millennial, but tend towards nihilism, i.e. they are nihilistigenic, and, as such, are paranoiagenic. Sartre's existentialism, for example, is un-grounding, unbalancing, and disorienting, for it removes all the familiar ontological and moral signposts that had existed in the past, whose purpose was to tell one who one really is, where one is going, and where one is supposed to be headed. (It is evident that Rajneesh, too, was lured to such ontologically disorienting ideas.)[36]

One can understand, then, the appeal of worldviews that promise to offer meaning, purpose and orientation. European intellectuals in particular have a proclivity to admire men of violence, such as Che Guevara, who seem to be able to act untroubled by hamstringing deeper questions. Sartre fell prey to this, as did Camus initially, but Camus eventually woke up. In a recent New York Times review of Ronald Aronson's new book on *Sartre and Camus,* Edward Rothstein writes, "...Camus found himself ever more repulsed by Communism, which he called 'the modern madness.' He saw Communism as a desperate attempt to create meaning and certainty. He wrote, 'Those who pretend to know everything and settle everything finish by killing everything.'" (2004, p. 2)

Now this is the curious thing: If Marxism was able to provide meaning and certainty there would be no ontological devolution, no moral sliding, from Marxism to the paranoid vision, but inevitably there is. Neither Marxism, nor fascism, nor any other radical ideology can successfully militate against the disorientation created by the real "specter haunting Europe," and America too, the specter of meaninglessness. Consequently, the paranoid vision always appears, for the paranoid vision is a desperate quest for reorientation. Pol Pot and his inner circle gave dramatic expression to this philosophical dialectic, whose last stage is often murder. In the next chapter, we shall see what happens when radical Islam attempts to flee the disorientation of the present age, by seeking to return to their own mythic vision of an imagined glorious age.

---

36 As we stated in the introduction, we are neither recommending nor not recommending a return to lost values. We are merely observing the connection between their loss the emergence of the paranoid vision.

Afterword: Genocide as Symptom of Multiple Ailments

The ideological roots of the Cambodian genocide are obviously not the roots of all genocides. After all, genocide has been perpetrated since biblical times. The American massacre of the Indians, for example, was an "ethnic cleansing" whose cause was simply greed for land, and whose specious justification ranged from manifest destiny to racial superiority. Similarly, those who perpetrated the Armenian genocide, which claimed the lives of over a million Armenians, were not Marxists, but Turks.

It is, therefore, debatable whether genocide, and murder in general, is more prevalent today than in an age of faith. Philosophers —like Marx, Sartre, and Fanon—may have had a undermining influence on mores and morals, and therefore a pernicious influence on the social and political realm. But it is uncertain whether or not their ideas have actually added to the already murderous potential of human beings. There is always the temptation to imagine that the present age is entirely the root cause of present problems. It would seem, though, that human beings have not significantly changed in their most fundamental aspects—such as their destructive potential —despite great differences in places, times, and cultures, throughout history. Whether or not human beings are more murderous in the present age is, in any case, an important question, but one that won't be resolved here. Nor will it be resolved whether or not the paranoid vision is implicated in all genocides.

If genocide can arise in different times and places, all with different zeitgeists, it may then be that genocide is not a disease in itself, but a deadly symptom whose cause could be any of a variety of diseases, ranging from those that are ancient to those that are modern, from those that are related to religious beliefs to those that are products of a secular ideology such as fascism or Marxism. On the other hand, the fact that genocide may arise under very different circumstances —some of which are, for example, quite foreign to Marxism—does not nullify the fact that in the case of the Cambodian genocide, Marxist ideology, allied with other deadly factors, played a highly significant role. Certain ideologies, which are paranoiagenic, are not the cause of human destructiveness, but they can greatly exacerbate it.

Chapter 7

Islamism as Paranoid Reaction to Modernity

"This paranoid Islam, which blames outsiders, 'infidels,' for all the ills of Muslim societies, and whose proposed remedy is the closing of those societies to the rival project of modernity, is presently the fastest growing version of Islam in the world."

— *Salman Rushdie (2001)*

The previous case examples were about paranoid organizations. Now we shall explore an entire ideology, one that derives from the paranoid vision. Wherever Islamism has taken root, there has emerged a harsh Manichean duality of believers versus infidels, sinister conspiracy theories, apocalyptic fantasies, hate-filled screeds, rabid anti-Semitism, and vituperative propaganda.

Sometimes referred to as militant Islam, radical Islam, or Islamic fundamentalism, Islamism contends that Islam has lost its former glory because Muslims have neglected to follow the Shariah, or Islamic holy law. But Islamism not only demands that Muslims return to Shariah. It seeks to make the entire world Islamic, and to accomplish this mass conversion by means of jihad, or holy war.

The Qur'an highly praises jihad, but we contend that what primarily motivates those who do set out on that violent path, or who are sympathetic to those who do, is neither piety nor virtue, but the paranoid vision. Steeped in conspiracy theories and apocalyptic fantasies, Islamists believe that America, Israel, and other "crusader" nations have plotted to destroy Islam, and that they are called upon to defend it.

Islamism and Islam are, of course, different phenomena. Daniel Pipes clearly distinguishes between the two, in several important respects:

> Traditional Islam seeks to teach humans how to live in accord with God's will, whereas Islamism aspires to create a new order. The first is self-confident, the second deeply defensive. The one emphasizes individuals, the latter communities. The former is a personal credo, the latter a political ideology. (Pipes, 2000, p. 5)

The key difference, then, is that Islam is a religion, whereas Islamism is a political ideology. Pipes' observation that "Islamism aspires to create a new order" (1998b) refers to Islamism's utopianism. Paradoxically, the new order that it wishes to create consists of a revival of an old order, one dating back to the seventh century, which was the time when Mohamed was alive. Islamism provides an illuminating example of the paranoiagenic potential of such utopian revivalism, and its dangerous consequences.

Furthermore, Pipes mentions that Islamism is "deeply defensive." Consider, for example, Osama bin Laden's response when an interviewer asked him if he was a terrorist: "They rip us of our wealth and of our resources and of our oil. Our religion is under attack. They kill and murder our brothers. They compromise our honor and our dignity and dare we utter a single word of protest against the injustice, we are called terrorists." (1998b, p. 1) As we shall see, it is very common for terrorists[37]—who are often given the euphemism "insurgents," or "freedom fighters"—as well as those who commit genocide, to feel vindicated in committing murder because they are defending their culture, society, religion or way of life. Paranoid defensiveness makes the politics of identity a desperate affair.

---

37 For the sake of clarity, we shall be using "terrorism" to mean acts of aggression against unarmed civilians that are not state-sponsored.

Although preoccupied by religion, it will be evident that Islamists are primarily motivated not by a theology, but by an ideology, a fundamentalist form of totalitarianism. We shall then consider the arguments, put forth by some scholars, that Islamism is a recrudescence of a set of certain anti-Western notions stemming from a variety of sources—from German romanticism to the Russian Slavophiles.

Theocratic Totalitarianism

Islamism has been referred to as "theocratic totalitarianism," to distinguish it from the secular variety, which gained notoriety in Nazi Germany and the Soviet Union. Whether secular or theocratic, totalitarian societies are, to use Popper's term, "closed societies," meaning that they are ideologically monistic, allowing for only one set of ideas, the so-called party line, to be believed, discussed, and implemented. What is known as "religious fundamentalism" is essentially theocratic totalitarianism. It is the wish to have an entire society and polity strictly conform to a certain set of religious rules, usually rigorous ones, which are held to be absolute. As in all forms of totalitarianism, questioning the existing social and political order is not tolerated. Opinions that are contrary to those of the ruling religious authorities are regarded as heresy, and draconian punishments are meted out.

Totalitarianism is the antithesis not only of pluralism, but also of individualism, the belief that each person should be free to decide how to live his or her life. In a democracy—one that is founded on the rule of law and that allows for free speech, freedom of worship, and freedom of the press—diverse opinions and individual goals are sanctioned. The state's function (at least under the social contract notion of government of John Locke) is limited to protecting the life, liberty, and property of its citizens. Totalitarianism, by contrast, is the belief that the members of a society or nation have no reality or value in themselves. The source of true reality and value is the state or in the case of theocratic totalitarianism, the church/state. A member of a totalitarian nation has the status not of a citizen, but of a subject — and sometimes merely that of a servant, or of a slave — of the state. As Trifkovic (2002) maintains, in regard to Islamism, "...at all times

Allah is the master and man is the slave." Appropriately enough, totalitarian social organization has often been compared to that of an ant colony, for all "thinking" and action are monolithic. It is guided by one intelligence, one purpose, one goal. At least that is the ideal.

That particular totalitarian vision then becomes a battle cry. Trifkovic quotes V.S. Naipaul as stating that, "There probably has been no imperialism like that of Islam and the Arabs…Islam seeks as an article of faith to erase the past; the believers in the end honor Arabia alone; they have nothing to return to…" (qtd. in Trifkovic, 2002, p. 89) The implications for individuality, ego-identity and selfhood are devastating, for as Trifkovic states, "The vanquished were 'culturally disemboweled,' condemned to the enforced psychosis of renouncing their old and highly developed identities for a crude and violent desert blueprint that regulated the minutest details of their personal lives" (2002, p. 90).

One is reminded, in this regard, of Arendt's distinction between tyranny and totalitarianism. The former only demands one's material goods and political allegiance, but the latter demands all that as well as one's individuality, mind, and soul.

For Islamists, the non-separation of church and state means that there is no secular realm, for the existence of such a realm would limit Allah's sphere of influence, thus fragmenting the overarching totalitarian unity. In some of the most repressive totalitarian dictatorships, even a person's leisure time is controlled, as it was under the rule of the Taliban in Afghanistan. Nor is a separate economic realm allowed to exist. Some Islamist thinkers, such as Sayyid Qutb, advocated the abolition of free market capitalism altogether. Qutb would have even abolished the interest on loans, for he considered it usury, and in conflict with Islamist morality. So it is that totalitarianism, with its ideological monism, requires that all domains of human existence — from marriage to morality, from child rearing to economics — conform to a single uniform theme, i.e. the social and political ideology dictated by the state.

It would be naïve to think that, in most cases, totalitarian regimes are simply imposed upon peoples longing to be free. As excellent a thinker as Natan Sharansky is, one derives a sense from his book *The*

Case for Democracy (2004) that people just want to be free. They often do want very much to be free. But, because human beings are creatures of contradiction, they can also wish to jettison the burden of responsibility that comes with being free. Thus one learns from writers like Huxley, Orwell, Fromm, and Hoffer about the inner wish to conform, not to have to think for oneself. As Camus observed, "The real passion of the twentieth century is servitude" (1951; 1956, p. 54).

That passion for servitude is related to the flight from freedom, as analysts like Fromm (1941; 1996) point out, but it runs deeper than that. The lure of totalitarianism derives from an inner epistemological demand. At the core of "totalitarianism" is the notion of "totality," which Kant regards as a category of reason.[38] A totality is, of course, a unity of the many in the one. The quest to make sense of it all, to render the world intelligible, to give coherence and shape to one's experience, to "get it together" so to speak, i.e. to organize it all into a totality, is one of the most fundamental of human longings. It is not that one has any choice in the matter; one must continually seek order, intelligibility, unity, totality, and self-identity, for that, according to Kant, is how the mind operates.

In some spheres of human existence, the use of the category of totality is not problematic. For example, the mind unconsciously employs that category when it requires that paragraphs cohere into a chapter, and that chapters cohere into a book. Similarly, a living room has aesthetic appeal when the furniture is arranged into a grouping, which is the aesthetic manifestation of a totality; people say that it all comes together. But human beings are neither chapters in a book, nor pieces of furniture, nor parts of any whole. This is not to deny that they can willingly participate in a larger whole. And, in doing so, they need not lose their integrity as individuals. But in totalitarianism that integrity is not respected. Thus the unconstrained use of the notion of totality is a dangerous affair. Kant had warned that the uncritical use of pure reason leads to dogmatic theories in science and philosophy, but Kant lived before the category of reason would enter into the political realm, i.e. before the advent of totalitarianism.

---

38 Cf. Kant's "axioms of intuition," from his *Critique of Pure Reason*.

Camus sees a connection between the philosophical longing for unity and its political expression, in the form of totality. He observes, "Totality is, in effect, nothing other than the ancient dream of unity common to both believers and rebels, but projected horizontally onto an earth deprived of God" (1951; 1956, p. 233). The totalitarian dream to which Camus refers is to replace unity in God, which is always an individual matter, with the ersatz unity of everyone acting totalistically, i.e. in accord with the same idea. The latter totalitarian dream of unity is that of human society made into something akin to an ant colony.

Apropos are Dostoevsky's insights from that chapter of *The Brothers Karamazov* entitled "The Legend of The Grand Inquisitor." Dostoevsky's story suggests that theocratic totalitarianism, or fundamentalism, is really the longing to replace God with "the Grand Inquisitor," a religion/ideology that offers one material and spiritual security. Most importantly, the Grand Inquisitor offers one freedom from all the doubts that are intrinsic to having a true relation to the divine, by telling everyone what to believe. After all, true religious faith does not bring certitude but often brings, according to Kierkegaard, "fear and trembling" before the unknown. Again, one recalls that even Christ was subject to doubt, which is the reason for his asking God why he had been forsaken.

But theocratic totalitarianism goes beyond the desire for material security and spiritual certitude. The command to conquer the world through holy war is an unholy command, predicated upon something akin to a Faustian bargain. Of course, it is not quite the same. One rejects the promise of Heaven, but not for the material joys of this world—Helen of Troy, and all the rest—that Faust demanded. Here is a different sort of deal, one whose consequences are not just foolish like the deal that Faust struck, but downright horrifying. Satan realizes that the fatal flaw of theocratic totalitarians is their impatience. They do not seek the heavenly state of being that is a function of a transformation of consciousness. They seek the millennium, and they seek it now, on this earth. If they cannot have the millennium now, then death for themselves and for everyone else is the only other alternative.[39] And so it is a vision of the millennium that Satan offers them. They imagine that the manifestation of God's glory would consist in a world in which everyone unquestionably obeys the laws of Shariah, or the laws of any other totalitarian doctrine, and where there are no infidels to ruin the image of perfect harmony.

The image of human beings blindly obeying, like a colony of ants, or bees, or obedient bureaucrats—the will of the Grand Inquisitor, or the Fuehrer or the Grand Ayatollah—s a truly banal image of perfection. It is banal for it seeks totality by negating the richness, plenitude, and diversity of human beings, as well as that which distinguishes human beings from all other beings, the capacity for free choice. Freedom cannot be valued if the notion of predestination is a fundamental tenet of a theology.

The idolization of earthly images of totality absorbs the energies that might have been devoted to an encounter with God. Of course, one could object that the Islamist is truly religious, for Islamism is very much concerned with having its votaries devote themselves to sacred law, and would abolish the secular realm altogether, if it could. But human beings are infinitely clever in their self-deceptions, and an adherence to law and rituals—and Islam is a thoroughly legalistic religion (Gould, 2005)—can be a way of protecting one from an encounter with the sacred, which Christ recognized long ago.

As Laqueur writes, "Radical Islam is a new religion characterized by an absence of love and true piety that have been replaced by the strict observation of religious rituals" (1996, p. 167). There cannot be much love and piety when one's energy has been channeled into a paranoiac hunt for infidels. Furthermore, some of the most extreme Islamists have perverted religion by reifying, objectifying, or

---

39 Amir Taheri, the Iranian journalist, analyzes the impatience of the terrorist with great clarity, "Politics is a serious business which requires hard work. It needs to find ways of keeping society in harmony while meeting its basic needs and creating conditions for economic, social and cultural development. Writing a poem, erecting a building, composing a symphony, painting a miniature, compiling a theological study, and making a film are not easy. But making a car-bomb is....The terrorist has no need of developing policies, building alliances, and mobilizing popular sentiment for his program. All that is hard work, just like winning free elections. The terrorist does not like hard work; he is in a hurry and wants a short-cut, even if that means turning himself into a human bomb. The terrorist has no patience with the lesser mortals who argue, answer back, and refuse to commit to anything unless convinced by rational analysis. All that means politics; something the terrorist is afraid of. He has no time to brew a proper coffee; an instant coffee is all he seeks" (2005, p. 2).

materializing it. An example of such materialization is a notion that seems to be particularly popular amongst suicide bombers: the reward for martyrdom is the gift in heaven of seventy-two black-eyed virgins.

What is the essential reason why totalitarianism ends up creating so much misery, if not a downright hell on earth? Human reason, operating uncritically, creates a gap, or a disproportion, between what the mind believes the world should be—i.e. a utopian dream of everyone and everything joyfully organized into a harmonious totality —and the way that the world actually is, i.e. forever recalcitrant to any effort to bring it all together into any sort of overarching totality. For example, it is absurd to think that most human beings are going to work extra hard and be entrepreneurial, without the chance of individual gain. Maybe some monks will, but few people are willing to live like monks. Is it any surprise, therefore, that totalitarian societies —particularly those that are communistic or theocratic—often end up impoverishing the lives of their citizens?

The gap between the ideal and the actual grew to immense proportions in the first part of the Twentieth Century, for that was a time in which dictators sought to make their societies conform to their utopian visions of goodness, beauty, truth, and reality. Despite the power of these dictators and their hordes of true believers, they could not bridge the gap between their utopian ideals and the actuality of lived life in the totalitarian state. Islamism creates this same gap. As Fukuyama writes:

> An Islamic theocracy is something that appeals to people only in the abstract. Those who have had to live under such regimes, for example in Iran and Afghanistan, have experienced stifling dictatorships whose leaders are more clueless than most on how to overcome problems of poverty and stagnation. (2002, p. 14)

If the effort to bridge the gap between the ideal and the actual is undertaken with a fanatical zeal, it invariably proves socially, economically and politically disastrous, as would be any effort to place life upon the procrustean bed of a totalitarian theory. It also creates a great deal of cognitive dissonance. This is where the paranoid vision enters the stage. It is an effort to explain why the gap between the ideal and the real exists.[40] It always comes down to assigning blame; a certain group of nefarious individuals has conspired to subvert what could have been utopia. Islamists blame "the infidels." Consequently, if absurdly convoluted conspiracy theories abound in the Middle East—Daniel Pipes provides ample evidence that they do—it is because these theories are attempting to bridge the impossibly wide gap between visions of Islamist glory and the actual state of Islamist societies today. Furthermore, those under the sway of the paranoid vision concoct apocalyptic fantasies, mad dreams of a time when there will no longer be a gap between the ideal (totality realized) and the real. Islamism is highly apocalyptic.

Rising expectations, by their very nature, widen the gap between what people believe is possible and the present state of affairs. If that disproportion becomes too extreme, it leads to a dangerous state of social and political dissatisfaction. That is what happened in Iran during the time of the Shah of Iran. Those on the side of greater democracy and freedom — and who were impatient with its gradual evolution in Iranian society and politics — sought the Shah's overthrow. But the result was, as in many revolutions, the emergence of a far more repressive regime, namely that of Ayatollah Khomeini. Something similar happened in Algeria, according to Laqueur:

> If the masses turned to the Islamists, it was more because of a feeling of having been betrayed by the old leadership, of poverty and resentment. It was the result of excessive expectation and a lack of elementary self-criticism, that is, the inability to understand Algeria after liberation was by no means the fault of imperialism and modernism but the responsibility of leaders and masses alike. (1996, p. 166)

It would seem that political leaders who have blatantly unrealistic objectives add fuel to the flames of social and political paranoia by increasing the width of the gap. The career of Egyptian president

---

40   The perception of the gap need not lead to the ersatz explanations of the paranoid vision. The perception of the gap can also lead to the comic vision. Much of comedy is founded on the discrepancy between the ideal and the real. This line of thought will be explored in Chapter Nine.

Gamal Abdul Nasser is a case in point. Nasser made grand promises to his people about the Aswan Dam, so much so that he felt that he could not reverse course when it became clearly necessary to do so without feeling disgraced. As the historian of the Middle East David Pryce-Jones describes it:

> From the moment that Nasser had staked his prestige on the dam, practical considerations became irrelevant because the shame of abandoning the scheme would have made his position untenable. Nothing less than the nation's foreign policy was swung by a shame-honor response. Sure enough, the Aswan Dam has spread bilharzia in exact accordance with the 1944 warning. Other consequences of this planned and forcible freeing of the peasants from age-old living patterns were more incalculable. (2002, p. 52)

The failure of the dam project was attributed, as were all other failures in the Middle East, then and now, to Zionist conspirators (Pipes 1998a, p. 104). In 1967, Nasser made the same type of grand claims, followed by the same humiliation when he promised to destroy Israel, but was defeated in six days. Naturally, when there are no grand expectations the size of the gap shrinks, and there is then no need to bridge it with paranoid explanations. As Winston Churchill said, "There is no worse mistake in public leadership than to hold out false hopes soon to be swept away." That is why Churchill, during some very dark times, told the British people, "I have nothing to offer but blood, toil, tears, and sweat."

The effect of Churchill's honesty was to maintain public morale. The effect of Nasser's braggadocio was demoralizing, creating a culture still imbued today with bitterness, resentment, and hatred, and a fertile ground for terrorism. It is not insignificant that four of the September 11th hijackers were from Egypt. The moral of the story is this: just as nature abhors a vacuum, so it is that the paranoid vision seeks to fill the gap between the totalitarian ideal and the less than glorious reality. Because totalitarianism, whether secular or theocratic, creates a large gap between utopian desires and actual realities, it is paranoiagenic.

Democracies, too, can create a gap, but the gaps that they create are, generally, far less extreme than those created by totalitarian political regimes. This is because democracies are generally not energized by millenarian images of Heaven on earth. It is enough for most people to find some modicum of happiness through owning a home, having a relatively satisfying marriage, and sending one's children to college. Those sorts of goals do not create heaven on earth, but they are realizable. Consequently, democracies are far less paranoiagenic.

Islamofascism

Fascism[41] and communism are often regarded as the two types of totalitarianism. Our previous discussion suggested, though, that theocratic totalitarianism—of which Islamism would be an example —is a third type. Or is it the case, as Laqueur contends (1996), that theocratic totalitarianism is essentially a form of fascism? By that logic, Islamism would not only be a form of totalitarianism but would, more particularly, be a form of fascism. All this is quite important because, for reasons that will be explored, fascism is very much a product of the paranoid vision.

Laqueur actually refers to Islamism as "clerical fascism," and notes that the term "clerico fascisti" was coined back in 1922 to refer to "...a group of Catholic believers in Rome and northern Italy who advocated a synthesis of Catholicism and fascism" (1996, p. 147). Laqueur indicates that he is not the first historian to make the connection between Islamism and fascism, "The affinities between the Muslim Brotherhood and fascism were observed in the 1930s, as was the fact that the extreme Muslim organizations supported the Axis powers in World War II" (1996, pp. 147-148). These affinities were not coincidental, for, as Laqueur observes, Hitler himself apparently drew inspiration from Islam:

> In a remarkable book published in 1937, a German Catholic writer labeled Nazism a new political Islam and Hitler-Mohamed its prophet. Why this "new German" (neudeutsch) Islam? According to Hitler from Mein Kampf onward, the

---

41   There certainly are distinctions between Fascism, as it existed in Italy, and then in Spain, and Nazism in Germany. Such distinctions are not essential to this argument.

sword has always been the carrier, prophet and propagator
of a new religion: "Hatred was always the main moving force

of all revolutionary change, persuasive fanaticism and even
hysteria were compelling the masses rather than any scientific
perception." (1996, p. 148)

One should note that although fascism certainly had been
foreshadowed historically, it did not become a movement until the
1920s, making it a relatively modern phenomenon. As the historian
Robert O. Paxton states: "Fascism was the major political innovation
of the twentieth century..." (2004, p. 3) Thus it would appear that the
emergence of Islamism as a movement was coeval with the emergence
of fascism. Historians, such as Francis Fukuyama (2002), have much
more recently observed the connection between Islamism and fascism.
He has used the neologism "Islamofascism," which has also been used
by Christopher Hitchens. It should be added, though, that Paxton has
argued that Islamism is not a form of fascism:

> The principal objection to succumbing to the temptation to
> call Islamic fundamentalist movements like Al-Qaeda and
> the Taliban fascist is that they are not reactions against a
> malfunctioning democracy. Arising in traditional societies,
> their unity is, in terms of Emile Durkheim's famous distinction,
> more organic than mechanical. Above all, they have not "given
> up free institutions," since they never had any. (2004, p. 204)

Walter Laqueur, to a certain extent, had anticipated Paxton's
argument. He agrees with Paxton, up to a point, but then disagrees:

> Indeed, with greater justification, it could be argued that the
> strengthening of fascism, then and now, was the result of the
> failure of democratic systems to resolve the problems facing
> them. The breakdown of democratic institutions — the failure
> of the democratic spirit — opened the doors to fascism. This
> generalization should not, however, be pushed too far, for
> even though it may apply to much of Europe, it is not valid in
> countries that never knew democracy. (1996, p. 5)

Laqueur is suggesting that thinkers like Paxton are over-generalizing a rather narrow notion of fascism, the one that Durkheim had developed. Durkheim's argument is sociological, predicated on how fascism comes into being in a society. It is not a philosophical argument over what fascism essentially is. In regard to origins, there is no intrinsic reason why fascism (and communism too) cannot be, and has not been, imported into societies that were never democracies, or which had very limited and unsuccessful experiments with democracy, such as Egypt. Paxton is correct that fascism arises out of discontent, but it need not be about a malfunctioning democracy. Iran, during the time of the last shah, was a dictatorship. Discontent there led to the Islamofascism of Khomeini. Furthermore, the Taliban in Afghanistan were thoroughly fascistic, but Afghanistan was never a democracy. Consequently, we would disagree with Paxton's conclusion that Islamic fundamentalist movements are not examples of fascism.

There is at least one other objection that comes to mind in regard to the notion that Islamism is a species of fascism. Fascism has historically been associated with nation states, often those that have transformed civilian life into a giant paramilitary organization. Examples include Mussolini's Italy and Hitler's Germany, as well as Iraq under Saddam Hussein. An Islamist terrorist organization like Al Qaeda, on the other hand, is not a nation state, but is in some ways akin to a holding company for other terrorist organizations (Bergen 2001), and in other ways it is akin to a large gang. But the Nazis too were very much like a gang before they became a political party, and then a government. And all along they were thoroughly fascistic in their viewpoint.

What we are contending, then, is that fascism is not merely a system of government. *Apropos* is an essay that Umberto Eco wrote for The New York Review of Books, entitled, "Ur-Fascism." He defines Ur-fascism as "eternal fascism." One may gather that Eco means that fascism is not merely an ideology created by Mussolini, which has had a certain historical expression. Its eternality is that of an essence, a prototype, or a Platonic Form. We are, though, thinking of it here not metaphysically, but epistemologically. Fascism is, most fundamentally, a vision of life, a worldview. Its central preoccupation is the polis, but it interprets all of human existence, from relations between the sexes to art, music, and architecture, to food and diet, to religion, in terms of a certain way of seeing, a vision of life, which Eco regards as fascistic. It will have to be determined what that vision of life is. Along these same lines, Roger Griffin distinguishes "Fascism" (which specifically refers to Mussolini's Italy) from "fascism." The latter, which he calls "generic fascism," is synonymous with Eco's Ur-Fascism.

Griffin contends that what inspired Mussolini was a vision of renewal, in the sense in which Mircea Eliade uses the word, one involving an evocation of mythic origins, which have the mystique of eternality. As Griffin suggests, "...it was the vision of renewal itself which became the linchpin of Fascist ideology rather than any particular set of policies or clearly conceived theory of state" (2005). So here again it is a vision of life that precedes its objectification in a social and political ideology.

Some psychologists—most notably Reich (1933; 1980), Fromm (1941; 1996), and Adorno (1950; 1993)—have also sought to understand the social and political manifestations of fascism as derivative of something prior, which for them is a certain psychopathology, which makes one prone to fascism as a political ideology. For example, Adorno, who influenced Fromm, contended that the type of person prone to fascism has an "authoritarian personality." A person of that sort is a conformist, rigid in his or her thinking, intolerant, and submissive to authority. As the previous case examples have indicated, worldviews are at the root of psychology and psychopathology. Thus what is of interest here is not a fascism-prone personality, but fascism as a way of seeing, as an epistemology.

It is necessary, then, to clarify the meaning of fascism, before seeking to determine its precise relation to Islamism. But rather than attempting to immediately define fascism, one can acquire a richer and more nuanced sense of its meaning by exploring what historians of ideas generally consider to be its intellectual origins. Of course, in referring to fascism's intellectual origins, we are not implying that Fascism arose because Mussolini or Hitler deliberately set out to create an ideology. They did create an ideology, but that was after the fact. More than anything else, fascism is not a set of consciously articulated ideas but, as Paxton rightly points out, a mood, and one that is thoroughly anti-intellectual.

A mood can be understood as the psychophysiological concomitant of a way of seeing, which itself is founded on certain philosophical assumptions. The word "Fascism" was coined by that theorizer and practitioner of Fascism, Benito Mussolini. He made Italy into a fascistic state in 1922. Mussolini had been a Marxist, but Fascism's theoretical origins lie not so much in Marxism or any other prior political theory as in philosophical ontologies, particularly in the philosophy of voluntarism. Simply stated, voluntarism is the belief that the will is both prior to and superior to the intellect. Philosophers like Schopenhauer, Nietzsche, and Bergson, although their philosophies are quite different from each other, share voluntaristic assumptions.

Romanticism can also be considered an influence on fascism. Romanticism is concerned, not with the will, but with the feelings, which it valorizes. Both voluntarism and romanticism are reactions to Kant's critique, which limited the legitimate range of reason. Of the different varieties of post-Kantians, one strain of thinkers—of which Bergson was the most notorious—concluded that if reason could not allow one access to true reality, then the will or the feelings, or other newly discovered faculties could be the road to reality and truth (Lovejoy 1961). Isaiah Berlin sees fascism as romanticism taken to its limit: "...[the] embodiment of the romantic ideal that took more and more hysterical forms and in its extreme ended in violent irrationalism and Fascism" (2001, 204).

There was a sense, shared by many of these post-Kantian philosophers, that culture and society, as they presently exist, are the products of the tyranny of intellect, or reason, to the exclusion of the vital elements of existence—those that are concerned with the body, from dancing to boxing to warfare—and that this has led to cultural decadence. There emerges nostalgia for a supposedly simpler age, one in which will and feelings held sway. Nietzsche, for example, wrote of the "undermen," men of the past, such as the Vikings, who were able to act directly without their actions being mediated and enervated by an excess of reflection. Rejecting the intellect in favor of the will was a revolutionary idea, whose fascistic implications Umberto Eco draws out:

> Action being beautiful in itself, it must be taken before, or without, reflection. Thinking is a form of emasculation. Therefore culture is suspect insofar as it is identified with critical attitudes. Distrust of the intellectual world has always been a symptom of Ur-Fascism, from Hermann Goering's fondness for a phrase from a Hanns Johst play ("When I hear the word 'culture' I reach for my gun") to the frequent use of such expressions as "degenerate intellectuals," "eggheads," "effete snobs," and "universities are nests of reds." The official Fascist intellectuals were mainly engaged in attacking modern culture and the liberal intelligentsia for having betrayed traditional values. (1995, pp. 12-15)

One might think of fascism as voluntarism and romanticism, with a utopian plan of action. It is not content to criticize the "degenerate intellectuals," and to affirm the virtues of un-self-critical willing. It seeks to revive and reestablish the supposed past greatness of a certain nation, society, culture, or religion, that supposedly existed before the slide into decadence. This revivalism, which is a key element of fascism, is captured in the historian Roger Griffin's definition:

> Used generically, fascism is a term for a singularly protean genus of modern politics inspired by the conviction that a process of national rebirth (palingenesis) has become essential to bring to an end a protracted period of social and cultural DECADENCE, and expressing itself ideologically in a revolutionary form of integral NATIONALISM (ultranationalism). (2003, p. 1)

So it is, as Griffin points out, that the fascist views the present age as the time of social and cultural decadence. Of course, there is always a tendency—by intellectuals of the certain pessimistic sort, form Hesiod to T.S. Eliot—to view the present age as decadent, as a product of moral decay and intellectual and cultural degeneration (Sandall, 2005). That in and of itself is not fascistic, but merely part of the mythos of the "fallenness" of the present age in relation to a supposed golden age.

For fascism, that golden age was a time of national grandeur. The cause of decadence, furthermore, is attributed to a certain group of people. Because it would be impossible to imagine fascism without delusions of historical grandeur and everything that follows from them, one may conclude that fascism is, at its very core, a product of the paranoid vision. Of course, dangerous utopian delusions are not the exclusive province of fascism. Communism, for example, also entertains such delusions. There are other factors that make utopian dreams distinctly fascistic rather than socialistic, communistic, etc. Griffin mentions, for example, ultranationalism. Those factors will be elaborated on shortly.

Berman (2003) points out that Islamism shares with other fascist movements the desire to resurrect an ancient empire. Mussolini, for example, wanted to restore Italy to the glory of the ancient Roman empire. And Hitler wanted to revive what he imagined to be a Nordic culture that had belonged to Germany's ancient past.

Islamism's revivalism consists in seeking to restore Islam to the greatness that it supposedly knew in the seventh century, during the time when Mohamed was living. The sense of "fallenness" and decadence, in regard to present-day Islam, is attributed to various historical events. For example, in one of the videotapes that bin Laden had sent to news stations, he alluded to something terrible that had taken place eighty years earlier. It would appear that that event was the abolition of the caliphate — in the early part of the twentieth century, by Kemal Ataturk, the former leader, modernizer, and secularizer, of Turkey. Bin Laden viewed this secularization as devastating to Islam.

Thus it is that revivalism is often allied with delusions of persecution —with their tone of resentment, self-pity, righteous indignation, and victimhood—which is a key aspect of the paranoid vision. Apropos is an article entitled "The New Fascism" by the military historian Victor Davis Hanson. He writes, "History was to be made up and distorted —the First World War was not caused by an aggressive Germany, but surely lost by a 'stab in the back' by Jews at home" (2002, p. 1). Hanson contends that the sense of being a victim is endemic to fascism, in all its varieties, including the "new fascism," which is present day theocratic fascism. Worst of all, the sense of victimhood becomes "a warrant for genocide," to use Norman Cohn's expression. Furthermore, the sense of victimization often leads to the propagation of malicious conspiracy theories, and all else that belongs to the paranoid vision.

Nationalism, as Mussolini indicated by his words and his actions, is a key component of fascism. It differs from communism in that respect, for communism's primary interest is not nations, but classes —the proletariat and the bourgeoisie. Thus communism tends to have not a national, but an international focus. It might seem, though, that the Islamists, whom we are deeming to be fascists, are not primarily concerned with nationality. But if one reads the words of Osama bin Laden one discovers that he and his ideological cohorts are indeed nationalistic, but not in the way that is usually meant by nationalistic:

> The call to wage war against America was made because America has spearheaded the crusade against the Islamic nation, sending tens of thousands of its troops to the land of the two holy mosques over and above its meddling in its affairs and its politics and its support of the oppressive, corrupt and tyrannical regime that is in control. (1998a, p. 1)

"The Islamic nation"? Apparently, bin Laden viewed all of Islam as a single nation. This is, of course, absurd, for within the Islam world there are many different nations, each with its own social and political goals, and opinions on how to be a true Muslim. The notion that there is an Islamic nation is part of Islamism's "fantasy ideology." In any case, one discovers here an example of the jingoism that is endemic to fascism. The aggressive nationalism of fascism does not, though, appear to be, for example, the self-confident nationalism of Napoleonic France or America under Theodore Roosevelt. Fascism, on the contrary, always blends nationalism with the perception of victimhood, which derive from paranoid delusions of persecution. Consequently, there is an undertone of vengeance in Islamism, and in fascism in general. That blend of resentment over persecution and the desire for vengeance is evident in bin Laden's speeches, as it was in those by Hitler, those by Milosevic, and by other fascists.

Not surprisingly, militancy is endemic to fascism. One must, though, be careful of distinctions here. Paxton points out that while fascism is invariably militant, not all military dictatorships are fascist. Paxton contends, for example, that Chile under Pinochet was not fascist. As Paxton argues, "...however odious [Pinochet's regime] cannot legitimately be called fascist, because they neither rested on popular acclaim nor were free to pursue expansionism" (2004, p. 201). Of course, popular acclaim and expansionism are not sufficient to make a regime fascistic, for Soviet communism rested on popular acclaim and was certainly expansionistic. A terrorist organization, like Al Qaeda, is not, of course, a dictatorship, but it could be argued that it is fascistic in its way of seeing. Their power has rested on popular acclaim, certainly by those within their organization, and by many people outside their organization as well. Indeed, Osama bin Laden had been hugely popular in the Muslim world.

In any case, the militancy of such Islamist organizations derives not only from ultranationalism but, more fundamentally, from fascism's voluntaristic and romantic roots, its rejection of intellect and thinking in favor of the life of instinct, feeling, and action unmediated by consideration of thought and conscience. From this militancy emerges the mystique of the warrior. If one reads transcripts of the speeches of Osama bin Laden, one hears about the virtues of being a holy warrior, of sacrifice and martyrdom. Bourgeois life is rejected in favor of that creed. Civilian life disappears as everyone becomes the equivalent of a soldier. This is not viewed as a temporary state of affairs, but one founded on the belief that war is good in itself. Islamists find scriptural support for warfare in the Qur'an, which commands that true believers go on a Jihad, or holy war.

The cult of the supreme leader is also endemic to fascism. Walter Laqueur describes the veneration, indeed the apotheosis, of Mussolini, as typical of totalitarian fascist leaders:

> Mussolini was predestined, elected by God and history. He was the greatest man who ever lived, the highest incarnation of the Italian race. He was alone and sad, a colossus, a titan, a cyclops, a giant — he could and should not be measured by ordinary standards. He was infinite, like the sky or the ocean, and for that reason it was impossible to describe or define him...Like Stalin, he was omnipresent and virtually never

slept...He was infallible, greater than Caesar, Augustus, and
Napoleon, and throughout the years more and more attributes
of God were bestowed upon him. Predappio, his birthplace,
became a place of pilgrimage. (1996, p. 32)

Islamism also has had its cult of the leader, from Nasser to
Khomeini to some of the current leaders in the Middle East. Bin
Laden was not, of course, the head of an Islamic state, but the head of
a terrorist network. He represented himself as more the Robin Hood
type of leader, who defends an Islam supposedly under attack by the
West, and many in the Islamist world saw him as a heroic savior,
although at the time this is being written his star has not been shining
quite so brightly. The flipside of the apotheosis of the supreme leader
is a denigration of the individual, but that denigration is not unique to
fascism. It is endemic to totalitarianism in general.

From Manichaeism to Apocalypticism

Islamism vilifies and dehumanizes certain groups of people. A
typical example of this can be seen in Wahhabi Sheikh Mustafa Bin
Sa'id Aytim, offering a sermon in Mecca: "It is no surprise that the
Jews and Christians deny the Koran. What is amazing is that some
ignoramuses and traitors from among the Muslims say: 'The Jews
and the Christians are our brothers.' By Allah, who told you that wild
animals can become human?" (qtd. in Spencer 2003, p. 19). Why,
then, is it that the votaries of Islamism regard certain groups of people
—Jews, Christians, pagans, moderate Muslims, Americans and, most
generally, Westerners — as their enemies? The answer to that question
brings us to that which lies at the core of Islamism's paranoid vision,
namely its radical Manichaeism.

In his essay, "The Roots of Muslim Rage," published in the
September 1990 issue of *Atlantic Monthly,* Bernard Lewis contends
that it is not primarily what Westerners do, or what they did, that
enrages Muslims, i.e. their alleged imperialism, colonialism, and
foreign policies, such as supporting Israel. These factors certainly are
significant, but the Soviet Union's foreign policy had been far more
egregious in regard to the Muslim world—the repression of Islam in the

Soviet Union, the invasion of Afghanistan, and the suppression of the revolt in Chechnya, for example—and yet the Soviets, as well as other hegemonic nations, were never hated with anything approaching the fury of many Muslim's anathema towards The United States. China's foreign policy has similarly been far from humanistic, but China has never been condemned with the vitriol reserved for the United States, and Israel too.

The real source of Muslim rage, according to Lewis, lies in who Americans are, the basic cultural values that define them, for these defining values are antithetical to the defining values of Islamism. That is why he believes that what is at issue here is a conflict of civilizations, a notion that has been expatiated upon by political scientist Samuel Huntington. In order to understand present-day Islamic rage, it is necessary, therefore, to understand how the U.S. and, more generally, the West, is perceived by much of the Muslim world, particularly by Middle Easterners. It is, furthermore, necessary to understand the intellectual origins of such perceptions.

Who, then, are Americans, such that their very identity is perceived to be antithetical to the identity, or selfhood, of many Muslims? Now here is a clue: there is a tradition of criticism of America by other groups of peoples—including the English, Germans, Russians, French, and Japanese—dating from the early part of the nineteenth century. Curiously enough, these criticisms are the same as those levied against America today. According to Bernard Lewis, German criticism of American culture—which includes a wide range of sources, such as Heidegger, Junger, Rilke and, of course, the Nazis—was particularly influential among Muslim intellectuals, such as Qutb, founder of the Muslim Brotherhood, in the nineteen thirties and forties, and still strongly influences current views of America. Lewis succinctly states the core of their criticism:

> In this perception, America was the ultimate example of civilization without culture: rich and comfortable, materially advanced but soulless and artificial; assembled or at best constructed, not grown; mechanical, not organic; technologically complex but lacking the spirituality and

> vitality of the rooted, human, national cultures of the Germans
> and other "authentic" peoples. (1990. p. 7)

But despite the alleged influence that these criticisms have had on the Islamic world, and the fact that these very same criticisms are being levied against America today—by Muslims, Europeans, and by others as well—Lewis concludes:

> But though these imported philosophies helped to provide intellectual expression for anti-westernism and anti-Americanism, they did not cause it, and certainly they do not explain the widespread anti-westernism that made so many in the Middle East and elsewhere in the Islamic world receptive to such ideas. (1990, p. 8)

What, then, does Lewis believe to be the real cause of Islamic hatred of the West? He contends that fundamentalist religious leaders see capitalism, democracy, and Western civilization in general as an appealing alternative to their way of life. That explanation does make a certain sense, for clergy who are threatened by losing power amongst their flock will fulminate with hatred against a rival, i.e. Western civilization.

All the same, Lewis may be too quick to dismiss the possibility that these imported criticisms really have done more than "provide intellectual expression for anti-westernism and anti-Americanism." It may be that these criticisms of American culture—that it is soulless, artificial, mechanical, and lacking in spirituality and vitality — really have resonated on a primal level with Islamists and not just with their leaders, for these criticisms have given voice to the psychological strains that some people can suffer when they are dislocated from their traditional way of life.

In an article that appeared in *Reason Online,* just a few months after the 9/11 attack, Charles Paul Freund explored what has come to be called "Occidentalism,"[42] the notion that the enemies of the West

---

42   "Occidentalism" is, no doubt, a confusing word for, if one did not know better, one would think that it meant a pro-Western stance, rather than the opposite. But "Occidentalism" is being deliberately used by way of contrast to "Orientalism," which means a set of misleading assumptions about the East. The notion of Orientalism was popularized by the critic of the West, Edward Said (2003).

have a set of misconceptions regarding what the West is all about. Freund quotes Nadje Al-Ali, a social anthropologist, who has done a study of the subject of Occidentalism:

> It has resulted in what she calls the construction of "an imperialist, corrupting, decadent and alienating West." If you attach that description to an empowering eschatology and arm it with explosives, you end up with something very like an angry Islamism contemplating its "corrupt, decadent and alienating" enemies. (qtd. in Freund, 2001, p. 14)

The Occidentalist is, then, a person who hates America and the West based upon a whole set of perceptions and misperceptions. Furthermore, Al-Ali is perceptive in seeing that such conceptions of the West are being motivated by an eschatology. More will be said about the apocalyptic and millennial aspect of Islamism later on in this chapter. Suffice it to say that what is required for there to be this apocalyptic drama is a Manichean duality. Occidentalism creates that duality, and thus sets the stage for apocalypticism, as well as all of the other manifestations of the paranoid vision.

Ian Buruma and Avishai Margalit, authors of *Occidentalism: The West in the Eyes of Its Enemies* (2004), confirm that there is an affinity between Islamist critics of the West, and those of the West's other critics. The authors, indeed, claim that Occidentalism is not just indigenous to Islamists, but became the mindset, in the early twentieth century, of the Japanese, the Nazis, the Maoists, and other groups, all of which are otherwise quite different.

One may note that nations like Germany, France, and England, who have an Occidentalist tradition, are, of course, Western nations! So there is a certain obvious lack of clarity in the term "Occidentalism." It could be rightfully argued, though, that the criticism that these European countries have levied against America has essentially been criticisms of their own Western mentality. We shall try to acknowledge these dualities in our analysis.

Fundamental to Occidentalism is the notion that Western civilization is alienating and dehumanizing, that it is a fall from the state of purity, wholeness, and goodness that supposedly had once existed in the world. Here, again, one finds the notion of paradise lost, a nostalgia for a state of affairs that never existed. It would be helpful to examine the criticism of the West, and consequent hatred, in more detail.

If Occidentalists view Westerners—including Americans, Jews, Christians and Europeans — as representatives of modernity, they see themselves as upholders of traditional values, as defenders of a rapidly eroding virtue. Modernity, which simply means the quality of being modern, is a word that has been used to contrast Western societies to those that are more traditional. Those who speak of modernity with disdain are critical of those forces in Western societies, or Westernized societies (like Japan), that disrupt the way of life of more traditional societies, causing a loss of community, as well as alienation, materialism, hedonism, and anomie. The critics of modernity are often members of modern societies themselves. In any case, what makes this duality, between traditional and modern, Manichean is that traditionalists are regarded as good, perfect, noble, wise and holy, but Westerners, because of their modernism, are bad, weak, shallow, foolish, decadent, degenerate or downright evil. This critique of the West, for its valorization of modernity, has also been made by fundamentalist Christian groups, and by some conservatives, a brilliant example of which is Richard Weaver's *Ideas Have Consequences* (1984). Many of the Occidentalist's criticisms are quite perceptive, and may be justified; others are simply misperceptions, or libelous. What concerns us here is not the accuracy of the Occidentalist's criticisms, or lack of accuracy, but its paranoiagenic potential.

Both the Occidentalist's self-exaltation—which, of course, is a paranoid delusion of grandeur — and his or her demonization of Westerners, are insidious fantasies, for vilifying Westerners vindicates murdering them. This fundamental duality between traditional and modern has a number of components, or sub-dualities. As one explores each duality, it becomes evident that the values that the Occidentalist holds dear are essentially the values of totalitarianism! Often, more precisely, they are the values of fascism.

1. We are whole / Westerners are fragmented

Occidentalists believe that their society was originally whole before Westernization shattered, fragmented, and splintered that wholeness. According to Buruma and Margalit, some Japanese intellectuals held a conference in Kyoto, in 1942, shortly after Pearl Harbor, in which they blamed science, technology, capitalism, individual freedom, democracy and other dimensions of Western civilization for having "...splintered the wholeness of Oriental spiritual culture" (2004, p. 2). The purpose of their conference was to decide how to overcome this Westernization, and restore the "holistic" and "organic" quality of Japanese culture. Apparently, Islamists, Chinese nationalists, and even some groups in the United States now share these same sentiments. If Buruma and Margalit are correct, then the sources of Islamism are, indeed, surprisingly modern, i.e. the valorization of the organic, the holistic and the natural, that emerges out of the Romantic movement of the late eighteenth century, although the seeds of it go back much further.

This romantic longing—to recover a supposedly lost wholeness, and thus inhabit a unified world, in contradistinction to a world that is either compartmentalized or downright fragmented—can find expressions in many ways. The popular interest in organic foods and in holistic health is one manifestation. Fascism is another way. Fascists seek to obliterate divisions that they perceive to be artificial, or due to the cultural fragmentation caused by the encroachment of Western ideas. They are especially intent on obliterating what they conceive to be a very primary source of division and separation, namely individuality. As Mussolini wrote, "If the nineteenth was the century of the individual it may be expected that this one may be the century of 'collectivism' and therefore the century of the State" (1932). Of course, Islamists have no interest in worshipping the state unless, like bin Laden, they view the Islamic world as one big state, to be ruled by the Caliphate.

For theocratic totalitarians, the church/state separation is viewed as artificial. Qutb had made that separation the gravamen of his critique of the West. According to Paul Berman, Qutb described this experience—of having to lead a double life, as a religious person and a secular person—as "the hideous schizophrenia of modern life." (qtd. in Berman 2003, 75) Qutb perceived that the Muslim world was riddled by that duality, and the question arose for him why this was so. As Berman expresses it:

> Qutb had described a universal experience. But he described it in a specifically Muslim version, which put the explanation not on anything vague such as modernity or human nature but on something specific and identifiable—namely on Christianity, and its doleful influence on modern culture, as exported by the power of Western countries. (2003, p. 76)

Blaming the existence of the duality, as it exists in the Muslim world, on the exporting of the sacred/secular duality from Christianity into the Muslim world, is, first of all, shallow, as are all explanations that attribute the emergence of individuality, and of a separate secular realm, to contingent causes, rather than to necessary psychosocial stages in human development. Secondly, it is a manifestation of the paranoid vision, for it finds a devil to blame for the fall into division and duality. The fact that the source of the problem is "specific and identifiable" makes it an example of what Sowell calls "the localization of evil" (1987), which is the basis of conspiracy theories.

Blaming the problem on Christianity is a way of drawing attention away from the internal conflicts and contradictions that exist within all human beings, including those who are Islamist. By way of contrast, an example of a profound explanation of the emergence of this duality of sacred and secular is Buber's theory of the twofold manner of knowing the world, namely I-Thou and I-It. The latter mode of knowing would be responsible for the existence of the secular realm. An explanation of that sort goes deep, for it sees the dialectical inevitability of the division of existence into the realms of the sacred and the secular. It sees it as due to the development of human consciousness. Berdyaev's notion of the fall of spirit into objectification is similarly profound. Sufi mysticism is an effort to overcome one's fallen condition through a change in consciousness. In any case, the claim that one's culture or society possesses wholeness and organicity—or had possessed these attributes, before it became corrupted by the West—coupled with a disdain for the supposed fragmentation of Western society, is a sociopolitical expression of Occidentalist Manichaeism.

We can conclude that totalitarianism is a futile effort to put Humpty Dumpty (i.e. a symbolic image of an original, unbroken, cosmic unity) back together again, while blaming another group of people—Americans, Jews, etc.—for Humpty Dumpty's fall.[43] More fundamentally, the preoccupation with one's culture, society, or world being natural, organic, and whole, is the outer expression of the longing to annul the divisions and dualities, and the consequent feeling of isolation and alienation that is a function of emerging self-awareness.

The totalitarian solution to the burden of individuality is to jettison one's own will and conscience, in an effort to live in accordance with the will of the leader, the nation, and the movement. Sartre saw the totalitarian longing for group identity as an inauthentic flight from the responsibilities of being a person. Wilhelm Reich attributed that species of totalitarianism, fascism, to the wish to be told what to do. Fromm saw the lure of totalitarianism as a flight from freedom. It is all these things.

2. We are rooted / Westerners are rootless

Related to the Occidentalist accusation that Westerners lack wholeness, or organicity, is the claim that Westerners are rootless and, consequently, abstract, mechanical, excessively rational, artificial, and superficial. If Occidentalists are not Westerners, they criticize Westerners. But if they are themselves Westerners, they criticize Americans in particular — but other groups as well, such as the Jews — for possessing all of the negative qualities associated with rootlessness. As Buruma and Margalit state in regard to the Nazis' belief in their rootedness: "Membership in a Volk was 'organic' and by definition exclusive, while citizenship in the French republic, the United States, or Britain was, like their cities, theoretically open to all" (2004, p. 34).

It is important to get to the philosophical origin of the mystique of rootedness, for here is an idea that has had very dangerous

---

43 This paranoid sentiment is expressed in the not altogether facetious bumper sticker, "Humpty Dumpty was pushed."

The Paranoid Vision

consequences. The Nazis found in Heidegger—who was already Germany's leading philosopher, and who had became a member of the National Socialist Party—a philosophical framework as well as an intellectual respectability for their anti-rationalism, anti-humanism, anti-intellectualism, and anti-enlightenment attitudes. Heidegger was a philosopher of rootedness, a notion that found expression in the Nazi mystique of blood and soil, and their hatred of Jews for their cosmopolitanism, which was regarded as the antithesis of rootedness.

Heidegger sought to provide the philosophical basis for reestablishing an organic relation of human beings to the world, a relation that supposedly had once existed. The connections that George Steiner finds between the Nazi's valorization of rootedness and a similar valorization of rootedness by Heidegger are as disturbing as they are illuminating:

> Both Nazism and the ontological anthropology of Sein und Zeit stress the concreteness of man's function in the world, the primordial sanctity of hand and body. Both exalt the mystical kinship between the laborer and his tools in an existential innocence which must be cleansed of the pretensions and illusions of abstract intellect. With this emphasis goes a closely related stress on rootedness, on the intimacies of blood and remembrance that an authentic human being cultivates with his native ground. Heidegger's rhetoric of "at-homeness," of the organic continuum which knits the living to the ancestral dead buried close by, fits effortlessly into the Nazi cult of "blood and soil." Concomitantly, the Hitlerite denunciation of "rootless cosmopolitans," the urban riffraff, and unhoused intelligentsia that live parasitically on the modish surface of society, chime in readily with the Heideggerian critique of "theyness," of technological modernity, of the busy restlessness of the inauthentic. (1980, p. 122)

Steiner refers to Heidegger's rhetoric of "at-homeness." In Freud's essay, called "The Uncanny," he referred to the uncanny as the absolutely frightening feeling of not being at home. Also apropos is Buber's sense that modern human beings no longer have a home but inhabit an open field. Is it modernity that has created this feeling of

238

ontological homelessness or uprootedness? We referred earlier to an essay by Roger Sandall, where he contends that the nostalgia over the noble savage is a notion that is over 10,000 years old and can be found in relatively primitive societies. They too, to varying degrees, felt alienated, not at home in the world. Consequently, it would be naïve to blame the alienation of human beings simply on the coming of all that is associated with modernity, such as the development of technology and the loss of community. Alienation is really a function of emerging self-awareness. Romanticism, and fascism too, grow out of the longing to return home, to return to Eden, despite the closed iron gates and the angels with the flaming swords preventing reentrance.

Rene Guenon was a thinker with a much different intellectual project than Heidegger. He offered a brilliant critique of the modern world from the standpoint of traditionalism and the perennial philosophy, an intellectual movement that sought a unity of all religious traditions, founded on mystical insight. Guenon, too—when he looked at the modern world, and tried to conceive why it was ailing —hopped on the "rootlessness" bandwagon. He believed that the ultimate cause of the problems of the modern world was due to the arrival of the Kali Yuga, the very worst age for the universe to be in, in terms of the meta-cosmic Hindu cycle of creation and destruction. But Guenon also localized the source of evil by blaming a particular group of people. He uses the word "nomadism" to describe what he believed to be Jewish rootlessness, more specifically the supposed rootlessness of contemporary Jewish intellectuals. Guenon believed that their nomadism, or rootlessness, is the source of their materialism, and that it has had an undermining impact on traditional life:

> The case of Freud himself, founder of psycho-analysis (sic), is quite typical in this respect, for he never ceased to declare himself a materialist. One further remark: why is it that the principal representatives of the new tendencies, like Einstein in physics, Bergson in philosophy, Freud in psychology, and many other of less importance are almost all of Jewish origin, unless it be because there is something involved that is closely bound up with the "maleficent" and dissolving aspect of nomadism when it is deviated, and because that aspect must

inevitably predominate in Jews detached from their tradition?
(1972, p. 355)

To blame the loss of traditional life on a certain group of modern Jewish intellectuals is farfetched. For one thing, there have certainly been modern Jewish intellectuals who were not materialistic, and there have been a great many non-Jewish intellectuals who were materialistic. What is clear, though, is that Guenon's notion that the Jews are nomadic — when read and interpreted by those who are under the sway of the paranoid vision — opens itself to nefarious purposes. Furthermore, the often-strident tone of Guenon's polemic against Western civilization, coupled with an apocalyptic vision of life, reinforces its paranoiagenic potential. In his later years, in the early 1950s, Guenon left his native France, became a citizen of Egypt, and converted to Islam. There his ideas were not unwelcome by those wishing to vilify Jews as being nomadic, rootless, and counter-traditional. One discovers a modern day exponent of Guenon's type of Occidentalism, its anti-nomadism, in Islam's famous present-day philosopher, Seyyed Hossein Nasr (2000), who quite plainly states that the West is evil.

3. We are pure / Westerners are impure

We have already analyzed purity seeking, in relation to the dread of defilement, which is an anxiety at the core of the paranoid vision. We offered the examples of Mohamed Atta's relation to the feminine, and Osama bin Laden's feeling that the existence of American troops stationed in Saudi Arabia was defiling the land.

What makes the pure/impure duality so dangerously paranoiagenic is that it represents evil on the defilement level of consciousness, which renders it more visceral and emotionally powerful, and less open to illumination than evil viewed as sin or guilt. Furthermore, the representation of evil as something external and extrinsic to who one is — i.e. whole, pure, and perfect—lends itself to ignoring "the beam in one's own eye," as one projects one's own faults onto other people.

Here one finds the effort to return to a supposedly purer state of being by means of terror and violence. The notion is, as Newell states, that, "A purifying violence would purge the people of egotism and hedonism, and draw them back into a primitive collective of self-sacrifice." (2001, p. 1) It is this Manichaean division of the world into the pure and the impure that is of relevance to an understanding of the paranoid vision.

4. We are heroic and spiritual. / Westerners are bourgeois, materialistic, and idolatrous.

To Islamic Occidentalists, whose consciousness is predominantly mythic, the city, particularly the Western city, has many negative symbolic connotations. Most generally, it symbolizes individual autonomy, experienced in all domains: intellectually, politically, socially, spiritually, artistically, culturally, and economically. The freedom that women know in Western cities is particularly galling to Islamic fundamentalists, with their strong patriarchal allegiances. The Western city also symbolizes debauched pleasure seeking, materialism, decadence, and idolatry.

What is New York City to Islamists? Buruma and Margalit claim that it symbolizes Babylon, the tall towers of the World Trade Center symbolizing the Tower of Babel, a hubristic assault on Heaven. Buruma and Margalit regard the myth of the Occidental city as a variant of the Promethean myth. As they express it:

> Since ancient times, humans have lived in terror of being punished for their effrontery in challenging he gods, by stealing fire, or gaining too much knowledge, or creating too much wealth, or building towers that reach for the skies. The problem is not with the city per se, but with cities given to commerce and pleasure instead of religious worship. In the case of Osama bin Laden and Mohamed Atta this religious impulse curdled into a dangerous madness. (2004, p. 16)

Related to the Promethean myth is the myth of the golden calf, to which the authors also refer. The notion here is that an idol has taken the place of God. To religious fundamentalists, idolatry is considered the equivalent to a mortal sin, for it is challenging the ultimacy of God, which is the very foundation of their faith.

There is much substance to the Islamic critique. After all, Westerners, like all people, are tempted by idols. All the same, resentment is evident here, for were religious fundamentalists truly religious, the Twin Towers would either have had no significance or been considered a pitiable attempt by the benighted to rival God, in which case it would inspire pity, not hatred. But the Twin Towers intimidated those who are insecure and envious. It seemed humiliating that materialist infidels should be surrounded by grandeur, while their own Islamic cities were centers of poverty and backwardness.

Furthermore, Occidentalists see themselves as heroic, with lofty utopian ideals, and view the West as a bourgeois society of merchants. The Occidentalist concludes that the Westerner is addicted to comfort and security, is excessively practical, and is soft and decadent. A young Taliban fighter, at the beginning of the war in Afghanistan, is quoted as saying, "The Americans would never win, for 'they love Pepsi Cola, but we love death.'" (qtd. in Brooks 2002, p. 5) The Japanese and the Germans had the same view of Americans prior to attacking them.

Related to the notion that the West lacks heroism, is the notion that it is bourgeois and lacks spirituality. Apropos is David Brooks' use of the term "bourgeoisophobe" to describe the reaction of Occidentalists to those in the West — particularly Americans and Jews — who are materially successful. Those who are successful are viewed by the bourgeoisophobe as "spiritually stunted" (Brooks 2002). It is true that capitalism and democracy are neither spiritual nor heroic creeds (although some, like Ayn Rand, would argue that capitalism can be heroic).

Consequently, in America, at least, it is up to the individual to search for deliverance, to discover the wellsprings of courage, and to seek out those situations that call for heroism. The state cannot be depended upon to provide direction in that regard, nor should it, although Mussolini argued that it should. Furthermore, the citizens of liberal Western democracies have invariably been able to rise to the occasion, becoming heroic when necessary, and have become fierce adversaries, defending democratic values against autocratic regimes (Hanson 2001).

This species of Occidentalism, like all Occidentalism, is founded on a misperception of the West. But there is a virulence to that misperception that suggests it is not founded on a simple misunderstanding. On the contrary, it is founded on the type of distorted perception that is a product of paranoia-infused Manichaeism.

5. We are soulful / Westerners are soulless

Westerners have been accused of being excessively rational, leading them to mechanize and commercialize all aspects of human existence. In placing their faith in science and reason, they supposedly lack feelings, intuitions, and wisdom. Buruma and Margalit trace these criticisms of the West's dehumanizing intellect to the 19th Century Russian Slavophiles, who derived their ideas from German Romanticism. They also state that the Western city has often been compared to that of a prostitute who makes basic human relations into a commodity, and is thus soulless. Radical Islamists are now levying these same criticisms against the West.

The resultant attitude might be expressed as, "Westerners may be rich and powerful, but they are soulless, mechanical, materialistic, shallow and devilish idol worshipers. We, on the other hand, are poor, but we are spiritual." If the Islamists truly believed that spiritual values were more important than material objects and worldly power —and did not secretly hanker after them—their attitude towards Westerners would certainly not be virulent hatred. If anything, it would be pity, sympathy, or perhaps the loving-kindness that the Mahayana Buddhists seek to display towards those whom they regard as suffering under materialistic delusions. The hatred towards Westerners for their lack of spirituality would appear to be a function of resentment, or envy.

Both paranoid defensiveness and envy—which are factors that transform Manichean dualism into murderous rage—have this in common: they are manifestations of an insecurity, a lack of faith in the worth of one's own values and in the ability of one's group to resist alien ideas and values. The psychologist Ervin Staub proposed that societies or nations who commit genocide suffer from a lack of self-esteem (Staub, 1992). Staub's notion is relevant to our discussion, for societies that are breeding grounds for terrorists may suffer from the same insecurities. As far as genocide goes, Straub believes that the Germans, after World War I, would be a case in point of an insecure people. The same might hold true, more generally, of those who, under the sway of the paranoid vision, become violent. Paranoid defensiveness, mixed with envy, makes for a very lethal combination.

What is the source of this defensiveness? To a large degree, it stems from the fact that Moslems know that Islam had once produced a great civilization, one that had spread to much of the globe, but that supremacy has eroded over the centuries, so that they are now in a subordinate relation—culturally, politically, and militarily—to infidels. As Bernard Lewis states:

> For a long time now there has been a rising tide of rebellion against this Western paramountcy, and a desire to reassert Muslim values and restore Muslim greatness. The Muslim has suffered successive stages of defeat. The first was his loss of domination in the world, to the advancing power of Russia and the West. (1990, p. 5)

This loss of cultural dominance is experienced as all the more galling to the Islamists, because they see themselves as having been defeated by an enemy whom they regard as fragmented, impure, rootless, idolatrous, bourgeois, and materialistic. The assumption, on the part of the Islamists, that makes for their bitterness, is that hegemony is an indication of moral superiority. After all, Mohamed was a hugely victorious general and leader, in contradistinction, for example, to Jesus. And so, not surprisingly, Mohamed becomes the paradigm for the right life. Consequently, if they do not see themselves as having been betrayed by fate, history, or conspirators, they are in danger of falling into doubt about their alleged moral superiority. It is possible, though, to challenge the equation of might with right, as did Socrates in Plato's *Republic*. To challenge that equation would be to challenge the very worldview that Mohamed bequeathed to them, but that is a risky business.

The Islamic Apocalypse

The dehumanizing caricatures of the West that are the product of these five Manichean dualities set the stage for the growth of apocalyptic fantasies. In this scenario, one sees the final battle. It is between the forces of good (the traditionalists) and the forcers of evil (the modernists). Like other apocalypticists, whether secular or theocratic, Islamists believe that their attack on the enemy could precipitate the apocalypse.

Of course, Islam was strongly apocalyptic right from the beginning, as were Judaism (in the book of Daniel, for example) and Christianity, long before the advent of modernity and Occidentalism. One of the foremost experts on Islamic apocalyptic literature, David Cook, stated in a recent interview that, "The *Qur'an* is filled with predictions about the end of the world. The prophet Mohammed envisioned the end as being very close, within a few years after receiving his revelation." (Cook, 2001) How prevalent is apocalyptic literature in the Muslim world today? Cook's assessment is rather unsettling:

> Modern Muslim apocalyptic literature is highly popular and derives its sources from three different influences. The first source is the framework provided by the *Qur'an* and classical Muslim literature. The second source is anti-Semitic conspiracy theories based on The Protocols of Elders of Zion, [a spurious Russian document]. The third source is Evangelical Protestant expectations of the return of Christ and the End of the World. The "Hal Lindsey" of modern Muslim apocalyptic (sic) is an Egyptian named Said Ayyub. In 1987 he wrote The Anti-Christ. This was an extremely powerful political and social apologetic for Muslims, identifying the United States as the Great Satan. (2001, p. 2)

One would have hoped that The Protocols of Elders of Zion was gone forever, along with the Nazis and the pogroms in Europe and Russia, but, according to Klinghoffer (2005), in Arab lands as well as in Iran, it ranks number six on the best seller list, along with the *Qur'an* and *Mein Kampf*. Furthermore, one is surprised to learn that Muslims would be drawn to a notion that belongs to Christian theology, namely the Antichrist, demonstrating that they can be eclectic in their theological references. Unfortunately, this popularity is not merely among Islamists, but among ordinary Muslims. The same interviewer then proceeded to ask Cook whether apocalyptic belief was more intense among the Islamic Jihad subculture. According to Cook:

> Yes. Without a doubt it influences terrorist sub-culture. Holy War and End of the World themes run together throughout this literature. Sometimes the Anti-Christ is identified as a U.S. president, other times it is western civilization in general. This literature freely uses predictions about End of World or Israel's demise to recruit followers and prove they need to be working for God, instead of their own purposes. (2001, p. 2)

Finally, the interviewer asks Cook about the apocalyptic beliefs of Osama bin Laden, and Cook quotes what bin Laden said in 1998, in an ABC News interview:

> "The Hour [of Judgment] will not arrive until the Muslims fight the Jews, and the Muslims will kill them until the Jew will hide behind rocks and trees, and the rock and the tree will say: O Muslim, O servant of God, there is a Jew behind me—come and kill him!" (2001, p. 3)

In the above passage, bin Laden is quoting the Hadith, sayings ascribed to the Prophet Mohamed. Richard Landes, a scholar of millennialism, confirms that bin Laden sees himself, and many Muslims also see him, as "...a central player in a cosmic battle that pits warriors of truth against the agents of Satan and evil in this world" (2005, p. 1). September 11th was, then, a product of Islamism's apocalyptic imagination, one in which America became the projection of the terrorist's own unmitigated malevolence.

Terrorism: Rational Decision or Symbolic Fantasy?

Not everyone would agree that terrorism is the product of the distorted thinking and the dark emotions endemic to the paranoid vision. Suicide terrorism would seem to be the type of terrorism most under the sway of fantasy thinking, and the paranoid vision in general, but there are those who argue that suicide terrorists are motivated not by paranoid lunacy or by fanaticism, but by strategic objectives. The most persuasive argument for this school of thought comes from Robert A. Pape, a political scientist, who wrote a well-circulated article for the *American Political Science Review* entitled "The Strategic Logic of Suicide Terrorism." As Pape expresses it:

> Most suicide terrorism is undertaken as a strategic effort directed toward achieving particular political goals; it is not simply the product of irrational individuals or the expression of fanatical hatreds. The main purpose of suicide terrorism is to use the threat of punishment to change policy, especially to cause democratic states to withdraw forces from territory terrorists view as their homeland. The record of suicide terrorism from 1980 to 2001 exhibits tendencies in the timing, goals, and targets of attack that are consistent with this strategic logic but not with irrational or fanatical behavior. (2002, p. 5)

There would appear to be much truth to Pape's thesis. Hezbollah, for example, was able, through a series of calculated suicide attacks, to get the United States and Israel to leave Southern Lebanon. Similarly, the Tamil Tigers—the terrorist separatist organization seeking the independence of Tamil Eelam from Sri Lanka—were able to bring Sri Lanka to the bargaining table.

There are, though, certain anomalies that would appear to qualify the validity of Pape's theory. Take, for, example, Pape's well-documented argument to prove that the various Palestinian terrorist organizations were able to get Israel to make concessions, which consisted in letting go of the Gaza Strip and the West Bank. Here is where the rationality thesis gets strained. Israel finally agreed, in 1993, during the Oslo Accords, to allow the Palestinians to be given the Gaza Strip, ninety-five percent of the West Bank, and half of Jerusalem. That would, in essence, have given the Palestinians just about everything that they had demanded. But to the surprise of everyone—including President Clinton, Israeli Prime Minister Ehud

Barack and, no doubt, many of the Palestinians—Yasser Arafat, who represented the PLO, rejected the deal. Hamas then launched a fierce infitada of suicide bombings.

In his essay, Pape does not explain how the PLO's rejection of the peace treaty with Israel served their strategic objectives of establishing a Palestinian state. But in *The Case for Democracy* (2004), Natan Sharansky—who was then serving as a member of the Israeli delegation at the Oslo accords—offers his opinion on what was Arafat's primary, but unstated, objective in turning down Israel's generous deal: "Arafat rejected countless projects Israel proposed that would have served to decrease tension between Israelis and Palestinians and release his hold on Palestinian economic life" (2004, p. 181). Sharansky then explains that it was necessary to keep Israel as an enemy because, as has been said before, having an enemy has always been the cynical method used by autocrats to maintain control over a group of people. Creating an enemy creates a scapegoat for their nation's social, economic, and political failures, and deflects criticism from their own corrupt regime. The suicide bombings served to keep the tensions with Israel at a feverish pitch. But would the suicide bombers have sacrificed their lives had they deciphered Arafat's real objectives? If Sharansky is correct — that it was all about Arafat maintaining power and control — then does it make sense to talk of the suicide bombings as fulfilling a strategic objective?

Do the car bombings in Iraq have a strategic objective? In an article in the *New York Times* entitled "The Mystery of the Insurgency" (May 15, 2005), James Bennet interviewed a number of counterterrorism experts, in an effort to make sense of the insurgency there. Most of the experts interviewed are more than a bit puzzled, hence the title of the article. They are puzzled by the fact that the widespread murdering of civilians is not winning hearts and minds. Indeed, it is having the opposite effect. Bennet also reminds us of something that Che Guevara believed. Quoting Guevara, Bennet states:

> "Where a government has come to power through some form
> of popular vote, fraudulent or not, and maintains at least an
> appearance of constitutional legality," he wrote, "the guerrilla

outbreak cannot be promoted, since the possibilities of peaceful struggle have not yet been exhausted." (2005, p. 2)

Hence, if Guevara is correct, because of the free elections, the insurgency cannot win in Iraq. But Bennet quotes Bruce Hoffman who, like Pape, is convinced that terrorists have rational motives. Bennet contends that the Iraqi insurgent's motives are like that of the IRA in Ireland; it is to get a foreign power to leave their country. Of course, the suicide bombings are also the result of a civil war, of Sunnis seeking to regain supremacy. In any case, as Bennet points out, after many years, the IRA is no closer to driving the English out of Ireland. As a matter of fact, an article in The New York Times read, "I.R.A. Renounces Violence in Potentially Profound Shift" (July 28, 2005).

Anthony James Joes, an expert on guerilla warfare, leaves open the possibility that we simply do not understand the insurgents' strategy, but suggests that what is going on is "wanton violence" (Bennet, 2005), and that the insurgents are simply "losers." Bennet also interviews Steven Metz, of the Army War College of Strategic Studies Institute. Metz believes that most insurgencies do have a certain goal, and so agrees with Pape on that point.

In regard to the Iraqi insurgency, on the other hand, he states, "It really is significant that even two years in there hasn't been anything like the kind of political ideology or political spokesman or political wing emerging. It really is a nihilistic insurgency" (qtd. in Bennet, 2005, p. 1). If nihilism is what is motivating the insurgency, then sending one's recruits to blow themselves up in a car bomb that indiscriminately kills as many civilians as possible is not a strategic plan.

Pape's thesis is, of course, only about suicide terrorism. Certainly, terrorism, in general, is primarily driven by strategic objectives. Or is it? Throughout history, there have been many terrorist organizations and individual terrorists—from the Hindu Thugs of the nineteenth century who murdered strangers to honor the goddess Kali, to the anarchist who assassinated President McKinley—whose motivations could not be regarded as strategic in Pape's sense of the word. After all, what was the political motivation for Timothy McVeigh for destroying the Federal Building in Oklahoma City? It would appear that he was motivated by vengeance for the disaster at Ruby Ridge and was on an apocalyptic mission inspired by his reading of the notorious book *The Turner Diaries*. For that matter, what was the strategic motivation of Aum Shinrikyo—a cult regarded by the United States government as a terrorist organization—for having released the poisonous gas Saran into the Japanese subways? Their motivation was similarly part of an apocalyptic fantasy.

This is not to deny the obvious fact that terrorists are often strategically motivated. It is just to suggest that non-strategic motives also play a crucial role, and it would behoove us to examine some of these motives, for they may help us not only to understand terrorism, but also to more deeply understand Islamism and, more ultimately, the paranoid vision.

Several years ago, Binyamin Netanyahu, the former prime minister of Israel, gave a speech entitled "The Root Cause of Terrorism is Totalitarianism." This is certainly an intriguing hypothesis, but was Netanyahu correct? After all, terrorism, at least as it is being defined here, is not state sponsored. Organizations like Hamas and Al Qaeda act independently. Is it fair, then, to connect terrorism to totalitarianism?

There may, though, be some truth to Netanyahu's statement. After all, Middle Eastern terrorists are radical fundamentalists and, as such, are foes of individual freedom, human rights, and all else that one associates with liberal Western democracy. For example, it is clear that Sayyid Qutb profoundly influenced Osama bin Laden, whose writings clearly espouse authoritarian and totalitarian values. Bearing this in mind, what then might be the connection between totalitarianism and terrorism? As Netanyahu sees it:

> [For terrorists], the cause they espouse is so all-encompassing, so total, that it justifies anything. It allows them to break any law, discard any moral code and trample all human rights in the dust. In their eyes, it permits them to indiscriminately murder and maim innocent men and women, and lets them blow up a bus full of children. (2002, p. 1)

This totalization, or absolutizing, of one's cause may make one a true believer, and perhaps a fanatic, but does it make one a totalitarian? It may or may not. And it may or may not make one a terrorist. But we would contend that fanaticism is a cause of terrorism, if "fanatic" means a person acting solely out of an end justifies the means ethics, i.e. a person who has lost all sense of proportion. It became evident, from the three previous case examples, that there is a connection between teleological ethics and antinomianism, nihilism, and the paranoid vision. One can, then, discern a common theme here. Needless to say, fanatics are dangerous, for their all-important cause vindicates any sort of action, including terrorism.

This brings us back to Pape's essay, "The Strategic Logic of Suicide Terrorism." Pape states that, "...all suicide terrorist campaigns in the last two decades have been aimed at democracies, which make more suitable targets from the terrorist's point of view" (2003, p. 5). Pape is making a very interesting point here, but one must ask: What about nations like Egypt, Saudi Arabia, and Sri Lanka? They have experienced terrorist attacks, and they are not democracies. Russia, too, as suffered terrorist attacks, and it is barely a democracy. Each of these cases is different, but it would seem that a recent phenomena are non-democratic countries that have dealings with democratic counties being attacked by terrorists. The July 26th 2005 terrorist attack in the Egyptian city of Sharm el-Sheik, Egypt, where there exists a vacation resort that caters to English tourists, and has been the site of meetings of international conferences, would be an example. All the same, Pape is mostly correct in his assessment. Why, then, do democracies make good targets? According to Pape:

> ...democracies are often thought to be especially vulnerable to coercive punishment. Domestic critics and international rivals, as well as terrorists, often view democracies as "soft," usually on the grounds that their publics have low thresholds of cost tolerance and high ability to affect state policy. Even if there is little evidence that democracies are easier to coerce than other regime types (Horowitz and Reiter, 2001) this image of democracy matters. (2003, pp. 7-8)

Pape's reasoning does make a certain sense, but overall it seems unconvincing as an explanation of why democracies have been most frequently targets of terrorists. It could be argued, though, that the essential reason is not practical, like Pape contends, but ideological. If democracies are a target for terrorism it is because democracies, quite naturally, stand for democratic freedoms, liberty, individualism, human rights, the separation of church and state, and all else that terrorists, who are invariably totalitarians, reject. Terrorist fear that such liberal values will invade their nation. This fear, and all else that follows from it, is a paranoid reaction to the dread of modernity.

The notion that what is really dreaded is democracy and liberty could explain why democracies are by far the most prevalent targets for terrorism, but how can one explain the act of terrorism itself, now that we have rejected Pape's rational motive thesis? One thesis is that suicide bombing, terrorism in general, and genocide, are part of a cult of death, i.e. a perverse mythicizing, glorification, and worshiping of death. As the counter terrorism expert Shmuel Bar expresses it: "Along with the renewal of the jihad, the Islamist Weltanschauung, which emerged from the Afghani crucible, developed a Thanatophile ideology in which death is idealized as a desired goal and not a necessary evil in war" (Bar, 2004. p. 3). Bar's cult of death hypothesis is akin to what Steven Metz suggested is at play in the insurgency in Iraq — nihilism. At its most extreme, nihilism is not just a doctrine advocating the complete destruction of social and political institutions, which is what some revolutionaries have sought, but the negation of all values. The love of destruction becomes a surrogate for value.

Lee Harris has a different take on the motives for terrorism. He too, contrary to Pape, believes that terrorism is an end in itself. But Harris believes that the end of terrorism is something other than pure nihilism:

> But in the fantasy ideology of radical Islam, suicide plays an absolutely indispensable role. It is not a means to an end but an end in itself. Seen through the distorting prism of radical Islam, the act of suicide is transformed into an act of martyrdom — martyrdom in all of its transcendent glory and

accompanied by the panoply of magical power that religious
tradition has always assigned it. (2002, p. 13)

It is not exactly clear what Harris means by the transcendent
glory of martyrdom. Does he mean earthly renown? Does he mean
heavenly bliss? It is not unusual for both motives to be conflated in
the self-exultation of the fanatic. Furthermore, self-exultation is easily
allied with nihilism. One is reminded, in that regard, of the film *White
Heat* (1949), starring James Cagney who, as usual, plays a gangster. In
the apocalyptic climax of the film, which became iconic, he is standing
on top of a giant gas tank, which has caught on fire. Right before being
blown to smithereens, he yells in glory, "Look Ma, I'm on top of the
world!"

Indeed, a third thesis is that apocalypticism is what motivates
the terrorist. Apropos is Jeffrey Herf's contention that, "Terrorists
have repeatedly attacked those who seek to find negotiated and
non-catastrophic solutions to difficult problems." (2002, p. 3) Herf
mentions, as examples, the assassination of the Austrian Archduke
Ferdinand for the reason that the Archduke sought a negotiated
solution to the serious political problems that Europe was facing.
Herf also points out that Anwar Sadat was similarly assassinated by
the forerunners of Al Qaeda, and Yitzak Rabin by a Jewish fanatic,
because these political leaders sought out solutions to conflict by
means of diplomacy and compromise, the type of solutions that lie at
the core of liberal Western democracy. In the minds of fanatics, such
compromises prevent the apocalypse from coming, and ultimately
forestall the arrival of utopia. Furthermore, they remove the terrorist's
raison d'etre. Consequently, as Herf points out, it follows from the
logic of terrorism that compromisers are counterrevolutionary and
must be killed.

Which view, then, is correct? Is terrorism all about nihilism,
or is it about martyrdom, or is it about apocalypse? It would seem
that all three views are correct, if one adds a few qualifications. First
of all consider the notion that the desire for martyrdom is what is
motivating terrorists. If this is martyrdom, Islamists are defining it
in a strange new way. After all, the notion that a martyr is a person

who, through the act of suicide, kills as many innocent civilians as possible, is outrageously absurd. If anything, martyrs recognize the sanctity of human existence. Furthermore, the *Qur'an* clearly prohibits suicide and it also prohibits the killing of noncombatants. Apparently, the suicide murderer is not a person prone to theological precision. Potential suicide murderers are bolstered in their belief that they will be martyrs by belonging to societies, or groups within those societies, that interpret suicide-murder as a glorious act of self-sacrifice. The martyrdom thesis applies not only to suicide-bombers, for all terrorists know that they are engaging in very risky behavior, and thus inviting death.

The contemporary French philosopher Andre Glucksmann would seem to be supporting the nihilism thesis in regard to terrorism. He states, "In Dostoevsky's The Possessed there are atheists and believers (a figure like Shatov for example) who have very different outlooks on the future. But they share one thing in common: the right to kill, to burn, to overturn, in order to achieve a tabula rasa" (2003, p. 1). Glucksmann identifies the attitude that "anything goes" when it comes to achieving one's objectives—which inevitably come down to destroying everything so as to turn the world into a tabula rasa—as being the essence of nihilism.

One might wonder, though, whether there is really any pure nihilism. It may be that the desire for complete destruction, for a tabula rasa, is itself prompted by a paranoid purity-seeking. The hope is that terror will precipitate the Gotterdammerung, and then the world, having been cleansed through destruction, will be ready for renewal, and for utopia. Underlying nihilism, then, may be apocalyptic fantasies, which would suggest that the nihilist is under the sway of the paranoid vision.

Terrorism is also motivated by the paranoid defense mechanism of projection. Consider, for example Osama bin Laden's opinion about who are the real terrorists: "The truth is that the whole Muslim world is the victim of international terrorism, engineered by America at the United Nations" (bin Laden, 1998b, p. 4) Then a good measure of envy is added to this psychosocial witches' brew, for those who are envious will readily sacrifice themselves if, in doing so, they can destroy the object of their envy. Envy, coupled with projection of one's shadow, can lead to the worst sort of sadistic schadenfreude. Putting it all together, the murderous martyrdom that terrorists seek might be called, for want of a simpler term, and a more parsimonious explanation, "apocalyptic, nihilistic, sadistic, envy-inspired, pseudo-martyrdom."

It can be concluded, then, that terrorism is not fundamentally strategic, even though, on a surface level, it appears so. It is, on the contrary, the product of a number of un-strategic elements, all of which are under the sway of the paranoid vision, combining together.

Concluding Thoughts: Islamism, Anxiety, New Learning

The rule of tyranny has been the norm since the earliest civilizations, but that special species of tyranny, totalitarianism, is a phenomenon that only really emerged, as Hannah Arendt tells us, in the twentieth century. There is, though, at least one important exception, the significance of which political scientist Scott Talkington discerns:

> But it seems that, ironically, the most virulent and world-threatening forms of the malady have coincided with the rise and spread of liberal democracy. I would almost suspect that the mere presence of a system seeking to institutionalize the optimization of liberty gives rise to an opposing ideal that seeks to control every thought and act through terror. And the first manifestation of this ancient rivalry may have been in the epic Peloponnesian Wars between Athens and Sparta. (2003, p. 3)

How is it that Athens and Sparta are mutually arising? Why, in other words, would the advent of liberal democracy coincide with the advent of totalitarianism? Arthur Schlesinger proposes an answer to that question. "The whole purpose of totalitarianism," Schlesinger wrote in 1949, "was to combat the 'anxiety' that is aroused by the lure of other, better ideas" (qtd. in Berman 1993, p. 190). Schlesinger is certainly right that totalitarianism is a response to anxiety, but the notion of better ideas being a lure does not get to the heart of the matter. If ideas cause anxiety, it is not necessarily because they are seen as better. It is because their very existence relativizes the supposed absoluteness of one's own ideas. Furthermore, new ideas suggest the perspectival quality of one's worldview, unmooring one from the solidity of the familiar. Totalitarianism is really a demonic flight from openness, freedom, and possibility. One might say that in each person there exists an inner Peloponnesian War, a series of battles between the forces of freedom and those that lure one to psychological slavery. The drama of history is the externalization of this inner warfare.

An encounter with the forces of change can create a sense of uprootedness, alienation, and ontological insecurity, all of which are experienced with much anxiety. Totalitarianism—of which Islamism is a form—is a desperate effort to quell those anxieties. Anxiety need not result in desperation, reactionary closure, and social and political malevolence. It can spur a people on to new learning, to an expansion of self-awareness, the result of which is a more conscious and more creative relation to the realities of human existence. It can, indeed, lead to a cultural renaissance. But if the "opportunity knocks card" of new learning is rejected, this anxiety will find release in outlets that are pernicious, including the paranoid vision in its various manifestations.

Islamism, therefore, and all the monstrous phenomena that are associated with it—from conspiracy theories to anti-Semitism, from totalitarianism to terrorism—is not the direct result of the anxiety-producing forces of modernity, for anxiety can have positive results. Islamism is an indirect result of that anxiety. The anxiety of modernity must first be appropriated and processed by the paranoid vision before it emerges as Islamism, or any other malevolent phenomena.

Some moderate Muslims, following the tradition of the Sufis, have interpreted the call to Jihad to mean the call to spiritual warfare, i.e. the conquest of one's weaknesses. A spiritual Jihad is, indeed, necessary if the temptation to accept the facile answers proposed by Islamist totalitarianism, and other paranoid phenomena, are to be overcome.

Part III:

Transcendence
of the
Paranoid Vision

Chapter 8

Paranoia in a New Key

---

*"...in the end all your passions became virtues and all your
devils, angels. Once you had wild dogs in your cellar, but in the
end they turned into birds and lovely singers."*

— *Nietzsche (1891; 1970)*

The ideas and beliefs of neurotics, including those who are
paranoid, are not downright delusional. They are, rather,
distortions of consensual reality. Our purpose in stating this
is not to lend credence to the cliché that "sometimes paranoids are
right." We aren't interested in assessing the validity of particular
paranoid narratives, but rather in discerning the truth that lies at the
core of the paranoid vision itself. As we hope to show, those who are
under the sway of the paranoid vision have reminiscences of a very
real conspiracy, and intimations of a very real apocalypse!

There is, though, a catch, which is where the distortion enters
in: The conspiracy and apocalypse to which we are referring do not
exist in the outer world, but belong to a different ontological realm
— to the realm of psyche, mind, or spirit. For a variety of reasons,
paranoids mistake symbolic and mythic truth for actual events in the
spatiotemporal world. That is the fundamental source of their folly.
Here, again, one finds the defense mechanism intrinsic to paranoia:
projection. Earlier, we explored what it means to project one's

"shadow" onto another group of people. Now, we shall explore the projection of inner events onto the outer world.

To arrive at the truth of the paranoid vision requires de-literalizing paranoid narratives, deciphering their symbolic language so as to extract their true import. Although our focus here is not psychopathology, our objectives would appear to be in accord with what Donald Carveth, a Freudian psychoanalyst, contends to be the goal of traditional psychotherapy—the de-literalization, disillusionment, or deconstruction of delusional beliefs, ideas, ideologies, and worldviews (Carveth 1999).

Disillusionment is key to psychological change, but when patients begin to suspect that the ontological foundations of their life are hollow, it can leave them feeling disoriented and anxious, and then depressed. This is true not only of the various schools of psychoanalysis but of all therapies—such as those which are existentially oriented—that seek to free people of their illusions. Consequently, according to Carveth, disillusionment needs to be coupled with supportive, nurturing therapy, so that the patient has the strength to continue to be disillusioned.

What we are proposing, though, is disillusionment of a different order than what Carveth correctly posits to be the foundation of psychotherapy. De-literalization and disillusionment need not involve a loss of one's beliefs, but rather a transcendence of the level on which one had held them to be true. More specifically, if those under the sway of the paranoid vision are to be disillusioned, it is healing if they can see that their worldview is essentially true, when raised to a "higher level."

In The Symposium, Socrates asserts that the usual objects of human love are but inadequate apprehensions of the real object of human desire, which Plato regarded as the Form of the Good. We are following Socrates' lead, at least in spirit, in suggesting that the usual sort of conspiracies, delusions of grandeur, and apocalyptic fantasies are but inadequate apprehensions, or representations, of "the true conspiracy" and "the true apocalypse," which are manifestations of the paranoid vision in its highest key.

Earlier, we concluded that conspiracy theories, apocalyptic fantasies, and other paranoid phenomena are a desperate flight from the temporality, relativity, and contingency of existence. The flip side of that is that they are a search for intelligibility and meaning. Now, we are suggesting that conspiracy theories, apocalyptic fantasies, and other paranoid phenomena might result from an inadequate apprehension of certain deep truths, or insights, about life.

How do these two different notions of the origin of the paranoid vision jibe? Those intimations of life's deeper truths are ontologically disorienting, which means that they open the door to the anxious awareness of temporality, relativity, and contingency. The resulting disorientation can inspire one to quest deeper into the mystery, in the hope of gaining illumination and deliverance. Or it can tempt one to seek the intelligibility and meaning promised by the paranoid vision in its lower representations. It is, therefore, the frightful intuition of the "real conspiracy" and the "real apocalypse" that tempts one to the more psychologically manageable ersatz conspiracies and ersatz apocalypses that are the product of the paranoid vision.

The reason for the distortion that is indigenous to the paranoid vision, then, is not only because the high-level representations of the paranoid vision are being "seen through a glass darkly," i.e. inadequately grasped. It is also because the psyche is censoring those high level insights, for they are too ontologically un-grounding in their raw form. Thus, our guide here is not only Socrates; it is also Freud, with his notions of censorship and repression, although here what is being censored or repressed is not sexual in nature.

Is it really the case, then, that the person under the sway of the paranoid vision has a sensitivity to life's deeper truths? If anything, paranoids tend to be narrow-minded ideologues, irascible hotheads, suspicious, grandiose, distrustful, and malevolent—not exactly the profile of a person open to deep questions. Those negative personality traits have, though, a function in the psychic economy of the paranoid. They are a defense mechanism, a bulwark against insight's dangerous assaults. Insight is dangerous because it corrodes one's beliefs, creating psychic instability. In any case, those under the sway of the paranoid vision may be off center to varying degrees, if not downright crazy, but they are not dullards. They are intuiting something true about life, even if it enters their conscious mind distorted beyond recognition. Shapiro (1965) contends that paranoids are sharply perceptive. Indeed, some of the most seminal minds of the nineteenth and twentieth centuries have, as Farrell (1996) has observed, been paranoids. What, then, is the truth that is being distorted by the paranoid vision?

The Ultimate Conspiracy Theory

Plato's Allegory of the Cave, from *The Republic,* has had an enormous influence. Its enduring message is that the world that we perceive is not the real world:

> Picture men dwelling in a sort of subterranean cavern with a long entrance open to the light on its entire width. Conceive them as having their legs and necks fettered from childhood, so that they remain in the same spot, able to look forward only, and prevented by the fetters from turning their heads. Picture further the light from a fire burning higher up and at a distance behind them, and between the fire and the prisoners and above them a road along which a low wall has been built, as the exhibitors of puppet shows have partitions before the men themselves, above which they show the puppets... See also, then, men carrying past the wall implements of all kinds that rise above the wall, and human images and shapes of animals as well, wrought in stone and wood, and every material, some of these bearers speaking and others silent. (p. 747)

Thus, for Plato, the human condition, in its immediate, uneducated state, is akin to prisoners viewing shadows on the wall of a cave, deluded from birth into thinking that the shadows are actual objects. The amazing thing is that Plato's allegory is, essentially, a conspiracy theory! Like all paranoid narratives, it is about the loss of autonomy, although in this case the loss of autonomy is not merely a fear, but a fait accompli. Of course, Plato's story is allegorical, unlike a run-of-the-mill conspiracy theory that claims to be literal. Furthermore, Plato's allegory is not about an event in the world, such as the clandestine meeting of two powerful leaders. It is, on the contrary, about a metaphysical event: human bondage to the transient and deceptive realm of appearances.

Plato's allegory is, therefore, a conspiracy theory in a higher key, for its claim to validity is founded, not on empirical facts, but on a certain intuition, or insight, that Plato had about the human condition: the world that we experience is delusory, and not the real world. We are suggesting, then, that the person under the sway of the paranoid vision is having the same intuition that Plato expressed in his allegory, but that he or she is literalizing, and therefore distorting, the significance of that truth.

The millennialism scholar Carol Matthews discovered this conspiratorial sense in Gnosticism. She came upon it reading Bentley Layton's book *The Gnostic Scriptures*. "...I was struck" Matthews states, "with how similar the 'grand Gnostic' myth which Layton described resembled in many ways a modern secular conspiracy theory" (2000, p. 1) What particularly intrigued Matthews were the powers that the Gnostics describe, whose intent is to deliberately deceive human beings.

> ...there are powers "out there/in here" who intend to deceive and conceal the deception. In ancient "Gnostic" texts, these powers were called "archons" and they were virtually "cabals" organized by and loyal to the keeper of the secret and the deception, the Demiurge. In a sense, "Gnostics" affirm what Descartes in his meditation most feared: there is a provisional 'god' of the world, and it is a spiteful, deceptive, control-hungry deity. In other words, the sense that some individuals have that they are exiled from their 'true' natures and that something is keeping them from that knowledge, is for the "gnostically" inclined, an intuition that is based on something "real" — yes Martha, there is a conspiracy of sorts. (Matthews, 2000, p. 2)

Matthews reminds us that Descartes' *Meditations*—which is what really initiated modern philosophy, with its shift from metaphysics to epistemology—belongs within the genre of philosophical conspiracy theories. Furthermore, just about every religion, both East and West, has a comparable notion of cosmic conspiracy. For example, Mara, the deceiver, seeks to distract the future Buddha during his meditation, and thus discourage him from awakening. Similarly, in Christianity, the devil tries to tempt Christ while he is praying in the desert. Of course, it is true that a conspiracy, by definition, requires more than one person, or being, and there is only Mara in the Buddha story, and only the devil in the Christ story. All the same, the key element that all such stories contain is the deliberate effort on the part of some power in the universe to deceive. That is why it would still be fair to call them metaphysical, or cosmic, conspiracy theories. Cosmic conspiracy theories can be found in a secular context as well, for example, in such popular films as *The Truman Show* (1998) and *The Matrix* (1999).

Let us return to Plato's cave. There is a great deal that is perplexing about the whole situation that he describes. Why, for example, have the prisoners been chained? What are the guards supposed to represent? What is their motivation? Who are they working for? Why is a prisoner allowed to go free, indeed dragged to the light? These are not questions that Plato asks in the dialogue. Nor do classical scholars —such as Francis Cornford, Benjamin Jowett, A.E. Taylor, Paul Shorey, Edith Hamilton, and Harold Bloom—explore such questions. Nor do philosophers, like Martin Heidegger, who takes Plato's allegory very seriously, explore them. We are, then, proceeding beyond the limits of existing scholarship, and perhaps beyond the limits of both discriminative understanding and metaphorical representation. Viewed as a conspiracy theory, Plato's allegory certainly leaves a lot of loose ends. Consequently, in an effort to give a metaphorical picture of the human predicament though his allegory—which he does superbly well—Plato ends up revealing the existence of a deeper mystery.

Of course, if the guards in Plato's cave are puzzling, one is equally puzzled as to why the grand deceivers of other traditions—the Demiurge and the Archons, Mara, and Satan, for example—are intent on deceiving human beings. Here may be the key to understanding "human bondage," to use Spinoza's phrase, but the explanations offered for this deception are not altogether satisfactory. There have, though, always been anthropomorphic explanations offered, which consist of attributing human motivations—including envy, and the other six deadly sins—to the forces of darkness.

For example, in Milton's *Paradise Lost,* Satan is primarily consumed by envy, but also by pride, ambition, and self-pity. In the film *The Matrix* (1999), the rulers, machines possessing artificial intelligence, enslave humans in an illusory world because humans supposedly are able to furnish them with energy. The hope, in anthropomorphizing the forces of darkness or positing a utilitarian motive, is to render the situation intelligible. But such flimsy accounts fail to convince anyone who, like the proverbial detective of film noir, is too skeptical to accept pat answers that bespeak a cover-up. Thus the mystery remains uncanny and metaphysically unsettling.

There was, no doubt, a certain wisdom in Socrates' not having addressed the question, for there are mysteries that are beyond rational knowing, and even metaphor or allegory can only go so far by way of explanation. Might it also be possible that what the dialogues reveal is far from all that was said and done in Plato's academy? There may have been secrets kept, but the real source of esotericism derives from the fact that there are mysteries that can only be solved by entering into them oneself. Actually, "solved" might not be the right word. After all, these are neither detective mysteries nor scientific mysteries where there exists a clear solution, either arrived at through a ratiocinative process or an empirical investigation.

These are mysteries that must be entered into, not just with the intellect, but with one's entire being, which is then transformed in the process. Consequently, only those who have entered into the mystery in that way can know the answer. That explains the problem of communicability. What is discovered, to the degree that it is communicable, is best expressed through myth or allegory.

Bearing these limits in mind, what are we able to understand about the resistance to knowledge, symbolized by the prisoner in Plato's allegory, who must be forcibly dragged out of the cave to the light? To answer that question, one must turn inward, where one might encounter something akin to the perverse willfulness that Saint Augustine wrote about in his Confessions. But it is not so much a force that wills evil as a force that wills "sleep," although the two are often conflated.

For example, the resolutions that one makes in the evening, during a moment of clarity, are often forgotten the next day when that clarity is no longer present.[44] Is it laziness that ails one? Not really, for the resolution may have been to ease off on the intensity of one's work, and to spend more time relaxing. Is it the force of habit? To a large degree, it is indeed a function of the inertia arising from old habits, a resistance that weighs on a person like a heavy anchor, discouraging forward movement. But whereas habit is merely a passive force, what we are referring to here is experienced as an active force, one that is diabolically clever.

At such moments of perplexity, it can happen that one has an intimation of a cosmic conspiracy, of a Mara, or a Satan, or some other cosmic deceiver, who is behind it all. The twelfth century Zen master Honen must have suspected as much when he said, "It is a terrible fact that devils always get in the way of those who are striving for Buddhahood." (qtd. in Perry 1971, p. 369) Some of the most perceptive philosophers, religious leaders, and saints have had this sense, and have struggled to unriddle this cosmic mystery and to unmask the cosmic conspirators. What happens, though, in the case of the paranoid, is that these intimations of a deeper mystery get distorted and literalized such that what emerges is a conspiracy theory, one that is only remotely related to the cosmic conspiracy to which Plato and other thinkers refer.

The Distortion that is Paranoia

Plato's theory of reminiscence contends that knowledge consists in remembering what has, at birth, been forgotten. Extending that notion a bit, one might say that even amidst this world of shadows, to use Plato's cave metaphor, a shadow may prompt a person to vaguely remember that this is not true reality. Such a perception is not necessarily true in an objective sense, but Plato has articulated a certain vision of life—that the world that one perceives is not true reality—that anyone, who begins to have metaphysical doubts, is likely

---

44 Bearing in mind how easy it is to fall asleep, there is much wisdom in orthodox Muslims having set times in the day to pray, so as to remind themselves what needs to be remembered.

to share. Thus when we speak of "the truth," in this context, we mean the truth of this vision.

The intimation that the world is but a shadow realm may be occasioned, for example, by a haunting dream, by the off-putting smile of a stranger, taking a wrong turn whereupon one travels down unfamiliar streets, by the candid observations of a child, or by the message on the side of a bus that communicates to one far more than it was intended to. These intimations may, in certain respects, be akin to what Martin Buber (1965) called "signs."

Most people seek to avoid the emergence of such unsettling intimations, clues, signs, doubts, and metaphysical suspicions, and if they do arise, they seek all the more desperately to absorb themselves in the familiar. Why this flight? As Buber indicates:

> Each of us is encased in an armor whose task it is to ward off signs, for we are afraid that to open ourselves to them means annihilation. Signs happen to us without respite, living means being addressed; we would need only to present ourselves and to perceive. But the risk is too dangerous for us, the soundless thunderings seem to threaten us with annihilation, and from generation to generation we perfect the defense apparatus. (1965, p. 10)

What, then, is this dangerous knowledge that, according to Buber, appears in the form of signs? Certainly self-knowledge is destructive. The light of self-knowledge, for example, blinded Oedipus, at least in the symbolic sense. Scrooge in Dickens's *Christmas Carol* was frightened by what he saw about himself. In the musical Man of La Mancha (1965), the Knight of the Mirrors finally defeats Don Quixote, for what he sees in the mirrors is himself, a demented old man. It would, indeed, be fair to say that nothing is as terrifying as self-knowledge, which is why there exists an immense resistance to it. But there are also metaphysical insights that are equally dangerous. Nietzsche seems to have had a special fondness for them; his notion of "eternal recurrence" would be one such example. Then, of course, there is that metaphysical suspicion that Plato articulates in his cave analogy. In any case, Buber argues that if the light of self does manage to break through the layers of defense mechanisms it is experienced as the world communicating with one, in the form of a sign.

This refusal to acknowledge a sign is not always successful. Sometimes the river of doubt can cause the dam of denial to finally crack, precipitating a flood of overwhelming questions, otherwise known as a crisis. But denial is not the only way in which people deal with metaphysical doubts. Just as the emotions find expression in music, opera, and drama, so it would seem that these amorphous suspicions find expression in novels and in films about conspiracies, and in rumors of conspirators involved in various forms of political skullduggery. For most people, conspiracy-infused novels and books provide adequate outlets for their metaphysical suspicions, and even then they indulge these suspicions only on occasion.

Those with paranoid proclivities seem to lack the ability either to repress or to adequately sublimate such deeper suspicions into more innocent channels, such as artistic or philosophical endeavor. One might think of a person under the sway of the paranoid vision, indeed any neurotic for that matter, as an artist manqué, to use Freud's term, or perhaps as a philosopher manqué. As we have suggested, paranoids may be more intuitively aware than are other people of life's metaphysical mysteries even though these insights come to them filtered through a grossly distorted lens.

Of course, the fact that one is an artist or philosopher does not make one any saner. It only means that one's lunacy has found a socially acceptable outlet. In a book entitled Freud's Paranoid Quest (1998), John Farrell begins by mentioning the fact that some of the great minds of modernity were paranoid, in the clinical sense. Over time, they became obsessed with delusions of persecution and of grandeur:

> Henry James spent his last afternoons as Napoleon, ordering furniture by imperial fiat. Friedrich Nietzsche late in his career assumed the titles Caesar and of "The Crucified." August Strindberg, exhilarated by a letter from "Nietzsche Caesar," signed his reply "The One and Only God."

Hobbes was pathologically timorous, given to sudden flights. Maupassant suffered from bouts of persecution, as did E.T.A. Hoffman. Schopenhauer slept with a gun beside his bed. "Stendhal" kept changing his name. Imaginary enemies pursued Hemingway. Rousseau believed that he was being persecuted by the entire generation of living Frenchmen... (Farrell 1996, p. 1)

It could be argued that if art and philosophy had successfully raised paranoia to a higher key, then these thinkers would have maintained their sanity. On the other hand, the fact that, as thinkers, they were immensely productive, despite either flirting with madness, or being half mad during their creative years, or eventually fully mad, would support the notion that the elevation of their paranoia into art and philosophy was successful, at least for a time.

What makes some of the most creative thinkers go mad is their perception of the delusory nature of human existence, of the cosmic conspiracy (the one that has to do with Plato's Cave) and of the inner apocalypse (which we shall discuss shortly). The naked truth disorients them, creating what R.D. Laing called "ontological insecurity," such that they seek to find order in events, by means of paranoid narratives. Thus the metaphysical openness of the person under the sway of the paranoid vision seeks closure through distortion and literalization.

The paranoid, therefore, literalizes the intuition of a metaphysical conspiracy and the intuition of a cosmic force of evil, imagining that what is at issue is an actual conspiracy involving real people — the Trilateral Commission, the Jews, the Illuminati, or some other group. Even better than acquiring "understanding" through uncovering conspiracies would be the ability to control events, indeed to create events. Then one's omnipotence will be put to the service of creating a world that is congruent with one's image of intelligibility and meaning. That is why, then, psychotic paranoids are tempted to become Caesar, Napoleon, or "The One and Only God," in the case of Strindberg. Despite all such efforts to find coherence, order, and meaning, or to create it, usually through violence, "Things fall apart. The center cannot hold."

As suggested earlier, in our discussion of Feuerbach, there are actually two reasons for this reification, or literalization. First of all, reification or objectification is the mind's effort to represent this intuition to itself, and thus understand it. The problem is that, in doing so, the mind distorts what it seeks to represent. But this mistake cannot be avoided. We referred earlier to Socrates' ladder of love. One must go through the educative dialectic, from puerile lust, and through many other, increasingly clarified, objects of love, before one knows that it is really the Form of the Good that one has been seeking all along.

Religion offers other examples of this phenomenon. Here, too, there is a ladder from the usual anthropomorphizing of deity to such rarefied notions as Spinoza's "intellectual love of God." We might add that when the un-illuminated mind hears a high-level notion, it misinterprets it such that the high-level notion ends up sounding like something on the beginning rungs of the ladder. For example, it has made little difference that Sufism has elevated the notion of Jihad, or holy war, to mean a war against one's baser nature. The baser mind will continue to construe Jihad to mean a war against other people.

Now this is the point: there is, similarly, a kind of Socratic ladder in regard to the paranoid vision. There are, indeed, many levels on which the mind can represent to itself the sense of cosmic conspiracy and deception. Furthermore, on some levels it might not even regard the deception as evil. Hegel, for example, believed that Reason was the grand schemer, as evidenced by his notion of "the cunning of Reason." Simply stated, it means that people think that they are acting independently, but Reason exploits their passions and beliefs to advance history towards Reason's telos. Optimist that he was, Hegel believed that Reason's cunning was something good, for its telos was the self-realization of Spirit. Ironically enough—standing the usual notion of conspiracy theory, with its fear of loss of autonomy, on its head — the cunning of Reason is all about the emergence of freedom!

Adam Smith, similarly, had a notion of a relatively beneficent force, one that rules the economic sphere, which he called the "hidden hand." The idea here is that everyone acting out of self-interest ended up advancing the economic wellbeing of society as a whole, and advancing social progress.

A certain modern group of thinkers also had notions of a larger conspiracy, but they were not so sanguine regarding its outcome. These thinkers were involved with interpreting the world, and interpreting various texts as well, but their interpretative method was, according to Paul Ricoeur, a "hermeneutics of suspicion" (1970, p. 33). They were intent on unmasking hidden motives.

Take, for example, the Bible. Nietzsche detected in the Bible the hidden motives of power, and also resentment. For Marx, the hidden motive was economics. Thus, for Marx, the Bible is nothing but a devious means to economically exploit the peasants. Freud looked at the Bible and detected the Oedipal complex. For Althusser it was Ideology. For Foucault it was the establishment of legitimacy and power, or hegemony. Despite their immense differences, all of these suspicious philosophers, from Hegel to Foucault, share the notion that there are hidden forces in the world whose purpose is to keep one ignorant of what is really going on. All such hidden forces belie one's claim to autonomy, and thus these philosophies have the flavor of paranoid narratives. And although theories founded on the hermeneutics of suspicion are often profound, like all paranoid narratives they literalize and distort the cosmic conspiracy. Thus, in bringing some dimension of reality to light, such as power or sexuality, they obscure a great deal more.

If the first reason for the paranoid's literalization of the cosmic conspiracy has to do with the dialectics of coming to know anything, the second reason is not so innocent: taking what is really an inner sense of conspiracy for an actual outer event is a form of projection, which, after all, is a defense mechanism. We might, therefore, ask: against what is one really defending oneself?

A person transforms anxiety into fear, according to Freud, so as to make it more manageable. Similarly, those who have an inner intuition of an ultimate conspiracy, the one represented by Plato's allegory, transform it into an actual external conspiracy so as to make it tangible, and thus manageable. Action can be taken against an actual group of people, but encountering one's "shadow," to use Jung's term, is infinitely more challenging. This would mean that the person under the sway of the paranoid vision is not simply a philosophical or psychological ingénue, but is demonic, in the Kierkegaardian sense, i.e. a person who is in active flight from "the good," and from himself.

There are other reasons, too, why one would not wish to leave the cave. To do so would mean cutting oneself off from the rest of humanity, who are convinced that what they perceive on the walls of the cave is true reality. Consequently, one would find oneself profoundly alone. Furthermore, as Plato indicates, the light of the sun (i.e. the truth) is blinding, for one's eyes have not yet adapted to the light. That is an image of the sense of disorientation that ensues when one's usual dreams and schemes that belonged to life in the cave (the life of unconscious immediacy), are no longer regarded as real.

Apropos are what Louis A. Sass, in Madness and Modernism (1992), refers to as "...Apollonian or even Socratic illnesses whose central features are hypertrophy of consciousness and a concomitant detachment from instinctual sources of vitality." (1992, p. 74) According to Sass, schizophrenics suffer from that Apollonian or Socratic illness, which modern artists and thinkers, such as Kafka, Strindberg, Kandinsky, and Wittgenstein express in their creations. There is much to suggest that paranoia is a way of avoiding the loss of vitality by literalizing, reifying, and distorting what one sees. Thus the paranoid vision can be considered to be a way of protecting oneself from the harsh light of conscious awareness.

Non-Delusive Grandeur

We have suggested that one must be in touch with reality, at least to some degree, in order to be able to distort it. Could it be, then, that the delusions of grandeur, which are intrinsic to the paranoid vision, are a distorted perception of a fundamental truth? If that is so, then these delusions, when played in a higher key, are no longer delusions —paradoxical though it may sound—but indicative of true human grandeur. But before exploring true grandeur, let us consider a bit further the delusory grandeur endemic to the paranoid vision, for the false can, by way of contrast, indicate the nature of the true.

Grandeur is delusional when it consists in attributing ultimate significance to oneself alone. A person regards himself as a king, towering above other human beings, who are relegated to the position of admirers, servants, nonentities, or obstacles in the way to happiness. Ironically, nothing is more common, and more indicative of a pedestrian soul, than the claim to ultimate importance, not to being superior in a particular area, but to a universal superiority. Delusional grandeur is akin to hubris, or overweening pride, in so far as it consists of a refusal to acknowledge the finitude intrinsic to the human condition.

Such arrogance is evident in Dostoevsky's character Raskolnikov, who believed that he was a superman and therefore allowed to do anything, including murder. Ironically, the opposite is the case, for as Berdyaev points out, "The rare and notable man who is endowed with special gifts is not a man to whom everything is permitted. On the contrary, he is the man to whom nothing is permitted. It is fools and insignificant people to whom everything is permitted" (1944, 1980, p. 180). In Part Two, we observed the destruction created by those individuals who believed that everything is permitted, by virtue of the importance of their cause.

It would appear that the delusions of grandeur endemic to the paranoid vision are compensatory in the psychological sense. They recompense paranoids for the sense that they have of themselves as weak and ignoble. Raskolnikov again comes to mind — full of grand ideas, but hungry and cold in his tiny apartment. A person under the sway of the paranoid vision, feeling "in disgrace with fortune," looks at other people as somehow responsible. Millon, quoted earlier in the introduction, contends that, "Beneath the surface mistrust and defensive vigilance in the paranoid lies a current of deep resentment toward others who have made it" (1996, p. 701).

Millon is referring to paranoia in the clinical sense, but his observations are true of the paranoid vision of life in general. Again, some of the subjects of the case examples come to mind—Pol Pot, Duch, Rajneesh, Sheela (Rajneesh's disciple), Mohamed Atta, and Osama bin Laden. It begins with an a priori claim to grandeur, the assumption that one, or one's group, deserves everything, all the benefits that heaven and earth have to offer. The second proposition encapsulates the bitterness of the paranoid vision: If one does not have what one deserves, it is because others have stolen it. Envy's resentful finale is that if one cannot have what one deserves, then no one deserves to have anything.

That conclusion has had a great variety of manifestations, from the woman in the King Solomon story who would be willing to see the contested baby die, as long as the rightful mother did not get her baby,[45] to the suicide bombers who would gladly destroy themselves to deny other people the possibility of happiness. It is also not surprising that the envious long for the apocalypse. After all, if the world goes up in flames, then no one can have anything.

Those who are under the sway of the paranoid vision may have delusions of grandeur not simply about themselves, but about the group with which they are affiliated. When groups have delusions of grandeur, it often leads them to an antinomian disdain for rules, laws, and morality in regard to people outside the group, or even outside the group's inner circle. Not surprising, this double morality is endemic to utopian organizations. We might recall Orwell's nightmarish novel *Animal Farm*, with its murderous ruling pigs. The same ruthless exceptionalism, which one might call "group Raskolnikovism," has existed in a variety of groups, including cults, terrorist organizations, ruthless and repressive political regimes, rogue business management teams, and bumptious, jingoistic nations, all who eventually go the way of King Ozymandias.

Group delusions of grandeur are seductive, for they promise those who feel unhappy and unworthy that they can attain the power and prestige of the group, or so they imagine. Furthermore, such groups offer opportunities for ambitious true believers to attain immortality by sacrificing their life for the group. As Schopenhauer has been attributed as saying, "Martyrdom is the only way a man can become famous without ability." Invariably, group grandeur is premised on a lie, for what seems like transcendence is but an extended egotism, and what seems like grandeur is really narcissistic fantasy. In essence,

---

45 For a discussion of the King Solomon example, see: Solomon Schimmel. The Seven Deadly Sins. Oxford University Press. New York: 1997.

delusional grandeur is founded on a hubris that impotently rebels against the finitude of the human condition.

Our discussion of delusions of grandeur has been the propaedeutic to a paradox: when finitude is denied, it leads to envy, bitterness, the worship of death, and just plain misery. But when finitude and suffering, too, are accepted without regret, indeed embraced—in the sense in which Nietzsche meant "amor fati"—something else, quite wondrous, can emerge: grandeur in a new key.[46]* Those who have peered into the dark depths of life have discovered this grandeur. After all, how else could Sophocles write, in a heart-rending tragedy, no less: "Numberless are the world's wonders, but none more wonderful than man." Similarly, Shakespeare's *Hamlet,* a melancholy Dane who, on the one hand, views humanity as a "quintessence of dust," (Act II, Scene II) on the other hand offers this encomium: "What a piece of work is a man! How noble in reason! How infinite in faculties! In form and moving how express and admirable! In action how like an angel! In apprehension how like a god! The beauty of the world! The paragon of animals!" (Act II, Scene II) Whether or not Hamlet was being ironic, the images that he uses affect us with their sublime power.

Walter Kerr—whose book *Tragedy and Comedy* (1968) has prompted this reflection on these passages from Sophocles and Shakespeare — observes that it would appear to many readers to be counter-intuitive, and a bit surprising, that such elevated thoughts are found in tragedies. After all, one thinks that tragedies are pessimistic, for human aspirations inevitably smash into the limits of the world. Apropos are what Jaspers calls "boundary situations," which include: suffering, death, guilt, chance, and conflict. What they have in common is that they limit human existence; they are the unavoidable forces of finitude. All of these limiting conditions find expression in tragedy. And yet, there exists a curious optimism, not just in literary tragedies, but in the tragic vision itself. How is this possible?

---

46 'It might be advisable to employ a different word than "grandeur," when considering its transformation to a new key. After all, "grandeur" often connotes an egotism that is intrinsically delusory. There is no ideal word for this new key, but "dignity," "nobility," or "greatness" would be preferable. Sometimes, we shall use those words, but on other occasions we shall stick with "grandeur," so as not to lose the connection that we are trying to establish with the delusions indigenous to the paranoid worldview.

Tragedy's sad ending might lead one to believe that it is all about accepting finitude, but that is not true at all. Like everything else that is elevating, tragedy is predicated on an acknowledgment and glorification of the dual nature of the human being. Apropos is Friedrich Schlegel's theory of why tragedy, on stage, is ennobling. He believed that only by the tragic hero's choice of values—like honor, courage, love, and loyalty—over life itself, do those values become truly real, rather than mere sentiments or abstract possibilities (Hedge, 1849, pp. 423-444). The transcendence and grandeur that arise from the heroic affirmation of values, in the face of death itself, are anything but delusions. As Jaspers has said in a remarkable passage:

> Paradoxically, however, when man faces the tragic, he liberates himself from it... There is no tragedy without transcendence. Even defiance unto death in a hopeless battle against the gods and fate is an act of transcending: it is a movement toward man's proper essence, which he comes to know as his own in the presence of his doom." (Emphasis Jaspers') (1952, p. 41)

Jaspers seems to suggesting a duality at the heart of the human being, which might be represented, for example, as that between fate and freedom, or between body and spirit. True grandeur would consist of suffering this duality while affirming freedom or spirit. This perception of humans as dual beings is not the exclusive province of tragedy, but can be found in other visions of life as well, including those that are religious, humanistic, existential, comic, and mystical. Mircea Eliade's Yoga: Immortality and Freedom (1970) offers an intriguing example. Eliade refers to a "primitive" tribe who regard human beings as more worthy of esteem than even the gods! Their argument is that humans are able to do something of which no other being is capable, including the gods.

Humans can mediate opposites: the animal kingdom and the realm of the gods, earth and heaven, the profane and the sacred, the temporal and the eternal. How are humans able to accomplish this mediation? Sir Thomas Browne claimed that human beings are amphibious creatures. He didn't mean, of course, that we are frogs, who live on land in in the sea. Rather, he is using "amphibious" metaphorically. The two realms that humans inhabit are the earthly and the spiritual. As Browne states,

> We are only that amphibious piece between a corporal and spiritual Essence, that middle form that links those two together, and makes good the Method of GOD and Nature, that jumps not from extremes, but unites the incompatible distances by some middle and participating natures. (1643; 1972, p. 36)

There are those who might argue that the notion of humans inhabiting a middle realm, on a great chain of being, is nothing new, but can be found in ancient philosophy, especially in Aristotle. But the ancient understanding of human beings differs from the view of humans that we are presenting here, for the former implies that humans have a fixed place. Pico della Mirandola, in 1446, denied that this is so. He believes that "the dignity of man," i.e. human grandeur, arises from an indeterminacy—a person can descend to the animal or ascend to the heavens:

> You alone are nowhere restricted and can take to yourself and be whatever you decide according to your will. We have placed you in the center of the world, so that you can look in all directions and discover where you like it. We have created you not heavenly, not earthly. Not mortal and not immortal. For you yourself are, according to your will and your honor, to be your workmaster and maker...So you are free to sink down to the lowest level of the animal world. Yet you can also rise to the highest level of divinity. (qtd. in Landmann, pp. 123-124.)

For the existentialists, consciousness is key to human finitude and infinitude. As Maurice Friedman expresses it, "Indissolubly connected with the finitude which is given by the ability to know only this, there is a participation in infinity, which is given by the ability to know at all" (1965, p. 13). For Pascal, human greatness consists, paradoxically, in the knowledge of one's misery! That is why, according to Pascal, human beings are a hopelessly contradictory mélange of finitude and infinitude.

> What a chimera man really is! What an extraordinary monster, what a chaos, what a contradictory thing, what a marvelous oddity! Judge of all things. Helpless earth-worm; protector of truth, cess-pool of ignorance and error: glory and scum of the universe. Who will untangle this knot? (1660; 1979, p. 182)

These are just a few examples of thinkers who have seen human beings as amphibious creatures, to use Browne's term, and who derive the grandeur as well as the pathos of human beings from that very fact. Thus Kant's question—"What is man?" has immensely significant implications for unconsciously held worldviews, including the paranoid vision.

There is, though, a resistance to seeing oneself as an amphibious being. As the philosophical anthropologist Michael Landmann has astutely observed, "So for the most varied reasons man does not want to be himself, and therefore he is his own worst enemy and therefore he refuses to know himself. He finds every theory that tells him he is a fallen angel or a monkey preferable to the truth about himself" (1979, 178). That truth, of course, is that human beings are neither monkeys nor angels, but are the meeting place of the animal and the transcendent realms.

Why, then, do human beings seek to deny their dual nature? To answer that question, consider — by way of contrast to the amphibious vision — utopian thinking, in its purest form, unhindered by the limits of the possible. The millenarian fantasies that are a product of utopianism contend that finitude is not intrinsic to the human estate; they promise, in essence, "Ye shall be as gods." The manifestations of that worldview have included sanguinary revolutions, ideologically-caused famines, totalitarianism, political oppression, terrorism, and genocide. Why these dark consequences? First of all, the possibility of the millennium now provides those with an instrumentalist ethics a justification for any atrocity (Cohn, 1996). As for totalitarianism, Isaiah Berlin draws out the intrinsic connection between utopianism and the loss of liberty, as suggested by the ideas of the utopian thinker Saint-Simon:

> Again, Saint-Simon more than anyone else invented the notion of the government of society by elites, using a double morality. There is, of course, something of that in Plato and in previous thinkers, but Saint-Simon is the first thinker who comes out and says that it is important for society to be governed not democratically... (2002, p. 107)

Furthermore, as we have suggested, the deep disappointment that inevitably arises from utopian expectations is paranoiagenic. It leads to bitterness, hostility, blame, envy, and all the other malevolent feelings associated with the paranoid vision. The utopian vision has clearly left something out of the human equation, namely the fact that human beings are, as Kant said, "twisted timber" (Berlin, 1990, p. v), from which nothing straight can grow.

How ironic, then, that the utopian vision, with its unconstrained affirmation of humanity's godlike possibilities, leads to bitterness. But those visions of life that recognize the amphibious nature of human beings, and which are constrained in their hopes for humanity, lead to the affirmation of human grandeur, greatness, and nobility. Furthermore, the tragic vision leads to an optimism — not one founded on shallow hopes, but on ennobling endurance of suffering and triumph over adversity. It is paradoxical that the acknowledgement of finitude is a prerequisite for the realization of true grandeur.

If some thinkers have sought to deny the amphibious duality by positing that human beings are fallen gods or fallen angels, other thinkers deny the duality by positing that human beings are merely animals, although highly intelligent ones. The latter view ranges from the animal aggression studies of Konrad Lorenz to the behaviorism of B.F. Skinner. Here the duality is denied by a debasement of the human. Instead of delusions of grandeur, they offer delusions of animality.

The Freudian view of human beings, although far more complex than those other thinkers, is also a debased view of human beings, as is all such biological reductionism. It is also important to keep in mind, in regard to a cure for the paranoid vision, that "shrinking," forsaking the eternal and infinite for the sake of the "reality principle"—which is recommended by Freudian psychoanalysis, behaviorism, "reality therapy," and by other such therapies—is ill-advised, for it only leads to depression or to quiet desperation.

Why, then, are human beings so loath to accept their amphibious nature? It means being required to mediate contradictory terms, and suffering their incompatibility. It is immensely difficult to recognize oneself as a finite being, and yet, paradoxically, not merely a finite being, for one is required to live at every moment such that one's life bears witness to eternal values. Who would wish to make one's life the crucible wherein realms of reality—that are, in Kierkegaard's opinion, incommensurable — are wedded?

By way of contrast, viewing oneself as an exiled god—not on some higher plane as do the Gnostics, but merely on the level of ego—and blaming another group of people for one's fallen condition, is very easy. That is why utopian visions, with their paranoiagenic potential, are so tempting. It is also tempting to seek to deny the difficult task of mediating contradictions by means of the claim that humans are mere animals, a claim that reeks of sloth. Psychologically speaking, humans beings wish to deny their fundamental ontological duality, for that duality is the source of dread, or anxiety. As Kierkegaard states: "If a man were a beast or an angel, he would not be in dread. Since he is a synthesis he can be in dread, and the greater the dread, the greater the man" (1884; 1973, p. 139).

We have been making the case that the narratives that characterize the paranoid vision are an inadequate apprehension of that which is essentially true. It would, therefore, be fair to say that the person under the sway of the paranoid vision, who is having delusions of grandeur, is intuiting, but grossly distorting, that which is fundamentally true: there truly is a grandeur that belongs to the human estate. Consequently, a person's longing for the infinite cannot successfully be abandoned by psychotherapeutic shrinking or by any other means; it can only be performed in a new key. This transformation of a person —from having delusions of grandeur to recognizing the ground of true grandeur, the type that is befitting to that amphibious creature known as a human being—is the meaning of moral evolution.

An example of this evolution would be the transformation of King Oedipus from vain exaltation to possessing tragic grandeur by the end of Sophocles' trilogy. According to the French scholar of mythology, Paul Diel (1980), this moral and spiritual evolution is the fundamental theme of all Greek mythology and literature. Spiritual evolution of those who are under the sway of the paranoid vision would, to a large extent, consist in learning what it means to be an amphibious being; i.e. elevating the grandeur to a new key. This elevation would require a person—not just those who are under the sway of the paranoid vision —to learn to endure the anxiety intrinsic to the task of mediating incommensurate realms, such as the temporal and the eternal. Tillich (1952; 2000) calls this endurance, "the courage to be."

The Apocalypse Within:
Fantasy as Surrogate for Inner Change

Might it be that endtime narratives are but a distortion—through the processes of literalization and projection—of a high level inner longing or need? We contend that that need is for self-renewal, self-transformation, a radically new mode of existence. Its fulfillment is being mistaken for an event in the outer world, one that has not yet transpired. Raising apocalyptic fantasies to a new key consists, therefore, in recognizing what has been motivating them all along: the need for an apocalypse within. Were we to de-literalize apocalyptic texts, we would discern that self-renewal was really at issue.

This de-literalization has previously been undertaken in a different context. For example, Bernard McGinn (2000) informs us that Origen, Augustine, and other prominent early Christian theologians criticized the literalist interpretations of the books of Daniel and Revelation, recommending instead that these apocalyptic texts be read allegorically. How, then, to understand the millennium in the de-literalized sense? According to Harold Bloom, "For Augustine, the church was the Millennium already embodied, the true Kingdom of God already established upon earth" (1996, p. 222). And according to Boyer, "Origen...interpreted the prophesies allegorically: Antichrist symbolized evil; the thousand-year reign of righteousness described a spiritual reality achieved in the souls of individual believers, and so on" (1992, 47). Jungians, on the other hand, argue that apocalyptic texts are mythic, or archetypal, as opposed to allegorical, and that they arise out of the depths of the collective unconscious. Edward F. Edinger's analysis is particularly interesting in this regard:

> ...the "Apocalypse" means the momentous event of the coming of the Self into conscious realization. Of course, it manifests itself and is experienced in quite different ways if occurring in the individual psyche or in the collective life of a group; but in either case, it is a momentous event — literally world-shattering. This is what the content of the Apocalypse archetype presents: the shattering of the world as it has been, followed by its reconstruction (1999, p. 5).

There exists, though, according to historians (Cohn, 1959, McGinn, 1998), a literary tradition of using certain symbols to construct apocalyptic prophesies, which would seem to belie the notion that they are spontaneous, archetypal eruptions from the collective unconscious. Whether consciously constructed or not, these stories resonate with mythic meaning for—like all good poets, playwrights, and novelists — writers of apocalyptic fantasies are in touch with the deeper layers of their unconscious.

The fantasies that interest us here are those that discover signs of the coming apocalypse in contemporary events. The imagery—both horrifying and idyllic—that belongs, respectively, to apocalyptic and millenarian fantasies, suggests a psychological ambivalence towards the transformative forces that lead to self-renewal; they are both dreaded and desired. Why the dread? First of all, there is the Day of Judgment, an event that is found in *The Book of Revelation* and other apocalyptic stories. The psychological correlate to Judgment Day is clear enough: transitions to a new mode of existence require that one be judged and held accountable for how one has lived, the consequence of which is, most often, remorse.

The verdict might not mean that one is guilty of leading a life of iniquity; but how one has lived, and that for which one has lived, may often be regarded, from one's present standpoint, as a deep disappointment, in the sense in which Eliade meant it when he wrote,

...whatever degree of fulfillment it may have brought him, at a certain moment every man sees his life as a failure. This vision does not arise from a moral judgment made on his part, but from an obscure feeling that he has missed his vocation; that he has betrayed the best that was in him (1958, p. 135).

We are reminded, in that regard, of Tolstoy's *The Death of Ivan Ilyich*. Such heavy realizations need not be the final judgment—there was a light at the end of the tunnel for Ivan Ilyich—but remorse is an unavoidable stop on the road to self-renewal, for the past must be burnt away if something new is to emerge.[47]

After the judgment, there is, in apocalyptic fantasies, the actual cataclysm. It symbolizes the destruction of who one has taken oneself to be. To understand the resultant dread, we must bear in mind that significant inner change is a terrifying affair, for one's present self is threatened with nonexistence. As Edinger explains it: "'Apocalypse' bodes catastrophe only for the stubbornly rationalistic, secular ego that refuses to grant the existence of a greater psychic authority than itself. Since it cannot bend, it has to break" (1999, p. 13). Whether or not one agrees with the Jungians that apocalyptic fantasies are about the coming of the Self as a threat to ego consciousness, phenomenologically speaking, significant inner change is experienced as the end of the world. In reality, it is the end of the world that one's mind has constituted. So it makes sense that these terrors and anxieties find expression in apocalyptic fantasies.

Like nocturnal dreams, apocalyptic fantasies are a kind of psychic feedback system, expressing what one needs to undergo inwardly. But the fascination with apocalyptic fantasies ends up subverting the forces of inner-change. One looks out-there when one should be looking in-here, which is, of course, what happens in all psychological literalization.

This subversion is neurotic, in Tillich's sense of the word, for it involves a refusal to live so as to avoid the death that is intrinsic to life. But without death, there can be no evolution. Instead of despairing

---

47 Hollywood often presents the opposite vision: a person who feels like a failure comes to realize that he or she has really led a valuable life. We see this in such films as *It's a Wonderful Life* (1946), and *Mr. Holland's Opus* (1999).

and letting go of that which has been outgrown, i.e., one's old mode of existence, one makes a home out of one's despair. Apocalyptic fantasies are merely one of many modes of flight from self-transformation. The result of this refusal is a sclerosis of spirit, a malady that is so common that it is generally assumed to be normal.

It is true that there has been a great deal said and written about "growth." Thousands of books on the subject can be found in the self-help sections of bookstores. "Growth" is a vacuous notion, for real transformation is not about getting bigger and better. It is about death and transfiguration. If there has been a great deal written, in the last forty years, about the glories of self-transformation — especially by votaries of the New Age Movement—it is because, in a youth-worshiping culture that encourages the perpetuation of adolescence, so few people actually wish to undergo what it required to transform (Epstein, 2004).

Although human beings in the modern age may be more prone to the narcissism that retards inner-development, human beings have always been prone to forget that this world is not a home, but a road that one travels in search of oneself. This resistance to coming to terms with life's fundamental realities is evidenced by the fact that the prophets, both ancient and modern, need to continually remind their flock that life is about death and transfiguration to a higher plane of existence.

Ecclesiastes advises, "Remember thy creator in the days of thy youth." St. Thomas Aquinas states, "No creature can attain a higher grade of nature without ceasing to exist" (qtd. in Perry, 1971, 206). Angelus Silesius implores, "Die before thou diest, so as not to die when thou diest, or indeed must thou perish" (qtd. in Perry, 1971, 208). Mohamed shared the same idea, "Die before ye die" (qtd. in Perry, 1971, 206). Sri Ramana Maharshi, a Hindu, stated: "One cannot see God and yet retain individuality" (qtd. in Perry, 1971, 208). Zen, too, is about dying. The Zen master Bunan Zenji said, "While living be a dead man" (qtd. in Perry, 1971, 208). Yekiwo said, "If you are really desirous of mastering Zen, it is necessary for you once to give up your life and plunge right into the pit of death" (qtd. in Perry, 1971, 209).

But what is it that is really being advised by those sages? Should one remember one's physical death? Martin Heidegger, who stated that man is a "being-towards-death," believes that one should be aware of death, if one intends to live an authentic existence. Heidegger's philosophy—his understanding of the anxiety that lies at the heart of Dasein — may be profound, but it would have been far profounder had his being-towards-death been about the daily dying that is intrinsic to human existence.

Socrates' statement, in the Phaedo, that "Philosophy is the art and practice of dying," is infinitely more perceptive than Heidegger's, for it indicates that dying is not something that only happens at the very end of one's life. Life is always about dying, in the sense of undergoing transformations. What, then, is the art and practice of dying? To a large extent it consists in consciously acknowledging the truth that one suspects—that one's efforts to achieve happiness and fulfillment have no foundation. That type of honesty is the alchemy, which propels one along the "stages of life's way," according to Kierkegaard. To acknowledge what one really knows deep inside means that life won't have to drag one out of Plato's cave, and back into the sunlight, for the thousandth time, as one kicks and screams, weeps and denounces life, fornicates and litigates, putting up all manner of resistance, crying that one had been watching a play of shadows on the wall of the cave, and now won't know how the story ends.

Invariably, one will only seek a new life at the point of despair, which is the result of having achieved clarity regarding the impossibility of achieving happiness and fulfillment through one's present mode of being. Despair is not the last word, for as Eliade states, "In such moments of total crisis, only one hope seems to offer any issue—the hope of beginning life over again. This means, in short, that the man undergoing such a crisis dreams of new, regenerated life, fully realized and significant." (1958, p. 135)

We would, then, agree with thinkers, from Origen to Edinger, who contend that the new Heaven and new earth, i.e. the millennium, is but a symbol, a projection of the transformed existence that follows rebirth. Raising millenarian longings to a new key would, therefore, involve clarifying the object of longing. Instead of longing for Utopia, one longs for a transformed existence. And, of course, it must be more than just a longing.

The Apocalypse Within: Purification, Transcendence, Awakening

Apocalyptic fantasies are, then, the symbolic expression of the need for inner transformation. An exploration of this required transformation would reveal that it has three different, but intimately related, aspects: the needs for purification, transcendence, and awakening.

The interest in purity is a projection of a psychological and spiritual requirement onto the world. The dangerous delusion lies in thinking that the world needs to be purified through a flood or a fire, rather than, "I need to be purified, by changing who I am and how I live." Of what does the world need to be purified? That is where the paranoid vision enters in, for the answer is always a group of people upon whom one has projected one's own feeling of being defiled.

It is a significant moral achievement to realize that the person or group that one had vilified has really been one's projected shadow, that the impurity one thinks one sees is due to "the mote in one's own eye." But even if one were to see into this "shadow projection," own up to it, and disengage one's energy from it (Freud calls the process "decathecting"), one would still be involved with the type of projection that we discussed at the beginning of this chapter, the projection of psychological events onto the world. This is because the sense of outer physical impurity is itself a projection of a deeper level of inner moral impurity.

Apropos is the title of one of Kierkegaard's books that we have already referred to, *Purity of Heart* (1847; 1956). The impurity to which Kierkegaard refers does not really have a physical dimension to it; it is not about being defiled. It is an impurity that comes from the sense that one's life is dissolute, rather than resolute, meaning that it lacks direction, focus, self-identity. For Kierkegaard, purity of heart is "to will one thing." We earlier mentioned Rajneesh as an example of a person who lacked purity of heart. We also stated earlier, that the term self-identity, as used by Plato, means that something is the same with itself through time. It means, in regard to the possibility of selfhood, that one must have a direction that one maintains from day to day. Kierkegaard's aesthete, the seducer who writes his diary, illustrates this impurity founded on a lack of self-identity:

> My life is absolutely meaningless. When I consider the different periods into which it falls, it seems like the word Schnur in the dictionary, which means in the first place a string, in the second, a daughter-in-law. The only thing lacking is that the word Schnur should mean in the third place a camel, in the fourth, a dust-brush. (Kierkegaard, 1843; 1979, p. 35)

To overcome the sense of being a "Schnur," to gain purity of heart, is a far more difficult task than is the effort to overcome defilements on the physical level. This is not to suggest that obeying various religious prohibitions—such as those involving diet, sexual practices, and dress code—and having to arrange one's day so as to be in accord with religious laws, is an easy thing. Nor is it to suggest that it is a meaningless thing. All the same, it is far easier to be outwardly pure than it is to be inwardly pure; i.e. to conquer one's inner turbulence, so that one can truly will one thing.

Inward purity requires mastering one's heart and mind, and this is a very difficult affair. As Lao Tzu states, "He who conquers others is strong. He who conquers himself is mighty" (Lao-Tzu, 600 BCE; 1895). It is difficult to conquer oneself, for human beings are ontologically labile. Actually, Shakespeare said it best, "Man is a giddy thing" (*Much Ado About Nothing,* Act V, Scene IV). There is, though, another reason why purity of heart is difficult, at least for those who live in the modern and postmodern ages: it has become, to many minds, intellectually discredited. For how can there be purity of heart when the very notion of a unified self has fallen into question? But whatever arguments there may be to the contrary—by Hume, Nietzsche, Sartre, and many other thinkers—and no matter how philosophically antiquated the notion may be, self-identity through time is still an inner demand, making selfhood all the more challenging for those living today.

The effort to purify oneself of physical defilements is, on the one hand, a function of a lack of clarity regarding what really needs to be purified. On the other hand, it is a flight from the difficult effort to purify one's heart. The September 11th suicide terrorists were obsessed, as are many fundamentalists, by the dread of impurity. How curious that they carried on the way they did, with liquor and prostitutes, just days prior to their suicide mission. They must have believed that their martyrdom through a "baptism by fire" would burn away their physical impurities instantly. Martyrdom through suicide is far easier than years of difficult struggle to obtain true purity.

Referring to the various fascist movements that existed in Europe from the 1920s through the 1940s, Berman writes, "The unity of mankind, the reign of purity and the eternal—those goals were out of reach, in any conventional or real-world respect. But unity, purity, and eternity were readily at hand, in the form of mass death" (2003, p. 51). We may conclude that the paranoid's sense that the world needs to be purified, through an apocalypse, is a distortion of a fundamental inner need— the need to attain purity of heart.

A second inner requirement that is being symbolized by the apocalypse is transcendence. Raising the notion of ending the world to a higher key, in this sense, means seeking to transcend the world. Jaspers saw the philosophical enterprise as the effort to transcend the mundanity of the world, but Berdyaev is even more relevant because he considered himself to be an apocalyptic metaphysician and epistemologist. For Berdyaev, the apocalypse is not the literal end of the world, through fire or ice, but the end of one's attachment to what he calls the objectified world, the world that emerges by virtue of the object splitting away from the subject. The result of this split means that the material world grows in metaphysical prominence and importance, and enslaves the subject. What particularly prompts that enslavement is the lure of comfort and security, which means the loss of freedom and creativity. Berdyaev's notion of an objectified world is akin to Buber's "I-It" world; both are fallen worlds.

In *The Beginning and the End* (1952), Berdyaev states that, "The metaphysical and epistemological meaning of the end of the world and of history denotes the end of objective being and the overcoming of objectification. At the same time, it is the removal of the antithesis between subject and object" (p. 231). What it would mean to experience the world, apart from the subject/object duality, is unintelligible in the way in which a mystical insight is unintelligible. One might also wonder when the apocalyptic end of the objectified world is to come about. According to Berdyaev, "The end of the world is not to be conceived as occurring in historical time..." (p. 231) Elsewhere Berdyaev says, "The whole difficulty of eschatological thought lies in the fact that it is conceived in terms of past and future. But the outlook of Eschatology lies outside these categories" (p. 241).

Berdyaev posits the notion of a non-historical time, which he calls "existential time." That is the quality of time when there can be timeless moments, eternity in time, paradoxical though the notion may seem. It is also not clear in Berdyaev's work whether the apocalypse could come about for a single person or whether the apocalypse means the transformation of the entire world. There is much to suggest that Berdyaev means the latter, and that were it to come about an actual millennium would arrive.

In any case, our intent here is not to assess the validity of Berdyaev's ideas, but merely to indicate that the notion of apocalypse can be elevated to a much higher key, one in which questions are posed that are lofty and yet existential. Apart from whether one agrees or disagrees with the particular answers proffered by thinkers like Berdyaev, Buber, and Jaspers, the very asking of such questions can prompt an inner-apocalypse, a radical transformation of oneself.

There is a third inner requirement that is also being symbolized by the end of the world. It is the need to awaken, i.e. to become self-aware, conscious of who one is and what life is really all about. In Calderón de la Barca's play *Life is a Dream* (1636; 2005), awakening from one's egocentric dreams is viewed as the death that is a prerequisite for self-renewal. One of the characters in the play states, "Out of the ashes of my self-extinction...A better self revive" (2005, Act III, Scene 2, line 120). It is not surprising, therefore, that if awakening has this self-extinguishing aspect it would be symbolized by apocalyptic fantasies.

For the most part, people wish to do everything possible not to awaken, but rather to remain immediate, or unconscious. Nor do they think well of anyone who would attempt to inform them that they are asleep. Plato's Allegory of the Cave illustrates the fate of the awakened person. He goes back to the cave to awaken the prisoners to their plight. They do not appreciate his claim that they are prisoners of illusion. Indeed, they try to kill him. Plato was, of course, making an allusion to the death of his teacher, Socrates who, as "gadfly of the state," saw awakening people as his mission.

Many of the manifestations of the paranoid vision — including religious fundamentalism, fanaticism, anti-Semitism, xenophobia, witch-hunts, anti-intellectualism, anti-secularism, and a fear of "conspiring" secret societies—are reflective of this fear, hatred, and yet secret fascination with people who are thought to possess knowledge. It's really a dread and fascination with knowledge itself. Knowledge is indeed dangerous, for it corrodes beliefs, superstitions, and unexamined ideas. Thus it can precipitate the end of one's world, in a very real way. One is also reminded, in that context, that there was a time when explorers, like Columbus, set out on a journey to what was regarded—as was indicated by ancient maps—as the end of the world. Thus that which lay beyond the limits of (geographical) knowledge was viewed as the "end" of the world.

Despite the immense resistance to waking up and becoming self-aware, everyone has a desire, dormant though it may be, to know themselves. The primary motive why people seek self-knowledge lies in the hope that if one can diagnose the root of one's difficulties, suffering can be avoided. Thus Dostoevsky was perceptive when he wrote, "Suffering is the origin of consciousness" (1864; 1993, pp. 34-35).

Sometimes, though, what spurs the quest for self-knowledge is not just suffering—unless one would classify a general sense of dissatisfaction, or spiritual malaise, as suffering—but a lust for a true and real life. This lust sometimes feels like homesickness, driving one to forsake a comfortable life, in the hope of regaining the completeness—symbolized by home—that one has lost. We might recall how Odysseus' men wish to remain among the lotus-eaters, but Odysseus longs to return home. Apropos is a comment by Novalis, whom Heidegger quotes, "Philosophy is really homesickness, an urge to be at home everywhere." (qtd. in Heidegger, 1930; 2001, p. 6) Home is being understood, not as a physical place, but a state of the soul.

Raised to their highest key, apocalyptic anxieties are transformed into a journey of awakening. Self-knowledge is apocalyptic, for to break free of the bounds of one's worldview is most certainly to precipitate the end of the world. Carlos Castaneda, for example — an anthropologist who became an apprentice to a Yaqui shaman and sorcerer — wrote of a notion called "stopping the world." Castaneda's teacher, Don Juan Matus, describes it as, "...the moment when everything around us ceases to be what it's always been" (qtd. in Castaneda, 2000, p. 104). Zen has a similar notion of the end of the world. Rajneesh's description of this state of affairs is quite incisive:

> The whole teaching of Zen consists of only one thing: how to take a jump into nothingness, how to come to the very end of your mind, which is the end of the world. How to stand there on the cliff facing the abyss and not get frightened, how to gather courage and take the last jump. (Osho, 2001, pp. 142-145)

Apocalyptic fantasies reflect the ambivalence, within most people, towards the choice of continuing to dream the dream that is their life, or awakening from it. More than most people, those who are under the sway of the paranoid vision have an unconscious intuition of the requisite inner apocalypse, but they distort what they intuit, for all of the reasons suggested. The fantasy images of a literal apocalypse are testimony to what is still inwardly required of a person.

Raising the paranoid vision to a new key would, therefore, consist in de-literalizing conspiracy theories, delusions of grandeur, apocalyptic fantasies, images of the millennium, and other products of the paranoid vision, so as to extract their essential truth. Raised to a higher key, paranoid suspicions lose their malevolence. Instead, they invite one to journey into life's profoundest mysteries. It is sad that people turn down the invitation, instead investing their precious time in pseudo conspiracies and pseudo apocalyptic fantasies, which take the form of fictional novels and films, or supposedly real conspiracies, such as those involving political intrigue. Thus it is that they miss the real thing — the real conspiracy, the real apocalypse, the real grandeur, the real mystery, and the real adventure of life.

Chapter 9
From Paranoid Vision to Comic Vision

"I will sing a song...a dancing and mocking song on the spirit of gravity."

— Nietzsche (1891; 1970)

For reasons to be explored, the paranoid vision is the polar opposite of the comic vision. It will be necessary, of course, to explicate what we mean by the comic vision. We shall see that every salient feature of the one vision has a corresponding antithesis in the other. For example, whereas the paranoid vision is grimly serious, the comic vision is lighthearted and playful. Whereas the paranoid vision offers a simplistic and reductive view of people and events, the comic vision embraces ambiguity, incongruity, and absurdity. Whereas the paranoid vision views humanity in terms of a Manichean dualism, the comic vision promotes a sympathetic inclusiveness. We are not, of course, referring to the paranoid vision in its higher keys, but at its typical lower levels of representation.

It was suggested, in Chapter One, that the set of unconscious assumptions on which a vision is founded can be brought to light, the effect of which is to unfetter the mind from the vision. It would, therefore, be possible for a person to shift from the paranoid vision to the comic vision. That is, of course, no small matter, for it involves a metanoia, i.e. a radical change of heart and mind. For a group of people, such as an organization or a society, to undergo such a transformation would constitute a cultural revolution. The possibility of that sort of transcendence has been our overarching interest in these chapters.

In the pages that follow, we shall be examining some of the manifestations of the comic vision. The paranoid vision has its narratives, including conspiracy theories, apocalyptic fantasies, hate-infused screeds, and vituperative propaganda pieces. Likewise, the comic vision has its narratives, including comic plays, situation comedies, cartoons, comic strips, humorous films, burlesque and standup comedy routines, clown acts, jokes, satires, funny songs, etc. Our intent is to uncover what such narratives can tell us about this lighthearted way of seeing.

The Critique of Seriousness

Can the comic vision, which has traditionally been contrasted with the tragic vision, also be the antithesis of the paranoid vision? The tragic vision, the moral vision, various religious visions, communism, fascism, the utopian faith in science, indeed all ideologies, are species of "the spirit of seriousness," to use Nietzsche's phrase. The comic vision is, therefore, the antithesis of all worldviews that are riddled with seriousness, including the paranoid.

Few people are as earnestly grave as those who are paranoid. After all, what could be more humorless than the bifurcation of the world into the forces of God and Antichrist, or the perverse appearance/reality thinking that leads one to posit the enemy lurking behind the façade of respectability? Furthermore, what could be more un-playful than being gripped by the outcome of a series of events that involves, literally, the end of the world as is the case with a person preoccupied with an apocalyptic fantasy?

What, then, is the essence of seriousness? It consists in absolutizing the creations of time, all of which are intrinsically finite, relative, temporal, and contingent. In that sense, it is the attitudinal ground of both idolatry and fanaticism. Furthermore, it is founded on ignorance, in the literal sense. What is ignored is the obvious contradiction created by the apotheosis of the finite. Since contradiction lies at the very core of the comical, seriousness consists in ignoring those contradictory elements of reality, which, if consciously apprehended, could cause one to laugh. One might say that it consists in not looking down, for fear that one might apprehend the god's feet of clay.

But isn't what is being considered here really "over-seriousness"? Yes, but since Sartre and the other existentialists who have adopted Nietzsche's phrase, "the spirit of seriousness," do not distinguish one from the other, we shall follow suit, and use the former term as shorthand for the latter. It is seriousness itself that is synonymous with gravity and solemnity. What, then, do they mean by the term? They mean completely investing one's time and energy in the material world — in business, politics, social causes, family, sports, and the arts, for example — so that one lacks what Kierkegaard calls "subjectivity," or "inwardness," which consists in the separation, nonattachment, and freedom of the subject from the object. Those who are serious have, to use a phrase from an older conceptual framework, have, "gained the world but lost their soul."

Kierkegaard, though, does take certain things seriously, indeed, the very things to which most people are indifferent. As he states (using the pseudonym "Anti-Climacus"), "The biggest danger, that of losing oneself, can pass off in the world as quietly as if it were nothing: every other loss, an arm, a leg, five dollars, a wife, etc. is bound to be noticed" (1849; 1989, pp. 62-63). Conversely, what absorbs, upsets, and disturbs the rest of humanity, the true philosopher can regard as a trifle worthy of amusement, for there is something quite funny, to use Kierkegaard's metaphor, about being more concerned over losing five dollars than over losing oneself. Furthermore, Sartre states, "... mirth denounces false seriousness in the name of true seriousness" (1971; 1981, p. 185). Thus Sartre, like Kierkegaard, distinguishing between false and true seriousness, does believe that certain things should be taken seriously.

Owing to their different sense of what is and what is not to be regarded as serious, philosophers will often find themselves out of step with the rest of humanity. We are reminded, in that regard, of a Charles Addams cartoon of an audience of people viewing a film. Everyone looks stricken with sympathetic grief over the fate of the characters;

some men and women are wiping their eyes with handkerchiefs, etc. Well, almost everyone looks grief-stricken, for there is one fellow in the audience with a broad grin on his face, who appears to be laughing rather heartily. That fellow would appear to be either a sociopath or a philosopher.

In Nietzsche's *Thus Spoke Zarathustra,* Zarathustra declares, "I myself will sing a song... a dancing and mocking song on the spirit of gravity, my supreme and most powerful devil, of whom they say that he is master of the world" (1891; 1977, p. 220). For Nietzsche, the spirit of seriousness, or gravity, is synonymous with dogmatism, which finds expression in philosophy, religion, morality and science. He sees the intrusion of the seriousness of those realms into everyday existence, choking the life out of it.

In *Beyond Good and Evil* (1885; 1989), Nietzsche asserts that since all ideas are eventually proven wrong anyway, there is no point in taking them too seriously. Consequently, he considered Socrates foolish for not having skipped town, after being convicted. In that respect, Nietzsche is Falstaffian. After all, Falstaff — whom critics from Wylie Sypher to Harold Bloom have lauded as the embodiment of the comic spirit — counters the charge that he is a coward for having played possum during a battle by posing, as Sypher (1985) points out, a rather Socratic question to his accuser, "What is honor?" (Henry IV, Part I, Act V, Scene I). In truth, Falstaff is not a coward; he just knows that discretion is the better part of valor. In affirming the value of surviving, the comic spirit runs counter to ideologically driven fanaticism. The comic spirit is particularly antithetical to those paranoia-infused ideologues that worship death — one manifestation of which is suicide bombing — and to those who would gladly precipitate a literal apocalypse.

Of course, those who embody the comic spirit are not only content to survive, but wish to seize the day and not let opportunities slip by. Apropos is Suzanne Langer's observation that the comic hero, or trickster, exhibits a, "...brainy opportunism in the face of an essentially dreadful universe" (1981, p. 70). One might think, for example, of some of the clever and opportunistic characters of comedy, such as Gogol's comic character Khlestakov, played by Danny Kaye in the film

The Inspector General (1949), or of Groucho Marx playing Rufus T. Firefly in *Horse Feathers* (1932), or W.C. Fields in films like *You Can't Cheat an Honest Man* (1939). While tragic heroes, and fanatics too, are uncompromisingly true to the often rigid and dogmatic principles that define their identity, such comic imposters exhibit a fluidity of self. Like the cartoon character, who is flattened by a steamroller and then pops back into shape, they affirm the values of endurance and ingenuity, which are crucial for human survival.

The darker side of selfhood nourished by the comic spirit, with its opportunism, may be hucksterism, but the positive side of it includes entrepreneurial creativity. It could be argued, though, that the comic spirit, like all visions of life, has its horizons, and, as such, leaves out certain important elements of human reality, such as idealism, courage, honor, and sacrifice. After all, Falstaff may be a wonderfully human character, but not an embodiment of nobility of spirit. Even those critics who deeply love comedy (Kerr 1970) argue that something is missing from the comic spirit, and they are right. We would contend that the comic vision is of great value in tempering idealism, so that one does not become possessed by all the dark emotions and desires associated with the spirit of gravity, such as the vanity, self-importance, and self-righteousness, endemic to those who are chronically humorless, as well as inoculating one from more serious diseases of the soul, such as the paranoid vision. That is why the education of Shakespeare's *Henry IV*—that which would make him a complete man and a wise king—cannot be complete without the time that he spent, as a youth, as the raffish protégé of Falstaff. This path of inner development on the part of Henry, is, according to Sypher, consonant with Milton's notion of "purification by trial." The goal of comedy is not moral development; it is freedom. All the same, the effect of these trials on the protagonist of comedies, and vicariously on everyone else, is purifying and civilizing.

We have observed that the spirit of seriousness, in the Kierkegaardian sense, consists in an enslaved attachment to the material world, and in the Nietzschian sense is enslavement to ideology. But, the spirit of seriousness is, most fundamentally, an attitude of mind. After all, one cannot take the material world seriously, and ideology seriously, unless one first takes oneself seriously, i.e. too seriously. More specifically, such seriousness consists in regarding, with ultimate gravity, what psychologists refer to as one's scripts, but which may also be called one's stories or narratives. As a result, those who are serious have, by continuing to follow those tragic scripts, condemned themselves to psychological hell. John Tallmadge relates that aspect of the spirit of seriousness to that dreadful place that Dante imagined:

> In Dante, the people in Hell are all grand and fascinating characters who take themselves very seriously, and they tell Dante all sorts of seductive and heroic stories that are dangerous because they justify these people's self-image as victims of a hostile, inscrutable, and omnipotent God. In other words, the damned all see themselves as tragic heroes; they prefer to suffer rather than give up their self-image. So they are stuck in Hell. But the Christian message is that you can give up your self-serving self-image. (2004, p. 1)

It would appear, then, that what makes existence hellish is not what befalls one, but one's script, the story that one tells oneself about why the world is the way it is and why one is suffering. The way out of hell would consist in letting go of that story, i.e. no longer taking it seriously. Then, the illusory world that arose as a function of one's story would collapse. This letting go could be considered a disenchantment and a disillusionment. Is there a cure, then, for the seriousness that belongs to the paranoid vision? Donald Carveth, with great insight, makes the connection between paranoia, therapeutic disillusionment, and liberation from the spirit of seriousness:

> Here, of course, the sort of "knowing" and "belief" that must be therapeutically surpassed refers to what may otherwise be described as dogma, ideology or reification, or as an alienated or undialectical consciousness (characteristic of what Klein called the paranoid-schizoid position.) It concerns the human proclivity to take one's stories and oneself entirely seriously, thus succumbing to what Nietzsche called the spirit of solemnity characteristic of those whom Jean-Paul Sartre called *les salauds* (a difficult term to translate, although

perhaps "the bastards" or "stuffed shirts" will suffice). (1999, pp. 323-358)

Carveth is, of course, referring to paranoia in the clinical sense, but what he is suggesting equally applies to the paranoid vision. The key, then, to liberation from the paranoid vision consists in no longer taking seriously one's stories, scripts, or narratives—i.e. one's conspiracy theories, apocalyptic fantasies, as well as one's dogmas and ideologies, which means taking oneself far less seriously. The passage by Carveth suggests that the key to health of mind and spirit requires an epistemological shift, one from dogmatic belief, i.e. from the seriousness that lies at the heart of the paranoid vision, to critical awareness, critical in the Kantian sense of knowledgeable about the nature of dogmatism.

It should be added, though, that the world that stands before one is not merely a function of one's psychological scripts. It is also, to an obviously significant degree, the resultant objectification of billions of people taking themselves all too seriously. The world thus constituted has far-reaching social and political implications. In an essay that appeared in *The National Interest*, on the Orwellian dangers of political correctness, Roger Kimball refers to the Czech writer Milan Kundera, who wrote a novel called *The Joke* (1993). Kimball summarizes the premise of the novel:

> Milan Kundera's novel *The Joke* traces the fortunes and amours of a young student, Ludvik, after his exasperatingly earnest girlfriend decides to show the authorities a postcard he had written to her as a joke: "Optimism is the opium of the people! A healthy atmosphere stinks of stupidity! Long live Trotsky!" As a result of this whimsy, Ludvik finds himself expelled from the Communist Party and the university and is eventually conscripted to work in the mines for several years. (Winter 2003/04., p. 5)

What is key here, according to Kimball, is the incompatibility of the comic spirit—especially when it takes the form of satirizing the powers that be—with totalitarian thinking:

> Among other things, Kundera dramatizes the dynamics of
> political correctness. He is especially good at portraying one
> of its signal features, humorlessness. One of the points of The
> Joke is that totalitarian societies cannot abide a joke; humor
> is anathema; political correctness is a kind of Geiger counter
> that registers deviations from the norm of earnestness. Any
> deviation is suspect, any humorous deviation is culpable.
> The allergy to humor that is integral to political correctness
> is one reason the art of parody has suffered in recent years.
> (Kimball, Winter 2003/04, p. 5)

It is "earnestness," then, or the spirit of seriousness, that is key
to the repressive quality of political correctness and totalitarianism.
How did this state of affairs come about? Here is where Kimball is
most interesting. He suggests that it is due to making benevolence the
guiding principle of social policy and politics. People like Robespierre
and Lenin were initially motivated by a love of humanity. How ironic
that when they came to power the rivers flowed with the blood of
their countrymen, whom they executed for political reasons. It is also
ironic that an economic system founded not on benevolence, but on
universal egotism, i.e. capitalism, has, by contrast, significantly raised
the standard of living of great numbers of people.[48]

The problem, of course, is not with benevolence, but with the
spirit of seriousness—regarding one's goals for social reform with
deadly earnestness. When the spirit of seriousness enters, benevolence
invariably departs. Why should this be so? When one has been
seduced by the lure of a perfect, just, equitable, harmonious world,
the benevolence (that might have originally inspired one to become
involved with social reform) is lost. This is because the lure of Utopia
drowns out all other thoughts and feelings. When benevolence departs
it is often replaced by something far more congruent with the spirit
of seriousness, namely the malevolence intrinsic to the paranoid

---

48 Marxist critics would argue that capitalism has exploited people, and sometimes oppressed
them too. That cannot be denied. But the poor in nations where capitalism exists have enjoyed
a much higher standard of living, and have had far greater opportunities for educational, social,
and economic advancement, than in "primitive" societies or in nations that are socialistic or
communistic.

vision. This frightening drift into a malevolent humorlessness is akin to demon possession on an organizational scale. That is why Lance Morrow is correct that "Evil has no sense of humor. Evil takes itself seriously...Evil represents, among other things, the failure of humor" (2003, p. 22, 24).[49]

Might the contrary be true? Could it be the case that for benevolence to flourish in this less than perfect world, it must be rooted in the comic vision, where the quality of mercy is not strained by utopian delusions, or any other species of seriousness? More generally, might the comic vision be requisite for social and cultural renewal, sustenance, and survival? Perceptively drawing out the implications of Northrop Frye's theory of literature, George Aichele states, "Comedy thus possesses tremendous cultural power for Frye...For Frye, comedy provides the basic structures in terms of which human culture can endure and persist." (1998, p. 25) Aichele is referring to a transition and transformation that is typified in comedies, the passage from death to rebirth, from the old society, represented by the character in comedies of the senex, or old man—who is characterized by repressive rigidity and oppressive seriousness—to the life energy and creative possibilities resident in the younger generation. In our exploration of Islamic fundamentalism, we saw the ever-present figure of the senex.

This is not to suggest that a senex-controlled society should be replaced by a revolutionary youth culture. The ideal synthesis is the wisdom of age coupled with the energy and daring of youth. In any case, since so much of the world is deeply in need of healing, self-renewal, and rebirth, the comic vision, with its overthrowing of the senex, is of crucial importance.

Naturally, for the comic vision to flourish in a particular body politic, it must be in evidence amongst the individuals that comprise

---

49 Is Morrow correct that evil has no sense of humor? What about Mephistopheles? Furthermore, Hitler was said to be a fan of Laurel and Hardy, and every week would have private viewings of their films with his cronies. Historian Paul Johnson, in Commentary, informs us that Hitler, among his other abilities, possessed, "...a valuable talent for making people laugh." (2005, 35) Even if Stalin, Pol Pot, and Osama bin Laden too, have similarly had such comic capacities, it is certain that these mass murderers did not have the capacity to laugh at themselves, nor were they embodiments of the comic vision in any other sense. We must, then, distinguish enjoying comedies and getting laughs, from seeing in terms of the comic vision. Especially at its higher elevations, the comic vision is antithetical to malevolence.

that polity. We have explored what it is like to be under the sway of the spirit of seriousness; what, then, is it like to be free of the spirit of seriousness? Kierkegaard and Nietzsche use the metaphor of dance to describe that unserious, or playful, state of the soul, for dancing suggests being light on one's feet, lightheartedness, as well as both physical and psychological "levity." It also suggests moving through life without an ultimate purpose; one dances simply for dancing's sake. As Jaspers states:

> At the limits of life's possibilities came not any heavy seriousness, but rather a complete lightness as an expression of their knowledge, and both used the image of the dance. In the last decade of his life Nietzsche, in ever-changing forms used the dance as a metaphor for his thought, where it is original. And Kierkegaard said, "I have trained myself... always to be able to dance on the service of thought...My life begins as soon as a difficulty shows up. Then dancing is easy. The thought of dance is a nimble dance. Everybody is too serious for me." Nietzsche saw his archenemy in the "spirit of seriousness" — in morals, science, purposefulness, etc. (1935; 1971, p. 43)

Can the paranoid, indeed can anyone, learn to dance and thus be freed from the spirit of gravity? To better answer that question, it will be necessary to further explore the nature of seriousness, and its transcendence through the comic vision.

When Dreaded Contingency Gets Belly Laughs

In Chapter Two, we concluded that conspiracy theories are founded on the paranoid notion that everything is planned, that there are no accidents. We concluded that this disbelief in the influence of luck, accident, and contingency on the outcome of events stemmed from a misunderstanding of the forces of history. But the paranoid vision is really predicated on a far more fundamental misunderstanding, not just about history, but about the nature of spatiotemporal existence itself. Despite the paranoid's belief that there is a secret plot that explains it all, "this world," according to Santayana, "is contingency and absurdity incarnate, the oddest of possibilities masquerading as fact" (1922; 1981, p. 56).

Santayana's metaphysics of contingency is the antithesis of the apocalyptic view of the world. It is, indeed, blasphemous to anyone who believes that God has planned everything and knows the outcome of all future events. A world whose happenings are neither predestined by God, nor plotted by a cabal of conspirators, is a world full of surprises and infused with comic possibilities. Santayana criticizes other philosophers for having been blind to this fact: "That real existence should be radically comic never occurs to these solemn sages; they are without one ray of humor and are persuaded that the universe too must be without one" (1922; 1981, 56). Is Santayana correct that existence is "radically comic?" Certainly, existence is infused with contingency, accident, and chance. Accidents, whether positive or negative, always enter upon the stage — like Chance, the protagonist from Jerzy Kosinski's comic novel *Being There* (1970; 1999) — making one's life far different than one had intended it to be, although far more interesting. Apropos is Suzanne Langer's distinction of comedy from tragedy, "Tragedy is the image of Fate, as comedy is of Fortune" (1953; 1981, 72). Langer means "fortune" in the sense of chance or contingency.

What exactly, though, is it about the contingent quality of existence that is comical? Contingency, chance, luck, and fortune are the breeding ground of incongruities — brought on by the chance combination of people, things, circumstances, events, ideas, and universes of discourse—and incongruity is, according to one school of thought, the basis of the comical. Kant's theory of comedy, from his Critique of Aesthetic Judgment, may offer insight into the comic potential of incongruity. He stated that laughter is "an affectation arising from the sudden transformation of a strained expectation into nothing." (1790; 1982, 199) Kant is somewhat elliptical here in his use of the word "nothing." It might suggest, to existentialists, the nothingness that is at the heart of human existence, but, for our purposes, a more parsimonious explanation is in order: Kant meant by "nothing" the absence of that which had been expected or, perhaps, dreaded. That which had been expected disappears into nothingness.

Thus, for Kant, the two sides of the fundamental comic incongruity are: 1) the expectation 2) the "nothing", i.e. the letdown, disappointment or relief. An example of such humor would be Woody Allen's statement: "Not only is there no God...but try getting a plumber on weekends" (1978, p. 25). A line that has been attributed to Woody Allen is: "I don't believe in an afterlife, but I am bringing a change of underwear." What a precipitous descent there is from lofty theological speculations to the mundane concerns of everyday life! Another example would be Henny Youngman's: "I miss my wife's cooking... as frequently as possible." Here there is a descent from the ideal of romantic love to the sometimes dyspeptic realities of marriage.

Humor of this variety, which is known as "bathos," points to the discrepancy between the elevated ideals that human beings have — whether they be religious, philosophical, romantic, artistic, political, or of any other noble variety — and the actual course of human existence which is, not infrequently, mundane. It is, indeed, the remarkable singularity of the human creature to be capable of this disproportion between lofty concerns, on the one hand, and the mundanity of actual existence on the other. This is the same sort of incongruity, or disproportion — referred to in the last chapter, in regard to the amphibious nature of human beings — that Pascal, and the philosophical anthropologists, found so awe inspiring. Charles Baudelaire, in his essay on comedy, observed that that type of incongruity, disproportion, or contradiction was at the foundation of the comical. As Baudelaire states,

> And since laughter is essentially human, it is, in fact, essentially contradictory; that is to say that it is at once a token of an infinite grandeur and an infinite misery — the latter in relation to the absolute Being of whom man has an inkling, the former in relation to the beasts. It is from the perpetual collision of these two infinites that laughter is struck. (1855; 1981, p. 316)

We do not know why Baudelaire used "laughter," when "comedy" would seem to be le mot juste in that context, since laughter is but the physiological expression of the comical perception. Furthermore, we would contend that the clash is not between two infinites, but between the infinite and the finite (having a body, being subject to contingencies, etc.) But, apart from that, his theory gets to the very heart of the matter. We might add that it takes but a slight shift of awareness for this disproportion, which Pascal found so awe-inspiring, to inspire laughter. We shall seek to determine the nature of that shift.

The humor that emerges from this disproportion between the animal and god in human beings, between the demands of the spirit and the needs of the body, between the noble and the mundane, between freedom and facticity, would not come as a joyous relief because the effort to adjudicate such opposites is quite stressful. Often the failure of this adjudication is experienced as a sense of inadequacy or failure, as well as guilt and despair. Rather than questioning whether the task of unifying these opposites is even theoretically possible, one attributes the failure of the task to a personal failing on one's part. Accomplishments can offer little relief from the sense of inadequacy and guilt. Tolstoy is a case in point. His Confessions reveal that he felt like a failure on an inner level, despite the fact that outwardly he was hugely successful. One might also recall the quote by Eliade, in the last chapter, where he says "at a certain moment every man sees his life as a failure" (1958, p. 135).

There are many ways to deal with feelings of failure and inadequacy. Tolstoy, for example, went on a religious quest. The paranoid vision is also a way of dealing with feelings of failure and inadequacy. Paranoids delude themselves into believing that an imaginary state of grandeur had once existed for them, or for their people. They then blame another group of people for their fallen condition. Malevolence is the inevitable result of paranoia's deeply neurotic answer to the crisis of self-doubt.

The comic reaction to the incongruity—and to the subsequent feelings of inadequacy, guilt and despair—results neither in tragic grandeur, nor in an earnest religious quest like the one undertaken by Tolstoy, nor in paranoid malevolence. The comic reaction is to recognize the utter impossibility of overcoming the disproportion between the infinite and the finite, between one's ideal self and one's actual self, and to simply let go and laugh at oneself, and at the impossible project which, as a human being, one is involved. This laughter indicates one's capacity not just to suffer the impossible task of attempting to adjudicate contradictory terms, but to view the incongruity objectively, i.e. with something akin to an aesthetic distance. At such moments, one feels temporarily free of life's anguishing contradictions, curiously beyond the terms of the disproportion between the finite and the infinite, the temporal and the eternal, and similar pairs of opposites.

Kant can explain comedy in the temporal mode — how the discrepancy between one's expectations and what actually comes to fruition results in bathos — but not all comedy is of that variety. For example, the simple pairing of incongruous characters is absurd, as is the case of Don Quixote and Sancho Panza, or more popularly: Lucy and Ricky (*I Love Lucy*), Felix and Oscar (from *The Odd Couple*), Laurel and Hardy, all the Marx Brothers and Margaret Dumont, the cast of *Seinfeld*, as well as the cast of a thousand other situation comedies. Apart from the droll situations in which they find themselves, the very existence of these incongruous pairs and groups resounds more deeply than one consciously realizes, for they defeat all hope that there can ever be a harmonious world. In letting go of this impossible hope, one lets go of the discontent that is connected with it, which is a great relief. It also frees one of all utopian foolishness, which is a blessing because, as we have seen, utopian longings have a proclivity for being paranoiagenic, since they will inevitably be disappointed, and this failure will inspire an effort to assign blame and to find devils.

Arthur Koestler's theory of comedy is enlightening in this regard, but he contends that the essential incongruity in comedy is not just between different people—Ralph Kramden and Ed Norton, from the TV show *The Honeymooners*, for example—but between different frames of reference, or universes of discourse (Koestler 1964; 1970, p. 21). An example would be a typical Woody Allen essay entitled: "If The Impressionists Had Been Dentists." (1976, 199-204) The two universes of discourse that are contrasted are: the world of root canals, dentures, and tartar buildup on the one hand and the passionate life of Van Gogh and Gauguin, on the other hand. Dentistry represents the needs of the body, not as the vessel of the life-force, but as that which rots, decays, aches, and is in need of repair, thus pointing to one's mortality. The lives of these artists, on the other hand, represent the needs of the imagination, soul, and spirit. It is one's fate as a human being to be amphibious, to inhabit both realms. There is a human tendency, though, to seek unity of self either by denying one of the realms, or by seeking to reconcile them. In Woody Allen's essay, dentists acting like painters—for example, Vincent writing to his generous brother Theo, requesting funds for more dental floss, or writing him about how glorious it was doing root canals out in the fields with Gauguin —highlights the utter impossibility of the reconciliation of the needs of the body and those of the soul. Acknowledging the hopeless effort to deny one's amphibious nature, one is relieved, at least for a time, of the anxious striving that is the concomitant of that hope. This relief expresses itself as laugher.

That form of the comical known as irony points to a very fundamental incongruity. A common definition of irony is that irony consists of an "incongruity between what might be expected and what actually occurs" (Dictionary.com). Consequently, one's pretensions to theoretical knowledge are deflated in the light of empirical experience. An example of such ironical disillusionment is Lord Rochester's observation about child rearing: "Before I got married, I had six theories about bringing up children. Now I have six children and no theories." Comedy certainly offers a constrained view of the possibilities of theoretical knowledge! One might add that the conspiracy theorist — whose fundamental belief is that all can be known, planned and predicted — is in need of this type of philosophical therapy, created by Socrates, the great ironist of ancient Greece.

Schopenhauer's theory of comedy focuses on that same incongruity, "...laughter results from nothing but the suddenly perceived incongruity between a concept and the real objects that he had thought through it in some relation; and laughter itself is the expression of this incongruity" (1819; 1966, Volume I, p. 59). Basically, Schopenhauer is stating that humor results from an incongruity between intellectual ideas and the knowledge that we acquire through our senses. In German, the difference between the two forms of knowing is expressed through the words wissen and kennen. For example, Don Quixote sees everything that he encounters in terms of the romances of knighthood and chivalry. Where his senses perceive a windmill, his reason, mixed with his imagination, represents it falsely as a giant. The comical emerges when sensation and reason appear as incongruous. When the two collide, sensation wins out over intellect and the laughter is an expression of being released from "this strict, untiring and most troublesome governess, our faculty of reason, for once convicted of inadequacy." (Schopenhauer 1819; 1966, Volume II, p. 98) It is curious, though, that Socratic irony is founded on the notion that reason is the true source of knowledge and reality, and that appearances deceive. Thus, Socrates may appear to be an ignorant fool, but he is truly the wisest man in Greece. Schopenhauer, post-Kantian that he is, reverses matters, making reason the source of delusion. What emerges, then, is the type of humor predicated on the empirical observation that the emperor has no clothes. Whether the comical is Socratic or is Schopenhaurian, it is still predicated on an incongruity.

There have been many other incongruity theories, each focusing on a particular species of incongruity, ranging from Bergson's "the mechanical is incrusted on life," (1900; 1956, p. 66) in which the two terms of the incongruity are life (the élan vital, in all its fluidity) and mechanical reason, to Stephen Leacock's notion that the essential incongruity is between things the way they ought to be and things smashed out of shape. Benjamin Lehman believes that the essential incongruity is "...that mind should see clearly and sometimes soar but the body should feed and sleep; that the human spirit should feel perennial and the matter of which spirit is a function should be changing always..." (1854; 1981, p. 110)

Whether or not Lehman is correct about what he regards as the overarching incongruity, there are many incongruities, and each incongruity points to a different aspect of the human experience, in all of its absurdity. This leads us to enigma: What, is it about incongruity that makes one laugh? An incongruity is indicative of, or symbolic of, a contradiction. Indeed, it was Kierkegaard who perceived that contradiction is at the heart of the comical. Contradiction points to the impossible and, therefore, to the hopeless. What, though, is so funny about hopelessness? Paraphrasing Helmuth Plessner, the formula for comedy should be "Situation hopeless, but not serious" (1970, p. 141). The perception that something is impossible, and therefore hopeless, releases us from all the frustrations and anxieties involved with attempting to do that which is truly impossible. Thus, every time one perceives that which is incongruous, one sees it as indicative of an ultimate contradiction, suggesting the hopelessness of our efforts towards achieving happiness and fulfillment, thus liberating us from the effort.

For example, imagine a man who claims that he wants to be free of the falseness and phoniness of society. So he flees from his friends, who greatly admire his independence, honesty, integrity and nobility of character, and who chase after him, begging him not to leave society. But, as this man runs away from them—which he always seems to be doing—he is continually looking over his shoulder, so to speak, to make sure that his friends are still chasing after him. This is because the man—due to a hidden vanity in his nature—needs his friends to admire him for his independence, honesty, integrity, and nobility, and therefore, he cannot really leave them.

Thus the man is caught in a contradiction that he cannot admit, especially to himself: he needs to be independent, but he also needs the recognition of other people, which means that he cannot be independent. Furthermore, his absurd effort to combine his two desires through getting recognition for being independent is contradictory, impossible, hopeless, and wonderfully ironic. What we have been describing and analyzing is the premise of Moliere's play, *The Misanthrope*.

The play is very amusing, not only because one is observing the foolishness of a highly intelligent man. Its humor is liberating because it resonates with one's own inner conflicts. One might not be a misanthrope, but one does share in this universal conflict — needing to be autonomous, on the one hand, and needing other people, on the other — which is a hopeless contradiction. Indeed, Schopenhauer says that human beings are like porcupines on a cold winter's day. They huddle together for warmth, but then start pricking each other, and so need to separate, but then the cold gets to them again, etc. (1890; 1932, p. 305) The fact that people find various ways of combining these two needs—Thoreau is reputed to have gone home on weekends, or so the facetious bumper sticker informs us—does not make it any less of a contradiction. In any case, this is just one of the many contradictions belonging to the human condition that are ripe for comic treatment.

It is the perception of the hopelessness of one's plight that frees one from seriousness, and thus from the anxiety attendant upon the effort to achieve happiness and fulfillment. That is why hopelessness can be psychologically liberating. Of course, not all hopelessness has the power to free one from seriousness, for one may have too much invested in a situation, in which case hopelessness only leads to despair. But if a situation can free one from seriousness, than Plessner's formula for comedy holds true.

Freud, in his Wit and its Relation to the Unconscious, may have been on to something when he suggested that comedy was a release of repressed sexual feelings, but comedy is far more a release of repressed intuitions about life's absurdity. If laughter is healthy, it is not simply because it gives our lungs a workout, as Kant suggested, nor is it because it releases endorphins. It is healthy because it frees one from the stress of repressing contradictions from conscious awareness, and thus of repressing the ever-lurking suspicion of hopelessness, and this release expresses itself as laughter. Contradictions that are not transcended through laughter, or through any other means, lead to a dysphoria, which is ripe soil for paranoia and other demons.

One might object to Plessner's theory on the grounds that comedy generally has happy endings, and that these endings do offer hope. That, indeed, is true, but with an important qualification. The protagonists of comedies typically do not succeed in the way in which they set out to succeed. For example, they set out to get rich, only to fail, but succeed in acquiring self-knowledge or wisdom, or at least humility, in the process.

The film *Catch Me if You Can* (2002) is an example. The con artist protagonist of that film, Frank W. Abagnale Jr., finally gets caught, but he also ends up developing into an adult with a moral sense. Having spent his young life impersonating other people, he ends up finding himself, more or less. And although Frank goes from being a comical character, i.e. an imposter, to being a serious person, the film itself is a comedy, in the deeper sense, since it is about the possibility of self-renewal.

Or, the protagonist seeks to become happy, as Forrest Gump (1994) had hoped to by marrying Jenny, his childhood sweetheart. Sadly, Forrest's dream fails, for Jenny dies, but the film still retains the sense of thanksgiving endemic to comedies, for life has surprised Forrest with quite a number of gifts. He has acquired fortune and fame, and the pride of receiving a Congressional Medal of Honor. Secondly, Jenny has given birth to a son, who is now about seven years old, and so Forrest now knows the joys of fatherhood. Then, in the very last scene, we see that life has provided him with a great gift of a different sort: a deep philosophical question. That question happens to be about fate, freedom, and destiny, and we are prompted to ask —if we remember Langer's distinction between tragedy (fate) and comedy (fortune)—of whether the film is a tragedy or a comedy, and whether life itself is a tragedy or a comedy. Thus the hopelessness, experienced by Forrest and by everyone, has wings, and can give birth, paradoxically, to hopefulness, but one that is unanticipated. In that sense, the comic vision of life is akin to that religious vision that sees that God's providence manifests itself in ways that "defy augury."

But Jenny's death still makes Forrest Gump the cinematic equivalent of a problem play, for there is a certain truth to the platitude that comedies end in marriage, at least that many traditional ones do, from those of Plautus to those of Shakespeare. What is satisfying, though, about a play ending in marriage is not that they live happily ever after. Marriage will bring the optimistic newlyweds far more difficulties than they suspect and, within time, their future children will bring more conflicts, crises, and suffering into the world. But there is a hopeful side to all of this, for what the protagonists will lose in terms of youthful dreams, they will gain in terms of emotional maturity and wisdom. And they will gain by virtue of the deeper union that marriage has the potential to provide.

Thus comedy's good cheer is not founded on succeeding in one's egocentric ambitions; those hopes abort, and inspire a release from seriousness, expressed in laugher. Comic hopefulness is of a different order. It might be summed up by what Clara Claiborne Park said of Dante, "It was not out of his prosperity that Dante wrote of the good he found" (1979; 1981, pp. 62-3). The good that lies at the foundation of the comic vision belongs to a different dimension, that of spirit. As Christopher Fry has suggested, "Laughter inclines me to know that man is essentially spirit" (1951; 1981, p. 17). Judged from that lofty height, Fry is even able to regard the Book of Job as, "...the great reservoir of comedy" (1951; 1981, p. 18).

What is the foundation of Fry's belief that the Book of Job is a comedy? Fry's answer to Job is not the paranoid's answer: "Why do we suffer? It is because of 'them!'" Nor does Fry offer a theodicy arrived at by reason. Nor does he suggest that what happened to Job is something good, but wholly unknowable and, therefore, to be accepted through blind faith. Fry believes that comedy offers a special intuition, one that leads to faith, for he states that, "Comedy is an escape, not from truth but from despair: A narrow escape into faith" (1951; 1981, p. 18). That intuition, which lies at the comic vision, is his answer to Job.

What, though, is the nature of the intuition to which Fry refers? As Fry suggests, "...there is an angle of experience where the dark is distilled into light: whither here or hereafter, in or out of time: where our tragic fate finds itself with perfect pitch, and goes straight to the key which creation was composed in" (1951; 1981, p. 18). That intuition — which eludes reason, but informs the spirit — is resident in the comic vision. It tells us that life, despite its terrible suffering, is a great good, and is to be affirmed. That sentiment is echoed in a Sufi saying, "When the heart cries for what it has lost, the spirit laughs for what it has found."

This leads to the core of a fundamental contrast between the two visions. The paranoid vision rejects life. The world is unacceptable as it is, which is why there must be an apocalypse, followed by a millennium of perfect peace and prosperity. In contrast to the paranoid's world rejection, the comic vision reconciles one with the way the world has always been, and will always be, more or less, because human beings, since the time of Aristophanes, have always been the same. Rather than being concerned with the end of the world, the comic vision is about life — folly, suffering, learning, self-renewal, and laughter — continuing on through the generations, continuing on as long as there are human beings to fall into a ditch, and then to emerge out of it, all the wiser—and then to joyously celebrate their victory.

We must, though, qualify our statement that comedy involves an acceptance or affirmation of life. There does exist satire, a form of comedy that expresses dissatisfaction with the world as it is. There is much to be said in satire's favor, such as the fact that by exposing folly it acts as a civilizing force. But in desiring a better world, satire is not purely comic, for it has not accepted comic hopelessness, in Plessner's sense. Since all comedy has elements of satire, the purely comical is an ideal type, like a Platonic essence, rather than something that actually exists in the world.

Although satirists reject the world as it is, they are not otherworldly or apocalyptic. Jonathan Swift, for example, in Gulliver's Travels was thoroughly disgusted with human beings whom he regarded as Yahoos —filthy, odious creatures. He had a good deal of the "defilement consciousness" that is endemic to the paranoid vision. But Swift's defilement consciousness was not evidence of the paranoid vision, but of the comic vision wedded to what Norman O. Brown (1985) has referred to as "the excremental vision." Most importantly, Swift was a moralist and a humanitarian, who saw the possibility of improving the world rather than outright rejecting it, as do those who are under the sway of the paranoid vision.

Paranoid Emotionality Versus Comic Distance

Santayana, we recall, contends that the accidental, chance, or contingent, dimension of existence is intrinsically comical. But, needless to say, chance can also result in tragedy. Consider, for example, what befell Oedipus on the road to Thebes. He just happened to run into a man, whom he killed, who he later discovered was his father. It is ironic, for sure, but it is a dark, Sophoclean irony. Often what happens by chance is neither comic nor tragic, but just painful or annoying. That is why chance, or contingency, make existence only potentially comical.

Might it be the case that the accidents that occur and the situations that evolve in comedies are of a pleasant sort, in contradistinction to those found in other genres, such as melodramas or tragedies? On the contrary, the situations that are presented in comedies are usually very far from being enjoyable to the characters concerned. Physical punishment, slander, humiliation, and the overturning of good fortune, indeed all the painfully absurd, ironic and incongruous situations in which comic characters find themselves, would belie any notion that comedy deals with mere pleasantries. What, then, is it that transforms all these terrible hardships into laughter? We mentioned the perception of hopelessness as essential for comic release, but hopelessness does not always lead to comic release. Sometimes it leads to despair. Some additional factors must, therefore, be present to transform life's accidents, mishaps, and reversals of fortune, indeed all of life's adversities, into laughter. Let us consider what it might be.

It has been said, "Tragedy plus time equals comedy."[50] What happens, in effect, is that time aids one in becoming emotionally distant from the unhappy events. Almost any suffering, with enough distance added, has the potential to become comical. It would appear, then, that emotional distance is necessary for one's awareness to be able to shift to the comical mode of constituting a world. Kierkegaard stated that "The tragic and the comic are the same in so far as both are based on contradiction, but the tragic is the suffering contradiction, the comical the painless contradiction" (1846; 1992, p. 459). It is, therefore, distance that makes the contradiction painless and opens the door to the comical mode of apprehension.

There are forms of distance other than the distance created by the passage of time. For example, we laugh when these characters undergo slaps or kicks or untoward reversals of fortune on stage or in film, or when things happen in real life, but to someone else. We might call this the distance of non-involvement, or "aesthetic distance." Thinking tends to engender distance and thus removes us from emotional

---

50 A search on Google indicates that the saying is most often attributed to Steve Allen, but it has also been attributed to Steve Allen Jr. M.D. (the comedian's son, a physician who offers workshops on humor and health), to Woody Allen (a character from one of his films says it), to Bob Newhart, and to Mel Brooks, among others.

sorrows, as expressed in Horace Walpole's famous statement: "Life is a tragedy for those who feel and a comedy for those who think" (1840; 1926, p. 127).

Is the person who thinks really more open to the comic vision? As Baudelaire states, in his essay on comedy, "The man who trips would be the last to laugh at his own fall, unless he happened to be a philosopher, one who had acquired by habit a power of rapid self-division and thus of assisting as a disinterested spectator at the phenomenon of his own ego. But such cases are rare" (1855; 1981, p. 316). Needless to say, Baudelaire was not referring to professional philosophers — who can be as emotionally heavy as most everyone else teaching at universities today — but to true philosophers, which is why he was right in asserting that such cases are rare. According to Aristotle, ancient Greece had at least one such individual, Democritus, who became known as the laughing philosopher.

At the other extreme from the laughing philosopher is the person under the sway of the paranoid vision, who is driven by anger, fear, suspicious apprehension, envy, resentment, bitterness, self-pity, and vainglorious pride, which are the emotive concomitants of the paranoid's delusions of grandeur. Also significant is what Hofstadter refers to as the "heated exaggeration" of the person with the paranoid style, which stems from the paranoid's emotional extremism, the sense that the sky is falling today, not tomorrow or the next day, but today. Yeats summed it all up when he observed, "...the worst are full of passionate intensity."

Might we, then, infer that all emotions are negative, and that powerful emotions are all the more dangerous? Certainly not, for there are elevating emotions, such as bliss and divine ecstasy. Furthermore, Kierkegaard points to the necessity of feelings, emotions, and passions for the true thinker when he writes, "...there is required for a subjective thinker imagination and feeling, dialectics in existential inwardness, together with passion. But passion first and last; for it is impossible to think about existence in existence without passion" (1846; 1992, p. 312Fn). Kierkegaard is an heir to European romanticism, but he is also the father of existentialism, in seeing the need to have thought wedded to passion.

Perhaps, then, it is really dark emotions that are of issue here. They cause a cognitive closure, a narrowing of perspective, and a reduction of the subtleties, hues, and values of the world, such that it becomes rendered in black and white, indicative of the Manichean view of things. Being lost in the moment, past and future no longer exist as categories. One then lacks the distance to realize that, "This too shall pass," which is akin to the sense that Langer says is endemic to the comic spirit that, "There is no permanent defeat or permanent human triumph" (1953; 1981, p. 37). We might recall the discussion of apocalypticists. In their conceit, they imagine that the particular times in which they live is like no other. Consequently the supposed uniqueness of the time and situation justifies any sort of action, no matter how murderous it may be.

Might one conclude, then, that it is dark emotions that are the problem? Not just yet, for there are those champions of the comic vision, like professor of religion and comic theorist John Morreall, who are critical not just of dark emotions, but of any and all emotions. According to Morreall:

> Whether considered positive, like pride, or negative, like fear and sadness, emotions lock heroes into self-concern and into their own perspectives, just as they do in real life. In emotional states, we tend to act in automatic, habitual, less intelligent ways; and the stronger the emotion, the less rational our actions...Tragic heroes, driven by emotions, tend to be extremists: to reach the goal set by their emotions, they will sacrifice everything else, including their own lives and the lives of those they love. (1999, pp. 25-26)

Of course, pride is not the only positive emotion. There are also, for example, joy, selfless love, and heavenly yearning. Consequently, Morreall's critique is somewhat unfair. All the same, Morreall hason his side a most formidable thinker, Plato, who excluded the poets from his ideal republic, for their art is to evoke the passions, which he deeply distrusted. And, along with Plato, there are Spinoza, Kant, Sartre, and many other philosophers who have been critical of the passions. Plato may have been puritanical, but his warning against the emotions has proven prophetic. We read in Camus (1956) examples of the high idealism and noble feelings of those rebels who ended up becoming murderous nihilists. Again, Robespierre and Lenin come to mind. And Hitler and Stalin were known for their sentimentality. The problem is that emotions, by their very nature, are labile, and positive emotions have a curious way of opening a person to the whole spectrum of emotions as well.

Of course, Plato would have also excluded the comic poets from his ideal republic as well, for, in Book Three of *The Republic,* he looked upon laughter with suspicion, as a disruptive force, and as malicious —because he viewed the object of laughter as being the faults, deformities, and ignorance of other people—and would prohibit the guardians of his republic from engaging in it. For better or for worse, emotions are not about to go into exile from the human condition, despite Plato's animadversions. If anything, the comic vision can serve as a salutary counterbalance to them.

Might the comic vision, then, be the medicine that could neutralize the over-emotionality of the paranoid vision, and all over-serious outlooks on life? We must first, though, ask: Is the comic vision really one of emotional coolness? Joseph Meeker suggests that when he states, "...comedy normally avoids strong emotions. Passionate love, hate, or patriotism generally appear ridiculous in a comic context, for comedy tends to create a psychological mood that is incompatible with deep emotions" (1997, 15).

Of course, overpowering emotions often possesses the characters in comedies, indeed passions would be a better word, for what they feel is not just experienced internally, but is exhibited in action, often violently. But these characters are presented such that the audience's heartstrings are not plucked too powerfully. If anything, the audience is made to feel superior—as the critic George Meredith (1871) contended —to the characters and the folly they exhibit on stage. A good measure of sympathy will make for high comedy, but too much sympathy and the audience would lose their aesthetic distance.[51]

---

51 Drama, literature, and film often do, in point of fact, blend comedy with pathos. The films of Charlie Chaplin are an example. They can make one cry as well as laugh. But, in such cases, a work of art is blending different visions of life, and creating a chiaroscuro of pathos and comic lightness. The films of the Marx Brothers, on the other hand, are almost completely lacking in pathos. They are much purer embodiments of the comic vision.

We suggested that the difference between the paranoid vision and the comic vision hinges, to a large degree, on the element of distance. That is the factor whose absence leads to the heated emotionality of the paranoid vision, and whose presence leads to the emotional coolness of the comic vision. If there is a problem with distance it is this: it soon collapses. One finds oneself unable to maintain one's separation from the world that one is witnessing. Distance collapses because one gets sucked back into the vortex of one's life and its problems. But, to a large degree, the reason why one gets sucked back is because remaining distant, having the attitude of being a mere witness or an ironical observer to life's crazy pageant, begins to feel empty and unreal. And so one dives back into the "destructive element," i.e. one's life with all of its hardships. This does not mean that the moments of laughter did not have their value, and may even linger throughout the day, or even the week. But there exists a certain sadness in watching the distance collapse, and the laughter fade, as the burden of seriousness returns.

That emptiness, which causes distance to collapse, is actually a function of the fact that the comical does not exist in itself, but is dependent upon seriousness, for laughter is a relief from seriousness. But once seriousness is laughed away, i.e. once that relief known as laughter occurs, the laughter is gone, for comic relief is generally a momentary experience. One is then left neither with seriousness nor with laughter, but with a restless mind, hungering for another serious project with which to direct its energies. Consequently, the distant relation to the prior serious content collapses and one is back in the serious world. But, although any occasion of laughter is transient, and seriousness returns, the comic vision itself—that deeper vision of life that transcends life's vicissitudes—remains. This is because, far more than being about laughter, the comic vision is a way of seeing that finds joy in this less than perfect world of ours.

We might also add that there is more to the comic vision than distance and its collapse. Just as the paranoid vision has a scale of levels, or keys, it would appear that the same is true for the comic vision. In its higher keys, the comic vision is not founded merely on seeking distance from life's painful contradictions, but on the transcendence of them. Whereas distance collapses, transcendence does not. This is because transcendence is not founded on a psychological separation of oneself from the world, but on an illumination of one's relation to the world. A Zen master, named Kaziaki Tanahashi, wrote a book entitled *Penetrating Laughter* (1987). He explores a certain species of laughter, one that is the concomitant to deep insight into life. It would be more accurate, though, to state that there exists penetrating insight that expresses itself as laughter.

The Apocalypse of Custard Pie

If we examine the language that describes people's reaction to the comical, we are struck by the violent destructiveness of the images. For example, one speaks of "cracking up," or "splitting one's sides with laughter," or "laughing one's head off," or "exploding with laughter." Similarly, we tell a comedian who is on a roll, "Stop, you're killing me!" All of these expressions are indicative of an underlying psychological truth: the effect of comedy is highly destructive, although we shall have to determine in what way it is.

And yet, the contrary notion, that comedy is healing, is perennial. The Bible, for example, recommends, "A merry heart maketh for a cheerful countenance." Jonathan Swift wrote that, "The best doctors in the world are Dr. Diet, Dr. Quiet, and Dr. Merryman." How, then, is comedy healing? The healing may be to the spirit, for as Wylie Sypher contends, comedy is all about, "birth: struggle: death: resurrection" (1981, p. 33). He also suggests "Comedy is essentially a Carrying Away of Death, a triumph over mortality by some absurd faith in rebirth, restoration, and salvation" (1956; 1981, p. 34)

Clara Claiborne Park offers us a further insight to this spiritual healing when she states that, "...the experience of comedy [is] healing, restoration, winning through" (1958; 1981, p. 60). It is true that the social order is finally restored after the comic disturbance, the ensuing agon, and the comic hero's "rendezvous with madness," as Eric Bentley called it. All the same, there is reason to disagree with Park that the healing power of comedy is essentially restorative. If it is healing, it must have something to do with the destructiveness suggested by the language that describes the effects of laughter.

The healing that takes place within the comic realm does not restore people to who they were before a series of mishaps and misadventures upset their situational and psychological applecart. Comedy is really healing in the transformative sense. It involves a death (a destruction) and a rebirth, as Sypher suggests, in which something new emerges. Thus Park is correct that there has been a "winning through." The winning through is to a new level of awareness, a transfiguration into a new mode of being.

The destructive images that describe the reaction to the comical —exploding with laughter, for example — are therefore appropriate, because death and destruction are the prerequisites for transformation. One explodes with laughter, which means that the constrictions of one's worldview explode, freeing one from those limits, either for a time or permanently, depending upon the power of the insight that precipitated the laughter.

We have referred to the transformative power of the comic vision. Who, though, is being transformed? Where lies the winning through? Is it the comic characters in a play or film, or is it the audience? The characters could be suffering all sorts of agonies, torments and tortures; they are not the ones laughing. The audience, on the other hand, does not suffer anything, but they get to have the laughs. It may be the case that a comic character, having been through hell, is transformed. For example, the cynical newscaster in *Groundhog Day* (1993) has undergone a sea change by the end of the film. What transformed him, though, was not the comic vision, but a series of harsh beatings, which made him willing to learn life's lessons. Unfortunately, the members of the audience are not similarly transformed, which is not surprising, for they did not undergo the alchemy of suffering.

On the other hand, the members of the audience would not laugh unless the suffering and comic hopelessness that they witnessed on stage resonated, at least on some level, as a fundamental truth for their own lives. The audience members are, therefore, vicariously experiencing the protagonist's trials and tribulations. Vicarious participation can be quite powerful—whether it is cathartic, as Aristotle believed, or transformative, in some sense — which has been the intended effect of tragedians, from Aeschylus to Arthur Miller. But the authors of comedies encourage their audiences to simultaneously participate in the agonies of the comic characters, while being distant from them. This sort of dual state of being, created by the power of "self-division," to which Baudelaire refers—in which one experiences life's travails, even if only vicariously, and simultaneously views them from a distance—is what makes comedy potentially transformative, for the distance allows one to stay awake and aware to the painful lunacy that one beholds, without one's awareness becoming clouded by a surfeit of pity, disgust, or horror.

Thus, for comedy to be transformative, what one hears or sees must be engaging, such that one thinks, "Hey, wait a second, this is really about me! I'm the big fool who is about to walk off a cliff!" Unfortunately, though, audience members infrequently make that connection. Consequently, they are laughing at the protagonist, rather than at themselves. That may explain the secret sadness of the circus clown. Clowns are, essentially, mimicking human foolishness, but because of human vanity, few people recognize that the clown's riotous idiocy is really their own idiocy. But clowns should not feel alone, for Samuel Beckett had the same problem in getting audiences to realize that the existential clowning in his play, Waiting for Godot, was not just about the despairing antics of two bums but, most universally, about the human condition. Quite likely, though, comedy's revelation of foolishness dawns on people subliminally. Unfortunately, it is all too diluted when it is subliminal for it to be really potent. Perhaps, in the future, due to advancements in the science of virtual reality, everyone in the movie theater will get his well-deserved pie in the face.

Far more potentially transformative is when the comical is not vicarious, i.e. when it is induced neither by viewing a comedy, nor by listening to a standup comic, but is direct. It is, indeed, when one catches a glimpse of the absurd, incongruous, and contradictory aspect of one's own life that the comic perception has great alchemical potency. This is because when one has the requisite distance to be able to laugh, one is open and unguarded. It is then that one is most open to insight about oneself. For that reason, there are laughs that are powerfully transformative. Whether the perception of the comical be vicarious or direct, if such laugh-inducing insights continue over a period of time, and are deep enough, encouraging one to let go of tonnages of seriousness, what can emerge for one is a transformed view of the world, one characterized by lightness, i.e., the comic vision.

What, then, does the apocalypse have to do with the alchemical possibilities of comic insight? We referred earlier to the "destructive" dimension of the comical perception—exploding with laughter, etc. Essentially, it derives from the awareness of one's impotence to act decisively, purposefully and meaningfully, due to the hopelessly contingent and contradictory nature of the enterprise. But this recognition of the impossible comes, to reverse T.S. Eliot's phrase, not with a whimper, but with a bang, or at least with a rim shot, i.e. with the sudden explosive shock of recognition endemic to comedy. The resurrection, on the other hand, is the release that one experiences from the confinement of one's serious projects, whatever these projects may be—from realizing one's notion of true love, to getting rich, to being considered an important person, to the sanctimonious effort to be considered a saint, to saving the world. One loses one's seriousness, but gains an expanded sense of self. That is the essence of comedy's apocalypse. A very perceptive observation by Cedrick Whitman—regarding the outcome of a pie fight in a Laurel and Hardy film—can offer us further insight into the essential nature of comic apocalypse:

> By the end—though the scene does not seem to end, but to continue toward a glorious eternity—the total mise en scene, an everyday street corner, is draped, inundated, and festooned with the squishy viscosity of custard and cream; men, women, buildings, dogs, and automobiles are transfigured in a perfect apocalypse of pie. The feeling which overtakes the spectator is one of sublime peace, of an access of knowledge which is true, of a revelation of the essence of things. Custard pie has become a way of life, and the world has been transformed by it. (1964; 1981, p. 241)

Whitman may have been speaking metaphorically, but he has tapped into a symbolic and mythic truth, one that lies at the heart of the comic vision. He uses the word "revelation," which indicates that he means that an apocalypse has occurred in this Laurel and Hardy film in that sense too. Whitman says that the effect on the spectator is one of "sublime peace." He does not clarify why this is so, but it would be fair to say that the experience of peace is derived from the wholesale defeat of the spirit of seriousness.

This defeat of seriousness is symbolized by everyone, without exception, from the policeman who tries to reestablish order, to innocent bystanders, getting a custard pie in the face. It is significant that the world be inundated by that which is creamy, squishy, and viscous, i.e., by custard pies. It symbolizes that distinct form and structure—which distinguish and separate us from each other, and constitute the very foundations of self-identity, meaning, importance and seriousness—have been demolished. In other words, it is impossible to distinguish one person from another when they have a pie in their face.

Paradoxically, this universal custard sliming is the defilement, with its concomitant threat to identity that the paranoid dreads. Indeed, the fear of slime and viscosity is universal, according to Sartre, although he considers it to be a case of "the revenge of the in-itself," the material world grabbing and clinging to a person, thus denying his claim to freedom (1943; 1988, p. 138). The denial of everyone's claim to freedom may, therefore, be another factor symbolized by the custard pie attack. But the amazing thing about comedy is that by maintaining a certain distance to life's adversities, one laughs. The loss of separate identity, pride, dignity, self-importance and seriousness—precipitated by the custard pie sliming—comes as a relief, and is thus rendered as sweet as custard.

Furthermore, the "for-itself," or freedom, that Sartre states one has lost by being slimed is regained by virtue of the fact that one can laugh, which is an indication of one's superiority to the scene, and to the human condition itself. That ability to laugh in the midst of life's adversities, i.e. the power of transcendence, is one of the surest foundations for human dignity and grandeur. It is true of course, that the members of the audience, those watching this Laurel and Hardy film, do not get a pie in the face. But, once again, it is experienced vicariously.

The "revelation of the essence of things," to which Whitman refers, therefore consists in the knowledge of the inner formlessness and absurdity at the heart of human existence. This is not a heavy, existentialist absurdity, for if it were we would not laugh. Nor is it reflective of a regression to a materialistic metaphysics, one that discounts the significance of form and identity, nor is it intended to be a Marxist image of a society made classless by the equalizing power of custard pie. True comedy does not have any such serious agenda. The revelation is, on the contrary, far more fundamental. It is founded on the intuition, or at least the intimation, of the ultimate "emptiness" —in the Buddhist sense of the word—of the roles that one plays in life, as well as by a world thus constituted by forms, which the Hindus call the Veil of Maya. One might say that in the best comedies, the trickster sneaks up on Maya, lifts her veil, and gives her a kiss.

Is one, then, to conclude that the comic spirit, in its very essence, is apocalyptic? It is apocalyptic even if any particular comedy does not express such apocalyptic longings so dramatically as in a pie fight, or in the ontological anarchy that overflows in Marx Brothers' films. In such farces, we find the comic spirit in its essential purity. In other forms of comedy, it is subtler. Sometimes the apocalyptic revelation is whispered. But, in all cases, the apocalypse consists in a playful revelation of the emptiness of the world of seriousness, if only for a time. Of course, viewing a comedy is not going to defeat the spirit of seriousness, but it may loosen its shackles a bit, and ready one for a more fundamental liberation. When the world constituted by the spirit of seriousness is defeated, what reemerges is not a new and better world, but freedom from the world, i.e. subjectivity, or inwardness.

How different this is from the paranoid apocalypse. Such fantasies, of the paranoid variety, are very serious. This is because they seek to offer an explanation, and a justification, in the form of a telos, of why the world is the way it is. They promise that the world will be a true world by the end of time. The implication, of course, is that the present world is woefully inadequate. The comic spirit, on the other hand, does not seek to explain the world, nor does it seek to justify it. Furthermore, the comic apocalypse does not lead to a "real" world, i.e.

to a world that is intelligible, but to the end of one's bondage to one's worldview, as well as to any other possible worldview.

More essentially, the comic apocalypse leads to a release, temporary though it may be, from the need for intelligibility and justice, from meaningfulness and self-importance. It is, therefore, apocalyptic but, paradoxically, also accepting of the world, for it is not the actual spatiotemporal world that needs to end; it is one's ignorance, self-importance, and seriousness, which derive from one's worldview, that needs to end. That is how it is that the comic vision is both apocalyptic and life-affirming.

Another example of comic apocalypse, somewhat less symbolic than Whitman's custard pie example, might help clarify our point. The driving force behind the plot of the film *The Treasure of Sierra Madre* (Dir. Houston, 1948) is the increasing paranoia of Fred C. Dobbs, played by Humphrey Bogart. The film—which most critics would place in the genre of adventure film and certainly not regard as a comedy—is thoroughly infused with the comic vision. It presents an example of a person under the sway of the paranoid vision, viewed in the illuminating light of the comic vision. That the film's director, John Huston, was able to accomplish this is not completely surprising, for there is something intrinsically humorous about paranoia. The key here, as Morreall points out, is mechanical inelasticity, which Bergson regarded as the essence of the comical. As Morreall states:

> To highlight the disadvantages of stubbornness and other forms of mental rigidity, comedy presents as mental butts the miser, the paranoid, the pedant, and other characters whose wills or intellects are in ruts. The idée fixe that dominates the tragic hero is in comedy something to laugh at. Indeed, Henri Bergson based his whole theory of comedy on characters with idées fixes, who represent what he called "mechanical inelasticity." (1999, p. 28)

In many ways, it is what happens to the paranoid Fred C. Dobbs that acts as a catalyst for the transformation of one of the other characters in *The Treasure of Sierra Madre*, named Bob Curtin, and offers a profound example of release from a major species of the spirit of seriousness: the category of progress, goals, purpose, as well as concern about success and failure. The film is about three men—two of whom are relatively young, Curtin and Dobbs—and a third whom they meet, in Tampeka, Mexico, named Howard, an old man, who is an experienced gold miner. The three set out together for the hills of Mexico to find gold. After ten months of struggle, they do finally discover a huge quantity of gold. Now they need to bring it back into town. But Dobbs, drifting into a kind of paranoid psychosis, starts concocting conspiracy theories about his comrades and becomes convinced that they are plotting to kill him so that they can steal his share of the gold. Dobbs tries to kill Curtin but Dobbs ends up getting killed himself by Mexican bandits.

Curtin and Howard—after having faced all sorts of dangers, including the Mexican bandits, and the assaults by their murderously paranoid former comrade Dobbs — now finally head back to Tampeka to cash in their gold. They put the gold dust into sacks and load them onto their donkeys. When they reach town, they hitch their donkeys to a post and look for the banker. In the few moments that they are away, the now desperate Mexican bandits see the sacks, pour the gold onto the ground, but mistakenly conclude it to be sand, and so walk away. Then a sudden, powerful windstorm comes and blows all of the gold hither and yon. In the middle of the storm, the two miners rush back to their donkeys only to realize that all the gold has been lost and that they are back to where they were at the beginning of their journey.

Curtin starts to feel a sense of life's futility. He looks like it is the end of the world, to use an apocalyptic expression. At this point, the film could have had an existentialist ending, like Hemingway's *The Old Man and the Sea,* which is about affirming meaning in the face of absurdity. But Howard is a different sort of old man. He becomes overcome with hysterical laughter—not a cool, Hamlet-like, tragic-comic, laugher, nor Sartrean absurdist laughter, but a truly boisterous, exuberant laughter. Totally perplexed by the old man's laughter, Curtin asks Howard what is so funny. This is Howard's amazing response:

> Oh laugh, Curtin, old boy. It's a great joke played on us by
> the Lord, or fate, or nature, whatever you prefer. But whoever

> or whatever played it certainly had a sense of humor! Ha!
> The gold has gone back to where we found it!... (Curtin joins
> Howard in boisterous laughter.) This is worth ten months of
> suffering and labor — this joke is!

What has essentially happened is that Curtin's consciousness has
suddenly ripened to the level where he is liberated from slavery to the
categories of progress, goals, achievement, success and failure. He is
also liberated from the potentially paranoiagenic bitterness that can
result from failure. What Curtin has lost in terms of worldly success, he
has more than gained in joyful wisdom. His laughter is an expression
of his liberation. Here, too, is an example of death and transformation,
a comic apocalypse. Here the new millennium is not a new time and
place, but a new state of mind, which we are calling the comic vision
of life.

There is a deep sense of thanksgiving and renewal, which is
the result of having survived a terrible ordeal, and being somewhat
surprised to find oneself still alive. One realizes that the gift of life
is what really counts, not fame or fortune. Apropos is Nietzsche's
"eternal return," his notion that everything will be repeated in exactly
the same way, endlessly. Nietzsche is asking whether or not one can
truly free oneself from the category of progress. If one lets go of the
categories of progress and purposefulness, the Sisyphean sense of
futility — the sense of: "What good is it struggling to bring the gold
down from the mountain if it will only blow away again?"—disappears,
and playfulness emerges, as it did for Curtin.

What can also emerge—for those who begin to let go of the
trappings and entrapments of selfhood, and venture further into the
world constituted by the comic vision—is "reverse-paranoia." This is
the sense that although the universe has numbered one's days and can
destroy one at any moment, there is something, other than the will
to survive that is keeping one alive. Furthermore, whatever this force
may be, it is like a teacher who, with infinite patience, continually
seeks to bring one to enlightenment. Whatever it was, therefore, that
had played the joke on Howard and Curtin was not just playing an
ordinary practical joke, but was delivering, in its fashion, an insight

whose result was "penetrating laughter." There are some "signs," to use Buber's terminology, that are subtle, but sometimes signs take the form of God, nature, or fate delivering a good swift kick in the pants, as it did to Howard and Curtin. Thus reverse-paranoia is the valid suspicion that the universe is conspiring, day and night, to make all beings beneficiaries of its perfect wisdom.

The Manichean versus the Sympathetic Vision

We referred earlier to the paranoid's us/them, or Manichean, bifurcation of humanity into the forces of absolute good and absolute evil. The comic vision is founded on a very different perception of humanity, one that is akin to what Ernst Cassirer called "sympathetic vision:"

> Comic art possesses in the highest degree that faculty shared by all art, sympathetic vision. By virtue of this faculty it can accept human life with all of its defects and foibles, its follies and vices. Great comic art has always been a sort of encomium moriae, a praise of folly. (1944; 1979, p. 150)

Cassirer's notion of sympathetic vision leads to the question, "What is sympathy?" Schopenhauer, viewing sympathy from an epistemological perspective, claimed that it is a perception of the delusive nature of "the principle of individuation." That principle, named by Leibniz, is the notion that people are separate by virtue of their spatial separation. It is really the common sense view of self and other. To see through the principle of individuation is to know the underlying identity—experienced as a fellow-feelingvbetween oneself and other people.

In *The Nature of Sympathy* (1913; 1983), Max Scheler differed from Schopenhauer in contending that what is shared is not identity of selves, but identity of feelings between distinct selves. To better understand sympathy, Scheler distinguishes it from empathy. Seeking to clarify Scheler's distinction, Douglas E. Chismar states, "Empathy, on the other hand, as a vicarious imitation of another's feelings, leads to a confusion of egos, as witnessed in cases of 'emotional infection'" (2003, p. 1). We might add that this "confusion of egos" and "emotional infection" is at the heart of the "group mind" that social theorists like Lucien Levi-Bruhl (1910; 1985), and Gustave Le Bon (1897; 1982), analyzed.

It would seem to be the case, then, that mass movements of true believers (Hoffer, 1951; 2002) are founded on empathy, i.e. in terms of a group contagion. None of the group members really understands or really shares in identical feelings, although they imagine that they do. In truth, they remain isolated individuals. Extrapolating, we may say that the paranoid vision, when it expresses itself on a group level, unites people in a bond of empathy.[52]

The sympathetic vision—that lies at the foundation of comic art, according to Cassirer—is founded neither on a confusion of selves nor of feelings, but on a genuine identity of feelings with the other. As to how this identity of feelings is possible is another story. Maurice Friedman, for example — who has given much thought to that question in his effort to clarify Buber's notion of the I-Thou relation—contends that it involves an imagining of the feelings of the other, accompanied by a "bold swinging into the other" (Buber, 1965). In any case, we shall see whether it is not just particular comedies, but the comic vision itself that possesses sympathetic vision.

Sympathetic vision may derive from an epistemological intuition, or insight—one regarding the identification of self and other, as Schopenhauer suggests, or from shared experience, as Scheler suggests—but sympathetic vision would also appear to be founded upon an ethical insight, one regarding the nature of human faults and foibles. Sympathetic vision views people, even those who may deserve rebuke, neither as demons nor as conspirators. On the contrary, they are regarded as merely foolish, or in error. An exemplar of Cassirer's "sympathetic vision" is the character Prospero, from Shakespeare's play *The Tempest*. As the literary critic Wylie Sypher observed:

> Using the tolerance of high comedy, and its confidence, Prospero speaks gently to those who tried to kill him. In this

---

52   To overcome their isolation would require a genuine acknowledgement of otherness (Sartre, 1993) and a genuine meeting, or encounter, with another (Buber, 1971).

larger perspective, sin seems to be the last delusion of man's mind, an error that is absurd... tragic danger is here cancelled by a feat of moral insight. (1956; 1981, p. 49)

Cassirer used the words, "defects," "foibles," "follies" and "vices," and Sypher used the words, "delusion," and "error." We might contrast those words with words like evil, malevolence, malice, demonic, meanness, nastiness, wickedness, and cruelty. The former group of words suggests that people perform destructive acts out of ignorance, or foolishness. Consequently, one tends to regard such actions as venial, excusable, or forgivable. That is why Jesus prays, "Forgive them, Lord, for they know not what they do." Someone who does not know what he does, someone who is foolish, or ignorant, seems more innocent, and therefore more deserving of sympathy.

By contrast, the latter group of words suggests that the person performing the destructive act was fully conscious of what he or she was doing. It is the deliberateness of the action, the fact that it was intended to cause harm that seems to make the action inexcusable, or unforgivable. Apparently, the notion of intention enters into such moral judgments. Furthermore, because foolishness is regarded as a product of innocence, it is far easier to acknowledge foolishness in oneself, than it would be to acknowledge evil in oneself. Even those who are resistant to acknowledging their foolishness might at least be open to admitting that they had been foolish in the past. This enlightened view of human beings, which regards them as not evil but as foolish, mistaken, or in error, is expressed by Kenneth Burke in his Attitudes Towards History, whom Barnet, Berman, and Burto aptly quote in their anthology of great comedies:

The progress of humane enlightenment can go no further than in picturing people not as vicious, but as mistaken. When you add that people are necessarily mistaken, that all people are exposed to situations in which they must act as fools, that every insight contains its own special kind of blindness, you complete the comic circle, returning again to the lesson of humility that underlies great tragedy. (qtd. in Barnet, Berman, and Burto, 1958, p. 12)

What is central to Burke's analysis is the realization that folly is universal, and furthermore, that it is inevitable, because it is intrinsic to the human condition. As King Lear comes to realize, "When we are born we cry that we are come to this great stage of fools" (Act IV, Scene 6). This kinship of oneself and other people— founded upon an acknowledgement of one's membership in the universal brotherhood of fools — is very likely to promote humility, as well as sympathy and tolerance. Burke states that humility is the lesson both of comedy and great tragedy. That is, indeed, an intriguing observation, for it suggests that there is both a comic and a tragic road to wisdom and that they converge at the same place.

But whatever road one takes to reach the humility that is requisite for wisdom, whether it be the tragic road or the comic road, humility is an attitude that is antithetical to the delusions of grandeur characteristic of the paranoid vision. The problem of sympathy, more fundamentally for the paranoid, is that sympathy is not possible if one disowns one's shadow, projecting it onto others. Sympathy requires some sort of identification with the other person—whether in terms of feelings, experience, or actual being, as Schopenhauer suggests—but there cannot be identification if one regards oneself as all good and the other person as all bad.

Let us now return to Cassirer's observation. In addition to stating that comic art is sympathetic towards human folly, he states that it actually involves a "praise of folly." Of course, Cassirer is alluding to Erasmus' work, *In Praise of Folly*. Whereas, at certain times, Erasmus was being ironical in praising folly, and was using this literary conceit, ironically, as a vehicle to castigate the folly of his age, at other times he was genuinely sincere in seeing a great value to folly. Fundamentally, his point is that folly makes life livable. As Erasmus suggests, without folly there would be no marriage, and that institution is needed if the human species is not to die out. Besides, wisdom can make one sad, but folly adds joy to life. Erasmus reminds us that as the fool enters the stage everyone in the theater rejoices.

This cheerful attitude toward human foolishness, as well as the good-natured appreciation of how one has been the butt of a joke by the cosmic trickster (Remember Howard and Curtin?) is a sea change from the attitude that is most prevalent amongst people—that ranges from peeved and petulant annoyance at having to suffer fools all the livelong day, to downright loathing of people for the insult and injury that they have caused one — as well as resentment at life itself for having placed obstacles, at every twist and turn, on one's path to happiness. The praise of folly that finds expression in that narrative genre known as comedy, which derives from the comic vision, neutralizes all the paranoiagenic toxins—the anger, annoyances, frustrations, and resentments—that can build up in a person, organization, or in a society.

A related implication of this sympathetic vision is the tendency to include rather than to exclude. This follows from the perception of the universality of folly. As Northrop Frye expresses it:

> The tendency of comedy is to include as many people as possible in its final society: the blocking characters are more often reconciled or converted than simply repudiated...[It] is the reason for the traditional importance of the parasite, who has no business to be at the final festival but is nevertheless there. The word "grace,"... is an important thematic word in Shakespearian comedy. (1957; 1981, pp. 85-86)

Here, again, we find the inclusiveness of the comic vision to be the polar opposite of the radical self/other exclusiveness of the paranoid vision. We might also add that Frye uses the word "grace," which, in this case, should be understood as "a favor rendered by one who need not do so; indulgence" (Dictionary.com). It means, in other words, a forgiving and generous attitude towards those who really do not deserve it. There is a high-mindedness that belongs to grace, which is opposite to the malevolence and spiteful envy that belongs to the paranoid vision.

Is the Sympathetic Vision Viable in a Dangerous World?

The distinction between paranoid Manichaeism and the sense of sympathy that is allied to the comic vision obviously has social and political implications. As Benjamin Lehman, a scholar of comedy, stated: "It is in democracy that comedy particularly prospers, for true democracy and true drama are of an immense hospitality and have respect for all men" (1954; 1981, p. 103). Here we find the inclusiveness to which Frye was referring. Of course, it could also be argued that democracy depends upon democratic government, which depends on a balance of powers, which is founded upon a distrust and suspiciousness of one's fellows, all of which sounds closer to the paranoid vision. There is, though, a reasonable ground for distrust that is not paranoiac. Furthermore, just because a person is sympathetic, hospitable, and respectful to others, does not mean that he or she is a damn fool.

If Lehman is correct, a totalitarian organization of people, whether secular or religious, fosters neither mutual respect nor sympathetic vision and, therefore, cannot nourish the comic vision. It would be intriguing to consider whether the inverse of Lehman's notion might also be true. It may be the case, in other words, that certain illiberal ideologies, such as fascism, communism, and radical Islamic fundamentalism, draw their sustenance from the paranoid vision, whereas liberty, democracy, creativity, innovation, and entrepreneurial capitalism are nourished by the comic vision. If so, then success or failure in such critical endeavors as nation building, propaganda, and the war of ideas in general, may hinge on the degree to which a particular dysfunctional society is able to undergo this more primary shift, from paranoid vision to comic vision.

An important question naturally arises as to the limits of the comic vision in regard to the element of sympathy. As one recalls, Kenneth Burke stated that in comedy people are not viewed as vicious. It would seem, then, that the comic vision contains an element of unreality. After all, while it may be true that most people who harm other people are simply ignorant or foolish, only an unrealistic Pollyanna would deny that there also exist plenty of people who are malicious and downright evil. Does the existence of malice militate against sympathetic vision, and thus bring us to the limits of the comic vision? Have we then reached, in regard to the comic vision, what Jaspers called a "boundary situation?"

If the existence of evil does constitute a limit to the comic vision, then the best that can be hoped for is a compromise with seriousness. The wisdom of Ecclesiastes would then hold sway—there would be a time for war and a time for peace, a time for love and a time for hate, a time to hang terrorists and a time to offer sociological explanations after they have been pronounced thoroughly dead, a time for seriousness and a time for the comic vision. There are, indeed, those thinkers who have circumscribed the reach of the comic. Reinhold Niebuhr, for example, although appreciating and respecting the value of comedy, has a constrained view of its efficacy in regard to the moral realm, both in terms of fighting evil, as it exists in other people, as well as in oneself:

> Laughter is the vestibule of the temple of confession. But laughter is not able to deal with the problem of the self in any ultimate way...We have dealt thus far with humor as reaction to the incongruities in the character of self and its neighbors. We have discovered it to be a healthy, but an ultimately unavailing, method of dealing with the evils of human nature. But men face other incongruities than those which human foibles and weaknesses present. Human existence itself is filled with incongruities. (1969, pp. 141, 143)

Niebuhr contends that humor cannot handle life's big incongruities, but he does not say why. Perhaps it is because to allow humor this power would be to have it compete with faith. Ricoeur would also limit the range of the comic. It is not, in Ricoeur's opinion, the existence of evil that limits comedy's power, but the existence of suffering:

> Only the "seer" of Greek tragedy and the "fool" of Shakespearian tragedy escape from the tragic; the seer and the fool have ascended from the tragic to the comic by their access to a comprehensive vision. Now nothing is more likely

to destroy the comprehensive vision than suffering. (1969, pp. 322-323)

Ricoeur is on target in seeing that "a comprehensive vision" is essential for ascending from the tragic to the comic, for what we are calling "the comic vision" is not just a mood, but a way of seeing that is a function of knowledge, understanding, comprehension, and insight. But Ricoeur states that suffering destroys the comprehensive vision. Why would this be so? After all, if a comprehensive vision emerges at all, it emerges out of an encounter with suffering.

For example, Dante's vision of life, which is both comprehensive and comic, emerged out of his own midlife crisis about the meaning of human existence. Dante called his famous work *La Commedia*. What made it a comedy was not that it was humorous, although it certainly was at times, but that it had a happy ending: our struggles on this earth are not for naught, but are ultimately meaningful, for justice is found in the afterlife. Thus the human situation, far from being absurd, merits our good cheer, and even warrants joyfulness. Dante's comprehensive view of human existence is congruent with the sense of renewal endemic to the comic vision. This is a vision of life that is not destroyed by suffering, for it triumphs over adversity. Consequently, one must disagree with Ricoeur. And one must disagree with Niebuhr, as well, for he is focusing on laughter, humor and comedy, and does not see that the comic vision is far more fundamental.

The question of whether or not the existence of malice and evil destroys sympathetic vision—and thus undermines the power of the comic vision, and limits its range—is crucial, because the seriousness that results from the battle with evil could leave one prone to a new danger, which Nietzsche recognized when he wrote, "Whoever fights monsters should see to it that in the process he does not become a monster" (1885; 1989, p. 89). The danger is that in battling evil, one can fall under the sway of the paranoid vision. The film *Lawrence of Arabia* (1962) illustrates that point. Lawrence starts out idealistic, but he becomes cynical. Perhaps his cynicism was due to embarking on his mission with expectations that were too high, and which then came crashing down when he experienced the horrors of war. Eventually, he becomes bloodthirsty and vengeful.

Might it somehow be possible to maintain sympathetic vision while acknowledging the existence of malice, even when engaging in mortal combat with those who are evil? For something like that to be achievable there must exist some level of consciousness in which what is apparently contradictory—sympathy and mortal combat—can either be reconciled, or else transcended. The Bhagavad-Gita points the way to such transcendence. Arjuna is about to go into battle, but he does not want to fight, for he sees that the enemy includes people whom he knows and is close to, such as his cousins, uncles, and former teachers. Sympathy has rendered Arjuna unable to act.

Lord Krishna helps Arjuna out of his quandary by revealing to Arjuna that there is ultimately no death, no sorrow, and no fault, for only Brahman exists. The true self, Brahman, is imperishable. Referring to the warrior, Lord Krishna says, "Though he slays from the worldly standpoint, he does not slay in truth" (Radhakrishnan 500-200 BCE; 1994, p. 357). Having reached the level of "holy indifference," through the yoga of knowledge, Arjuna is able to slay the enemy, which includes his relatives and teachers, and yet keep his humanity. The comic vision is preserved, for it has shifted to a new key, one in which life, in all of its horrors, is seen to be a divine comedy. It is in this way that the Bhagavad-Gita seeks to reconcile the comic vision with the harsh realities of human existence. If the comic vision is to be preserved amidst such conflicts and crises, it must, therefore, ascend toward a mystical vision.

Even apart from the most promising possibility, although the most difficult—the elevation of the comic vision to a mystical key, where it can transcend mighty contradictions—there have been times, in the history of warfare, when sympathy arose amongst the fiercest combat troops engaged in mortal combat. Sometimes sympathy arose out of simple compassion, and sometimes out of respect for a worthy adversary. In an article for the Joint Service Conference on Professional Ethics, Chaplain Scott Sterling, of the United States Air Force, contends that there is a long history of soldiers showing respect for worthy adversaries. (2003, pp. 1-16) Sterling quotes St Ambrose —

who wrote a book called Duties of the Clergy during the forth century — where he states that the notion of worthy opponent goes back to the Bible. Referring to King David, St Ambrose states:

> When he showed that he loved valor even in an enemy. He had also thought that justice should be shown to those who had borne arms against himself the same as to his own men. Again, he admired Abner, the bravest champion of the opposing side, whilst he was their leader and was yet waging war. Nor did he despise him when suing for peace, but honored him by a banquet. When killed by treachery, he mourned and wept for him. (qtd. in Sterling, 2003, p. 6)

Of course, it is easier to be sympathetic towards an enemy after they have been vanquished. Prospero, for example—whom Wylie Sypher admired for his tolerance, high-mindedness, and moral insight—forgave his enemies, but only after he was in full control of the situation. Apropos is the fact that Americans have a unique history of subsequently raining CARE packages down on their defeated foes. Lincoln encapsulated the sentiment behind such generosity when he said, "With malice toward none, with charity for all." Here, then, exists a people who, although far from perfect, possess the ability to immediately return, after the hostilities have ended, to the beneficent realm of the comic vision, where they are energetic in their largess of spirit. It would appear, then, that sympathetic vision, which lies at the core of the comic vision, is congruent with the realities of human existence and remains a powerful antidote to that most pernicious form of the spirit of seriousness, the paranoid vision.

Chapter 10
Conclusions and Lingering Conundrums

---

*"Man is a riddle in the world, and it may be, the greatest riddle...
Man lives in an agony, and wants to know who he is, where he
comes from and where he is going."*

— *Nikolai Berdyaev*

In the course of this investigation of organizational malevolence
and the paranoid vision, a larger question has gradually emerged:
What does the existence of the paranoid vision tell us about what
it means to be a human being? We addressed that question throughout
this work, and more particularly in the chapter entitled, "Paranoia in
a New Key." We suggested that the paranoid vision is a flight from the
task of living life at the intersection of time and eternity, of the finite
and the infinite. It is a refusal to be the crucible of transformation,
where these polar opposites seek integration.

All of the manifestations of the paranoid vision make sense, and
are of a piece, when considered from that perspective. Delusions of
grandeur are an obvious enough refusal to acknowledge one's finitude.
The sense of evil that is endemic to the paranoid vision has a similar
ground. After all, evil—represented as defilement, possession, or as
a devil (projected onto a vilified group of people)—has the aspect of
externality. The implication is that one is inwardly pure and perfect.

This arrogation of absoluteness to oneself is a refusal of the task to mediate the finite and the absolute. Conspiracy theories, apart from their vilifying function, fail to acknowledge the limits of the knowable. They derive from a refusal to acknowledge the uncertain, contingent, and chance dimension of spatiotemporal existence. Apocalyptic fantasies are founded on a rejection of the world, with all of its imperfections. Rather than taking up the arduous task of being the crucible, one longs for the day when this imperfect world will be destroyed, and a less demanding mode of existence will appear, i.e. at the millennium.

The paranoid vision can be viewed as one modality of the flight from the inner demand to live at the intersection (of time and eternity, of the finite and infinite.) Might all psychopathology, and all immorality, consist in various forms of flight from that difficult task? The evidence would suggest that they are indeed a flight, but a detailed exploration of this phenomenon must be deferred for another time.

For now, it will be enough to propose an answer to the question that began this chapter: What does the existence of the paranoid vision tell us about that amphibious creature known as a human being? It bespeaks of the difficulty of living at the intersect. After all, if mediating opposites were not thoroughly problematic, there would be no paranoid vision, nor would there be the ten thousand other ways in which human beings flee their special calling. It is because the task is arduous that there has always been admiration for such virtues as saintliness, nobility, and heroism. As Spinoza said, "All things excellent are as difficult as they are rare."

The Origin of All Narratives

This investigation raises a number of intriguing questions that lie beyond the purview of the present work. They are worth considering here, if only briefly, for they require us to now step back and view the paranoid vision from a larger perspective. One such question involves whether there are ways of seeing corresponding to the other personality disorders. Does there exist, for example, an obsessive-compulsive vision, a schizoid vision, and a hysterical vision?

Indeed, is all psychopathology founded on ways of seeing? If such is the case, which is what we would suspect, clinical psychology could take a quantum leap forward by uncovering those ways of seeing. Consequently, instead of regarding psychopathology as a concatenation of symptoms, one would be able to grasp an underlying essence, and thus gain true understanding. The key, then, is to deepen the level of investigation by shifting from a psychological to an epistemological plane of inquiry, one where visions of life are central.

A similar advance might also be made in the field of social, political, and organizational psychology. That an organization can become possessed by the paranoid vision should now be clear enough. Can an organization be possessed by other ways of seeing as well? Might there be, for example, manic-depressive organizations, impulsive organizations, schizotypal and passive-aggressive organizations?

There is, though, something perplexing here: Evidence exists that paranoia is contagious, but such evidence would seem to be lacking in regard to the other personality disorders. This is important because we have taken the fact that paranoia is communicable as evidence that it is founded on a vision of life, the assumption being that visions of life are akin to cognitive viruses. How, then, is one to understand this anomaly? One possibility is that there is something unique to paranoia as a way of seeing that makes it communicable. If so, what it might be has still not been determined. Another possibility is that the other personality disorders are contagious, but in ways that have not yet been discerned.

In her book, *Hystories: Hysterical Epidemics and Modern Media* (1997), Elaine Showalter does, in fact, contend that the personality disorder known as "hysteria" is contagious. She regards a number of disorders that became prevalent in the 1990s—alien abduction, chronic fatigue syndrome, satanic ritual abuse, recovered memory, Gulf War syndrome, and multiple personality disorder—as contemporary manifestations of hysteria. If hysteria is contagious, how does it spread? As Showalter states:

> Infectious epidemics of hysteria spread by stories circulated through self-help books, articles in newspapers and

magazines, TV talk shows and series, films, the Internet, and
even literary criticism. The cultural narratives of hysteria,
which I call hystories, multiply rapidly and uncontrollably
in the era of mass media, telecommunications, and e-mail.
(1997, p. 5)

Here, again, a distorted view of the world is being communicated
through certain narratives. Whereas the narratives of paranoia are
conspiracy theories, apocalyptic fantasies, angry screeds, vicious
rumors, etc., those of hysteria are psychosomatic diseases. Both
paranoia and hysteria are transmitted through the media, although
the choice of media is different. Paranoia seems to find its home, for
example, on websites or blogs devoted to disseminating conspiracy
theories. The ideal medium for the spread of hysteria seems to be
Oprah-style TV talk shows.

Showalter sees hysteria as a "false explanation." It is false because
it does not get to the real ground of a person's difficulties. One can
gather that she regards certain forms of hysteria as akin to the
paranoid vision, in so far as they involve finding a scapegoat for one's
troubles. Recovered Memory Syndrome, a form of hysteria, illustrates
the explanatory and justificatory power of hysteria. Those who suffer
from this malady supposedly come to painfully remember what they
had long been repressing from memory, that their father had raped
them as a child, and that is the reason for their present emotional
difficulties. Thus instead of some conspiring cabal, it is one's father
who is to blame for paradise lost.

Some of the other disorders that Showalter associates with
hysteria — such as chronic fatigue syndrome, and Gulf War syndrome
— are simply regarded by hysterics as being caused by a virus of some
sort, one that doctors have thus far not been able to discover. We
must note, though, that these are not simply forms of hypochondria,
for those with these psychogenic illnesses can come down with real
symptoms, and suffer terribly.

Showalter does not, though, refer to hysteria as a vision of life, but
merely as a psychological malady with various somatic manifestations.
But we would contend that psychological maladies are communicable
only in so far as they are founded on visions of life. The logic here

is that communicability requires narratives, and narratives are the product of ways of seeing, or visions.

A person with the type of psychogenetic illness derivative of hysteria is really a rhetorician, for their malady is the language that they use to persuade other people of the truth of their worldview. Thus paranoids, hysterics, and people with other ways of seeing as well, are only too happy to tell their stories to whoever will listen. But all that hysterics really need to do is to tell other people the name of their malady. They might, for example, state, "I am a victim of alien abduction." That statement alone carries with it an entire ontology. Why, though, the need to persuade? Certainly, misery loves company, perhaps because one's conviction seems truer if other people also believe in it.

Throughout these chapters, we have been dwelling on some rather dark stories, or narratives. To put matters in perspective, most of the narratives that human beings use to render their experience intelligible are more mundane, and far less malevolent. There are, for example, the workaday narratives that get one through the day, of which there would appear to be two types. The first offers direction. It is a story that one daily repeats to oneself, like a mantra, and often to other people. It may sound like: "Today I am going off to work, so that I can retire from teaching in only twenty-four more years." Or perhaps, "I am going to marry my sweetheart, so that I can live a life of happiness and joy in the suburbs." Such stories provide the thread, tenuous though it may be, with which our days are linked together, thus serving to organize our energies and to provide direction. That type of narrative is most efficacious in what C.G. Jung calls the first half of life, before the arrival of life's major disappointments, which come from not getting what one had hoped for, as well as from life's major disillusionments that come from getting what one had hoped for.

The second type of workaday narrative, which sets the tone for the second half of life, seeks to explain the reason for one's failure to have achieved happiness. Such stories sound like: "I am not successful because my spouse has held me back. Maybe I should get a divorce." Or, "I feel bitter because I do not get enough credit from my boss at work." Or, "How can anyone not be depressed with the world being in the sorry shape that it's in?" This type of narrative is darker than the first type, and can easily lead to paranoid explanations. In all cases, the explanation for unhappiness is a contingent cause.

Settling on contingent explanations—those that do not seek the necessary and essential source of the negative dimension of one's existence, and of human existence—one never arrives at the profound question that prompted the Stoic philosopher Epictetus to ask, "What is it about life that there is always something missing?" Or that prompted the Zen master Hakuin to inquire, "At this moment what is there you lack?" If the ever-present sense of lack is the mother of all narratives, including those that are paranoid—for narratives seek to explain what is lacking and why it is lacking—then ultimate liberation from narratives, whether they be paranoid, hysteric, prosaic, or of a thousand other varieties, would require solving Hakuin's riddle. But that is a journey beyond the limits of the present inquiry.

Highly Subversive Agendas

We have been interested in the conditions that foster the emergence of the paranoid vision, and have uncovered a diversity of such paranoiagenic factors, which can be thought of as subterranean motives, or hidden agendas, especially hidden to those who are under their sway. That these agendas operate unconsciously follows from the fact that leaders of organizations, although they may be intelligent and idealistic, are often blind to their own darker motives and unaware of their ontological assumptions. Furthermore, followers are resistant to seeing the emperor's new clothes, which means that an organization's real agenda usually remains hidden from them too.

These hidden agendas (i.e. paranoiagenic factors) are invariably at loggerheads with the stated aims of an organization. For example, the hidden agenda of Freud's inner circle was not about developing and promoting psychoanalysis. On the contrary, it was all about Oedipal warfare between Freud (the father) and his disciples (the sons). As for Rajneesh, he had a long list of hidden agendas—from those that were mercenary to those that were millenarian—that were antithetical to the stated mission of helping his disciples to attain enlightenment.

The stated mission of the Khmer Rouge was to bring about a new and better society, but their hidden agenda was bloodthirsty revenge.

Hidden agendas interfere with accomplishing the stated objectives of an organization because, as the saying goes, when one pursues two birds at the same time, one ends up catching neither. But, far worse than that, an organization's hidden agenda often turns out to be paranoiagenic. If it is seriously paranoiagenic, it not only retards the progress of the organization, or seriously weakens it; it ends up destroying it.[53]

This leads us to an intriguing question: Is it relevant—from the standpoint of the emergence of the paranoid vision—whether an organization's mission is to promote psychoanalysis, to coordinate a bowling league, to fight disease, to commit genocide, to invest in stocks, to stage a coup detat, to defend freedom, or to perform jazz together? Or is there is always a danger of subterranean motives creeping into any organization—no matter how beneficent a mission statement is posted on their meeting room door—to subvert, like fifth columnists, the direction of its member's energies?

Some organizations, because of their totalistic ideology or their millenarian ambitions, are natural candidates for the paranoid vision, as are organizations whose credo is antinomian or nihilistic. But even an organization devoted to a charity, or to any noble cause, can become a hotbed of egotistical rivalry, suspicion, hostility, envy, and treachery. Disagreements will often result in such a group splintering into warring factions. The spirit of distrust then gives rise to slander and to that cousin of the conspiracy theory, the vicious rumor. Such troubled groups, as they become increasingly insular, will similarly evince a Manichean suspiciousness towards other groups or organizations who are viewed as adversaries, even those organizations that share similar goals.

---

53 Needless to say, an organization can have an agenda that is not hidden, but is clearly manifest, and which is not just paranoiagenic, but downright paranoid. Nazi Germany would be a case in point. Far from being hidden, its agenda was clearly stated by Hitler in Mein Kampf. The problem is that the rest of the world did not want to believe that a person or a nation could have such an evil agenda until the damage was already done. All the same, it would appear that Hitler actually did have a hidden agenda. His stated agenda -- apart from exterminating people -- was the creation of a thousand year Third Reich. His real agenda, though, which he hid from himself, was precipitating the Gotterdammerung.

Therefore, as high-minded as an organization's mission may be, it often takes a backseat to hidden agendas of all sorts that may emerge over time. For example, national security and the safety of a nation's people are generally regarded as vitally important objectives. But it came to light, after September 11th, that the FBI and the CIA had long regarded each other as rivals, if not enemies. Consequently, each organization had a policy of not sharing vital information with the other. By some accounts, this lack of a coordinated intelligence effort contributed to the failure to prevent the September 11th disaster (Riebling, 2002, Posner 2003). To offer another example, the purpose of President Nixon's cabinet was to assume the duties of elected office of a democracy. But as the Watergate conspiracy revealed, another agenda had emerged, one that was a product of the paranoid vision, with its virulent us/them view of politics, and its apocalyptic the-end-justifies-the-means fanaticism.

Ironically, even an organization whose core value is rationality can devolve into a very repressive, apocalyptic, paranoid cult, thus becoming a hothouse of irrationality. That is what happened, according to Jeff Walker, in his aptly titled book, *The Ayn Rand Cult* (1999). Walker points out many similarities to another famous cult of intellectuals, namely Freud's inner circle.[54]

One would think that if a serious amount of money were involved, an organization would become very practical, eschewing any subterranean agendas that might undermine its practical efforts. But that too is not the case. An example of a CEO who was thoroughly possessed by the paranoid vision was Henry Ford. Ford's remarkable success in business and his rabid anti-Semitism were not unrelated. The reason for Henry Ford's success was mass production, which was based on uniformity. Ford once famously said that customers could have Ford cars in any color they wanted, just as long as it was black.

Ford enforced uniformity through the infamous Service Division of his company. Representatives could visit a worker's home at any time to make sure that the worker was living morally, i.e. in conformity and in uniformity with Henry Ford's values, and workers could be

---

54 It is not insignificant that Rand's philosophy of Objectivism disdains any gesture of altruism. Indeed Rand wrote a book entitled, The Virtue of Selfishness (Signet, 1989). Here, again, is the modern intellectual's antinomian contempt for goodness.

fired if they failed to conform (Halberstam, 1986, Baldwin, 2001). This rage for uniformity was part of what was behind Ford's anti-Semitism. He wrote a bestseller called *The International Jew*, which was essentially one long conspiracy theory. Hitler quoted it in *Mein Kampf* (1925), and Ford subsequently received an award from Hitler. It would seem that the Jews did not conform to Ford's constricted image of an American citizen, for they refused to assimilate and become Christians. Furthermore, they represented, to Ford, the forces of cosmopolitanism, internationalism, and all that was foreign. Their alien nature was an assault on Ford's need for homogeneity.

Henry Ford's fetish about uniformity was a manifestation of the paranoid quest for purity, whether in the ideological or the quasi-material sense. That which is homogenous was pure; that which was unique or different was impure, or evil. Ironically, that which was the source of Ford's success, mass production in the service of uniformity, was also his nemesis; for it blinded him to the demands of consumers.

Alfred P. Sloan Jr., the CEO of General Motors, had no such fetish about uniformity. Consequently, he welcomed the idea of offering cars in all shapes, sizes, and colors. Furthermore, one learns from, *My Years with General Motors* (1964; 1990) that Sloan developed the idea of market segmentation, i.e. creating cars for different income groups — Chevy, Buick, Oldsmobile, Cadillac, etc. That is why the Ford Motor Company lost its predominance in the auto industry to General Motors, and never recovered.

The point, then, is that an organization's stated mission, noble though it may be, or practical though it may be, cannot prevent it from becoming subverted by subterranean motives. It can devolve, spawning the intra-group and inter-group malevolence endemic to the paranoid vision. Only psychological maturation, self-knowledge, and devotion to a higher calling on the part of individual members of any organization, can hope to prevent the paranoid vision from emerging and catching hold. Of course, that is a tall order.

The Paranoiagenic Power of Insularity & Authoritarianism

All of the organizations examined here were insular in nature, as are all cultish organizations. Freud's psychoanalysis, although popular with the public, had its inner circle. They were an in-group, with their own private language, making no effort to become part of mainstream psychology. Some critics of psychoanalysis, exasperated by psychoanalysts' refusal to test their theories by verifiable experiments, have contended that the various psychoanalytic societies are not scientific organizations, but essentially part of a mystery religion. It has also been compared to the type of secret controlling cabal that is found in dictatorships.

Our study of the Rajneeshees offered another illustration of the potentially pernicious effects of insularity. They were certainly not on the best of terms with their neighbors in India, but when they emigrated to the gigantic ranch in Oregon they became far more alienated psychologically and socially from the outer world. The mostly hostile dealings that they had with their neighbors only increased their siege mentality and sense of isolation. Furthermore, the Rajneeshees, having been discouraged to leave their commune in Oregon, or simply not permitted to do so, only knew what the Rajneesh's inner circle told them, or what they read in their own newspaper which, needless to say, was tendentious and highly distorted. As FitzGerald points out:

> The constant prodding and poking of the Antelope people were creating ripples of hostility across the state; it was turning the politicians and bureaucrats against them and slowly strangling the commune in litigation. With all the great ambitions the Rajneeshees had for the commune, they seemed quite unconscious of this banal form of danger: what they saw was merely the mythopoetic world the guru had created around them. (1986, p. 343)

FitzGerald's notion of the "mythopoetic world" that Rajneesh had created for his disciples in Oregon is akin to Lee Harris' notion of "fantasy ideology," that he used to describe the mythic world inhabited by the September 11th terrorists. When a group of people inhabits a world constituted by dream images and paranoia-infused nightmares, their insularity and alienation from the rest of humanity transforms their world into a stagnant swamp which breeds infestations of the soul.

As for the Khmer Rouge, during its reign of terror Westerners were not allowed into Cambodia; those people who chose to flee the country could only do so at great peril to their lives. Consequently, the international community had only a vague idea of what was occurring there. And when reports of the terrible genocide began to leak out, conspiracy theorists like Noam Chomsky obstinately contended that the reports of a genocide were merely bogus. Consequently, as Morris (2004) and Paddington (2004) indicate, the atrocities continued without interference from other nations. In any case, the insularity of organizations like the Khmer Rouge prevents the existence of "checks and balances," i.e. criticisms, or interventions, from other nations.

As for Islamic terrorist groups, their "fantasy ideology" grows in a manure rich with conspiracy theories and other paranoid narratives, hidden from the light of reason, lacking contact with what Buber called, "the word that is common to all," i.e. universal discourse. The radical Islamists burn books, destroy religious monuments, and murder people who have contrary opinions, for fear that they might be affected by contact with other ideas. We see here, then, a paranoid fear of defiling the supposed purity of their beliefs.

E.M. Forster once wrote, "Only connect...live in fragments no longer" (1986, p. 148). Insularity is a failure to connect with the larger world. Without that connection, one lives a fragmented, isolated, alienated, and dissolute existence, and one becomes a candidate for possession by the paranoid vision.

There is another comparison that one can make: all the organizations that we examined were authoritarian. Of course, Freud's and Rajneesh's were not technically so, but they were in point of fact. Disagreement in regard to ideology or policy meant losing favor with the master, ostracism, and possibly excommunication.

Of course, in some organizations, such as those involved with education, a certain level of autocracy is necessary. In Zen monasteries a very high degree of autocracy is required. Zen masters cannot, for example, engage in debates with their students about whether or not a certain student's answer to a koan is correct. Furthermore, metaphysical trickery is necessary, on the part of the Zen master, in order to arrange for students to have insights. Similarly, for Socrates' teaching to be effective, he could not tell potential students beforehand that he was going to be ironical. Such deception could be considered a form of manipulation, but it is certainly necessary.

All the same, it is always better if the guru, or teacher, is accountable to other such teachers who belong to larger tradition. Rajneesh, we might add, lacked such accountability. According to Storr, "No wonder that he became inflated with his own importance. Even the Pope has his own confessor; but Rajneesh had no-one to whom to confess, no-one to point out his faults or restrain his excesses" (1996, p. 63). Without such controls, students can only hope to avoid rogue teachers and dysfunctional spiritual groups with sinister agendas that, over time, become increasingly infused with the paranoid vision.

In any case, it could be objected that democracies are really no more paranoia-free than are authoritarian regimes. We learn from Hofstadter's seminal essay that since America's founding in 1776, and probably long before then, conspiracy theories, and paranoia in general, have been rife. The political rhetoric was at least as virulent and paranoia-infused in the 1770s, with political opponents calling each other skunks and worse, and getting into brawls and duals with each other. A strong democracy is usually able to contain the paranoiagenic effect of partisan politics. Indeed, the United States has survived a number of serious internecine conflicts, since its inception in 1776 that threatened, like the Civil War, to tear it apart.

At times, something more than a tradition of strong democratic institutions has been necessary to prevent conflicts from getting dangerously out of hand. President Kennedy's Profiles in Courage offers examples of individuals holding political office who, at critical moments in America's history—at great sacrifice to their careers— did what they could to prevent paranoia-infused partisanship from wreaking massive damage to their country. Thus, if the paranoid vision has already gained strength in an organization, courage is needed to forestall its spread before it becomes a conflagration that destroys everything in its path. Despite the imperfections of democracy, a democratic nation has a better chance of surviving such crises than one that is authoritarian.

The Paranoid Vision Versus the Borderphobic Vision

In the last chapter, we suggested that the antithesis of the paranoid vision is the comic vision. In a different sense, though, the antithesis of the paranoid vision is, for want of a better term, "the borderphobic vision." Consider, by way of contrast, the concern that paranoids have with maintaining their autonomy. Strong psychological barriers are erected so that the "not-I" does not possess, dilute, infect, or defile the purity or the integrity of the "I."

To a certain extent, the separation of the "I" from the not-I, the subject from the object, is a universal concern. But it is particularly, to use Jungian terminology, a "masculine" concern. This does not mean that it is not a concern for women, but it is intrinsic to masculinity to clearly differentiate the "I" from the not-I. The masculine is neither prone to I-Thou relations with the world, nor to a sharing in feelings with other people. It has, rather, a sharp sense that "I'm me, and you're you." It certainly does not tend towards inclusiveness. William James is reputed to have said that "the key to wisdom is knowing what to exclude." That gets to the heart of masculinity.

Femininity, by contrast, tends to be inclusive, and is thus more prone to sympathy, and it would be fair to say that it has its own wisdom in that regard (Dillof, 2000, pp. 23-45). For the paranoid, though, the need to erect a barrier between the "I" and the not-I is extreme. Since the need for that separation is, essentially, a masculine concern, it is not surprising that there are far more men than women who are clinically paranoid.

The borderphobic vision, by contrast, is extreme in the other direction. It is predicated on the belief that borders, of any sort, are fundamentally unreal. Borders are, consequently, experienced negatively, as limits to one's true identity. Thus the direction that the quest for selfhood takes lies not in emphasizing the distinction of the subject from the object, but in abolishing the distinction. The hope is that by abolishing such dualities as self/world, I/you, and subject/object, a global sense of self can be achieved. Again, one thinks of Walt Whitman, with his sense of containing multitudes. Of course, this is true of "femininity," in the Jungian sense, in general.

Just as paranoia tends to be a masculine pathology, so it is that borderphobia can be considered to be a feminine pathology. It is not just a dislike of borders, but a serious dread or revulsion to them. To speculate a bit, it may be that certain personality disorders—such as hysteria and the borderline disorder, which are far more common to women than to men—are essentially disorders of the borderphobic vision. A woman suffering from the borderline personality disorder has a curious ontological predicament in regard to the question of borders. She finds it painful to separate from another person, her husband for example. But when she is with her husband she can feel that her own sense of identity is in danger of being merged and lost in the other person.

It is important to understand borderphobics because they are often in conflict with paranoids, and that conflict is expressed, writ large, on the body politic. An example of political borderphobia is an indifference to maintaining cultural, language, and geographical borders. The latter is expressed, for example, in a refusal to protect one's nation's borders from illegal aliens. If the paranoid maintains extreme vigilance, the borderphobic is not merely indifferent to such borders, but often wishes to abolish them. The borderphobic is similarly in denial over the fact that the nations of the world can have very different and often opposing political interests. If the paranoid is over-suspicious, the borderphobic is under-suspicious Thus if the danger of a paranoiac foreign policy is a bellicosity predicated on a misperception of threat, the danger of one that is borderphobic is a foolish naiveté that is blind to genuine threats.

Sexual identity is another example of a domain in which these contrasting visions come into play. The borderphobic would seek to eradicate the distinction between male and female. Borderphobics would also seek to negate the distinction between the human realm and the animal realm, for they see humans as essentially no different from animals. Thus if the paranoid establishes harsh Manichean divisions of self/other, or of us/them, in all domains, the borderphobic seeks to completely abolish such distinctions.

It is possible to be under the sway of the paranoid vision in certain areas of one's life, but under the sway of the borderphobic vision in other areas. Rajneesh, for example, may have been borderphobic in regard to his ideal of selfhood, but paranoid in regard to the outlying community in Oregon. Ironically, the borderphobic can be paranoid in regard to those who seeks to establish or protect borders of an sort. The Khmer Rouge, certainly an extremely paranoid organization, with their murderously Manichean distinction of the pure from the impure, had a borderphobic vision of a classless (borderless) society.

The fact that it is not uncommon for a paranoid and a borderphobic to end up married together—upon which there is a real conflict of visions—indicates that the representatives of each vision unconsciously know its own worldview to be one-sided and limited. Thus the paranoid and the borderphobic seek to compensate for their limited apprehension of reality by joining with their missing half (Dillof, 2000).

A full examination of the borderphobic vision is beyond the purview of the present work. We mention it, though, to suggest that the antithesis of the paranoid vision is not always the liberating comic vision. Often, it is but another problematic, overly serious way of seeing, namely the borderphobic vision.

On the Futility of Superior Intelligence and Psychiatric Knowledge to Forestall the Paranoid Vision

The story of Freud's inner circle is important, not just for what it has revealed to us about the paranoid vision, but because it now allows us to raise a larger question: What is required to transcend the paranoid vision in any organization?

Of the different case examples considered in these pages, the one about Freud's inner circle is, in a certain respect, the most unsettling, for there is a sense that if it happened there, it could happen anywhere. After all, they were not a gathering of lost souls, consumed by a millenarian fantasy, led by a lunatic, such as a Charles Manson, a Jim Jones, or a David Koresh. On the contrary, although some of the members of the inner circle had their psychological problems, some of which were serious enough to lead to suicide, the group mainly consisted of highly capable and, for the most part, psychologically centered individuals. Sigmund Freud, who, although a genius, visionary, and rather difficult person with a strong nihilistic streak, had his feet on the ground, and was certainly quite sane.

Furthermore, almost all of the members of this group were trained in psychiatry and psychoanalysis, so they must have understood something about the obscure emotions that can plague the psyche. Some of them had a profound understanding in that regard. But their level of knowledge and personal development did not militate against the paranoid vision emerging among them, for there existed more powerful forces at play that set the stage for their devolution into a cultish or totalistic organization, and then for the onset of the paranoid vision.

In order for something different to have been possible, for the story of the inner circle to have had a different ending—and, again, this is applicable to all types of organizations—it would have required, at least theoretically, that the inner circle become aware of the nature of the psychological dynamics of cultish organizations. Most importantly, they would have needed to understand those factors in their own personality that made them susceptible to being a "son" in Freud's inner circle. With all the talk about transference, those powerful transferences and counter-transferences never ended, but continued to endure in all its outlandishness. And, as psychoanalysts, they should have known something about the father complex. Furthermore, Freud had written about the conflict between the father and his sons in a number of his works, including *Group Psychology and the Analysis of the Ego* (1975) and *Totem and Taboo* (1962). As Freud and his followers knew — from their work with patients who were intellectuals—for knowledge to liberate a person, intellectual ideas are insufficient. The knowledge must become existential. The Buddhists would say that the knowledge must descend from the head to the gut, for it to be transformative. Apparently, it had remained in their heads, and was thus ineffectual.

Furthermore, the members of the inner circle would have needed to understand the psychological dynamics of the paranoid vision, those factors that can precipitate it, and those elements in their own makeup that rendered them susceptible to it. Freud had written some brilliant things about paranoia, such as his book about Schreber and in his essay, "Mourning and Melancholia." (1997) But the paranoid vision had not yet been known and formulated as such, by Freud or by anyone else.

It could also be argued that knowledge is necessary, but is not sufficient to vanquish the passions of the soul, for "only perfect love can cast out fear." Perhaps only perfect love can cast out that malevolent fear known as paranoia. Although necessary, love is not sufficient. Each person, when the time comes, must solve the sphinxlike riddle of the paranoid vision—in the context of his or her own life, amidst all the confusion and adversity that often darkens and obscures the light—or else be consumed by the paranoid vision. Of course, paranoia is only one of many passions. Each is its own riddle, which must be solved if the soul is to be victorious over that which would enslave it.

The Amphibian's Balancing Act

Part III explored two different forms of the transcendence of the paranoid vision, one involving its elevation to a new key, and the other involving a shift to its antithesis, the comic vision. What is the relation of these forms of transcendence to each other? If paranoids, and anyone else for that matter, ascend from delusory grandeur to true grandeur—by seeking to live at the intersect of the temporal and the eternal—they will be attempting to do what, from the standpoint of rational understanding, is unintelligible and, therefore, impossible. It is unintelligible because, as Kierkegaard indicates, the two realms, the temporal and the eternal, are incommensurate. How can one live in the light of that which eludes finite understanding? Here, then, is an insuperable contradiction.

Are not all contradictions, though, when viewed at a distance, subject to comic release? Indeed, Kierkegaard indicates that the religious life (where one surrenders all hope at understanding the eternal, infinite, absolute) is no stranger to the comical:

> The more thoroughly and substantially a human being exists, the more he will discover the comical. Even one who has merely conceived a great plan toward accomplishing something in the world, will discover it...But the resolution of the religious individual is the highest of all resolves, infinitely higher than all plans to transform the world and to create systems and works of art; therefore must the religious man, most of all men, discover the comical... (1992, pp. 413-414)

That is quite a relief, for the alternative, having to seriously endure a contradiction, without the respite provided by laughter, might well lead to utter exhaustion or to madness. Furthermore, in opening oneself up to mystery — including the mystery that we referred to when discussing Plato's Cave—there is a danger that the power of the sacred, which Otto (1958) says is experienced as a mysterium tremendum, can be overpowering, deranging, and shattering. That is where laughter, along with wonder and amazement, all of which allow for distance, become invaluable in maintaining equipoise in the face of such mysteries. What about the transformations that are intrinsic to human existence, i.e., "the apocalypse within"? The deaths necessary for rebirth are never amusing, but the comic vision, with its abiding confidence in the possibility of renewal and rebirth, can help one endure those difficult times in life.

It is necessary, though, to issue a caveat. As valuable as the comic spirit is, a laughter that avoids the depths of human existence is shallow. As Conrad Hyers, a scholar of humor in religion states, "The Comic, therefore, requires the sacred as much as does the sacred the comic...Humor turns into despair if it is not essentially and inwardly related to holy things. But if it has this foundation, it can play its own peculiar role in the inner dialectic of the sacred and the comic" (1969, p. 27). So here it is, in Hyers' opinion, that true seriousness must be balanced with comic lightness for human existence to avoid nihilistic despair.

Perhaps, then, the comic spirit cannot save one from nihilism, but it is very much an antidote to that which, in some sense, appears as the antithesis of nihilism, namely dogmatism and fanaticism, although we have argued they are essentially a species of nihilism. As William F. Lynch, another scholar of humor in religion felicitously states, "The comic is par excellence the great enemy of the unequivocal mind" (1969, p. 40). That is why the comic vision is the great enemy of the paranoid vision.

Awe, wonder, and amazement at the mystery of human existence, and laughter at one's very existence, are modes of transcendence that reflect two different sides of the human condition. Perhaps that is why there have always been tragedy and comedy. Apart from all of its other functions—from catharsis to a dramatic imitation of the mythic ritual of propitiation of the gods—tragedy, according to Northrop Frye (1973), is an encounter with life's mysteries. Comedy also encounters these mysteries, but its primary mode of transcendence involves a joyous acceptance of life, as well as liberation from excessive seriousness.

One may conclude, then, that there is a reason why there are these two forms of transcendence. A life that is neither prey to the paranoid vision, nor to any other of the myriad forms of human bondage, is one that is balanced—however precariously at times—between gravity and levity, between awe before the mysteries of existence and laughter at the unique peculiarity of one's amphibious being.

BIBLIOGRAPHY

Adorno, T.W. (1993). *The Authoritarian Personality*. (Abridged/Rei. edition) New York: W. W. Norton.

Aichele, George. (2002). *Theology as Comedy: Critical & Theoretical Implications* Lanham, MD: University Press of America. Online PDF edition: 9 May 2004

<http://home.comcast.net/~gcaichele/writings/comedy. pdf>

Allen, Gary. (April 1969). "The CFR., Conspiracy to Rule the World." American Opinion, XII. 56.

Allen, Woody. (1976). "If the Impressionists Had Been Dentists" From: *Without Feathers*. New York: Warner Books.

Allen, Woody. (1978). "My Philosophy" From: *Getting Even*. New York: Vintage.

Anzulovic, Branimir. (1999). *Heavenly Serbia: From Myth to Genocide*. New York: University Press.

Augustine, St. (1998). *Confessions*. (Oxford World's Classics, Reprint edition) New York: Oxford University Press.

Aurelius, Marcus. (1964). *Meditations*. Translated by Maxwell Staniforth. London: Penguin Books.

Baldwin, Neil. (2002). *Henry Ford and the Jews: The Mass Production of Hate*. New York: PublicAffairs.

Bar, Shmuel. (June & July 2004) "The Religious Sources of Islamic Terrorism." Policy Review.. Number 125. Published by Hoover Institute.

Barkun, Michael. (2003). *A Culture of Conspiracy: Apocalyptic Vision in Contemporary America*. Berkeley: University of California Press.

Barnet, Sylvan, Morton Berman, and William Burto, Editors. (1958). *Eight Great Comedies*. A Mentor Book. New York: New American Library.

Baudelaire, Charles. (1981). "On the Essence of Laughter, and, in General, on the Comic in the Plastic Arts." In: *Comedy*

Meaning and Form (Second Edition) by Robert W. Corrigan. New York: Harper and Row.

Becker, Elizabeth. (1986). *When the War Was Over: The Voices of Cambodia's Revolution and Its People*. New York: Simon and Schuster.

Becket, Samuel. (1997). *Waiting for Godot*. New York: Grove Press.

Bennet, James. (May 15, 2005). "The Mystery of the Insurgency." *The New York Times*. The Week in Review.

Bentley, Eric. (Editor) (1985). *Life is a Dream and Other Spanish Classics*. New York: Applause Theatre Book Publishers.

Berdyaev, Nikolai. (1944). *Slavery and Freedom*. New York: Charles Scribner's and Sons.

Berdyaev, Nikolai. (1952). *The Beginning and the End: An Essay on Eschatological Metaphysics*. (trans. by R. M. French) New York: Harper.

Bergen, Peter L. (2001) *Holy War: Inside the Secret World of Osama bin Laden*. New York: The Free Press.

Bergson, Henri. (1956). *Laughter*. Garden City, NY: Doubleday Anchor Books.

Berlin, Isaiah. (1990). *The Crooked Timber of Humanity: Chapters in the History of Ideas*. Princeton: Princeton University Press.

Berlin, Isaiah. (Henry Hardy, Editor.) (2001). *The Power of Ideas*. Princeton, NJ: Princeton University Press.

Berlin, Isaiah. (2002). *Freedom and Its Betrayal*. Princeton: Princeton University Press.

Berman, Paul. (2003). *Terror and Liberalism*. New York: W.W, Norton and Company.

Bettelheim, Bruno. (1983). *Freud and Man's Soul*. New York: Alfred A. Knopf.

Beyond the Stars Productions. (Nov. 2003).
4 June 2005 <http://home.pages.at/stargazers/endworld/fin-signs/05-the-ac.htm> Deep Truths. Articles from David Berg and the Family International.

bin Laden, Osama. (1998a.) Speech. <http://www.pbs.org/wgbh/pages/frontline/shows/binladen>

bin Laden, Osama. (May 1998b). Frontline interview. 4 June 2005 <http://www.pbs.org/wgbh/pages/frontline/shows/binladen/who/interview.html>

Bizot, Francois. (2003). *The Gate.* New York: Alfred A. Knopf

The Bhagavad-Gita. (1994). (Trans. by S. Radhakrishnan.) New Delhi: Indus. An imprint of Harper Collins.

Bloch, Ernst. (1995). *The Principle of Hope,* Vol. 1 (Studies in Contemporary German Social Thought) Reprint edition. Boston: The MIT Press.

Bloom, Harold. (1996). *Omens of Millennium.* New York: Riverhead Books. A division of G.P. Putnam's Sons.

Boyer, Paul. (1992). *When Time Shall Be No More: Prophesy Belief in Modern American Culture.* Cambridge Mass: The Belknap Press of Harvard University.

Brooks, David. (April 15, 2002). "Among the Bourgeoisophobes: Why the Europeans and the Arabs, each in their own way, hate America and Israel." *The Weekly Standard.*

Brown, Dan. (2003). *The Da Vinci Code.* New York: Doubleday.

Browne, Sir Thomas. (1972). *Religio Medici.* Oxford: Clarendon Press.

Buber, Martin. (1953). *Good and Evil.* New York: Charles Scribner's Sons.

Buber, Martin. (1965). *Between Man and Man.* New York: Collier Books. Macmillan.

Buber, Martin. (1971). *I and Thou.* New York: Free Press.

Buruma, Ian and Avishai Margalit. (2004). *Occidentalism: The West in the Eyes of Its Enemies.* New York: The Penguin Press.

Calderon. (July 29, 2005). "Life is a Dream." *The Harvard Classics.* (Volume 26. Part I.) <http://www.bartleby.com/26/1/32.html. >

Camus, Albert. (1956). *The Rebel: An Essay on Man in Revolt.* New York: A Vintage Book.

Carey, Benedict. (February 8, 2005) "For the Worst of Us, the Diagnosis May Be 'Evil.' The New York Times..

Carter, Lewis F. (1990). *Charisma and Control in Rajneeshpuram.* New York: Cambridge University Press.

Carveth, Donald L. (February 27, 1999) "Is There a Future in Disillusion? Constructionist and Deconstructionist Approaches in Psychoanalysis." Journal of the American Academy of Psychoanalysis: 325-358.

Cassirer, Ernst. (1979). *An Essay on Man.* New Haven: Yale University Press.

Castaneda, Carlos. (1991). *Journey to Ixtlan.* Washington Square Press.

Castaneda, Carlos. (2000). *The Active Side of Infinity.* New York: Harper Perennial.

Cervantes, Miguel. (2001). *Don Quixote.* New York: Modern Library.

Chandler, David. (1992). *Brother Number One: A Political Biography of Pol Pot.* Boulder: Westview Press.

Chandler, David. (1999). *Voices from S-21: Terror and History in Pol Pot's Secret Prison.* Berkeley: University of California Press.

Chase, Alston. (June 2000) "Harvard And The Making Of The Unabomber." *Atlantic Monthly* v285 no 6 p41-65

Chismar, Douglas E. (Nov. 16, 2003). "Heidegger's Critique of Empathy." From Chowan College website. Department of Religion and Philosophy. <http://www.chowan.edu/acadp/Religion/pubs/heidegger.htm.>

Cohn, Norman. (1961). *The Pursuit of the Millennium. (Second Edition)* New York: Harper Torchbooks. Harper and Brothers.

Cohn, Norman. (1993). *Cosmos, Chaos and the World to Come.* New Haven: Yale University Press.

Cohn, Norman. (1995). "How Time Acquired a Consummation." In Bull, Malcolm. (ed) 1995. *Apocalypse Theory and the Ends of the World.* Oxford: Blackwell Publishers.

Cohn, Norman. (1996). *Warrant for Genocide: The Myth of the Jewish World Conspiracy and the Protocols of the Elders of Zion.* (New edition) Serif Publishing.

Connolly, Cyril. (1983). *Enemies of Promise.* New York: Perseas Books.

Conrad, Joseph. (2002) *Heart of Darkness.* London: Hesperus Press.

Cook, David. (Sept. 12, 2001). "Islam's Apocalypse: An Interview with the Editorial Staff of *Presence Magazine.*" <http:www.CBN.com.> The Christian Broadcasting Network. 4 June 2005 <http://www.cbn.com/SpiritualLife/understandingislam/ Islam's_Apocalypse.>

Coomaraswamy, Ananda K. "Who is Satan and What is Hell." From: *Metaphysics.* (Edited by Roger Lipsey) Bollingen Series/ Princeton University Press. Princeton: 1977.

Copper, William. (1991). *Behold a Pale Horse.* Flagstaff, AZ: Light Technology Publications.

Corrigan, Robert W. (Editor) (1981). *Comedy Meaning and Form (Second Edition)* New York: Harper and Row.

Courtois, Stephen, et al. (1999). *The Black Book of Communism: Crimes, Terror, Repression.* Cambridge, Massachusetts: Harvard University Press.

Crews, Frederick C. (Editor) (1998). *Unauthorized Freud: Doubters Confront a Legend.* New York: Viking.

Daniels, Anthony. (October 2003). "History by other means." *The New Criterion.* Volume 22. No. 2.

Dante. (2003). *The Divine Comedy.* (Translated by John Ciardi) New York: NAL Trade.

Dean, Jodi. (2002). "If Anything Is Possible." In: *Conspiracy Nation.* By Peter Knight. 2002. New York: New York University Press.

Descartes, Rene. (1999). *Discourse on Method and Meditations on First Philosophy, 4th Ed.* (Trans. Donald Cress) Indianapolis: Hackett Pub Co.

Diel, Paul. (1980). *Symbolism in Greek Mythology: Human Desire and Its Transformations.* Boulder, CO.: Shambhala.

Dillof, Mark. (2000). *Awakening with the Enemy: The Origin and End of Male/Female Conflict*. Binghamton, New York: Philosophy Clinic Press.

Dostoevsky, Fyodor. (1993). *Notes from Underground*. New York: Vintage Classics, Vintage Books. A Division of Random House.

Dostoevsky, Fyodor. (1999). *Devils*. (New edition) New York: Oxford University Press.

Dostoevsky, Fyodor. (2002). *The Brothers Karamazov*. New York: Farrar, Straus and Giroux.

Dowbiggen, Ian. (2000). *Suspicious Minds: The Triumph of Paranoia in Everyday Life*. Toronto: Macfarlane Walter & Ross.

Eco, Umberto. (1990). *Foucault's Pendulum*. New York: Ballantine Books; Reprint edition.

Eco, Umberto. (June 1995) "Ur-Fascism." *New York Review of Books,* 22.

Edinger, Edward F. (1999). *Archetype of the Apocalypse*. Chicago: Open Court

Edmunds, Lavinia. (April 1988) "His Masters Choice." Johns Hopkins Magazine,: 40-49. Anthologized in: Frederick C. Crews. (Editor) Unauthorized Freud: Doubters Confront a Legend. Viking. New York. Pages 260-276. In Crew's book as "The Marriage Counselor."

Eliade, Mircea. (1958). *Rites and Symbols of Initiation*. New York: Harper Torchbooks.

Eliade, Mircea. (1970). *Yoga : Immortality and Freedom. (2nd edition)* Princeton, NJ: Bollingen/Princeton University Press.

Eliade, Mircea. (1978). *The Myth of the Eternal Return*. Princeton: Bollingen. Princeton University Press.

Emerson. Ralph, Waldo. (1983). "Self Reliance." *Ralph Waldo Emerson: Essays and Lectures*. New York: Library of America.

Epstein, Joseph. (March 15, 2004) "The Perpetual Adolescent and the triumph of the youth culture." *The Weekly Standard*. Volume 009, Issue 26.

Fanon, Frantz. (1965). *The Wretched of the Earth*. New York: Grove Press.

Farrell, John. (1996). *Freud's Paranoid Quest: Psychoanalysis and Modern Suspicion*. New York: New York University Press.

Faulkner, William. (1950). "Nobel Prize Acceptance Speech." In: Carroll, Andrew, Robert Torricelli, and Doris Kearns Goodwin. 2000. *In Our Own Words : Extraordinary Speeches of the American Century*. Stockholm. Washington Square Press. Page 179.

Ferenczi, Sandor. (1998). *The Clinical Diary of Sandor Ferenczi*. (Ed. By Judith Dupont) Cambridge Mass: Harvard University Press.

Festinger, Leon., Henry Riecken, and Stanley Schachter. (1956). *When Prophesy Fails*. New York: University of Minnesota Press/ Harper Torchbooks, Harper and Row.

Feurenbach. Ludwig. (1989). *The Essence of Christianity*. Prometheus Books.

FitzGerald, Francis. (1986). *Cities on a Hill: A Journey Through Contemporary American Cultures*. New York: Simon and Schuster.

Forster, E.M. (1986). *A Room with a View and Howard's End*. New York Signet Classics; Reissue edition.

Foucault, Michel. (1995). (Reprint edition) *Discipline & Punish : The Birth of the Prison*. New York: Vintage.

Frederick C. Crews. (Editor) (1998). *Unauthorized Freud: Doubters Confront a Legend*. New York: Viking.

Freud, Sigmund. (January 3, 1913). Letter to C.G. Jung. Manuscript Division, Library of Congress.

Freud. Sigmund. (1962). *Totem and Taboo*. W.W. Norton.

Freud, Sigmund. (1966). *On the History of the Psychoanalytic Movement*. New York: W.W. Norton.

Freud. Sigmund. (1975). *Group Psychology and the Analysis of the Ego. (Revised Edition)* New York: W.W. Norton:

Freud, Sigmund. (1989). *Civilization and Its Discontents. (Reissue edition)* New York: W. W. Norton & Company.

Freud, Sigmund. (1993). *Wit and Its Relation to the Unconscious.* New York: Dover Publications.

Freud, Sigmund. (1997). "Mourning and Melancholia." *General Psychological Theory.* (Reprint edition) New York: Touchstone.

Freud, Sigmund. (2003). *The Schreber Case.* New York. Penguin Books.

Freund, Charles Paul. (December 2001). "2001 Nights: The End of the Orientalist Critique." Reason Online.

Friedman, Maurice. (1965). "Introductory Essay" from *The Knowledge of Man* by Martin Buber. New York: Harper Torchbooks.

Fromm, Erich. (1973). *The Anatomy of Human Destructiveness.* New York: Henry Holt and Company.

Fromm, Erich. (1996). *Escape from Freedom.* New York: Owl Books.

Fromson, Brett D. (February 23, 1997). "Plunge Protection Team." The Washington Post. <http://www.washingtonpost.com/wp-srv/business/longterm/blackm/plunge.htm. 8/8/05.

Fry, Christopher. (1981). "Comedy." Vogue (January), 1951. Anthologized in: *Comedy Meaning and Form (Second Edition)* by Robert W. Corrigan. New York: Harper and Row

Frye, Northrop. (1981). "The Mythos of Spring: Comedy." From *Comedy Meaning and Form (Second Edition)* by Robert W. Corrigan. New York: Harper and Row.

Fukuyama, Francis. (Winter 2002). "Has History Started Again?" Policy.

Fulghum, Robert. (2004). *All I Really Need to Know I Learned in Kindergarten.* New York: Ballantine Books

Gay, Peter. (1988). *Freud: A Life of Our Time.* New York: W.W. Norton and Company.

Girard, Rene. (1979). *Violence and The Sacred.* Baltimore: Johns Hopkins University Press

Gleik, James. (1988). *Chaos: Making a New Science. (Reprint Edition)* New York: Penguin.

Glucksmann, Andre. (March 3, 2003). "Bin Laden, Dostoevsky and the reality principle: interview with André Glücksmann." openDemocracy. 4 June 2005 <http://www.opendemocracy. net/debates/article-5-107-1111.jsp>

Goethe, Johann Wolfgang von. (1999.) *Maxims and Reflections*. New York Penguin Classics.

Gordon. James. 1987. *Golden Guru: The Strange Journey of Bhagwan Shree Rajneesh*. Brattleboro, Vermont: Stephen Greene Press.

Gould, Mark. (February-March 2005.) "Understanding Jihad." Policy Review Online.

Gracian, Balthasar. (1993). *The Art of Worldly Wisdom*. Boston: Shambhala.

Graumann, Carl F. (1987). "Conspiracy: History and Social Psychology." From *Changing Conceptions of Conspiracy,* by C.F. Graumann and S. Moscovici. New York: Springer-Verlag.

Gray, Chris Hables. (July 2005). Personal correspondence: dissertation report.

Griffin, Roger. (1991). *The Nature of Fascism*. London and New York: Oxford University Press.

Griffin, Roger. (Spring 2003) Revised articles on 'fascism' and 'totalitarianism' for new edition (ed. William Outhwaite) The Blackwell Dictionary of Modern Social Thought. Blackwell, , pp. 231-34; 697-99.

Griffin, Roger. (May 2005.) "'I Am No Longer Human. I Am A Titan. A God!' The Fascist Quest To Regenerate Time." Institute of Historical Research website. 26, 4 June 2005 <http://www. history.ac.uk/projects/elec/sem22.html#9t.>

Griffin, Roger. (1993) *The Nature of Fascism*. London and New York: Routledge.

Groh, Dieter. (1987). "The Temptation of Conspiracy, Part I." From *Changing Conceptions of Conspiracy,* by C.F. Graumann and S. Moscovici. New York: Springer-Verlag.

Grosskurth, Phyllis. (1991). *The Secret Ring: Freud's Inner Circle and the Politics of Psychoanalysis*. New York: Addison-Wesley Publishing Company, Inc.

Guenon, Rene. (1972). *The Reign of Quantity and The Signs of the Times*. Baltimore, Maryland: Penguin Books.

Halberstam, David. (1986). *The Reckoning*. New York: William Morrow & Co

Halkin, Hillel.(July-August, 2005). *Eichmann: The Simplicity of Evil*. Commentary.

Hamilton, Edith. (1937) *Three Greek Plays*. W.W. Norton Company.

Hanson, Victor Davis. (2001). *The Soul of Battle : From Ancient Times to the Present Day, How Three Great Liberators Vanquished Tyranny*. New York: Anchor.

Hanson, Victor Davis. (April 26, 2002). "The New Fascism." *The National Review*. Online Edition.

Harris, Lee. (2002 Issue). "Al Qaeda's Fantasy Ideology." Policy Review. Stanford: Hoover Institute.

Hayek, Friedrich A. (1978) *The Constitution of Liberty*. Chicago: The University of Chicago Press.

Haynes, John Earl and Harvey Klehr. (1999). *Verona: Decoding Soviet Espionage in America*. New Haven: Yale University Press.

Hedge, Frederic H. (1849). *The Prose Writers of Germany*. Philadelphia: Carey and Hart.

Hegel, G.W.F. (1990). *The Philosophy of History*. Reprint Edition. Amherst, NY: Prometheus Books.

Heidegger, Martin. (1962). *Being and Time*. (Revised Edition) San Francisco: HarperSanFrancisco.

Heidegger, Martin. (2001). *The Fundamental Concepts of Metaphysics: World, Finitude, Solitude*. Indiana University Press; Reprint edition.

Heidegger, Martin. (2002). *The Essence of Truth: On Plato's Cave Allegory and Theaetetus*. Translated by Ted Sadler. New York: Continuum.

Hemingway, Earnest. (1996). *The Old Man and the Sea*. (Reprint edition) New York: Scribner.

Herf, Jeffrey. (2002) "What is Old and What is New in the Terrorism of Islamic Fundamentalism?" *Partisan Review*. PR 1/ 2002 . VOLUME LXIX NUMBER 1

Herman, George. (1997). *The Idea of Decline in Western History.* New York: The Free Press.

Herman, George. (2000). *Joseph McCarthy: Reexamining the Life of America's Most Hated Senator.* New York: The Free Press.

Hitler, Adolph. (1999) *Mein Kampf.* New York: A Mariner Book. Houghton Mifflin Company.

Hoffer, Eric. (2002). *The True Believer : Thoughts on the Nature of Mass Movements.* New York: Perennial Classics.

Hofstadter, Richard. (1966). *Anti-intellectualism in American Life.* New York: Vintage Books.

Hofstadter, Richard. (1996). *The Paranoid Style in American Politics and Other Essays.* Cambridge Massachusetts: Harvard University Press.

Hyers, Conrad. (1969). "The Comic Profanation of the Sacred." Anthologized in *Holy Laugher: Essays on Religion in the Comic Perspective.* Conrad Hyers (Editor). New York: The Seabury Press.

Nasr, Seyyed Hossein. (2000). (Editor) *Philosophy of Seyyed Hossein Nasr* (Library of Living Philosophers Series) New York: Open Court Publishing Company

Jackson, Karl D. (1989). Cambodia, 1975-1978: *Rendezvous With Death.* Princeton, NJ: Princeton University Press

Jaques, E. (1976). *A General Theory of Bureaucracy.* New York: Halstead.

Jaspers, Karl. (1952). *Tragedy is not Enough.* trans. H. A. Reiche, T. Moore, and W. H. Deutsch Boston: Archon Books.

Jaspers, Karl. (1971). *Reason and Existentz.* New York:. The Noonday Press. A Division of Farrar, Straus and Giroux.

Johnson, Paul. (1988). *Intellectuals.* Harper Perennial, A Division of Harper Collins.

Johnson, Paul. (June 2005). "The Anti-Semitic Disease." *Commentary.* Pages 35-38.

Jones, Ernest. M.D. (1955). *The Life and Works of Sigmund Freud. (Volume 2: 1901-1919. Years of Maturity).* New York: Basic Books Publishers.

Jung, C.G. (1968). *Man and His Symbols.* (Reissue Edition.) New York: Laurel. Edition. Cambridge Mass: Harvard University Press.

Kant, Immanuel. (1982). *The Critique of Aesthetic Judgment.* New York: Oxford: Clarendon Press.

Kant, Immanuel. (2003). *Critique of Pure Reason.* (2nd Rev edition) New York: Palgrave Macmillan.

Kazantzakis, Nikos. (1996). *Zorba the Greek.* Touchstone; 1st Scribner Paperback Fiction ed edition.

Kennedy, John. (2003). *Profiles in Courage.* New York: HarperCollins.

Kermode, Frank. (1985). "Apocalypse and the Modern." In *Visions of Apocalypse: End or Rebirth.* Editor: Saul Friedlander. New York: Holmes and Meier.

Kermode, Frank. (1995). "Waiting for the End." From: *Apocalypse Theory and the Ends of the World.* Edited by Malcolm Bull. Oxford: Blackwell.

Kernberg, Otto, M.D. (1998). *Ideology, Conflict, and Leadership in Groups and Organizations.* New Haven: Yale University Press.

Kerr, Walter. (1968). *Tragedy and Comedy.* New York: A Clarion book/ Simon and Schuster.

Kierkegaard, Soren. (1956). *Purity of Heart.* Harper Torchbooks

Kierkegaard, Soren. (1979). *Either/Or. Volumes One and Two.* (trans. Joseph Lowry.) Princeton: Princeton U. Press.

Kierkegaard, Soren. (1973). *The Concept of Dread.* Princeton, NJ: Princeton University Press.

Kierkegaard, Soren. (1989). *The Sickness Unto Death.* (trans. Alistair Hannay). London: Penguin.

Kierkegaard, Soren. (1992). *Concluding Unscientific Postscript.* Princeton NJ: Princeton University Press.

Kiernan, Ben. (1996). *The Pol Pot Regime : Race, Power, and Genocide in Cambodia under the Khmer Rouge, 1975-79.* New Haven: Yale University Press.

Kimball, Roger. (Winter 2003/04). "Political Correctness, Or, the perils of benevolence." The National Interest.

Kirsch, Adam. (September 2, 2005). *Against Purity.* September 2, 2005. The New York Sun. Arts and Letters. <http://www.nysun.com/article/19510>.

Klinghoffer, Judith Apter. (May 26, 2005). "Blood Libel." History News Network. 4 June 2005 < http://hnn.us/articles/664.html>

Knight, Peter. (2000). *Conspiracy Culture: From Kennedy to the X-Files.* London: Routledge.

Kobrin, Nancy. (August 12, 2005). *Symposium: Through the Eyes of a Suicide Bomber.* By Jamie Glazov. FrontPageMagazine. com. 12 August 2005 <http://www.frontpagemag.com/Articles/Printable. asp?ID=19110.

Koestler, Arthur. (1970). *The Act of Creation.* Macmillan Publishing Company.

Koestler, Arthur. (1976). *The Ghost in the Machine.* London; Hutchinson & Co.

Kosinski, Jerzy. (1999). *Being There.* New York: Grove Press.

Kraepelin, E. (1921). *Manic-Depressive Insanity and Paranoia.* Edinburgh: Livingstone.

Kressel, Neil J. (2002). *Mass Hate: The Global Rise of Genocide and Terrorism.* Cambridge MA: Westview Press.

Kuehnelt-Leddihn, Erik von. (1990). *Leftism Revisited: From de Sade and Marx to Hitler and Pol Pot.* Washington D.C.: Regnery Gateway.

Kuhn, Thomas. (1996) *The Structure of Scientific Revolutions. (3rd Edition)* University Of Chicago Press.

Kundera, Milan. (1993). *The Joke.* (Reprint edition) New York: Perennial.

LaHaye, Tim and Jerry B. Jenkins. (1996) *Left Behind.* Carol Stream, IL: Tyndale House.

Landes, Richard. (May 5, 2005). "Apocalyptic Islam and Bin Laden." Center for Millennial Studies at Boston University. website. 4 June 2005 <http://www.mille.org/whatsnew.html>

Landis, Mark. (1987). *Joseph McCarthy: The Politics of Chaos.* Selinsgrove, PA: Susquehanna University Press.

Landmann, Michael. (1979). *De Homine: Man in the Mirror of His Thought*. Applied Literature Press.

Langer, Susan. (1981). "The Comic Rhythm." Anthologized in: *Comedy Meaning and Form (Second Edition)* by Robert W. Corrigan. New York: Harper and Row.

Lao-tzu. (1891). *The Tao Te Ching*. J. Legge, Translator. (Sacred Books of the East, Vol 39) [1891] <http://www.sacred-texts.com/tao/taote.htm>

Laqueur, Walter. (1996). *Fascism: Past, Present, Future*. New York: Oxford University Press.

Layton, Bentley. (1995). *The Gnostic Scriptures : A New Translation with Annotations and Introductions*. (The Anchor Bible Reference Library) New York: Anchor Bible.

Le Bon, Gustave. (1982). *The Crowd: A Study of the Popular Mind*. (Reprint edition) Flint Hill, Virginia: Fraser Pub. Co.

Lehman, Benjamin. (1981). "Comedy and Laughter." Anthologized in: *Comedy Meaning and Form (Second Edition)* by Robert W. Corrigan. New York: Harper and Row.

Levi-Bruhl, Lucien (1985). *How Natives Think*. Princeton NJ: Princeton University Press

Lewis, Bernard. (1990). "The Roots of Muslim Rage." The Atlantic Online. September Volume 266, No. 3; pages 47 - 60.

Lewis. C.S. (1961). *A Preface to Paradise Lost*. New York: Oxford University Press.

Lifton. Robert Jay. (1989). *Thought Reform and the Psychology of Totalism: A Study of Brainwashing in China*. Chapel Hill: The University of North Carolina Press.

Lifton, Robert Jay. (2000). *Destroying the World to Save It: Aum Shinrikyo, Apocalyptic Violence, and the New Global Terrorism*. New York: Henry Holt and Company. An Owl Book.

Lipset, Seymour Martin., and Earl Raab. (1970). *The Politics of Unreason: Right-Wing Extremism in America, 1790-1977. (Second Edition)* Chicago: The University of Chicago Press.

Lovejoy, Arthur O. (1961). *The Reason, the Understanding, and Time*. Baltimore: Johns Hopkins University Press.

Lynch, William F. (1969). "The Humanity of Comedy." Anthologized in: *Holy Laugher: Essays on Religion in the Comic Perspective.* By Conrad Hyers (Editor). New York: The Seabury Press. Jersey: Barricade Books.

Man of La Mancha. (1965). Music: Mitch Leigh. Lyrics: Joe Darion. Book: Dale Wasserman.

Margolin, Jean-Louis. (1999). "Cambodia: The Country of Disconcerting Crimes." From: *The Black Book of Communism: Crimes, Terror, Repression.* By Stephen Courtois, et. al. Cambridge, Massachusetts: Harvard University Press.

Marsden, Victor. (2004). *The Protocols of The Meetings of the Learned Elders of Zion.* (Reprint edition) York, South Carolina: Liberty Bell Publications.

Maslow. Abraham. 1993. *The Farther Reaches of Human Nature.* (Reprint ed.) New York: Penguin Books.

May, Rollo. (1989). *Love and Will.* (Reissue edition) New York: Delta Books.

Matthews, Carol. (Jan. 12, 2003). "The Plate in My Head is a Government Plot: Visions of the Eschaton in UFO Conspiracy Theory." New World Orders. Journal of Millennial Studies. 4 June 2005.
<http://www.bu.edu/mille/publications/winter2000/matthews.PDF>

McGinn, Bernard. (2000). *Antichrist: Two Thousand Years of the Human Fascination with Evil.* New York: Columbia University Press.

McWilliams, Nancy. (1994). *Psychoanalytic Diagnosis.* New York: The Guilford Press.

Meeker, Joseph. (1997). *The Comedy of Survival: Literary Ecology and a Play Ethic. (Third Edition)* Tucson: The University of Arizona Press.

Meissner, W. (1978). *The Paranoid Process.* Lanham MD: Jason Aronson.

Merleau-Ponty, Maurice. (1990). *Humanism and Terror : An Essay on the Communist Problem.* Boston: Beacon Press.

Meyerson, Emile. (1989). *Identity and Reality*. New York: Gordon & Breach Science Pub.

Miller, William Ian. (1997). *The Anatomy of Disgust*. Cambridge Mass.: Harvard University Press.

Miller, William Lee. (2002) *Lincoln's Virtues: An Ethical Biography*. New York: Knopf.

Millon, Theodore. (1996). *Disorders of Personality: DSM-IV and Beyond. (Second Edition)* New York: John Wily and Sons.

Mills, Judy, and John Kaplan. (1983b). "'Peace Force' blends mellow thoughts, tough tactics." Spokane Spokesman Review. September 11.

Milne, Hugh. (1987). *The God that Failed*. London: Sphere Books Limited.

Moliere. (2001). *The Misanthrope, Tartuffe, and Other Plays* (Oxford World's Classics) New York: Oxford University Press.

Molnar, Thomas. (1990). *Utopia, The Perennial Heresy*. Lanham Maryland: ISI: University Press of America.

Morreall, John. (1999). *Comedy, Tragedy, and Religion*. New York: State University of New York Press.

Morris, Stephen J. (2004). "Whitewashing Dictatorship in Communist Vietnam and Cambodia." Anthologized in: *The Anti-Chomsky Reader*. Peter Collier and David Horowitz (Editors). San Francisco: Encounter Books.

Morrow, Lance. (2003). *Evil: An Investigation*. New York: Basic Books.

Moscovici, Serge. (1987). *Changing Conceptions of Conspiracy*. Edited by C.F. Graumann and S. Moscovici. New York: Springer-Verlag.

Mussolini, Benito. (1938) *The Doctrine of Fascism*. (Translation by E. Cope)Vallecci.

Naipaul, V.S. (1998). *Beyond Belief: Islamic Excursions Among the Converted People*. New York: Random House.

Netanyahu, Binyamin. (May 2002). "The Root Cause of Terrorism is Totalitarianism." FactsOfIsrael.com News, Comments and Links. 21, September 2005.

<http://www.factsofisrael.com/blog/archives/000005-print.html>

Neumann, Erich. (1995) *The Origin and History of Consciousness.* (Reprint Edition)Princeton, NJ: Bollingen/Princeton University Press.

Newell, Waller. (November 26, 2001) "Postmodern Jihad: What Osama bin Laden learned from the Left." The Weekly Standard., Volume 007, Issue 11. Online Edition.

Niebuhr, Reinhold. (1969). "Humor and Faith." From M. Conrad Hyers. *Holy Laughter: Essays on Religion in the Comic Perspective.* New York: The Seabury Press.

Nietzsche, Frederick. (1970). *Thus Spake Zarathustra.* From: *The Portable Nietzsche.* New York: The Viking Press.

Nietzsche, Frederick. (1989). *Beyond Good & Evil : Prelude to a Philosophy of the Future.* New York: Vintage.

Orwell, George. (1973). *The Road to Wigan Pier.* Amer. ed edition Harvest/HBJ.

Orwell, George. (1996). *Animal Farm.* (50th Anniv. Edition) New York: Signet Book.

Osho (Rajneesh). (2000). *Autobiography of a Spiritually Incorrect Mystic.* New York: St. Martin's Griffin.

Osho (Rajneesh) (2001). *Osho on Zen.* Los Angeles: Renaissance Books.

Osho (Rajneesh) (2001). *Awareness: The Key to Living in Balance.* New York: St. Martin's Griffin.

Otto, Rudolph. (1958). *The Idea of the Holy. 2nd edition* New York: Oxford University Press.

Puddington, Arch. (October 2004). "Chomsky's Universe." Commentary Magazine.

Pape, Robert A. (August 2003). "The Strategic Logic of Suicide Terrorism." American Political Science Review. Vol. 97, No. 3

Park, Clara Claiborne. (1981). "No Time for Comedy." From: Robert Corrigan. *Comedy: Meaning and Form (Second Edition.)*

Pascal, Blaise. *Pensees.* (1999). New York: Oxford University Press.

Paxton, Robert O. (2004). *The Anatomy of Fascism.* New York: Alfred. A. Knopf.

Peck, M. Scott. M.D. (1998). *People of the Lie: The Hope for Healing Human Evil*. New York: Simon and Schuster (A Touchstone Book).

Perry, Whitall N. (1971). *A Treasury of Traditional Wisdom*. New York: Simon and Schuster.

Peters, Ralph. (2003). *Beyond Baghdad: Postmodern War and Peace*. Mechanicsburg, PA.: Stackpole Books.

Pipes, Daniel. (1997). *Conspiracy: How the Paranoid Style Flourishes and Where it Came From*. New York: Free Press.

Pipes, Daniel. (1998a) *The Hidden Hand: Middle East Fears of Conspiracy*. New York: St. Martins Griffin.

Pipes, Daniel. (1998b) "Distinguishing between Islam and Islamism." June 30, 1998. Center for Strategic and International Studies. From the website danielpipes.org. 4 June 2005 <http://www.danielpipes.org/article/954>

Pipes, Daniel. (Spring 2000). *Islam and Islamism - Faith and Ideology*. National Interest. Daniel Pipes.org. 31, 7, 2005 <http://www.danielpipes.org/article/366>

Pipes, Richard. (2001). *Communism: A History*. New York: Modern Library.

Plato. *The Republic*. (1969). Translated by Paul Shorey. The Collected Dialogues of Plato. Edited by Edith Hamilton and Huntington Cairns. Bollingen Series LXXI. New York: Princeton University Press.

Plessner, Helmuth. (1970). *Laughing and Crying*. Evanston Illinois: Northwestern University Press.

Ponchaud, Francois. (1989). "Social Change in the Vortex of Revolution." From:

Karl D. Jackson. Cambodia 1975: *Rendezvous with Death*. Princeton, NJ: Princeton University Press.

Popper, Karl. (2002). *Conjectures and Refutations*. New York: Routledge Classics.

Posner, Gerald. (2003) *Why America Slept: The Failure to Prevent 911*. New York: Random House.

Price, Ruth. (July 29, 2005). "Agnes Smedley, an Example to Whose Cause?" The Chronicle Review. The Chronicle of Higher

Education.
<http://chronicle.com/temp/email.php?id=48hp3hjj3me9w
lihltj3hdmvaex1ws10>

Pryce-Jones, David. (2002). *The Closed Circle*. Chicago: Ivan R. Dee.

Queenan, Joe. (2002). *Balsamic Dreams : A Short But Self-Important History of the Baby Boomer Generation*. New York: Picador.

Quinn, Kenneth M. 1989. "Explaining the Terror." From: Karl D. Jackson. *Cambodia 1975: Rendezvous with Death*.: Princeton, NJ: Princeton University Press.

Radhakrishnan (Translator)1994. *The Bhagavad-Gita*. Indus (An imprint of Harper Collins) New Delhi.

Raggio, Rev. Ken. 2003. "The Last Remaining Superpower A Look at the United Nations in a Biblical Role." 5 Oct. 2004 <http://www.endtimeinfo.net/Government/oneworld.php>

Raszelenberg, Patrick. (Fall/Winter 99) "The Khmers Rouges and the Final Solution." History & Memory, , Vol. 11 Issue 2, p62.

Reich, Wilhelm. (1980). *The Mass Psychology of Fascism (Third Edition)* New York: Farrar, Straus and Giroux.

Ricoeur, Paul. (1969). *The Symbolism of Evil*. Boston: Beacon Books.

Ricoeur, Paul. 1970. *Freud and Philosophy: An Essay on Interpretation*. New Haven: Yale University Press.

Riebling, Mark. (1994). *Wedge: The Secret War Between the FBI and CIA*. New York: Knopf.

Rieff, Phillip. (1979). *Freud: The Mind of the Moralist. 3rd edition*. Chicago: University of Chicago Press.

Rieff, Phillip. (1987). *The Triumph of the Therapeutic : Uses of Faith after Freud*. University edition Chicago: University Of Chicago Press.

Roazen, Paul. (1971a) *Freud. and His Followers*. A Meridian Book: New York: New American Library.

Roazen, Paul. (1971b) *Brother Animal: The Story of Freud and Tausk*. New York: Vintage Books. A Division of Random House.

Robins, Robert S. and Jerome M. Post. (1997). *Political Paranoia: The Psychopolitics of Hatred*. New Haven and London: Yale University Press.

Robins, Robert S. and Jerome Post. (1997). "Political Paranoia as Cinematic Motif: Stone's JFK." Paper presented at the August/September, 1997, meeting of the American Political Science Association. Washington, D.C

Rodman, Peter W. (March 1996) *Commentary*, Vol. 101 Issue 3.

Ronson, Jon. (2002). *Them: Adventures with Extremists*. New York: Simon and Schuster.

Rosenbaum, Ron. (1999). *Explaining Hitler: The Search for the Origins of His Evil*. New York: HarperCollins

Rothstein, Edward. (February 7, 2004). "Camus and the New-Cons: More in Common Than They Might Suspect." The New York Times. Connections.

Roustang, Francois. (1982). *Dire Mastery: Discipleship from Freud to Lacan*. Baltimore, MD: The Johns Hopkins University Press. Chapter called "Sons and Killers" anthologized in: Crews, Frederick C. (Editor) 1998. *Unauthorized Freud: Doubters Confront a Legend*. New York: Viking.

Rushdie, Salman. (November 1, 2001). "Yes, This Is About Islam" Faithfreedom.org. 4 June 2005 <http://www.faithfreedom.org/Articles/rushdie/yes_its_about_islam.htm>

Said, Edward. (1979). *Orientalism*. (1st Vintage Books ed edition) New York: Vintage.

Sandall, Roger. (June 2005) "10,000 years of nostalgia." <http://www.culturecult.com/spiked.htm#nostalgia.>.

Santayana, George. (1981). "The Comic Mask and Carnival." From Robert W. Corrigan. *Comedy: Meaning and Form*. Publishers. New York: Harper and Row.

Sartre, Jean-Paul. (du 15. oct. 1972). "La Cause du peuple." Originally published in J'accuse, No. 29, Reprinted in: Sartre Studies International, Volume 9, Issue 2, 2003. Translated by Elizabeth Bowen.

Sartre, Jean-Paul. (1981). *L'Idiot de la famille, vol 1.* From: Robert W. Corrigan. *Comedy: Meaning and Form.* New York: Harper and Row Publishers.

Sartre, Jean-Paul. (1988). *Existential Psychoanalysis.* Washington, DC: Regnery Gateway.

Sartre, Jean-Paul. (1991). *Critique of Dialectical Reasoning.* New York: Verso.

Sass, Louis A. (1994). *Madness and Modernism: Insanity in the Light of Modern Art, Literature, and Thought.* Cambridge, Massachusetts: Harvard University Press.

Scheler, Max. (1983). *Nature of Sympathy.* Nottingham, England: Shoe String Press.

Schilpp, Paul Arthur. (1951). (Editor) *The Philosophy of Alfred North Whitehead.* New York: Tudor Publishing Company.

Schimmel, Solomon. (1997). *The Seven Deadly Sins.* New York: Oxford University Press.

Schoeck, Helmut. (1987). *Envy: A Theory of Social Behavior.* Indianapolis: Liberty Press.

Schopenhauer, Arthur. (1932). *The Works of Schopenhauer: The Wisdom of Life and Other Essays.* New York: Black's Readers Service Company.

Schopenhauer, Arthur. (1966). *The World as Will and Idea.* (Volumes I and II) New York: Dover Publications.

Schreber, Daniel Paul. (2000). *Memoirs of My Mental Illness.* New York: New York Review Books.

Schwartz, Hillel. (1989). *Century's End.* New York: Doubleday.

Shapiro, David. (1962). *Neurotic Styles.* New York: Basic Books.

Sharansky, Natan. (2004). *The Case for Democracy: The Power of Freedom to Overcome Tyranny and Terror.* New York: Public Affairs.

Short, Philip. (2004). *Pol Pot: Anatomy of a Tragedy.* New York: A John Macrae Book. Henry Holt and Company.

Showalter, Elaine. (1997). *Hystories: Hysterical Epidemics and Modern Media.* New York: Columbia University Press.

Siegel, Ronald K. (1996). *Whispers: The Voices of Paranoia* (Reprint Ed.) New York: Simon and Schuster.

Sloan, Alfred. (1990). *My Years with General Motors*. (Reissue edition) New York: Currency

Smith, Adam. (1994). *The Wealth of Nations*. (Editor: Edwin Cannan) New York: Modern Library.

Sophocles. (1947). "Antigone." (Translated by Dudley Fitts and Robert Fitzgerald.) *Greek Plays in Modern Translation*. New York: Dial Press

Sowell, Thomas. (1987). *A Conflict of Visions*. New York: William Morrow.

Spence, Donald P. (1984). *Narrative Truth and Historical Truth: Meaning and Interpretation in Psychoanalysis*. (Reissue edition) W. W. Norton & Company;

Spencer, Robert. (2003). *Onward Muslim Soldiers: How Jihad Still Threatens America and the West*. Washington: Regnery Publishing Company.

Stanton, Gregory H. (April 1989). "Blue Scarves and Yellow Stars: Classification and Symbolization in the Cambodian Genocide." Occasional Paper of the Montreal Institute for Genocide Studies,. <http://www.genocidewatch.org/bluescarves.htm> 23 July, 2005.

Steiner, George. (1980). *Martin Heidegger*. New York: Penguin Books.

Sterling, Chaplain Scott. (2003). "An Analysis and Application of the Moral Equality of Soldiers Or Lifestyles of the Just Warrior." JSCOPE. A Joint Services Conference on Professional Ethics. Anti-Terrorist Operations and Homeland Defense. 36 Apr. 2005
<http://atlas.usafa.af.mil/jscope/JSCOPE03/Sterling03.html.
Also see:
http://atlas.usafa.af.mil/jscope/.>

Storr, Anthony. (1996). *Feet of Clay: A Study of Gurus*. New York: Simon and Schuster.

Staub, Ervin. (1992). *The Psychological and Cultural Roots of Genocide*. New York: Cambridge University Press.

Swift, Jonathan. (2003). *Gulliver's Travel's*. (Revised edition) New York: Penguin Books.

Sypher, Wylie. (1981). "The Meanings of Comedy." In Robert W. Corrigan. *Comedy: Meaning and Form*. New York: Harper and Row.

Taheri, Amir. (August 1, 2005). "Terrorism Cannot Win." FrontPageMagazine.com 8, 1, 2005. <http://www.frontpagemag.com/Articles/Printable.asp?ID=18965>

Talkington, Scott. (October 19, 2003). "Totalitarianism 3.0." Demosophilia. <http://demosophia.typepad.com/demosophia/2003/10/totalitarianism.html>

Tallmadge, John. (March 2004). Personal correspondence via. e-mail.

Tanahashi, Kaziaki. (1987). *Penetrating Laughter*. New York: Overlook Press.

Tillich, Paul. (2000). *The Courage to Be*. (2nd edition) Yale University Press.

Tillich, Paul. (2001). *The Dynamics of Faith*. New York: Harper Perennial Modern Classics

The North American Jaspers Society. (April 3-6, 1996) "Karl Jaspers: Metaphysics, Ontology, and Periechontologie." Seattle, WA.

Tolstoy, Leo. (1981). *The Death of Ivan Ilyich*. (Reissue edition) New York: Bantam Classics.

Tolstoy, Leo. (1996). *Confession*. (Reissue edition) New York: W. W. Norton & Company.

Trifkovic, Serge. (2002). *The Sword of the Prophet: Islam, History, Theology, Impact on the World*. Boston: Regina Orthodox Press.

Tucker, Robert C. and Stephen F. Cohen. (1965). *The Great Purge Trial*. New York: Grosset and Dunlap.

Vickery, Michael. (2000). *Cambodia 1975-1982*. Chiang Mai, Thailand: Silkworm Books.

Von Eckardt, Barbara. (1982). "Can Intuitive Proof Suffice: The Scientific Status of Psychoanalysis," from *Introducing Psychoanalytic Theory*, Sander L. Gilman editor. New York: Bruner/Mazel. In: Crews, Frederick C. (Editor) 1998. *Unauthorized Freud: Doubters Confront a Legend*. New York: Viking.

Walker, Jeff. (1998). *The Ayn Rand Cult.* New York: Open Court Publishing Company.

Walpole, Horace. (1926) *Selected letters of Horace Walpole.* English: E.P. Dutton.

Weaver, Richard M. (1984) *Ideas Have Consequences.* Chicago: University of Chicago Press; Reprint edition.

Webster, Richard. (1995). *Why Freud Was Wrong: Sin, Science, and Psychoanalysis.* New York: Basic Books.

Whitman, Cedrick. (1981). "Aristophanes: Discourse of Fantasy." *In: Comedy Meaning and Form (Second Edition)* by Robert W. Corrigan. New York: Harper and Row.

Wolfe, Tom. (2004). *I Am Charlotte Simmons.* New York: Farrar, Straus and Giroux.

Yahoo.com. (July 12, 2005). "Suspect in Dutch filmmaker's murder makes dramatic court room confession". http://sg.news.yahoo.com/050712/1/3tfgc.html

Youngman, Henny. (1998). *Take My Wife, Please!: Henny Youngman's Giant Book of Jokes.* New York: Citadel Press; 1st Carol Pub. Group ed edition.

Zonis, Marvin. (1993). "Leaders and Publics in the Middle East: Shattering the Organizing Myths of Arab Society." From: Renshon, Stanley A. 1993. *The Political Psychology of the Gulf War.* Pittsburgh: University of Pittsburgh Press.

Zukier, Henri. (1987) "Medieval Jewry in Western Europe." From *Changing Conceptions of Conspiracy.* Carl F. Graumann and Serge Moscovici. New York: Springer-Verlag.

Filmography

Blake, Henry (Producer), & Huston, John (Director). (1948). *The Treasure of Sierra Madre*. USA: Warner Brothers.

Capra, Frank (Producer & Director). (1946). *It's a Wonderful Life*. USA: RKO.

Cowen, Lester (Producer), & Edward F. Cline & George Marshall (Directors). (1939). *You Can't Cheat an Honest Man*. USA: Universal Studios.

Edelman, Louis. F. (Producer), & Walsh, Raoul (Director) (1949). *White Heat*. USA: Warner Bros.

Field, Ted. (Producer), & Herek, Stephen. (Director) (1996). *Mr. Holland's Opus*. USA: Hollywood Pictures Home Video.

Goodloe, J. Mills. (Producer), & Donner, Richard (Director). (1997). *Conspiracy Theory*. USA: Warner Brothers.

Grillo, Michael (Producer), & Brooks, Albert. (Director). *Defending Your Life*. (1991). USA: Warner Brothers.

June, Ray (Producer), & Norman Z. McLeod. (Director) (1932). *Horse Feathers*. USA: Image Entertainment.

Ramis, Harold. (Producer & Director). *Groundhog Day*. (1993). USA: Columbia/Tristar Studios.

Rudin, Scott. (Producer), & Weir, Peter (Director). (1998). *The Truman Show*. Paramount Studio.

Silver, Joel (Producer), & Wachowski, Andy, & Wachowski, David (Directors) (1999). *The Matrix*. USA: Warner Studios.

Spiegel, Sam. (Producer), & Lean, David (Director). (1962). *Lawrence of Arabia*. USA: Columbia Tri-Star.

Spielberg, Steven. (Producer & Director). (2002). *Catch Me if You Can*. USA: Umvd/Dreamworks.

Wald, Jerry, (Producer), & Koster, Henry (Director). (1949). *The Inspector General*. USA: Madacy Entertainment.

Wanger, Walter (Producer), & Siegel, Don. (Director) (1956). *Invasion of the Body Snatchers*. USA: Republic Pictures.

Welles, Orson. (Producer & Director) (1941). *Citizen Kane*. USA: RKO.

Wise, Robert (Producer & Director). (1966). *The Sand Pebbles*. USA: Twentieth Century Fox.

Zemekis, Robert. (Producer & Director). (1994). *Forrest Gump*. USA: Paramount Studio.

Index

Saint Augustine 265, 281
Saint-Simon, Claude-Henri 279
Sandall, Roger 226, 239
Sand Pebbles, The 165, 384
Santayana, George 303, 313
Sartre, Jean-Paul 100, 202–208, 237,
    287, 295, 298, 316, 323, [329]
Sass, Louis [18], 272
Satan 9, 13, 23–24, 52, 55–56, 78,
    86, 95, 98, 216–217, 245–247,
    264
satanic 21, 35, 341
Schachter, Stanley 107
Scheler, Max 328–329
Schimmel, Solomon 9, [274]
Schlegel, Friedrich 276
Schlesinger, Arthur 91, 255
Schoeck, Helmut 199
Schopenhauer, Arthur 38, 225, 269,
    274, 307–309, 328–329, 331
Schwartz, Hillel 82
Scofield, C. I. 99
Seinfeld 306
Serbia 3, 67
Shakespeare, William 49, 72, 170,
    176, 275, 287, 297, 311, 329
Shapiro, David 45–46, 68, 83, 92,
    129, 262
Sharansky, Natan 214, 248
Sheela 160, 164, 166, 178, 273
Short, Philip 185, 188, 201, 205
Showalter, Elaine 341–342
Siegel, Ronald K. 83
Silberer, Herbert 131
Sloan Jr., Alfred P. 347
Smedley, Agnes 19
Smith, Adam 19, 270
sociopath 1, 296
sociopathy 167
Socrates 110, 171, 174, 177, 244,
    260–261, 265, 270, 285, 290,
    296, 307–308, 350

Sophocles 3, 65, 170, 275, 281
Sowell, Thomas 74, 236
Spence, Donald P. 126
Spencer, Robert 230
Spinoza 3, 264, 270, 316, 340
Stalin, Joseph 18, 50, 55, 70, 76,
    108, 122, 130, 147, 184–185,
    191–192, 195–197, 200–201,
    204, 229, 301, 317
St Ambrose 336–337
Stanton, Gregory H. 202
Staub, Ervin 243
Steiner, George 238
Stekel, William 116, 119, 121, 131,
    133
Sterling, Chaplain Scott 336–337
Storr, Anthony 115, 157, 166–168,
    172, 350
Swift, Jonathan 313, 319
symbolic thinking 52, 53, 56
Sypher, Wylie 319–320, 329–330,
    337

T

Taheri, Amir [217]
Talkington, Scott 255
Tallmadge, John 298
Tanahashi, Kaziaki 319
Tausk, Victor 131, 138
teleological ethics 147, 158, 251
terrorism 3, 11, 14–15, 56–57, 83,
    162, 204, [212], 220, 247–248,
    249–256, 278, 395
Tillich, Paul 94, 146, 281, 283
Tolstoy, Leo 283, 305
totalism 58, 104, 125, 127, 129
totalitarianism 14, 23, 55, 118, 195,
    213–216, 218, 220–221, 230,
    234, 237–238, 250, 255–256,
    278, 300
Treasure of Sierra Madre, The 325,
    383

About Mark Dillof

Mark Dillof, Ph.D. offers consulting to organizations, throughout the world, seeking to combat political fanaticism, terrorism, cult indoctrination, school shootings, and other dark matters. As this book indicates, he plunges into the depths, to unlock the puzzle of malevolent phenomena. He could accurately be described as a psychological detective.

In a previous work — *Mysteries in Broad Daylight: A Journey into the Deeper Meaning of Everyday Life* (Mystical Kentuckian Press, 2012) — Dr. Dillof explored the deeper meaning of everything from our food preferences to the current fascination with zombies, from the game of golf to the deeper meaning of popular jokes. He reveals that even the eggs on our breakfast plate or the drink in our cocktail glass can be a doorway into who we are and life's profoundest questions.

In *Awakening with the Enemy: The Origin and End of Male Female Conflict* (Philosophy Clinic Press, 2000), he analyzed relationship conflicts from a philosophical perspective, using literary classics, popular TV shows, films and songs as examples. His book remains one of the most illuminating explorations of the problematical dimension of erotic love ever written.

Dr. Dillof is director of **Plato's Attaché: Life & Business Advisory** and **The Dillof Institute for Transformative Knowing,** both located in Louisville, Kentucky. For over twenty-five years, he has offered philosophical counseling for people undergoing a life transition, or an existential crisis, or who have suddenly become perplexed about the meaning of it all.

Dr. Dillof offers a variety of popular seminars, the newest of which is, "From Paranoid Vision to Comic Vision."

For more information: www.platosattache.com or www. deeperquestions.com. Or you can e-mail Dr. Dillof at: mdillof@ me.com or at mdillof@verizon.net.

www.ingramcontent.com/pod-product-compliance
Lightning Source LLC
Chambersburg PA
CBHW031457270326
41930CB00006B/133